The New Asian Renaissance
From colonialism to the post-Cold War

François Godement

Translated by Elisabeth J. Parcell

London and New York

The New Asian Renaissance

In the global race for growth, the Asia–Pacific region is emerging as the front runner. This study provides a comprehensive history of today's East Asia, tracing the essential stages in the rise of the region, from its birth under colonial rule to the post-Cold War period. *The New Asian Renaissance* recounts the evolution of:

- China
- Japan
- North & South Korea
- Malaysia
- Singapore
- Burma
- the Philippines
- Thailand
- Vietnam

François Godement outlines the major forces that have led to the present economic, political and social shape of East Asia. Originally published in French, this work is an essential tool for understanding the past, present and future of a region that has become a significant actor in the international political economy.

François Godement is a Professor of Contemporary Chinese History at the National Institute of Oriental Languages and Civilization, Paris. He is also senior research associate at the Institut Français des Relations Internationales.

First published in English in 1997
by Routledge
11 New Fetter Lane, London EC4P 4EE

Simultaneously published in the USA and Canada
by Routledge
29 West 35th Street, New York, NY 10001

First published in French by
Editions Odile Jacob
© Editions Odile Jacob, mai 1993
La Renaissance de l'Asie

This edition © 1997 Routledge

Translated by Elisabeth J. Parcell

British Library Cataloguing in Publication Data

A catalogue record for this book is available from the British
Library

Library of Congress Cataloging in Publication Data

Godement, François.
  [La renaissance de l'Asie. English]
  The new Asian renaissance / François Godement.
    p. cm.
  Includes bibliographical references.
  1. Asia–History–20th century.
DS35.G57 1997   96–20090
950.4–dc20   CIP

ISBN 0–415–11856–5
     0–415–11857–3 (pbk)

Published with the help of the French Ministry of Culture

For Ning and Olivier

Contents

Introduction

In the global race for growth, the Asia–Pacific region is emerging as the front runner. For over ten years now, trade between the two shores of the Pacific has outstripped transatlantic levels, while trade within maritime Asia has in turn exceeded the volume of transpacific trade. As European trade, to a far greater extent than that of the United States, was long sheltered from Asian competition by both direct and indirect protectionism, the current catching-up process has come as even more of a severe shock, as though a tidal wave of goods were welling up from Asia's industrious societies and swamping European consumers. Even manufacturers have been overwhelmed: Germany's dominance of the machine tool industry, traditionally the mainstay of its economy, has been wiped out by Japanese competition.

We have still not yet fully grasped this phenomenon. American studies clearly show that, on the whole, the Japanese schoolchild in Nagoya, the Chinese pupil in Peking and the average Japanese or Chinese high-school student perform far better than their American counterparts, especially in mathematics. While we in Europe have been harking back nostalgically to the Latin lessons of our parents' generation and the traditional teaching of classical literature in a few privileged institutions, almost no research has been carried out to compare our own educational results with those of Asia. Furthermore, while we remain obsessed with the perpetual reform of our educational system, how many studies have addressed the issue from the point of view of individual or family motivation, rather than simply assuming that our educational system must have the answer to all society's ills?

Both old political hands and industrialists in search of scapegoats still point to the low salaries paid to the Asian workforce, the lack of social welfare and the authoritarian nature of Asian politics as being the negative factors which fuel the region's economic dynamism. If this argument were true, many a South American republic would be overdeveloped by now. Yet in actual fact, Japanese salaries are among the highest in the world, while those of Taiwan or Korea have already caught up with, or surpassed, the levels found in Spain and Portugal. Admittedly Asia – even capitalist Asia – is still divided between dictatorship and democracy. Yet the quantity and quality of the information carried by the press in the most advanced Asian countries is far superior to that found in Europe, and the readership of books and newspapers is also higher there.

Granted, Asia's developed societies still harbour certain flaws, such as underinvestment in public infrastructure (for example housing and transport), the high cost of health care for individuals (though not for society as a whole), and the maxim that work must come before private life. Other weaknesses, such as the existence of mafias, corruption and the narrow range of political choice, are better assessed in the light of the deficiencies in our own society. Are these problems really unique to Asia? Can we generalize? Should we, for instance, take General Suharto's Indonesia as being truly representative of Asia as a whole? If so, then perhaps we should take a closer look at the quality of public life in Greece, or in Hassan II's Morocco which has such strong links with the European Union.

This book has grown out of a sense that when it comes to discussing or judging present-day Asia, we have a tendency to jump to conclusions. Admittedly, we could easily be led astray by the criteria which some of Asia's despotic régimes set for themselves: taking a country's growth rate as the sole index of human development would be tantamount to rejecting our own values and their claim to universal validity. Accordingly, the impressive nature of Asia's successes must not lead us to tear up the political and social contract on which our own societies are based. On the other hand, we must not barricade ourselves behind that contract as though it were an impregnable fortification. Before we pass judgement we must understand. And it is vitally important that we understand Asia: we are heading for certain failure if we delude ourselves as to the reasons for its success, or reduce them to an over-simplistic formula. To take one striking example, it is worth noting that the pioneer of the concept of 'total quality', the American W.E. Deming, initially attracted media coverage and a large following in Japan, rather than in his native country. Yet this lesson teaches us little indeed unless we grasp why the Japanese were predisposed to take his message on board. Ultimately, history does matter.

This book sets out to trace the main stages in the rise of East Asia: its birth under colonial rule, followed by the symmetrical crystallizations of Asian nationalism and Asian communism, the precursory aspects of Japan's first attempt to create an Asian model, and the Cold War which was thrust upon the region. Each of these historical stages forms one of the separate strata making up contemporary Asia. Japan, the first country to catch up with the West economically speaking, remains a source of discovery and rediscovery. For example, the recent phenomenon of the vast speculative 'bubble' which occurred in Japan between 1985 and 1989, and the growth which it spawned, should remind us that Japanese economic thought was once just as far removed from monetary and financial orthodoxy as it was from the utopia of economic liberalism. As for the Asian model of communism, characterized by utopian and often bloody Maoism, it differs from

Stalinism in the sense that it has failed to halt the march of China's history. Throughout the turbulence of that history, there has always been an intense conflict over the political line to be followed. In 1978 this led to the emergence of the world's first post-communist strategy, namely that of Deng Xiaoping. After the industrialized nations and the Asian newly-industrialized countries (NICs), the third major centre of industrial revolution is to be found among the family workshops of the Lower Yangtse, the skyscrapers of Hong Kong-like Shanghai and Canton, and along the outer ring-road of Peking. While the ingenuity of the Chinese is astonishing, the political tightrope act performed by their leaders is a cause for concern. At any rate, elsewhere – in North Korea and among the Khmer Rouge – Stalino–Maoism has become fossilized once and for all in its most monstrous guises. Indeed the fact that these parties continue to exist as potential flashpoints is a further sign that Asia's history is still in the making.

Even before this history has finally been written, many different threads are coming together in Asia. The rise of Japan has meant that, realistically, it is obliged to act as the locomotive for the rest of the region. The rift created by the Pacific War is being bridged, as is that of the Cold War. China, and possibly also Vietnam in the near future, are starting to matter, not just on a geopolitical level as in the past, but also on a geoeconomic level. The flow of public opinion back and forth across borders is forcing governments to converge, or at least to promise convergence in the future. There is a Japanese parliamentary model which is close to providing a political framework for South Korea and Taiwan. The democratic jolt which Corazon Aquino gave to the Philippines had a seismic effect, triggering a series of similar movements from China to Myanmar. The Confucian despotism of Lee Kuan Yew in Singapore is a source of fascination for China's leaders and commands the respect of his neighbours in the Malay world, even though they are reluctant to consider a Sinocentric model. Similar attitudes, though rarely shared by all, can be seen in the trade difficulties encountered with the United States and Europe. As the result of labour migration and tourism by the new middle classes, the intermingling of nationalities, interrupted in 1945, has begun afresh. Of the many issues raised by these developments, I have selected those which, however dated, still serve to shed light on the future and enable us to understand the way in which East Asia will evolve in the years to come.

IS THERE AN ASIAN IDENTITY?

It is possible that an Asian entity might emerge in the future, just as the beginnings of European unity have emerged. Nevertheless, as recent problems in Europe have shown, unity requires agreement on some form of shared identity, or at least voluntary progress in that direction. Is there such a shared identity in Asia's case? The answer to this does not lie in triumphant generalities about the rise of the transpacific and Pacific Basin economies. Attempts to relate everything to a single factor, especially the economy, which has become the lowest common denominator for Asia's developing countries, make it easy simply to skim the surface and ignore the flesh-and-blood reality, rather as though the idea of Europe were to be reduced to plans for freedom of movement, motorways and gross national product (GNP) aggregates. Yet giving free rein to our cultural conceptions of Asia can lead us into trouble. The words 'Asia' and 'the East' are loaded terms from a fantasy seemingly woven from a Baudelaire poem, a melody by Ravel, a short story by Somerset Maugham and a James Ivory film. It would certainly be hard to find an Asian equivalent to the 'Ode to Joy' among the work of Asian writers, composers and filmmakers. Whereas Beethoven was European, they are Chinese, Japanese, Vietnamese or Indonesian. The very idea of Asia is clearly a mirror-image based on the idea of Europe: the East as conceived by the West, as Edward Saïd (1978) trenchantly argues. Saïd also points to the fact that, for Europeans, the term 'East' primarily denotes the Near East, which they believe should fit their own conceptual framework, while the very term 'Far East' reflects the region's remoteness. The Americans, on the other hand, first encountered Asia by way of the Far East, with which they are more familiar. *Orient extrême* (Extreme East) was the title given to the memoirs of Robert Guillain (1986), an old hand at Asian journalism, who began his career back in the 1930s: with this pun he emphasized how foreign, indeed extreme, the Far East (in French, 'Extrême Orient') must be to citizens of the Old World.

Accordingly, we would like Asia to create itself, or at least arrive at its own sense of identity. Yet the idea of Asia was not taken up by the Asians themselves until the period of nationalist and anti-colonial resistance to the influence of the West and of Japanese militarism. If we ask ourselves whether Bukharin and General Tojo were fighting on the same side, the answer is obviously no. Theirs was merely an imaginary alliance, a mirage dreamt up by nationalist Japan which quickly paled into insignificance beside the latter's own ascendancy. Yet the similarity between the rationale put forward by the architects of the Comintern's anti-colonial Asian strategy and that of the ideologists behind Japan's pan-Asian thrust was by no means coincidental. The former wanted to stir up turmoil in Asia in order to finish off the global revolution which had become bogged down in Europe, while the latter championed the cause of 'Asia for the Asians'. The former pressed this strategy into the service of Russian Bolshevik interests, while the latter did the same on behalf of imperial Japan. Some Japanese militants, convinced that Soviet internationalism offered the only path to Asian unity, even established a famous network of Soviet spies, led by Richard Sorge under cover of the Imperial Army staff headquarters. Japanese intellectuals and young officers in the Imperial Army often combined extreme right-wing nationalist ideas with an admiration for Soviet-style collectivism, all of which was set in contradistinction to the pervasive climate of racketeering which accompanied imported democracy, and to the influence of the great Western powers. Many other more conservative Japanese feared Moscow-style communism above all else. They even interpreted the multi-racial society which evolved between 1941 and 1945 as the first sign of Japanese-style collectivism. In actual fact, Japan's pan-Asian militarism arose out of the melting-pot of nationalism and modern state-building. This conjunction is just as important as that embodied in European fascism, which simultaneously grew out of European communism's disintegration into populism and the anti-communist counter-revolution which followed 1917. Furthermore, the Soviet Union signed a non-aggression pact with both militarist Japan and Hitler's Germany in April 1941. All three, as respective partners, took the view that any system was preferable to democracy. Judging from these events, we would do well to ponder the dangers of premature unification for large regions which have yet to define themselves, whether it be fuelled by political or by hegemonic ambition. It was Leninist communism which spawned the Soviet Union's Eurasian empire, now overthrown, Nazism which led to the unification of Europe for the first time in modern history, and Japanese militarism which marked the first embodiment of an Asian identity.

JAPAN: PART OF ASIA OR PART OF THE WEST?

If Winston Churchill – the man who spoke of democracy as the worst form of government except all those other forms that have been tried from time to time – had not been chosen as Prime Minister, and if Britain had not decided to go to war in 1940, the expression 'Anglo-Saxon', so beloved of the pro-Nazi Vichy government and a certain French chauvinist tendency, would have taken on a new, unexpected connotation. In France, the historical fact that a silent majority supported the Vichy government has since come to light: France's destiny was shaped just as much by pre-eminent figures such as Winston Churchill and General de Gaulle as it was by the course of the Second World War.

However, the history of modern Japan has not been marked by the decisions of providential individuals: on the contrary, the traditionally diffuse nature of decision making, stemming from the Japanese system of consensus, patronage and denial of responsibility, has often made individual accountability impossible. Even today, the part played by the Emperor Hirohito in Japan's downfall is still unclear. The rest of Asia has a whole host of military leaders, charismatic politicians and despots, yet Japanese history, particularly post-1945, has apparently been shaped entirely by what seem to us to be the anonymous armies of civil servants who spill out of Kasumigaseki underground station in central Tokyo each day to occupy the offices of the main ministries, in other words bureaucracy, the collective hero of Japanese history. Yet at the heart of Asia's recent history (and no doubt at the heart of its future too), there lie Japan's uncertainties and the choices it has made over the course of time. Japan certainly does not control the rest of Asia and has never quite succeeded in doing so, even at the height of its power in 1942–3. Yet the other countries of the region have often defined their position, or set their course, in relation to Japan. Whether Japan adopts the stance of a shogun on horseback as in the past, or of a mikado veiled behind a curtain as it does today, whether it aspires to direct domination (as in the days of imperial Japan) or indirect influence (as in parliamentary Japan), it casts a shadow across the rest of Asia. The Chinese world has feared Japan considerably in the past and is still wary of it today, as reflected, for example, in the blunt comments made by Singapore's statesman Lee Kuan Yew who, during talks on whether Japan should provide troops for UN peacekeeping operations, is said to have remarked that it would amount to giving liqueur chocolates to a reformed alcoholic. Yet anti-Japanese patriotism, a prominent feature of all Chinese régimes, did not stop Chinese politicians from forging alliances with Japan in the past, while Chinese businessmen overseas are currently the leading partners of Japanese firms in the rest of Asia. Other Asian politicians currently want and expect Japan to play an even wider role that will dovetail with their own ambitions for Asia.

The most obvious example of this is Muhammad bin Mahathir, the Islamic nationalist Prime Minister of Malaysia. Mahathir advocates East Asian unity, occasionally requests Japanese military support for regional security and criticizes appeals for democracy and protectionist tendencies on the part of the West. He is the herald of a philosophy of history which draws on many sources: anti-British feeling in Malaysia, Islam, the collective community as opposed to the individualism represented by the Chinese business community, and the cult of near-militaristic efficiency surrounding the Japanese economy. For a long time, Mahathir's key political slogan was 'Look East', a term which owed its origins to imperial Japan in precisely the same way that the phrase 'Fortress Europe', so popular with the pro-ASEAN (Association of South-East Asian Nations) press, was in fact a creation of the Nazi ideologist Joseph Goebbels. Like Lee Kuan Yew, Mahathir is a complex phenomenon. He is indubitably an agitator who is guaranteed to raise the hackles of Western liberal governments, especially when he decides to enforce the Arab League's boycotts. Yet Malaysia is one of South-East Asia's success stories, not only in economic but also in social terms. Malaysian 'communalism', which once alternated between fatalism and violent revival, has taken a constructive turn under the guidance of men like Mahathir, while the development of the Chinese and Malaysian communities, sometimes separately, sometimes in unison, offers a positive example. Both Lee Kuan Yew and Muhammad bin Mahathir share the view that the Age of Europe, if not the Age of the West, is over. Mahathir and some of his fellow leaders in the Near East and Asia are now looking to Japan. But is Japan really what they imagine it to be? This question is crucial for our future. In fact, Japan has never been able to answer the question of its identity: is it the model partner of the West, emulating it to the point of assimilation? Or is it the model pupil of the West, but one which is striving to become the master in its turn, taking the first step by offering a lead to the other Asian countries coming up in its wake? Only fanatical 'Japan-bashers' could take the second of these two possibilities seriously. On the other hand, only a naïve observer would imagine that there was no evidence or potential in Japan for such a view, or that there would be no increased danger of this happening if the West were to make the Japanese success story a scapegoat for all its own problems.

Japan's attitude to the West has effectively dominated its political shifts over the past century. These shifts began in the 1880s, during the Meiji era, when Japan felt the impact of Western influence, while continuing to widen the gap between itself and its Asian neighbours. In Japan it is sometimes said that 'Japanese are not Asians'. This paradox is true in the sense that Japan saw a more profound transformation at an earlier stage than the other Asian countries, creating 'a modern system which both emulates and competes with the West' (Pons, 1988: 10), and because feelings of mutual hostility existed with the rest of Asia from the time of the collapse of the imperial dream of a Greater East Asia Co-prosperity Sphere. Japan's pan-Asian vision was clearly destroyed by the final act of the Pacific War, but it had already been rejected on numerous occasions within Japan itself. In 1885, in the face of the failure by China and Korea either to resist the West or to implement reform, the educated son of a samurai named Yukichi Fukuzawa called on his fellow countrymen to 'separate from Asia'. One Japanese minister put this advice into concrete terms in 1886 when he advocated 'establishing a Western-style empire at the gates of Asia'. Throughout the history of Japanese foreign relations, this pull towards the West has meant attempting to comply with Western expectations while negotiating pragmatic compromises with the other great powers. These subtle, agile manoeuvres were frequently counterbalanced by the view that Japan, while ahead of China, formed with it a single, complementary whole, justifying a common stance *vis à vis* the rest of the world. At the very heart of this pro-Western diplomacy lay the germ of what was clearly the deep-seated notion of pan-Asianism. The great Shigeru Yoshida, who served as Prime Minister in the years following the Japanese defeat, was capable of holding both positions simultaneously. In any case it was not so much a matter of choice as far as Japan was concerned, but rather of creative adaptation to the demands of the United States.

That other great Japanese Prime Minister of recent times, Yasuhiro Nakasone, was the man who came closest to being a national saviour. At any rate, he broke with the tradition which stated that no policy could be decided individually but should instead be subject to the collective decision-making process operating both before and after the Pacific War. Nakasone was one of those rare Japanese politicians who seemed to want their decisions to leave their mark on post-war history. In fact, his decision making had a decidedly Western slant, while retaining a peculiarly Asian, and above all Chinese, quality. The 1980s are an excellent example of the first type of Japanese foreign policy stance, with Japan acting as the model pupil of the United States within the Western alliance, sometimes taking a harsher anti-Soviet line than its master. At that time, out of all the G7 nations, it was the French government, at the Versailles summit of 1982 and even at the Williamsburg summit in 1983, which wanted to prevent Japan from joining in any Western declaration of collective security. Yet this kind of involvement offered the chance for Japan to become firmly anchored and to broaden its relations beyond the United States. At any rate, Yasuhiro Nakasone and his successors managed to overcome this obstacle. The second type of Japanese stance may be seen in its special relationship with China and in the first signs of the formation of an Asian regional community, particularly in the face of the trade problems encountered with the United States and the European Union. Finding itself under considerable pressure from these quarters, the Japanese government has so far responded with great caution, but it is fully aware that within its global trade strategy it holds an Asian card.

WILL THE TWENTY-FIRST CENTURY BELONG TO CHINA?

If we were to imagine the countries of maritime Asia as the tip of an iceberg, mainland China would be the bulk below the surface. This image almost holds true in population terms, but it is notoriously dangerous to draw geopolitical conclusions solely on the basis of demographic trends. The same image might one day prove valid in economic terms, even though for the time being Japan's GNP alone accounts for two-thirds of the Asian economy. If we pursue this notion to its conclusion, the GNP for the Los Angeles area is equal to that of India, showing the kind of conjuring trick which can be performed with GNP statistics. Since 1911, China has been the object of severe mood swings in the West, over-optimism alternating with phases of intense disillusionment. China's fortunes actually picked up in 1978, but then they had already done so after 1911, as well as in the early days of communism in 1949, irrespective of the errors committed at that time. The evolution of an unofficial post-communist régime, sometimes encouraged, sometimes tolerated in silence by Deng Xiaoping and reformist leaders, has unleashed unprecedented 'forces of production' (in Marx's words, though he was referring to machines rather than human beings) formerly blunted by collectivism. As with everything else in China, this development is not without its dangers, given the unstable nature of Chinese society. Also, as throughout Chinese history, these dangers are ultimately greater for the Chinese themselves than for the outside world. The Chinese iceberg is so vast that it moves with glacial slowness, shedding only minute fragments of itself, in the form of economic migration from certain geographic areas and professions, the brain drain (or at any rate an outflow of students) and political exile.

We should therefore ignore the famous Hun (not Chinese) invasions which gave rise to the old European (or Eurasian) myth of the Yellow Peril. The Great Wall of China, a multi-purpose structure, was also built to keep Chinese citizens inside the empire, for the celestial bureaucracy feared nothing so much as the loss of its subjects. At times, the Chinese government skilfully plays on Western fears: for example when Deng Xiaoping was asked in 1978 if his fellow citizens were free to emigrate, he replied 'How many million do you want?' It is the minorities, the Chinese first cousins of Hong Kong and Taiwan, and the old imperial dependencies of Korea and Vietnam, which must fear the wrath of the empire. Yet these manifestations of Chinese nationalism are epiphenomena compared with the central fact of the transition to post-communism. They would only have any significance if this transition were to fail and Western nations (the only ones likely to take the risk) were to cross swords with the régime over matters deemed by the latter to be internal to China.

For a long time, China was the mirror image of certain Western utopias. The legacy of neo-Confucian culture both in China and, even more noticeably, in North Korea, gave Maoist ideology a more highly-structured, totalitarian quality than Leninism itself. Conversely, the dismantling of this ideology from 1978 onwards led to the negation of all political and social models. This development was already implicit in the authoritarian, narrow definition of the 'four principles of socialism' formulated by Deng Xiaoping in 1979, which could be summed up in a nutshell as the monopoly of the communist party. The deconstruction process is even more noticeable in current ideology and speech. This catharsis, following in the wake of decades of Maoist stereotypes, has created untold confusion both in people's minds and in their writings. Although dictatorship still exists, the communist socio-economic system is already moribund. China is thus pitching and tossing, buffeted by two uneven currents. There is a transition underway from one mode of production to another: the transition from communism to capitalism, following on from an earlier, unfinished transition from feudalism to the development of capitalism. However, a process which in post-medieval Europe took several centuries, and in post-imperial China (1911–49) only went as far as the emergence of the 'buds of capitalism', is currently taking place in the post-communist era at almost lightning speed. Maoism locked China's social structures into the straitjacket of collectivization, managing, for example, to prevent virtually all rural–urban migration and minimize trade with the outside world. This will doubtless take up as much space in the history books of the year 3000 as the late manorial system does in our own textbooks on the Middle Ages. However, since the onset of de-Maoization, forces long pent up have been unleashed with incredible vigour.

Thus the divide between reformers and conservatives within the communist movement has ceased to be an issue in China since 1989, partly because the political alliance with the educated élite which had existed in the 1980s was destroyed by the denial of democracy, and also as a result of the death of reformism, in other words the belief in the possibility that communism might be reformed along a third path envisaged since 1956 and the time of Khrushchev. With the demise of communism in Europe, China's leaders have recognized the fact that their ideology is doomed and that reform will result in the collapse of the Leninist system. The now obsolete debate between reform and conservatism has been superseded by two much more urgent questions, the first of which is how to preserve Chinese national unity, given the rise of the many regional capitalist economies splintering the country. This is a vital issue, because ever since the beginning of the nineteenth century, whenever it has encountered pressure from its neighbours, China's destiny has traditionally been staked either on *de facto* dismemberment or on unity. While productive China (though not the dry, mountainous western part) is shielded from the ethnic question, the fragmentation of political authority is a fact accentuated by the recent economic boom. The second question is how to ensure the survival of the last group of communist rulers. It is a grouping unique of its kind, for it still includes members belonging to the generation of revolutionary founders, as well as their descendants, the sons of high-ranking cadres who wield so much power in China. As a result of the hybrid economy introduced from 1978, with bureaucrats fixing the rules of the market economy and taking their cut, this generation, which had originally come together following Mao's purges, formed into a quasi-bourgeoisie, not without certain social as well as political advantages: the chance to study abroad, the experience of power, including the running of the economy, and above all the keys to a network of personal contacts which owed as much to Chinese tradition as it did to communist power.

Deng Xiaoping was no Gorbachev: he had neither his tragic dimension nor his nostalgic kinship with the West. Yet neither was he a loser or a trustee in bankruptcy – a 'liquidator', to use the Leninist jargon. A central figure in the development of a Chinese brand of communism, Deng is a man whose career coincided with the rise of a revolutionary group. At the same time, his experience of violent turmoil, both as victim and perpetrator, made him into an anti-conformist: he had no regard for ideology, yet showed a will of iron when it came to preserving the legitimacy both of the nation and of the régime responsible for rebuilding it. This was capable of leading him into defiant gestures, as when, after 1989, he issued a threatening warning that he would forcibly put down another democratic movement. He was too openly contemptuous of foreign pressure to be wholly immune from it, whereas Mao deceived 'friends of China' throughout the world. Yet he was also stubbornly determined to transform the very foundations of the régime. He occasionally seemed very pressed for time, and even to have been overtaken by events, as in the spring of 1989. But Deng also used time as a weapon against his enemies, sometimes even going so far as to dictate the timescales for the end of their hostility. Thus, in 1979, he declared 'ten years of punishment' for Vietnam, a schedule that was subsequently adhered to. In 1989, despite scepticism from the West, he countered the claims of the urban, educated classes with the reimposition of the iron hand 'for two or three years'. This deadline was also upheld, with economic and social controls later being relaxed in 1991. Meanwhile, there was a change of objective: Deng Xiaoping no longer wanted to preserve the system through reform via a communist-style New Deal such as he launched in 1978. Instead he aimed, on a massive scale, for the same historical shift embarked upon by Yeltsin in Russia, Kravchuk in Ukraine, Nazerbajev in Kazakhstan and others elsewhere. The former communist leadership, forcibly restrained by the army (as prefigured by General Jaruzelski of Poland, for whom Deng Xiaoping declared his admiration from 1987 onwards), has turned into a Janus-like class, for the sake of the nation and in order to preserve vital state power. This élite is the custodian of the economic legacy of communism, in other words the state-owned enterprises. Either *de facto* or as a result of deliberate privatization, these enterprises are due to become genuine limited companies which will actually be owned by former communist cadres. Yet the other face of this ruling class safeguards national order by co-ordinating the interests of the military and state bureaucracies. Indeed there is already a huge civil society in China, fragmented and anarchic, and the post-Maoist state is hard-pressed to find the non-despotic means to hold it together and form an administration. Deng Xiaoping possessed a major asset in this respect: the vitality of the Chinese economy, which has been casting off the shackles of bureaucracy since 1978, cancelling out all Prime Minister Li Peng's efforts at authoritarian recentralization in 1988–90. As this economic reform has been underway for over fifteen years, the rising tide of administrative and economic chaos across China does not have nearly the same significance as the total breakdown of Gosplan and the former Soviet economy. Even though the fall of fixed incomes and the rise of mafias distorting the rules of the market economy are as much a feature of Peking as they are of Moscow, they have not impaired the economic boom, but have simply helped to establish an embryonic capitalist class, albeit one which is heavily tainted with corruption. In fact, the huge inflow of foreign investment (mainly by overseas Chinese) has transformed what might easily have been a mere mafia battleground like Uzbekhistan and Sicily into a genuine capitalist game. Given that 40 per cent of the total money supply of Hong Kong dollars is in circulation in southern China, that region clearly constitutes a hinterland of the global market rather than a mere epiphenomenon. From Vietnam to the states of the former Soviet Union, ghost investment zones are springing up in search of potential, albeit extremely cautious, capitalist partners. Yet China itself has succeeded in luring its prey – international investors who have put down 100 billion dollars of foreign investment since 1979.

The second asset which Deng Xiaoping sought to preserve and exploit was the fact that among China's immediate neighbours, political democracy and its supporters have not been on the march up until now. It is only developments in Taiwan that give China cause for concern, as the political and cultural rift between the two Chinese societies presents a challenge which could well prevent reunification. Yet Japan is relatively close, and so are the countries of South-East Asia which have yet to depart from the national security states constructed after the Second World War. These societies are torn between a deep-seated yearning for democracy and the perpetuation of authoritarian governments capable of using Tiananmen-style tactics against any threat of instability, as with the Rangoon junta (an extreme example ever since the demonstrations of 1988) and the repression on the streets of Bangkok in 1991, a miscalculation on the part of yet another military establishment which found itself up against the Chinese–Thai middle classes. The ideology that favours the big stick is usually ersatz, conveniently abstracted from real society, whether it be the four principles of socialism in China, 'king and country' in Thailand, *pancasila* in Indonesia, Islam and the *bumiputra* principle in Malaysia or neo-Confucianism in Singapore. All these régimes are the products of national security factors, and the Chinese government can base its hopes on its affinity with castes which either have not yet fully accepted elective democracy, or distort it. Yet this Holy Alliance is a fragile one: it does not include all governments even in South-East Asia alone. Public opinion, as reflected for example in the Indonesian, Malaysian and Thai press, has now had enough of this state of affairs and is ready for change.

Even though China's economic dynamism constitutes an asset for Deng Xiaoping and his successors, its political kinship with the rest of Asia offers a less secure anchorage. Modern Asian societies, having survived the ideological rivalry of communism, are keen to put their authoritarian rules behind them just at a time when communist China is attempting to justify a political dictatorship that has lost its Marxist–Leninist legitimacy once and for all. China's leaders were unfortunate enough to come to power over a century after Meiji Japan transformed itself into the Prussia of Asia, and thirty years after the military régimes of maritime Asia spawned economic tigers. As long as these régimes have yet to complete their own transformations, Deng Xiaoping and his successors can still hope to contain pressure for democracy and manage China's transition to capitalism. The winding trajectory followed since 1978 suggests that this will prove a feat as difficult as that portrayed in the genre scene from the Peking Opera, in which the ferryman mimes the crossing of the river in his boat. It is a capitalist revolution without violence and without utopia. Both for Deng and for the opponents of the régime, feudalism had never disappeared from China but was reincarnated as Maoism. However, Deng countered the possibility of a Western-style political revolution by gradually merging China's élites, including the various bourgeoisies (the old educated one, the capitalist one and the overseas one), the communist cadres and a host of new entrepreneurs, and by preserving China's founding political legitimacy of 1949 as a political touchstone, contrasting patriotism with a symmetrical fear of chaos. This vision differs from the democratic political strategy which prevailed in Moscow after 1989, but it foreshadows radical change none the less. It guarantees a safe haven for all communist veterans, just as the ferryman promises the 'lords and fine ladies' when they board his boat in the scene from the Peking Opera. Deng rebuilt a political alliance whose themes were straightforward: a gradual downscaling of the state-run economic sector, a transition to a 'socialist market economy' as the propaganda now states, and a move to open the doors to capitalism; however it also includes the preservation of a dictatorship reduced to a narrow range of objectives. He wished to avoid any outbreak of political rivalry and to maintain both a unified national government and an army that would enable China to play a major role on the international stage.

Does this strategy mean a return to traditional society? That is the theory supported by the majority of historians, especially Sinologists. They have a preference for repetitive and therefore predictable cycles, and are frequently attracted by the idea of a traditional China whose endless decay neither challenges the outside world nor disturbs academe. Yet this cyclical vision is false, just like the mid-1970s' idea of the perpetual renewal of Mao's political campaigns, or routine revolution. In the first place, the bureaucratic capitalism propounded by the Soong sisters, the Kung brothers and other Kuomintang leaders, which serves as a model from the past to describe the present, only existed on a very small scale, both financially and geographically. The individual and cultural responses are similar in some cases, but the scale of events does matter. This fragile form of capitalism survived under the political domination of the West and of Japan, a fact which apologists for the ten-year Nanjing Republic (1928–37) continue to conceal. The era of Maoist dictatorship in all its totalitarian despotism subsequently spawned a modern social structure, with nuclear families, divorce, a falling birth rate and a state-dependent salaried class now so prevalent that it is even hindering economic transformation. Maoist brainwashing was so thorough that it left behind a modern state of ignorance, a gaping void which the electronic media are now rushing to fill. Furthermore, the possibility of a peaceful transition to capitalism also hinges upon the latent potentiality of an authoritarian régime and society, both of which are rooted in tradition. Yet there is no longer any consensus for this. Given the clash of ideologies and social interests and the potential violence caused by very disparate rates of change, it is more probable that events will follow a spasmodic, if not chaotic, course: after several boom years a new internal crisis will occur, followed at best by further progress. However, Deng Xiaoping is already no longer in a position to influence events: it is highly likely that he will have been China's last Great Helmsman.

POLITICAL DEMOCRACY: WESTERN MODELS AND AN ASIAN PATH

Democracy is, of course, never finer than when we are demonstrating it to an outsider. Like the white plaster Statue of Liberty erected by the Tiananmen demonstrators in 1989, it appears as a *deus ex machina*, a goddess armed top to toe, or – to use the legal Newspeak – an indivisible 'constitutional bloc'. Of course, the only real danger lurking beneath the ugly term 'human rightsism' (the opposite of Third Worldism) is that we may fail to spot the minor, sometimes even major, flaws which mar the face of our own democracy.

Yet the converse attitude, which exploits the practical limitations of our own values in order to deny the universal validity of democracy and human rights, is even more absurd. Instead we should recall La Rochefoucauld's famous maxim that 'hypocrisy is a tribute which vice pays to virtue'. Although it has become hard to find either advocates of the dictatorship of the proletariat or enemies of 'bourgeois law' (to use the terminology of the former Maoist extremists of 1974–6), there has been an increase in the number of those in favour of Plato's tyrannical city of Syracuse, where harmony prevailed under a benevolent despot. Maritime Asia offers them a positive model, in contrast to Africa where dictatorship is generally defended and exemplified in terms of default arguments such as 'the time is not yet ripe'. In so doing, it is following in the footsteps of Japan, which has finally been recognized as free and democratic, warts and all. The authoritarian states undergoing rapid growth, their despotism attenuated by the educational influence of Confucianism, and their impressive economic successes have generated new arguments in favour of authoritarian pragmatism. Furthermore, whereas in Europe 'the invention of liberty' (Starobinsky, 1964) either preceded or coincided with industrial revolution, maritime Asia's economic miracle often seems to be rolling back the growth threshold even further, to a point beyond which democracy becomes a need as staple as bread or rice. For example Singapore, with a per capita income of US$25,000, still apparently falls short of this threshold, although some tensions are detectable and electoral democracy has been authorized. This example prompts the notion, particularly among defenders of the existing arrangements, not that democracy must wait, but that it would quite simply be pointless to introduce it. Western-style political debate, so it is argued, would lead to decline, just as in the past the welfare state made workers in the old Europe idle.

Let us admit the inadmissable: although the idea may primarily be a convenient shield for the militaristic, nepotistic or ruthlessly inegalitarian classes which have laid the foundations for regional development, occasionally it is right on target. There are two dimensions to our sense of democratic superiority: first, there is the notion of progress enshrined in the ideals on which Western republics were founded, as distinct from democracy conceived of simply as a mechanism for keeping opposing sides apart.

With the demise of socialism and the eclipse of social democracy, progress is taking a back seat to the rule of law. Second, there is the fact (or the goal) of the separation of public and private interests, which from a European standpoint is often open to question today. This leads us to the reality of patronage, which is almost as much the bedrock of Latin societies as it is of traditional Asian societies. The key to escaping it lies not in some miracle discourse on the rule of law, but in a concrete principle as strong as the ill it is designed to cure: the primacy of checks and balances and the concept of due process of law. These elements, together with the bipartisan system, form the main foundations of the English parliamentary model and its American relation, in which democratic rivalry promotes a withering of the political Messianism which could prove so fatal to our own system. In other words, European countries based on Roman law are currently just as far removed from a fully-functioning, impartial system as many Asian semi-democracies. Both are undergoing transition. The primacy of due legal process over old ideologies is gradually gaining ground in all modern states, from the Italian judiciary to newly-internationalized Japan. At last we are able to witness the final stage in the separation of powers which is still such an imperfect feature of our own system. Many Asian countries are approaching democratization at such a rate and within such a short space of time that they will never know the long, gradual filtering of idealism which characterized the European experience, instead moving straight to the stage of procedural, arbitral democracy. This, at any rate, is the step which Japan is about to take, for no politico-financial scandal there seems likely to revive programmes and utopian schemes based on nineteenth-century European socialism. It would be surprising indeed if maritime Asia's arch-capitalist society were to show a different result.

At the same time, our political republic seems caught in a paroxysm of doubt, as reflected in the way that the postmodernist cult of consensus-building is replacing yesterday's intellectual battles. Admittedly, it also signals the end of the civil strife which has smouldered in the Latin world since 1793 and has exacted an even heavier tribute from the Slavic world since 1917. The politically utopian forces which have shaped the twentieth century, or at any rate its ideal, are now almost, if not entirely, extinguished. Curiously enough, once our ultimate political goal becomes that of balance and the alternation of power, our view of political history reverts to being static. It thus turns into a closed system such as is represented by American politics in spite of its civic innovations, or even a cyclical one, as with the Confucian idea of human government, whose aim is to arrive at, or rather to return to, good governance. Confucianism teaches that public life thrives on the virtues of its leaders rather than on the application of positive law. There is no question whatsoever of any programmes, utopias or social transformations, but simply the preservation of civilization. One of the most famous tales of Hu Shih, the sole liberal heir to May Fourth 1919, describes Karl Marx entering the temple of Confucius, borne along by merchants, and how Confucius confounded him with his ironic scepticism. In 1983, in his quest to replace Maoism, Deng Xiaoping hit on the idea of introducing the concept of 'spiritual civilization' in order to thwart the democratic movement in his own country, so Hu Shih actually had the last word as far as China was concerned. It would certainly be presumptuous to claim to know which of these two visions will prevail. At any rate, the crisis in our own vision encourages us to be more tolerant of arguments at variance with our own values.

Unless we want to trap Europe in a nineteenth-century mentality, we must acknowledge that our 'issue-based democracy', rooted in political debate, also marked the high point of our own industrial revolution. Another revolution is currently taking place in Asia with Japan at its head, albeit ambiguously given the country's pull towards the West. For the time being, this revolution is seizing the practical benefits of democracy rather than its intrinsic principle. In Asia, politics is a matter of personalities, the alternation of power a means of electoral sanction rather than a 'choice of societal models', and parliamentary representation a mechanism for the safe venting of ethnic and social tensions. The range of political choice available in Asia is perhaps less broad, yet information is clearly more freely accessible there, as witnessed by the content and circulation of the principal media, at least in the more advanced countries: an over-informed, under-motivated brand of democracy, one might argue. In all these societies there is less abstention – that stage of supreme indifference to politics – than in some of the major Western democracies.

In any event, we must do away with ready-made explanations which attribute the 'Asian miracle' to an absence of democracy and social rights. Asian societies are prone to evolve and adapt and, like Japan, they are virtually all attracted to Western transculturalism in varying measures. Asia's small element of political opposition (constitutional jurists, lawyers and dissidents) seeks its inspiration and its models in the Western democracies, usually of the Jeffersonian variety, sometimes of the Diderot variety. Conversely, by drawing from these evolving societies some of the keys to their success we can avoid becoming fossilized in the next century: from Argentina to Portugal and even the United Kingdom, examples abound of countries which are slowly climbing back down the development ladder. If we are willing to acknowledge that in Asia's case economic growth offers the basis for the introduction of democracy, we must also apply the corollary of this at home: to deny the goal of economic growth means jeopardizing our own democratic framework.

SELECTED READING

Guillain, R. (1986) *Orient extrême: une vie en Asie*, Paris: Arléa-Le Seuil.
Guillermaz, J. (1989) *Une vie pour la Chine: mémoires (1937–1989)*, Paris: Robert Laffont.

Johnson, C. (1964) *An instance of treason: Ozaki Otsumi and the Sorge spy ring*, Stanford: Leland Stanford Junior University.

Pons, P. (1988) *D'Edo à Tokyo: mémoires et modernités*, Paris: Gallimard.

Saïd, E. (1978) *L'Orientalisme: l'Orient créé par l'Occident*, Paris: Le Seuil.

Waldron, A. (1990) *The Great Wall of China: from history to myth*, Cambridge: Cambridge University Press.

1 The colonial era

Enormous contrasts are not hard to find in Asia, ranging from the nomads of the Mongolian steppes to the sedentary farmers of the Tonkin rice fields, from the city-dwellers of Tokyo to the fishermen of Bangladesh, and from Confucian North-East Asia to the Islamized world of Indo-Malaysia. Seen against this background, the region as a whole must primarily be defined in terms of international relations, without attempting to compare politics, cultures or societies. In France, this international perspective has traditionally been the dominant approach to the Far East question, both historically and more recently. As for the historians, political scientists and economists themselves, they are not so much Asia specialists as 'Sinologists', 'Indianists', 'Japanists' or 'Vietnamists' who traditionally pay little attention to international or comparative perspectives, except to reflect the influence of their own favourite culture.

At the other extreme, geographic tradition has rooted Asian history in the landscape of its rice fields and the destiny of its farmers. Temperature and rainfall levels were more significant there than the national borders which took shape during the nineteenth and twentieth centuries. As a result, geographers and ethnologists tend to transcend these borders which, to them, are of little significance. The spheres of influence of the great religions and quasi-religions, especially Hinduism, Buddhism and Confucianism, offer a far more meaningful point of reference. Viewed from this angle, the various sub-regional groupings and definitions, of which South-East Asia is the most common, seem alien and artificial. In fact, the very term 'South-East Asia' has merely been tacked on from outside: first it was the Chinese who coined a single name for the region with Nanyang, then the Japanese with Nampo, and lastly the Allies with their 'South-East Asia Command' during the Second World War. The term 'Indochina' is a French innovation, although the Vietnamese nationalists enthusiastically appropriated it to enhance their own expansionist dreams.

More specifically, however, the grouping that is modern East Asia possesses one unique feature: it is the product of recent history. The colonial period generally played a key part in the creation of borders and states. The major ideologies of the modern era – nationalism and communism – both had a decisive impact. The ambitions and excesses of imperial Japan likewise left a lasting mark. The Cold War forged new relationships, while the collapse of communism has opened the way for the economic boom originally generated by Japan and Asia's 'Four Dragons'. More than any other single factor, it is this recent history which has given East Asia a certain unity.

THE CONTOURS OF PRESENT-DAY EAST ASIA

But which Asia are we actually discussing? There is a wide variety of definitions and delimitations to choose from. From its base in Hawaii the United States CINCPAC (Commander-in-Chief for the Pacific) oversees a zone which stretches from the coast of California and the Bering Strait to the Persian Gulf and Afghanistan, and this meaning of the term 'Asia' has been reinforced by the strategic thinking of the 1970s and by more recent visions of the Pacific Basin. My aim, however, is to adopt the simplest possible definition and encompass the post-war history of the whole of East Asia. This includes, to the north-east, Japan, Korea and part of China; to the south-east, the remainder of China, Hong Kong, Taiwan, the former states of Indochina (Vietnam, Laos and Cambodia) and Burma, as well as the first generation members of ASEAN: Indonesia, Malaysia, the Philippines, Thailand, Singapore and the oil-producing sultanate of Brunei.

This definition corresponds to most of the major influences at work in Asia today, including those of Chinese language and culture, Japanese economic power, a region in the process of developing a regional structure and economies which are undergoing rapid growth, yet it also covers some underdeveloped areas and states which are still lagging behind. It may also be described in terms of what it excludes, namely Asia Minor – in other words the region known to us as the Near and Middle East. While there is no denying that the Turkish and Saudi versions of Sunni Islam radiate out as far as Xinjiang in China, nor that the Koranic universities of Cairo exert a powerful influence on religious teachers and political movements in Indonesia and Malaysia, this only leads us further away from Asia, rather than bringing us closer to it. Also excluded is the Pacific region, widely popularized by the term 'Asia–Pacific'. The 'white' states of the Pacific – Australia and New Zealand – are still a long way from being part of Asia, even though their ethnic fabric is beginning to change. The Polynesian and Melanesian microstates in the South Pacific, even though they were populated by island-hopping boatmen from Asia, also constitute a separate entity. As for the idea that the Western seaboard of the United States, possibly even the entire global economy, is gradually shifting towards the Asian shore of the Pacific, this is an inspired yet muddled notion better considered after, rather than instead of, an attempt to absorb a modicum of Asian history.

We may also exclude Central Asia or, more accurately, continental Eurasia: the region of steppes, nomads and also Himalayan tribes on the so-called 'roof of the world'. Although ties of trade, culture and tribute have long existed between that region and the rest of Asia, its peoples and cultures have none the less been regarded by the great agrarian, sedentary civilizations of Asia as symbols of the outside world, of the foreign and the barbarian, indeed just as they were viewed by European civilization. The borders of the Asian interior have varied throughout history, with Mongol invasions to the East and Hun incursions to the West, but their chief defining feature has indubitably been the freezing winter climate. This central continental area, which was first vassalized and later absorbed by the great twentieth-century powers, particularly the Soviet Union and China, is clearly heading for a future revival, given the current decline in the power of both these states. Kazhakhstan could already serve as a model, with its wily president who has managed the political feat of being advised by Turkey, Pakistan, Israel and Singapore simultaneously. Nevertheless, Central Asia is still marching to a different drummer from the rest of Asia.

It is not so easy to justify the exclusion of South Asia from our definition. It is a grouping dominated by India and Pakistan, around which are clustered the sub-Himalayan states (Nepal, Sikkim and Bhutan), Bangladesh and the countries of the Indian Ocean, notably Sri Lanka. Hinduism has left its imprint on the whole of South-East Asia, formerly dominating the Indochinese peninsula. Indians and Tamils (from southern India and Sri Lanka) spread to Burma, Singapore and Fiji, mirroring the pattern of Chinese emigration. India, the great regional power, could almost be categorized as part of South-East Asia by virtue of its maritime territory, which stretches to the easternmost boundaries of the Indian Ocean, as far as the islands of the Andaman Sea and close to the Indonesian island of Sumatra and the Strait of Malacca. The philosophy of non-alignment, which became one of the guiding principles of the Third World after 1945, originated in India under Mahatma Gandhi's successor Pandit Nehru, and reached its zenith in Asia following the famous Afro-Asian Conference held in Bandung (Indonesia) in 1955. The five principles of peaceful coexistence originally formulated jointly by Nehru's India and Mao's China, developed into the doctrinal basis of Chinese foreign policy. Nevertheless, it remains true that India and Pakistan exist very much apart from the rest of Asia. This fact is evident in current commercial trends as well as on the strategic map: India has been the former Soviet Union's chief Third World ally, while following the Soviet invasion of Afghanistan, Pakistan became a custodian of Western interests to the south, in the Persian Gulf. The long-drawn-out dispute between India and China from 1959 to 1989, the still unresolved border question and the low volume of trade between the two countries all illustrate the fact that, culturally and politically, both have turned their backs on each other. The economic synergy currently driving what is, bluntly speaking, 'productive Asia' (in other words the maritime region of

Asia, now also being joined by the Chinese coastal economy) is only just beginning to touch India, still less its neighbours. Instead, since the 1960s, South Asia has suffered a string of natural disasters, ethnic unrest and political troubles. Today there is the prospect of renewal in the wake of the deaths of Indira and Rajiv Gandhi, whose murders marked a climax for the demons of the Indian subcontinent.

BUDDHISM, CONFUCIANISM, ISLAM AND CHRISTIANITY: THE SPIRITUAL DIVIDE

If geography is an inadequate criterion with which to define Asia, can religion be seen as playing a unifying role? Animism – a patchwork of beliefs and worship dedicated to the dead, household gods and nature spirits – is omnipresent in rural Asia and has permeated the popular form of Taoism also practised by modern city-dwellers. There exists an awe of the spirit world, and of the soothsayers and shamans who make contact with the beyond. Astrology and geomancy (the Chinese *fengshui* which, for instance, governs the design of new buildings) continue to influence the thinking of many people today. In 1991, the best selling work of fiction in Singapore, that most modern of South-East Asian cities, was a collection of ghost stories previously published in the local press. By and large, this mosaic of pantheistic beliefs has given Asia a high degree of spiritual tolerance, for the monotheistic religions have gained little ground there. The chief characteristic of Asian religious observance is the fact that an assortment of different beliefs can coexist within the mind of each individual, due to the way in which successive strata of religious influence have been superimposed on top of one another, ranging from the many different forms of Hindu Buddhism, through the successive schools of Confucianism, to the more recent arrivals of Islam and Christianity. Governments periodically contributed to this process: imperial China, for example, was instrumental in bringing Confucianism to the Vietnamese farmers by dressing it in what were, for them, the more evocative robes and rituals of Buddhism. Imperial Japan built up the Shinto faith, the personal cult of the Emperor, which also drew on Taoism, creating a system of national observance superimposed upon an assortment of existing beliefs. In Vietnam during the Second World War, the officials installed by the French Vichy government recreated all the pomp and ceremony of courtly Confucianism around the figure of the sovereign Bao Dai. This overlaying of diverse beliefs also involved compromise, as in the case of the many Javanese who were converted to Islam over the centuries, yet remained relatively untouched by its rigours, continuing to practise their traditional mysticism. Yet another example is that of many Chinese Christians, who often preserved their ancestor worship and other family rites at the same time.

The sphere of Buddhist influence is clearly very broad, but often very limited in intensity. The version of Buddhism known as *mahayana* (of the great vehicle) spread out from India, sweeping across Nepal, Tibet, Mongolia, China, Korea, Japan and Vietnam. Yet apart from some theocratic states such as Tibet, many of these countries have since experienced the decline of Buddhism to the status of a minority sect. Although it remained the dominant faith in China until the sixth century AD, it largely became superseded by Confucianism, so much so that there are now officially only 35 million Buddhists in China. Yet the cultural legacy of Buddhism is much greater than these figures suggest, ranging from the passage of many Sanskrit words into Chinese (including contemporary speech) to festivals and popular culture, as well as famous tales such as that of the Monkey King in *Xi You Ji* (The Journey to the West). Buddhism, being based on fatalism and a belief in reincarnation, has always been more popular with the rural population than with the intellectual élite. The latter, like the liberal thinker Hu Shih (1937: 247), bemoan the 'indianization of China' to which it has supposedly led, and especially the fatalistic outlook which it engenders. Having been brought to Korea by the Chinese in the sixth century AD and thence to Japan, Buddhism remained the dominant religion for a far longer period. It was adopted as the Japanese imperial religion from the seventh century AD onwards, and flourished in the form of several sects, including Zen. The philosopher-monk Nichiren was the first to develop the very idea of nationalism before it was ever conceived of in Europe. From time to time Buddhism combined with Shintoism, a faith deeply rooted in Japanese peasant culture, as well as being a variant of Chinese Taoism, albeit normally distinct from it. Thus, from the seventeenth century onwards, the rise of Confucianism in its neo-Confucian form and the re-emergence of Shintoism interpreted according to nationalist and authoritarian principles provided strong competition for Buddhism. As of 1945, Shinto was no longer the state religion, but merely that of the Japanese imperial family, and Confucian precepts ceased to be taught explicitly in schools. Japan, the most modern country in the world, still remains a patchwork of religions and curious observances: for example, propitiatory rites and geomancy regularly accompany the opening of new, ultra-modern Japanese factories. This is all, admittedly, accompanied by immense religious tolerance and a proliferation of diverse sects, the most important of which, the Soka Gakkai, numbered nearly one in eight of the Japanese population among its membership in the early 1970s, and even spawned a political party which was represented in the Diet. As for the form of Buddhism known as *theravada* (of the small vehicle), it spread from India to Sri Lanka, and thence across the entire Indochinese peninsula, where it exercises greater political influence on present-day society owing to the fact that it has, from the outset, always emphasized the existence of a formal priesthood set apart from the mass of believers. Over and above the ubiquitousness and importance of the monasteries, the saffron-robed monks have also been responsible for children's education over the centuries. The clergy often provides a focus for political support or opposition to the government, as was again the case in Burma after 1988. The architecture and art of Angkor, Ayut-thaya (Thailand) and Borobudur (Java) show how Buddhism in both its *theravada* and *mahayana* forms has perpetuated Hindu tradition and art.

As with Max Weber's analysis of Protestantism, Confucianism has become the favoured explanation for Asia's economic miracles. Though known in the West chiefly as the result of this much-exaggerated influence, Confucianism also has a long history. The original doctrine of Confucius, who lived during the sixth century BC, gave rise to many schools of thought, some of which were concurrent, some sequential. A school of wisdom centred chiefly on the family sphere, it favours government by élites wherever they consist of individuals of virtue and integrity. Even today, throughout the Chinese world, the 'rule of men' still takes precedence over the rule of law with a regularity deplored by pro-Westerners and democracy supporters. Under the Soong dynasty (960–1279 AD) Confucianism evolved into a neo-Confucian form which later had a decisive impact on Korea and Japan. Neo-Confucianism was philosophically more stringent and was also based on investigation as the means to knowledge, placing principles (*li*) at the forefront of its teaching, as well as being more rationalistic and con-cerned with civic and social matters. As such it dominated North-East Asia between the eleventh and nineteenth centuries. It was mainly used as a weapon by governments which derived a measure of philosophical legiti-macy from it, but its ethical rigour also enabled it to become an instrument of opposition or rebellion in the cause of right. It was surely no accident that the majority of Asia's peasant revolts were led by educated Confucians who had been marginalized and deprived of social status by the intrusion of the West. Differences in emphasis could also occur from one interpretation to the other, so for example the cardinal virtue of Chinese and Vietnamese Confucianism is humanity (*ren* in Chinese) whereas in Japan it is preceded by loyalty (*chu* in Japanese). As a state religion or moral code, Confucian-ism formed the backbone of the Chinese, Korean and Vietnamese bureau-cracies. It has resurfaced, encouraged to a small extent by propaganda, in some present-day régimes such as Singapore, which have drawn from it a heightened sense of civic order, an unrivalled degree of social engineering and also a certain condescension towards the neighbouring Malaysian and Indonesian peoples. It has also reappeared in various guises in the moral propaganda of Chinese Maoism and in Vietnamese and North Korean communism. The authoritarian North Korean form of Confucianism which underlies that country's hostility to trade and the free market, also embod-ies the stifling constraints of courtly Confucianism which was already being denounced by reformers at the beginning of this century.

The third great Asian religion, Islam, was introduced into Central Asia and South-East Asia simultaneously, via the Spice Road originally opened up by Arab navigators and merchants. This Sunni form of Islam then spread to conquer the Malay world and the southern part of the Philip-pines. Although initially tolerant and aimed at proselytism, in more recent times it has increasingly veered towards fundamentalism in Malaysia, Indonesia and southern Thailand. During the post-war era, with the emergence of the aristocratic founders of independent Malaya and the syncretic ideology of Sukarno, the father of Indonesian national unity, a compromise evolved between officially Islamic states and the other communities, particularly the Chinese. This balance was increasingly disturbed as governments embarked, often unsuccessfully, on power struggles with movements which supported *shariah* or religious government. Compared with this phenomenon, Christianity counts for relatively little in Asia. It secured a small yet firm foothold in Japan from the sixteenth century onwards and owes its status in China chiefly to nineteenth-century Protestant missionaries rather than to the Jesuits who preceded them. The only countries where it has been a decisive social and political factor are the Philippines and the two nations split by the Cold War: Korea and Vietnam. In these cases, Catholicism, originally a means of self-expression for the emerging urban middle classes, became an instrument of political opposition, first against communism, then increasingly against the authoritarianism of the local régimes. Like Tibetan lamaism, and for the same reason, in that it demands obedience to a religious authority independent of all temporal power, Christianity occupies an uneasy position in most Asian communist countries. Particularly in China, it periodically seems to fulfil the same kind of spiritual rallying function as it once did in Korea, with the result that a fresh wave of persecution has been inflicted on Chinese bishops and clergy since 1989. With equal inevitability, the political thaw in Peking in 1992–3 resulted in a number of priests being released from prison.

If there does indeed exist a coherent Oriental spirit, just as there exists a European spirit, it is not to be found in any religion or metaphysical morality. Asia has seen the broad spread of animist beliefs which form the bedrock of popular religion. It has also seen the evolution of religions and cults, both sequential and simultaneous. Dangerous fault lines still exist between these cults in Chinese Turkestan and along the maritime straits of Asia. The contemporary Western world now has little insight into the seething of religious movements in Asia and fails to grasp their indirect resurgence in such violent episodes as the Great Leap Forward in China in 1958 and Democratic Kampuchea at the hands of the Khmer Rouge from 1975 to 1978. The bizarre exploit staged by one Japanese Buddhist sect in 1995 further testified to this danger, which had previously been thought confined to the rural communities of Asia. Fanatical, yet with considerable intellectual resources in the shape of young university students and scientists, the sect committed the first terrorist attacks ever to use a poison gas, sarin, on the Tokyo underground. Although its lethal escapade sent shock waves through Japanese society and provoked a new hostility towards extreme religious sects and groups, this did not do any damage to the Buddhist Komeito in the subsequent elections. Religious phenomena are an important aspect of life in contemporary Asia, which modernity has sometimes obscured but never totally extinguished.

THE WEST AND ASIA: THE CASE OF CHINA

While religion plays little part in the overall structure of present-day Asia, colonial history continues to form one of its central pillars. However, this history has clearly varied according to the nature of the colonists and the people whom they colonized. It involves both action and reaction, for the majority of Asia's political movements and contemporary ideologies are rooted in anti-colonialism. Its fundamental starting-point is the impact of the Western intrusion and the resulting collapse of the existing traditional systems.

In 1800, despite the age-old rivalry between Spain and Portugal for the conquest of the globe, the only Asian territory to come under Western rule was the Philippines, a Spanish possession since the days of the Conquistadores, and a few scattered islands in what later became the Indonesian archipelago, which the Netherlands had annexed in order to maintain its monopoly over the spice trade. The key regional actors at this period were China, albeit in the throes of internal decline, Tokugawa Japan, named after the feudal dynasty which ruled from 1603 to 1868, the kingdoms of Korea and, in South-East Asia, the Vietnamese, Siamese and Burmese monarchies which were perpetually in conflict with each other. Yet in the course of the nineteenth and twentieth centuries the whole of Asia, with the exception of Japan and Thailand, was brought under colonial rule. Even then, Japan was forced to open its doors to the outside world by Commodore Perry's fleet in 1853, while the Siamese kingdom of Thailand, the weaker successor to the Ayutthaya era, was obliged to give in to numerous foreign demands in order to maintain its independence.

The process of colonization varied considerably both in its modalities and in its impact. In the case of China, Marxist–nationalist historiography uses the term 'semi-colonialism' to denote the complex web of influences resulting from Western aggression. The partial dismemberment of China and the unequal treaties which China, like Japan and Korea, was forced to sign in the mid-nineteenth century, first with Great Britain and France and later with Russia and Japan, did not destroy its political identity totally. The last great Chinese dynasty, the Qing, struggled, albeit somewhat inconsistently, against foreign invasion before agreeing to a compromise. The dynasty produced many national heroes, such as Lin Zexu, an imperial mandarin in Guangdong during the first Opium War against the British (1839–42). This war signalled the start of a series of unequal treaties, concluded first with Great Britain and later with the other great powers, including Russia and Japan. The first included war reparations, the surrender of Hong Kong in perpetuity, the creation of five British-controlled open ports with extraterritorial status, freedom for Christians to carry out missionary work, and compensation for the opium seized by the Chinese authorities. However, the most ingenious clause of all was that of 'most favoured nation', guaranteeing the British an automatic right to any concessions or privileges already granted to another country. By the terms of the Treaty of Tianjin in 1858, signed while the Qing rulers were being forced to contend with the internal Taiping rebellion, the number of foreign concessions was increased and imports of opium were subjected to open taxation. In order to enforce the terms of the treaty, the British and French burnt down the Summer Palace in Peking, after which the imperial government was forced to accept the annexation of the Kowloon peninsula to the colony of Hong Kong. In 1879, China was forced to surrender the Ryukyu Islands to Japan, while its newly-created southern fleet was sunk by the French navy at Fuzhou in 1884 and its northern fleet by Japan at Weihaiwei in 1894. There then came the scramble for the spoils: the British and the Germans split Shandong between them, and in 1898 Hong Kong was enlarged to incorporate the New Territories for a 99-year period. The Russians seized northern Manchuria, while the French laid claim to a large area of southern China: the country was being carved up like a watermelon. A fresh disaster occurred in the form of the Boxer uprising, an anti-Christian movement which originated in Shandong and, thanks to the thinly-veiled support of Empress Cixi and her more conservative courtiers, succeeded in taking Peking in June 1900. The defeat of the Boxers and a further humiliating treaty in 1901 left China virtually disarmed and forced it to pay a huge indemnity repayable over thirty-nine years. Yet the most concrete of all the West's misdeeds was undoubtedly the spread of opium, which was originally a monopoly of the British East India Company and its Dutch equivalent. In 1865 the annual volume of declared imports amounted to 76,000 'chests', each weighing approximately 75 kilos, equivalent to around 5,700 tonnes and enough to exhaust China's silver reserves. By the 1920s, opium-growing had reached endemic proportions and took up a considerable amount of the viable farmland in arid north-western China, where it contributed to food shortages. Certain Western historians, eager to disassociate themselves from communist historiography, turn a blind eye to this factor, which played a crucial part in China's decline. Others prefer to emphasize the traditionalism and xenophobia which dominated the Qing court at the expense of foreign policy and openness to the West, which would doubtless have been the more realistic stance. The controversy between preserving tradition and westernizing, and between perpetuating the bureaucracy and reforming the political system, has again resurfaced in post-Maoist China.

The country's decline and internal collapse after the failure of the first Chinese revolution in 1911 allowed the main extraterritorial privileges to survive until the outbreak of the Sino-Japanese War in 1937, although it is true that after Chiang Kai-shek's partial reunification of the country in 1926–7, his Republican government took up the nationalist baton once again. In addition, the Western powers handed back twenty of their thirty-three concessions in 1927, while over the next few years the Chinese municipality of Shanghai waged what amounted to a legal guerilla campaign against the concession and its privileges. The government in theory abolished the entire system of extraterritoriality in 1930 but was unable to implement the measure fully as it was subsequently distracted by growing pressure from Japan and by the anti-communist struggle. Finally, in 1943, in the midst of the Second World War, the Allies signed a treaty at Chungking declaring an end to the system of concessions and extraterritoriality.

The dismemberment of China fuelled nationalist feeling and spawned several revolutionary movements. Even imperial policy, from the time of Emperor Daoguang (1821–50) until the long reign of Empress Cixi (which ran in practice from 1861 to 1908), was dominated by the need for compromise and a desire to resist. The policy of *ziqiang* (self-strengthening), with its fostering of institutions imported from abroad and its creation of new industries, was followed by schemes on the part of the Republican government to win the support of one or other of the great powers. These efforts coincided with popular movements which frequently criticized the shortcomings of the central government. A campaign to nationalize the foreign railways and numerous nationalist boycotts launched by the Chinese traders from 1905 further galvanized public opinion. The slogan which accompanied the renewal campaign of the May Fourth Movement in 1919 – 'Save the Fatherland!' (*jiu guo*) – eventually resulted in the peasantry as well as most of the intelligentsia rallying to the communist cause. Communism became the standard-bearer for the mood of national suffering, reinterpreting for its own ends all the nationalist protests of the previous century. In circumstances like these, the positive effects of the Western intrusion – and there were some – could scarcely offset the mood of nationalist, even racial hostility. This was the case with Robert Hart, the remarkable administrator of the Imperial Maritime Customs Service, a government office set up in 1854 to extract from the Chinese Treasury indemnities payable as a result of the treaties, but which developed into a major source of revenue for the Chinese exchequer. Hart was the archetypal 'good modernizer' of Western history: yet in a manner typical of the English colonials portrayed in the works of Somerset Maugham, after fathering a young family by a Chinese concubine he abandoned them with compensation in the United States in order to be able to make a more suitable marriage in England – a tale which epitomizes the limits of good colonialism.

The impact of the intrusion by the West – and Japan – prior to 1937 was not entirely negative, however. Economically, China became integrated into the global market without continually facing penalties, as everything depended on fluctuations in the prices of raw materials. Furthermore, foreign firms in China expanded their activities significantly, creating a true Chinese market rather than merely a few small outlets for systematic export as often happened in South-East Asia. Admittedly, China in the 1930s remained a largely pre-industrial economy with a system of sectoral

distribution similar to that which operated in early Meiji Japan. Nevertheless, certain sectors boomed: China's production of spun cotton yarn, at
that time a staple consumer industry, almost matched Japanese levels, while
in the steel, cement, coal and electricity-generating industries China produced between a third and half as much as Japan. In addition, the rate of
growth in China's industrial production prior to 1937 was comparable with
that of a modern newly-industrialized country. The railway infrastructure
which Chinese and foreign firms vied with each other to build was a key
factor that, together with the navigable waterways, was the cause of China's
changing human geography. Shanghai, with its three million inhabitants,
was the location of 60 per cent of all company start-ups in the 1930s, ahead
of Peking and Tianjin. The degree of foreign control over the economy
varied, but was fairly limited across the industrial sector as a whole: it
affected less than 19 per cent of China's industrial production in the early
1930s, with the exception of Manchuria. However, it was much more significant in primary sectors such as coal, electricity, cotton and cigarette
manufacture, where it reached over 50 per cent. However, foreign enterprise
failed to take hold in the agricultural sector and consequently did not create
a plantation economy, despite the fact that foreign factories were dependent
on Chinese primary products. The major firms such as Jardine & Mathieson
and the Hong Kong & Shanghai Banking Corporation established themselves in all economic sectors, including the service industries, transport and
property. Yet they did not prevent the emergence of a growing class of
Chinese entrepreneurs, not to mention firms which had links with influential Republican factions such as the Soong and Kung families. After 1949,
the communist leadership began to condemn foreign domination and the
geographic concentration and outward orientation of the Chinese economy.
Yet in 1974, even after two decades of socialist planning, Shanghai and the
surrounding region still accounted for 45 per cent of China's industrial
production. The whole question of China's development after 1979 is bound
up with the key importance of the maritime region, the role of the main
urban centres and the restoration, in that form at least, of a foreign presence in the economy. Consequently there has also been an official rehab-
ilitation of the mandarins involved in the pro-westernization movement of
the later nineteenth century (*yangwu yundong*) and the urban bourgeois
dynasties of the early twentieth century.

In an even more complex way, a hybrid civilization evolved under partial
foreign domination. It survives today in architectural form, in the stones of
the Bund in the centre of Shanghai, which has remained unchanged since
1949. It is finding renewed expression along the whole length of China's
maritime border, strengthened by the influential overseas Chinese community and the capital it provides, and by the waves of Chinese students now
making their way to Japan, the United States and Europe. The idea of a
golden age has probably only ever existed in the memories of the Chinese
bourgeoisie, yet that extraordinary encounter between East and West finds

poignant echoes in the popular memory, in literature, in music such as the love songs of Zhou Xuan, and in Shanghai cinema, for example *Angel of the Boulevard*, with its moments when the actor Zhao Dan creates a pastiche of the young Charlie Chaplin.

China, even more so than the rest of Asia, embodies two contradictory phenomena. On the one hand, in the words of one historian of rural China, there is the 'chronic and ubiquitous propensity of China's peasants to take local power into their own hands in modern times rather than their poverty' (Kataoka, 1974: 311). This tendency to rebel, which was exploited by communism and tested to its limits by the Japanese invasion, brought about the success of the revolution. On the other hand, contrasting with this prorevolutionary sociology there is also the force exerted by the entrepreneurial bourgeoisie, which evolved first through contact with the West and later under the aegis of the nationalist government after 1927. After 1978 'the [communist] State took over many of the ideas and procedures that had characterised the triumphant bourgeoisie' (Bergère, 1989: 18).

COLONIALISM COMPARED: BRITAIN, FRANCE, HOLLAND AND THE UNITED STATES

In 1941, on the eve of the Japanese invasion, the map of South-East Asia showed colonies and newly-formed states whose outlines had changed many times since the beginning of the nineteenth century. Admittedly, Western colonialism managed to preserve the local monarchies of Vietnam, Laos, Malaya and Java in all their ritual and ceremonies, albeit with varying degrees of prestige, ranging from the Malay sultans and the emperors of the new Nguyen dynasty in Annam to the Indonesian rajahs. Yet this ingenious front, which helped to legitimize colonial power and create a measure of continuity between this power and the native populations, should not obscure the basic fact that most pre-colonial institutions disappeared, while others were created at the instigation of the new rulers. Before 1800, only the Philippines and part of what would later become the Indonesian archipelago had been colonized on any lasting basis. Following the ill-fated landing of Ferdinand Magellan, who met his death during the course of his adventures in 1521, the Philippines were conquered by the Spanish who created a hybrid culture or *mestizo*, combining Hispanic influences with Malay foundations as well as increasingly dominant Chinese elements. They never totally managed to subdue the Muslim Moro tribes in the south of the islands, with whom the Americans were forced to compromise after 1898. This tendency towards resistance is still an important factor in present-day Filipino politics. Meanwhile, in order to maintain their monopoly over the European spice trade, the Dutch, with their powerful East India Company (1602–1799), built up a plantation economy in the Malay peninsula and islands, starting with Malacca and their Javanese base at Batavia. Despite this, they did not control, let alone unify, the vast expanse of the Indonesian archipelago. With the Napoleonic wars, the English were given the opportunity to act as temporary governors of the Dutch colonies. They subsequently held onto the region stretching from Kuala Lumpur to Malacca and Johor, under the heading of the Straits Settlements, and founded Singapore in 1819, thus ending the Dutch commercial monopoly.

Discounting these colonial beginnings, the region was dominated by three powers: the Vietnamese empire, which had been reunified since the days of the Hué monarchy, the Siamese monarchy which had been forced to seek refuge in Bangkok after the fall of Ayutthaya into Burmese hands, and the Burmese kingdom of Mandalay. These states, with their indeterminate borders, vied for influence over the remnants of the Cambodian kingdom, which had been driven out of Cochinchina, and over the many small Laotian monarchies. The rest, especially the islands, was divided into sultanates and principalities with ever-shifting borders. The age of the nation state had not yet dawned. Pirates, adventurers and local conquerors fought for power, so much so that from 1839 until the arrival of the Japanese in 1941, a large area of Sarawak (now part of Malaysia) was ruled by the Brookes, a family of adventurers who became a unique dynasty of Malaysian chiefs known as the 'white rajahs'. The local potentates quite understandably had difficulty accepting Western notions of borders, treaties and extradition, whereas in contrast bonds of protectorship and suzerainty were more in keeping with their own view of the world.

During the nineteenth century, colonization progressed rapidly. Between 1824 and 1852 the British, the masters of the Indies, took control over the key Burmese region of the Rangoon Delta. By means of a series of negotiations and disputes, they seized the whole of Burma, finally annexing it in 1886. Between 1886 and 1895, they crushed all resistance, relying particularly on minorities such as the Karen. In Vietnam, the Nguyen dynasty founded in 1802 by Emperor Gia Long (1802–20) had unified the country with the help of French soldiers and missionaries, but the persecution of Christians provided France with a pretext to seize the entire southern half of the country (Cochinchina) in 1862 and establish a French colony there. In 1864 this base enabled France, after some hesitation, to impose its suzerainty on King Norodom of Cambodia, a country which had been torn apart over several decades by Vietnamese–Siamese rivalry for its possession. At the court of the Vietnamese emperor Tu Duc (1847–83), conflict raged between the anti-Catholic and pro-French factions and between the pro- and anti-Confucians. Vietnam, which showed itself more willing than the other cultures of the region to adopt modern Western ways, foundered on the reef of Christianity, which was promoted by the French but proved incompatible with the country's traditional bureaucracy. A number of military expeditions ensued, the last of which took place in 1884–5, triggering a war with China and bringing the entire country under French control.

Under French rule, Vietnam was divided, not to say fragmented, into three separate entities – Tonkin, Annam and Cochinchina – and sixty provinces. Within a few years, all authority had effectively been transferred to the Governor-General, based in Hanoi, and to the civil servants of the Colonial Ministry in Paris. This situation was epitomized to the point of caricature by Bao Dai, the last Vietnamese emperor, who, after being educated in France, was crowned in 1932 and 'reigned' until the declaration of independence in 1945. Colonization brought with it an economic boom. As a colony geared to 'exploitation' rather than 'settlement', Indochina numbered just 39,000 French citizens in total out of a population of 22 million, 13,000 of whom were French 'by assimilation'. As elsewhere in South-East Asia, Chinese immigration was encouraged, including 300,000 Hoas in 1939. They particularly controlled the rice trade and created the commercial centre of Cholon in Saigon. As in the other former colonies of South-East Asia, this led to severe ethnic tensions after independence. In Cochinchina the boom in the hevea plantations and in rice growing in turn had an impact on exports, yet it also led to the social exploitation of the contract-labouring 'coolies' by the Vietnamese foremen and small landowners. Three thousand kilometres of railway track were built, including the stretch from Yunnan to southern China and the Trans-Indochina line, still the only rail routes in Vietnam today. The mining industry flourished, particularly at the Honggai coal mines of north-east Tonkin. Public health also improved, thanks to the Pasteur Institute and the fight against malaria, although no statistics are available to pinpoint this progress at regional level.

The French promoted a tiny Vietnamese élite consisting of traditional mandarins, who continued to be awarded nominal posts via the system of Confucian examinations (which had actually been abolished in China since 1905), and a new élite educated in Hanoi or France. On the eve of the Second World War the latter constituted a 10,000-strong group, highly-educated and representing many different ideologies. In 1939, 450,000 children (approximately 9 per cent of the school-age population) were attending primary school, generally for a period of two years, and there were 600 university students in total, certainly far more than in Cambodia or Laos, where approximately 50,000 children attended school. The Dutch East Indies rated even less well in this respect: out of a population of 68 million in 1938, 93,000 children were attending primary school (45,000 of them in native schools for the non-Dutch population) and 496 were registered as students. The Dutch, even more so than the French, initially attempted to eliminate all local competition, then proceeded to regulate it. Yet it was difficult for an educated Vietnamese official to accept a salary below that of the most humble French worker, just as members of the Indonesian élite felt ill at ease alongside their traditional rulers and their better-placed Dutch counterparts. In contrast, the Philippines, like the Japanese colonies, opted for linguistic assimilation, and with two million children attending school and 7,000 students, not counting the large number of expatriates, they were a model society as far as education was concerned. However, the rest of the region lagged behind compared with Thailand and Burma, the countries of *theravada* Buddhism, where the educational role of the monasteries enabled approximately half of all children to be educated throughout the nineteenth century.

In Cambodia, the French introduced property law, abolished the traditional practice of serfdom, brought in foreign settlers and financed their cost through customs duties. Ironically, the abolition of slavery, which had been a Khmer tradition since the days of the kingdom of Angkor, provoked an uprising by supporters of the old order in 1885. King Norodom and his brother Sisowath were supplied with opium for their own personal use to the order of 113 kilograms per annum. King Sisowath and his successors down to Norodom Sihanouk (once a pupil at the French *lycée* in Saigon) were appointed as rulers from within the royal family by French officials. The authorities encouraged immigration from Cochinchina, and the Vietnamese farmers, merchants and interpreters who came to settle incurred the old enmity of the Khmers. Yet Cambodia's rice exports flourished notwithstanding. As in Vietnam, where French cartography and the work of the École française d'Extrême Orient marked positive innovations, the colonization of Cambodia was remarkable for the partial restoration of the vast complex at Angkor, a monument to the lost grandeur of the Khmer kingdom which had lasted from the eighth to the fourteenth century. In Laos, after shoring up the kingdom of Luang Prabang and in 1907 annexing several provinces which had previously come under Siamese rule, the French settlers did little to change the course of events. Laos was also the only colony in French Indochina to run a deficit. By the end of the 1930s, the French, content to rule both colonies with minimal resources through the agency of the local monarchs, had succeeded in enhancing the prestige of the latter.

From 1824 onwards, the division of power between Britain and the Netherlands resulted in the Malay peninsula being granted to the British, while the Indonesian archipelago fell into Dutch hands. Thanks to the large-scale immigration of Chinese labour, the British built up a prosperous plantation economy based on rubber, pepper and coffee. From 1850, in the interior which was still ruled by Malay chiefs, they obtained the concession on the vast tin mines, which notably formed the origins of the modern Malaysian capital, Kuala Lumpur. From 1874, by the terms of the Pangkor Engagement, they persuaded the Malay sultans one by one to accept the 'advice' of the British on all questions other than those touching Malay religion and custom. The following year, 1895, saw the establishment of the Federated Malay States into which all the sultanates were incorporated by 1910, even though some retained a greater degree of autonomy than others. North Borneo (now the Malaysian province of Sabah) formed part of this federation, with the Brooke family keeping control of their territory of

Sarawak. However, British policy embodied all the major problems which would later beset modern Malaysia. Although the status of the sultans and Malay customs was respected, allowing them to be preserved in ritual form, the majority of the population were actually Chinese (40 per cent) or Indian/Tamil (20 per cent). They were often plantation workers, but they also controlled trade as well as the local banking system. The Malays, on the other hand, amounted to less than 10 per cent of the urban population. Out of a mixture of political calculation and innate romanticism, the British kept the Malay villagers at arm's length, creating reservations for them as well as a separate education system to preserve their identity. Traditionalism, religious momentum and the dispossession of the Malays in their own country are the three major problems facing Malaysia today.

As for the Dutch, they steadily expanded their control over Java, Sumatra and the Lesser Sunda Islands. Following the Java War of 1825–30, they introduced forced labour for the local farmers on the plantations, a policy which proved a considerable economic success until the 1870s when the system was liberalized. Overwhelmed by an ethnic mixture which included Chinese of various origins, Malays, Javanese and Eurasians, the Dutch divided themselves into two groups, one being the *totoks*, or colonists of pure ethnic origin, whose racial superiority was increasingly accentuated, and who were further subdivided into long-established settlers and more recent arrivals, and the other being the local *indisch* of mixed race. Chinese immigrants throughout the region were similarly treated, the terms *baba*, *nonya* or *peranakan* still being used to distinguish the Chinese born locally and therefore more likely to be the offspring of intermarriage, from more recent settlers. In 1874, the British accepted a Dutch monopoly over Sumatra, where it took thirty years for the Dutch to win control over the kingdom of Aceh in the northern part of the island: even after 1945, this region would be the scene of two bids for independence. Being few in number, with approximately 100 senior officials to 17 million Javanese, the Dutch conserved the local power of the hereditary rulers and the *priyayi* aristocracy. Beyond Java itself, their rule was even more indirect, and the vast entity which resulted was generally referred to as *Kumpeni*, or 'The Company', after the old Dutch East India Company. Greater standardization was introduced at the beginning of the twentieth century, along with the teaching of Dutch. Driven by an increased concern for 'ethical policy' from 1901 onwards, the Dutch proceeded to invest in infrastructure, social welfare and education for the benefit of the Javanese peasantry. The Dutch East Indies nevertheless remained a major source of revenue, contributing between 12 and 15 per cent of the Dutch national income in 1928. The rapid population boom also had an adverse effect on the standard of living, as it would continue to do after independence.

The situation in the Philippines, unquestionably the most advanced country in South-East Asia at this period, presents a highly contrasting picture. However, American domination began with bloodshed. The United States seized the island from Spain by joining forces with the pro-independence movement, led by Emilio Aguinaldo. Together with the writer José Rizal (who was executed by the Spanish in 1896) Aguinaldo was involved in the creation of a nationalist movement, the Katipunan, and in June 1898 he proclaimed independence, establishing his capital at Malolos. After the American annexation of 1899 he led the resistance against the American forces during which nearly 200,000 Filipinos lost their lives. This experience of nationalism was significant, as it led to the restoration of both the Malay heritage shared by the entire island region from Malaya to the Philippines, and the *tagalog* or national language, as well as being deeply rooted in Catholicism, all forces which were to re-emerge in the second half of the twentieth century. The same forces also underlay the Malolos constitution of 1899, the second to be established in Asia after the Japanese constitution of 1889. However, the Americans, while turning a deaf ear to calls for independence, proceeded to establish a democratic system dominated by the Parti Nacionalista, which demanded independence by negotiation. In 1916, all Filipino males won the right to vote, and in 1920 the United States limited its authority to matters of defence and foreign affairs. This later served as the model for the independence agreements granted to other American-controlled islands in the Pacific. In 1921, 94 per cent of the country's civil servants were Filipino, a feature which in itself marked a radical difference between the Philippines and the other colonies. On the other hand, the Americans carried on the old distinction between the rural population and the educated élite (or Illustrados as they were called in the days of Spanish influence), thus strengthening the landowning oligarchy. In particular, the latter controlled the Senate, or upper chamber, as it continues to do today. Paradoxically, the democratic system introduced by the Americans played into the hands of the ruling families, who forged bonds of patronage with their rural electorates. In 1934, President Roosevelt declared a ten-year commonwealth between the United States and the Philippines, enabling the election of a president with far-reaching powers: Manuel Quezon, the leader of the Parti Nacionalista. This presidential structure was modelled on the United States executive branch, yet it also bore traces of the Latin American caudillo tradition, reinforced in this case by the undeniable charisma of Quezon and some of his post-war successors such as Ramon Magsaysay and Ferdinand Marcos. Thus, even as the country was in the process of acquiring political autonomy, the drift towards dictatorship was already beginning .

The colonial era caused total upheaval in Asia, eroding or destroying existing states such as China and Vietnam, and creating new states in South-East Asia, for example the Federated Malay States, Singapore, the Dutch East Indies and the Philippines, on top of societies dominated by local chieftains and traditional customs. Conversely, where the traditional local monarchs appeared absolutely compliant, as in Cambodia, Laos, the Malay sultanates and the Indonesian archipelago, they were carefully preserved in order to lend strength and legitimacy to colonial rule. By the end of this period, the Khmer and Laotian monarchies in particular seemed to have become virtually fossilized, while the Malay sultans and the aristocratic élite of the *priyayi* in Indonesia at least managed to preserve the status of their own customs. Ultimately, the colonial era generated three major social upheavals. First, it stimulated new trade, which although admittedly based on the exploitation of primary resources, also coincided with considerable improvements in infrastructure which guided the region towards the global market. Second, it simultaneously influenced and antagonized the most highly-educated members of the colonized populations who came into contact with it and who, as Frantz Fanon (1961: 143–6) predicted in another context, were the first to raise the nationalist or communist banner against the colonial powers. Finally, the colonial era served to draw most, though not all, the borders for the modern nation states of South-East Asia and Indochina, on a map that up to that point had only been roughly sketched. The colonial era unquestionably represents the true moment when modern Asia came into being.

SELECTED READING

Bergère, M. (1989) *The golden age of the Chinese bourgeoisie*, Cambridge: Cambridge University Press.

Berval, R. de (ed.) (1987) *Présence du bouddhisme*, Paris: Gallimard.

Fairbank, J.K. (ed.) (1978) *The Cambridge history of China*, vol. 10, *Late Ch'ing, 1800–1911*, Cambridge: Cambridge University Press.

Fanon, F. (1961) *Les damnés de la terre*, Paris: F. Maspéro.

Geertz, C. (1960) *The religion of Java*, Glencoe: The Free Press.

Gourou, P. (1972) *La terre et l'homme en Extrême-Orient*, Paris: Flammarion.

Joyaux, F. (1991) *Géopolitique de l'Extrême-Orient*, 2 vols, Brussels: Éditions Complexe.

Le Thanh Khoi (1981) *Histoire du Vietnam des origines à 1858*, Paris: Sudestasie.

Lombard, D. (1990) *Le carrefour javanais: essai d'histoire globale*, 3 vols, Paris: 'Éditions de' École des Hautes Études en Sciences Sociales.

Morishima, M. (1987) *Capitalisme et Confucianisme: technologie occidentale et éthique japonaise*, Paris: Flammarion.

Peyrefitte, A. (1989) *L'Empire immobile ou le choc des mondes*, Paris: Fayard.

Polachek, J.M. (1992) *The Inner Opium War*, Cambridge, MA: Harvard University Press.

Pye, L. W. (1985) *Asian power and authority: the cultural dimension of authority*, Cambridge, MA: Harvard University Press.

Rozman, G. (ed.) (1991) *The East Asian cultural region: Confucian heritage and its modern adaptation*, Princeton: Princeton University Press.

Sansom, G. (1988) *Histoire du Japon: des origines aux débuts du Japon moderne*, Paris: Fayard.

Sardesai, D. R. (1989) *Southeast Asia: past and present*, London: Macmillan.

Scammel, G. V. (1989) *The first imperial age: European overseas expansion c.1400–1715*, London: Unwin Hyman.

Sieffert, R. (1968) *Les religions du Japon*, Paris: Presses Universitaires de France.

Sinor, D. (1979) *The Cambridge history of early Inner Asia*, Cambridge: Cambridge University Press.

Spence, J.D. (1990) *The search for modern China*, New York: W. Norton.

Steinberg, D.J. (ed.) (1987) *In search of Southeast Asia*, Sydney: Allen & Unwin.

Vandermeersch, L. (1986) *Le Nouveau Monde sinisé*, Paris: Presses Universitaires de France.

Woodside, A.B. (1971) *Vietnam and the Chinese model: a comparative study of Vietnamese and Chinese government in the first half of the nineteenth century*, Cambridge, MA: Harvard University Press.

2 Nationalism and communism (1900–41)

The course of modern Asian history was determined by hostility to the incursion of the West, from its beginnings until the time of decolonization. In 1521, during his circumnavigation of the globe, Ferdinand Magellan landed on Mactan Island in the Philippines and attempted to intervene in a local conflict, with the result that he was killed in battle by a local chief named Lapulapu. It is Lapulapu's martial feat, rather than Magellan's arrival, which is commemorated on the plaque marking the site of their encounter. In 1906, the traditional chiefs of Bali committed mass suicide following their defeat by the Dutch, an act which went down in the long, macabre legend of that deceptive island paradise. These two dates mark approximately the beginning of the violent intrusion of the West and the onset of its decline with the First World War, which distanced the home countries from their colonies and coincided with a boom in the domestic economies of Japan, China and India. In the meantime there came what the historian Carlo Cipolla (1965: 5) calls 'the era of Vasco da Gama', when the West succeeded in subjugating Asia through a combination of force and guile, backed by its military and strategic superiority, particularly in fire-arms and warships. Countless confrontations arose with the indigenous populations which not a single Asian country escaped. Thus, in one sense, the birth of Asian nationalism cannot be attributed to any particular source, for its roots may be traced back to all the many acts of resistance to colonization from the outset. Yet modern nationalism could only materialize in the presence of two simultaneous conditions: first, the crystallization of a national community, if only in the form of an artificial grouping created by the colonial power itself, as in Indonesia, and second, the decline of the traditional monarchies and chieftaincies, causing a shift away from the tribal system and its diplomatic rituals towards new élites calling for complete equality and independence. At the end of the nineteenth century it was still the old élite which rose up against the West, for example in the Revolt of the Literati which marked the death throes of old Vietnam in 1885–6, and in a similar uprising by the Khmers in 1885.

Conversely, the great majority of Asian peasant movements were prompted, not by nationalist claims, but by food shortages and by efforts to bring about a return to fairer standards in dealings with the ruling powers, whether vested in the local landed élite or in the state. The bonds of patronage were generally cemented by what Scott (1976: 2–3) calls the 'subsistence ethic', implying a moral principle of reciprocity between the local rich and poor. From Annam in Vietnam to north-eastern Thailand and the arid region of Burma and from western Java, with its involuted economy (Geertz, 1963), to north-western China and some parts of the interior, there occurred a string of natural disasters, causing the collapse of this untenable contract and with it the outbreak of frequent rebellions. Punitive taxes and allowances (as in republican China), the gradual takeover of communal land by the notables (in Vietnam), the precarious existence of immigrants eking out a living on the fringes of the plantations and jungle (as in the case of the Chinese in Malaysia) and, more generally, the severance of traditional bonds of patronage caused by the growth of the Western-style trading economy, all provided the ingredients for revolt.

Yet this climate of revolt did not necessarily mean nationalism or revolution. In Vietnam, between 1930 and 1931, the Nghe Tinh and Nghe An soviets (*xo viet* in Vietnamese – revolutionary peasant councils inspired by the events of 1917) grew up in the wake of a natural disaster which exacerbated the burden of colonial taxation. With their communist leadership they are generally taken as the starting-point for the grassroots anti-colonial movement in Vietnam. Yet the role of the peasants in this instance was not especially different from what it had been in the earlier movements of 1900, which had been mere jacqueries without the political organization needed to provide new direction. In 1955, in the same Vietnamese provinces, there also occurred a number of uprisings against the Communist government itself as a result of its decision to collectivize the land. What is more, the social background to these movements also bears a resemblance to the peasant uprisings in the Chinese region of Hailufeng between 1920 and 1921, which were led by the intellectual Peng Pai against the landlords in the southern province of Guangdong in advance of any communist intervention. The Asian peasantry always had a strong propensity to rebel in order to preserve or re-establish its social status, yet this rebellious tendency did not necessarily imply any ideological or political commitment. In Asia, nationalism and communism both came into being not in a blaze of fire, but with a spark which needed intellectual momentum and organizational power to fan the flames. The mechanistic notion of a purely spontaneous socio-economic conflagration does not stand up to scrutiny. Moreover, the worst Asian famines of this century (in central China in 1921, 1928 and 1942, throughout South-East Asia and eastern India in 1945, in China in 1959–61 and in Cambodia in 1978–9) failed to provoke any specific uprisings, even when there was enough human suffering to create the necessary inflammatory conditions.

PEASANT MOVEMENTS, RELIGION AND NATIONALISM

There were two exceptions to the rule that traditional peasant protest against colonial taxation did not eventually lead to a nationalist movement: Sarekat Islam in Indonesia and the Cao Dai movement in the colony of Cochinchina during the 1920s. Both were religious in essence and nationalist in substance, drawing mass support from the peasantry. The Cao Dai sect, whose name may be translated as 'of the High Platform, above which only the divine spirit exists', was founded in 1925 and highlighted the Vietnamese tendency to syncretize Confucianism, Buddhism and Taoism (known as the *tam giao* or three religions) with added elements of Christianity. However, its followers also venerated Victor Hugo, Joan of Arc and Charlie Chaplin, attracting mockery from the colonial settlers who failed to grasp the popular significance of such figures. It recruited its converts from the old Chinese-style secret societies, but its capital was established at Tay Ninh, in the heart of Cochinchina's hevea plantations. Initially, it was the Vietnamese notables who joined the movement, especially employees of the colonial system with an eye to their status. Before long, however, it had attracted a huge following among the day-labourers and small landowners, as well as the rural teachers. It protected its members, dispensed justice between them, persuaded some of the larger landowners to join and respect its principles, and ultimately came to rival the colonial administration with over 500,000 followers in 1938. Its spiritual leader, Pham Cong Tac, predicted the outbreak of war, the arrival of the Japanese, the return of Crown Prince Cuong De from Tokyo and the coming of independence with the help of the Japanese. These prophecies proved more or less accurate and, from 1941 onwards, Admiral Decoux's agents were forced to hunt down the followers of Cao Dai as they did other nationalists, although they were protected by the Japanese *Kempetai* or military police. Already unstable, faction-ridden and just as much a vehicle for corporate advancement as a religious movement, the Cao Dai sect subsequently became even more discredited after 1945, when an increasing number of its leaders began to perform political about-turns. Yet its place in history is better judged in the light of the decision by the Vietnamese Communist government in 1991 to legalize the sect's activities once again after a sixteen-year ban. Before the war it was also rivalled by the Hoa Hao sect, led by Huynh Phu So, an illiterate peasant whom the French dubbed 'the mad monk': in fact, he also predicted the French defeat. Millenarian, egalitarian, violent, anti-French yet also anti-communist, the Hoa Hao commandeered land on behalf of the impoverished peasants during the war, while continuing to ensure the delivery of Japanese rice supplies. In 1946 the 'mad monk' founded a political party together with a group of former Trotskyists and was assassinated by the communists in 1947. Conscious of his personal magnetism, they dismembered his body into three as a precautionary measure, to prevent him coming back to life.

In Java, part of the Dutch East Indies, Sarekat Islam was the other great precursor of nationalist mass movements. The Sarekat movement, which began in 1908 as the Islamic Traders' Association, responsible for preventing the sale of *batiks* or local painted textiles by Chinese merchants, soon became the focus for anti-Chinese feeling, pro-Islamic support and anti-colonial hostility. It owed much of its success to the charisma of its leader Tjokroaminoto, a *priyayi* aristocrat who was educated at the training college for local civil servants. He also adopted the fourteen-year-old Sukarno, and the future founder of the Republic of Indonesia made the first of his five legal marriages to Tjokroaminoto's own daughter. The Sarekat movement proclaimed the impending advent of the Mahdi, the Islamic messiah, in the shape of the Ratu Adil or 'Just King', a belief which persisted as late as the mid-1920s. By 1919 it had amassed nearly two million followers, and Tjokroaminoto became the object of a major popular cult whose followers believed him to be the promised saviour. Sarekat's goals were syncretic and diverse, including the advancement of Islam, political autonomy, hostility to capitalism and defence of the Javanese traditions of dialogue and mutual co-operation, the *gotong rojong*. Today the latter remains one of the pillars of official Indonesian ideology, despite having been reduced to little more than the art of compromise and the practice of endless debate. These ideas contributed to the influence of European socialism within the Sarekat movement. Following its disintegration into factions, it spawned the Indies Social Democratic Association, founded in 1914 by a Dutch trade unionist named Henrik Sneevliet. Sneevliet, who later became a hard-line Comintern militant under the pseudonym of Maring, thus began his career within an Islamic association. The paradox of this situation is only superficial and serves to explain the rifts which characterize present-day Indonesia. Life in Java – poor, economically involuted and somewhat lacking in collective organization – revolved around the age-old conflict between two groups: the *abangan*, who were Muslims only in a purely formal sense and never gave up their other beliefs, including animism and Hindo-Buddhism, and the *santri*, who were devout followers of Islam. The founders of Sarekat Islam looked to Cairo and Istanbul for intellectual guidance and wished to extend the territory of the modernizing caliph Kemal Ataturk to include the entire Islamic world. As the harbingers of a modern anti-Western trend, they crossed paths with the Dutch-educated Javanese, who were drawn to the anti-colonialist political societies spawned by the social democratic movement. Yet this association was not to last. In 1920, the social democrats, who had tired of Islam and were now anxious to concentrate on their political battle with the Dutch, founded an Indonesian Communist Party (PKI), the first communist movement in Asia's history. The Islamic wing, including Tjokroaminoto, drove out the PKI in 1921 but subsequently failed to spread as quickly. The *santri* followed the Sarekat and its Islamic successors, while the *abangan* gravitated towards the modern, secular radicalism to which both the PKI and the nationalist movements laid claim.

This divergence was the underlying cause of the greatest confrontation in modern Indonesian history, which broke out literally between two rival brothers. In 1965, at the time of the coup which led to the physical elimination of the PKI, fanatical gangs of youths, stirred up by the *santri*, began hounding *abangan* members, whether they were communists or simply non-religious. The nationalists were constantly pulled back and forth between these two poles, which explains Sukarno's repeated alliances with the communists. In his first major political text, *Nationalism, Islam and Marxism*, published in 1926, he attempted to reconcile the three currents, telling his people that they should not wait for some caliph to come from Istanbul, or some aeroplane from Moscow, bearing independence (Sukarno, 1970). Syncretism and the shift towards secularism were thus already linked. It is therefore hardly surprising that Sukarno and his associates forged a number of further alliances with the PKI, nor that many Islamic nationalist leaders had their roots in socialism, for example Mohammed Hatta who was imprisoned for that very reason in 1927 and later became one of the co-founders of Indonesian independence, or even Adam Malik, who became General Suharto's foreign minister after the 1965 coup. The new officer class, while it benefited from the backing of the *santri* against the communists, was hostile to the idea of a specifically political role for Islam. Similarly, the present-day officers and technocrats of the Suharto régime are endeavouring to ride an Islamic wave emanating from Saudi Arabia and Cairo, which they perceive as a serious threat. This duality between a strictly spiritual Islam and one which seeks a universal role, in other words between fundamentalism and extremism, and the clash between these two forces and their Javanese setting with its syncretism and mysticism, both had their origins in the foundation of Sarekat Islam in 1908.

In addition to the Cao Dai and Sarekat Islam movements, is it possible to identify a third example of a nationalist movement arising directly out of the pre-colonial tradition? Can the Chinese Boxer movement, which besieged the foreign legation district of Peking between June and August 1900, possibly be considered a mass nationalist movement? The Chinese Boxers actually had their origins in the traditional secret societies as far back as the White Lotus sect of the 1770s with its anti-dynastic aims. Their numbers swelled as a result of economic crises and unemployment, due partly to natural disasters and partly to competition from new imported industries. Their impact also owed a great deal to the prevailing hostility towards foreigners and Christians. However, they chiefly owed their rise to the support of conservative imperial officials, who offered them protection and used them as a means to counter foreign pressure. Lacking any unifying political goal, they practised martial arts and magic rites which they believed would render them invincible in battle. Their celebrated fifty-five day siege of Peking was instigated solely by Empress Cixi and her courtiers. She faced the scramble by the foreign powers for territorial concessions at the expense of Chinese interests, and she also feared the consequences of pressure from reformists within her own court. The Boxers were very much a traditional response to the West, but had no strategy of their own. Overcome by a powerful foreign force, they were the last gasp of traditional society rather than the precursors of nationalism. Apart from subsequent eulogies by Marxist historians desperately seeking examples of mass anticolonial movements, they had little impact on posterity. All in all, the Taiping Kingdom of Heavenly Peace (1851–64) was a more ground-breaking movement, with its Christian affinities and its quest to revive the egalitarian society of a bygone era, although it was primarily directed against the Qing dynasty itself, rather than against the West.

THE ORIGINS OF ASIAN NATIONALISM

However, the birthplace of modern Asian nationalism was China. Even a party like Sarekat Islam owed its nationalist zeal to its Chinese enemies. The Vietnamese Nationalist Party from 1920 to 1930, the VNQDD (Vietnam Quoc Dan Dang), was modelled on the Kuomintang, while Phan Boi Chau, the figurehead of Vietnamese nationalism, mimicked the flights of oratory of Sun Yat-sen. Korea's anti-colonial struggle against Japan was strongly based on the Chinese model, while it was in Shanghai that the Catholic Syngman Rhee was proclaimed President of the Korean government-in-exile in 1919. This was also clearly the result of the influence of the Chinese community throughout Asia as a whole. Again, in the early 1920s, Chinese communism provided the main vehicle for the Leninist model which Chinese militants replicated throughout Asia.

Chinese nationalism was originally the product of an upsurge by the ruling classes, including the educated élite, but as it was invariably accompanied by its inseparable double, westernization, it took many different forms. The conservatives were either xenophobes or pragmatists, sometimes even both in succession, their chief priority being the preservation of the Confucian dynastic and bureaucratic order. As for the nationalists, their aim was to seize all weapons belonging to the foreigners, which following the failure of the initial reform phase of 1861–74 included their institutions and thought. Ultimately, after several fruitless attempts, they toppled the imperial régime with the 1911 revolution and condemned classical culture in the May Fourth Movement of 1919 with a zeal that strove to be patriotic and pro-Western at the same time. It is therefore hardly surprising that the key figures in the nationalist and communist movements were generally those who had already rubbed shoulders with the West and its ideas, nor that the initial social impact of their movements was chiefly felt among the entrepreneurial classes and by the urban bourgeoisie who lived in close contact with foreigners. After all, the political militants frequently encountered the new class of Western-trained officers who, while they had their roots planted deep in the soil of declining rural China, also found themselves confronted with foreign superiority. The early nationalist figures and leaders fitted this stereotype. Sun Yat-sen, the founder of the Revolution-ary Alliance (which became the Kuomintang after 1911), was born in the hinterland of Macao, in the Pearl Delta. He was educated exclusively abroad and, after taking part in his first political conspiracy, became a professional globetrotter, drumming up revolutionary support from the overseas Chinese community worldwide. He was an example of 'social types unknown in traditional China, the most striking of which were professional politicians and revolutionaries' (Bastid-Bruguière, 1980: 555). Countless Chinese thinkers, intellectuals and militants passed through Western-style educational institutions at the end of the last century, taking up law, medi-cine or, as in the case of the philosopher Yan Fu, naval construction, before arriving at their own vocation or philosophy. During this period the man-darins turned their hands to commerce, forming a class known as the *shenshang* (business aristocracy), and the first major challenges faced by the fledgling nationalist movement were of an economic nature. In particular, there was the question of the construction of Chinese railway lines to counter the foreign railways, which were spreading octopus-like throughout the country. This problem had remained unresolved since its first appear-ance in 1889 because of a lack of resources, and continued to fester until 1910–14, when the imperial court caused its own downfall by declaring its intention of using foreign loans to bail out the Sichuan Chinese railway.

This positivist, almost Saint-Simonian form of nationalism (Bianco, 1987: 53) was more important than the revival of traditionalism which ran paral-lel with it. Although many intellectuals, like Kang Yuwei in 1898, shied away from the consequences of their philosophy, the national crisis gener-ally led them to modify their positions and their actions. Radicalism often went hand in hand with patriotism, some examples being the two great imperial mandarins, Governor-General Li Hongzhang and Viceroy Zhang Zhidong, the intellectual reformists Kang Yuwei and Liang Qichao, Sun Yat-sen himself, and Li Dazhao and the other instigators of the May Fourth Movement. Historians have often stressed the intellectual rifts which existed between these highly diverse personalities, as though their 'solutions' followed one another in succession, yet they were in fact closely interrelated. It was Li Hongzhang to whom the young Sun Yat-sen addressed a memorandum on Chinese reform, while Zhang Zhidong and Liang Qichao backed the significant move to allow young people to travel to study in Japan, the breeding-ground of the 1911 revolution. Before communism caused an even greater rift between reform and social revolu-tion, only a very few, like the philosopher Hu Shih, remained purely liberal, pro-Western reformers without any vision of more radical solutions.

NATIONALISM: THE JAPANESE CONNECTION

Upon China's defeat by the West, Japan reversed the mirror which in the past had led it to prize its Chinese cultural and artistic roots above all else and revere the heritage of continental Asia. In future, it would be Japan which would provide the inspiration for the notion of Chinese renewal, while the vast numbers of Chinese students in Japan (approximately 20,000 in 1908) were frequently a target for the scorn of the Japanese people. Yet in actual fact, the ideas which Japan was exporting to China were often Chinese in origin. For example, it was the Chinese historian Wei Yuan in 1842 who first contrasted Western military and technical superiority with Chinese ethical and philosophical strength. In Japan he inspired Sakuma Shozan, the reformist philosopher of the Meiji era, who adopted as his precept the phrase 'Eastern ethics and Western technology'. He in turn was imitated by the modernizing Chinese mandarin Zhang Zhidong, who in 1898 coined a similar expression – 'Chinese wisdom as the base, Western knowledge as the instrument' (*Zhongxue wei ti, xixue wei yong*) – which became the most famous maxim in modern Chinese history. The story of these mutual borrowings has yet to be written, but it might well offer the starting-point for a culturalist approach to Oriental civilizations, based on their mutual kinship sustained via the continual interplay of their ideas and their insistence on a legitimacy equal to that of the West.

During this period, Japanese statesmen began to pay considerable attention to China as well as to North-East Asia in general. In 1898, following the failure of the Reform of a Hundred Days in China, the outlawed intellectuals Kang Yuwei and Liang Qichao fled to Japan, where they encountered Sun Yat-sen and his followers who were in the process of setting up their own political movement in Tokyo. They were welcomed with open arms by a number of the more senior officials in the Meiji administration, who conversely took a somewhat contemptuous view of the Qing predicament. In the years 1898–1911, Japan had a decisive influence on Chinese intellectuals in the broadest possible sense, from the army officers trained in Tokyo (the Russians generally being regarded as the common threat) to the Chinese interns who, within a few months, absorbed Meiji institutions and ideas. Such visits and experiences gave rise to countless writings and translations. The greatest anti-Manchu pamphleteers of the period either lived in Japan or had their work taken to Tokyo for translation, for example Chen Tianhua with his *Kill the foreign devils, kill the Christian converts, kill the Manchu mandarins!* and Zou Rong, the author of a 1903 essay attacking the Qing entitled *The revolutionary army*. More than half of these Chinese translations of Japanese works were on historical or legal topics. The nascent constitutionalism which developed towards the end of the Qing era, as well as numerous legal texts, were Japanese in origin, while three-quarters of the neologisms to enter the Chinese language during this period came directly from Japanese. The terms adopted for many Western philosophical concepts, such as individual liberty and the rights of man, as well as those pertaining to the fundamentals of Marxism, which were first translated from Japanese in 1906 in the

Min Bao (People's Journal), reflected the importance of this linguistic and cultural prism.

Japan also influenced Chinese nationalism in a more direct, political way. After the attempted Reform of a Hundred Days in 1898, the Ministry of Foreign Affairs hammered out the first of its 'doctrines' on Asia which were intended to guide its diplomacy. The Okuma Doctrine of 1898 argued that Japan, historically the recipient of Chinese culture, should now hold back the advance of the West long enough to allow China to build up new momentum. This magnanimous reasoning coincided with Japan's first pan-Asian theories, which combined defence against the West with support for the rights of Asian peoples, as well as incipient Japanese designs on Korea and Manchuria. The same circles were simultaneously sending aid to Aguinaldo's revolution against the Spanish in the Philippines. In 1898, this conjunction of a pan-Asian vision, anti-colonialism and Japanese ambition did not fail to make an impact.

Much later, Prince Konoe, Prime Minister from 1938 to 1941, surrounded himself with advisers who made up the Association for the Greater East Asia Co-prosperity Sphere, founded together with a group of left-wing intellectuals who felt called upon to support both their country and the Chinese revolution. Their anti-imperialism was exploited by the Japanese military for its own ends until these changed in 1940–1. However, the most famous member of the group, Hotsumi Ozaki, was the favourite informer of master Comintern spy Richard Sorge, who was arrested in October 1941. After the war, even the Japanese conservative parties, notably the Liberal Democratic Party, would each have their own lobby dedicated to the promotion of good relations with the People's Republic of China in defiance of United States policy, while similar links existed with Kim Il Sung's North Korea.

THE 1911 REVOLUTION AND ITS LEGACY

On 10 October 1911, following a series of abortive intrigues between 1895 and 1911, the Chinese revolutionaries provoked an uprising in the barracks of Wuhan, in Hubei province, and thereby succeeded in bringing down the Qing, who abdicated in the following year. Today, the 'Double Ten' (the tenth day of the tenth month, 10 October 1911) is commemorated only in Taiwan, but Sun Yat-sen, the roving doctor who briefly became the first leader of the Chinese republican government, is officially revered in both China and Taiwan. His three 'Principles of the People' – nationalism, democracy and socialism – are universally invoked as the justification for conservative régimes and Chinese progressivism alike. Yet the three terms are distorted in their translation from the Chinese. The first, *minzu*, primarily evokes the idea of race and implies something much broader than 'nationalism' in the European sense of the word. In all Sun Yat-sen's writings, *minzhu*, usually translated as democracy, signifies a system of government which enjoys popular legitimacy, rather than simply a system of electoral representation. The third term, *minsheng*, which means 'subsistence of the people' rather than socialism as such, denotes the classical duty of the mandarin élite towards the people, combined with assorted connotations of the British Labour movement, as opposed to Marxist socialism. It was ambiguities of this kind – as well as the eventual rallying of some of Sun Yat-sen's associates to the communist cause, among them his widow Song Qingling and Liao Chengzhi, the son of his political successor – which enabled the communist movement to reinterpret the tenets of 1911 as the mere precursor of their own ideology.

However, one further aspect of the 1911 revolution proved a much clearer portent of future events, and that was the role played by the officers and the modern army, with the rise of the first military régime in what would later be called the Third World. In comparison with the handful of élitist members of the Revolutionary Alliance, the soldiers and officers of the New Army, which was formed by the Qing from 1903 onwards, played by far the more decisive role. Better educated than their predecessors, they were deeply imbued with the new mood of intellectual and political unrest. The imperial General Yuan Shikai, who had already founded the Northern Army but was wisely kept well away from Peking by the mistrustful imperial rulers, was finally given orders to quell the uprising. It was he who later saved the situation by accepting the abdication of the Emperor in Peking and securing his own election as the first President of Republican China. Ahead of their counterparts at the Whampoa Military Academy, founded under the auspices of the 1924 Chinese Communist Party (CCP)–Kuomintang united front, the officers of the New Army played a key role in all the military governments which ruled China, both successively and concurrently, until at least 1927. Even in Canton, Sun Yat-sen, in the course of his attempts to form a government, was forced to contend with the local strongman, General Chen Jiong-ming, until 1923. This struggle led to the militarization of the Kuomintang as well as the rise of the former commandant of the Whampoa Military Academy, Chiang Kai-shek, following Sun Yat-sen's death in 1925. This process of militarization – the era of the 'warlords' – brought China to the brink of chaos. Yet from the outset, the dual identity of the Chinese republican government, torn between rival parties of political idealists on the one hand and hard-line militarists on the other, prefigured the military and nationalist régimes that were to emerge on left and right alike in the twentieth century. Chinese communism itself was primarily militaristic and nationalistic in nature, and it was probably this which constituted the main difference between it and the Bolsheviks and the Soviet bureaucracy. Particularly from the 1970s onwards, the army steered an uncertain course between conservatism and pro-nationalist modernism, between acknowledgement of its élite kinship with the rebellious student body and recognition of its role as the highly-paid guardian of public order. The communist forces and their republican contemporaries rubbed shoulders in the military academies and united fronts, and were actually very much alike.

The spirit of the clique or faction, bound up with traditional notions of loyalty, emerged all the stronger from the transition to a modern army with a political role. In China, the principal communist leaders – Mao Zedong, Liu Shaoqi, Lin Biao, Deng Xiaoping and even the veteran conservative Yang Shangkun of 1989 fame – all primarily owe, or owed, their power to the soldierly brotherhood established while they were in command of Red Army units prior to 1949. Indirect proof of this may also be seen in the relatively weak position of those leaders who could only claim a civilian base, such as the Gang of Four radicals in 1976 and Hu Yaobang and Zhao Ziyang, the two reformers sacked in 1987 and 1989. South Korea since 1960, Indonesia since 1945, Thailand since 1932 and Burma since 1962 have likewise been dominated by groups of officers whose ties of mutual loyalty were often cemented during their days as contemporaries at military academy.

THE RISE OF NATIONALISM IN SOUTH-EAST ASIA

The Great Depression which followed the crash of 1929, accompanied by falling demand and prices for raw materials from the colonies, created social instability and political tensions throughout South-East Asia. In certain places, such as the Malay states, these took the form of ethnic rivalry rather than a protest movement. Although Marxist historians have placed considerable emphasis on the condition and role of the plantation workers, particularly in Vietnam, it was the intelligentsia, some belonging to the pre-colonial élites, some from the westernized fringes of society, in contact with the colonial system, who were the fountainhead of modern nationalism across the whole of South-East Asia. This was particularly true of French Indochina: nowhere else was the tension so clearly marked between the natives' utopian expectations of the colonial power and the harsh, even racist reality. The Dutch and British, with their more strictly segregated educational and administrative systems, had raised fewer hopes than the French colonial government of Jules Ferry, Paul Doumer and Albert Sarraut.

Compared to the rest of South-East Asia, the rise of nationalism in Vietnam was also made smoother by the fact that it stemmed from the old national struggles waged against Chinese domination, ranging from the legendary Le Loi, who overcame the Chinese in 1427, to the revolt of the Tay Son in 1771. However, after attempting to claim equality and assimilation with France, its earliest twentieth-century exponents drew their inspiration from the doctrine of Sun Yat-sen and the political structures of the Kuomintang, already influenced by Leninism. Two intellectuals, Phan Chau Trinh and Phan Boi Chau, carried the movement between them. The former, imbued with French republican idealism and the legacy of 1789,

was exiled to France but he nevertheless helped to establish a fringe Constitutionalist Party in 1923 whose very name reflected the course of Chinese
and Japanese development at the end of the nineteenth century. His funeral
in Saigon in 1926 was marked by a major demonstration, and the ensuing
crackdown served to swell the ranks of future militants. Phan Boi Chau, the
more famous of the two, took part in the Revolt of the Literati in 1885 and
initially developed a fascination with Japan: in 1905, at the time of the
Franco-Russian alliance, he witnessed the Russian imperial fleet lying at
anchor in the bay of Cam Ranh before it was sunk by the Japanese navy at
Tsushima. He then founded the Dong Du movement, whose name meant
'Go East!' He subsequently focused his attention on the work of the
Kuomintang, which he planned to replicate in Vietnam. He advocated
violence and was the driving force behind a number of riots and assassination attempts in Vietnam itself. After being arrested in Shanghai by the
concessionary police he was condemned to death, but his sentence was
commuted by Governor-General Varenne, a member of the SFIO (the
French socialist party of those days) and an advocate of liberal colonialism.
These forerunners of nationalism soon fell by the wayside. The Constitutionalist Party was reduced to a small group which was preoccupied with its
own representation in the French National Assembly and backed the
French attempt to establish a separate government for Cochinchina in
1946. Phan Boi Chau's position changed considerably. Having followed in
the footsteps of their earlier counterparts, the first nationalist intellectuals
fell into the same trap as their nineteenth-century predecessors, who were
too full of admiration for Confucianism and the Chinese to put up any real
opposition to either.

In the wake of the extraordinary success of the Cao Dai and Hoa Hao
sects, two early manifestations of mass proto-nationalism, the political
momentum was taken up by a much younger generation with the creation,
in 1927, of the Viet Nam Quoc Dan Dang (VNQDD), a literal translation
of the Chinese Kuomintang in terms of both its organization and its ideology. Primarily a Tonkinese party, the VNQDD came to prominence in
1929 with its assassination of the director of the General Office of Labour, a
prime target. In so doing, it prompted the immediate mobilization of the
French security services which were less concerned about signs of burgeon-
ing communism than about this particular brand of unrest, so strongly
reminiscent of the groundswell of Chinese nationalism. In the following
year, the VNQDD inspired a bungled attack by the soldiers of Yenbai who
massacred their French officers, provoking a general crackdown. The leaders of the VNQDD were executed and the rest of its members deported,
often alongside the communist agitators responsible for the revolt (also in
1930) of the Nghe An and Nghe Tinh soviets. The future of the nationalist
movement was consequently hammered out within the confines of French
prisons and penal colonies, although it was largely dominated by the superior organization and ideology of the communists. The Vietnamese nation-

alist movement was thus weakened at birth, first by the conflicting influences of millenarian sects, then by communism. The most influential non-
communists of the post-war period, such as Ngo Dinh Diem, the Catholic
doctor who later became President of South Vietnam, were mere secondary
figures, even if they did manage to keep their distance from the colonial
administration.

Nothing of this sort occurred in Indonesia, where the rise of nationalism,
as already shown in the case of Sarekat Islam, was firmly anchored in the
extraordinary personality of Sukarno. Over and above his kinship with the
Sarekat movement, Sukarno (who like many Indonesians used only his first
name) proved an immensely gifted figure. He was educated in a predom-
inantly Dutch school along with a small number of other Indonesians, but
he clearly drew his inspiration and particularly his oratorial skills from his
father-in-law, the leader of the Sarekat movement. In order to avoid the
colonial administration, he studied as an engineer, thereby tapping into the
sociological vein of Indonesia's first small-scale nationalist movement, the
Boedie Oetomo (or 'Noble Enterprise'), which originated in the first Dutch
medical school established for the native population. Sukarno, a man of
prolific intellect, could already speak Dutch, so-called 'bazaar Malay' (the
forerunner of modern Indonesian), English, French and German as well as
Javanese. Familiar with the great political thinkers from Voltaire to Abra-
ham Lincoln to Karl Marx, he juggled an eclectic combination of their
ideas. Later, when in power, he not only coined a vast range of modernizing
acronyms, but also succeeded in slipping a medley of these languages into
his official speeches. Above all, the father of 'Third-Worldism' was an
unusually talented pupil of the Western world, which has never sufficiently
acknowledged this fact.

The successive failures of the Sarekat Islam movement and the embryonic
PKI in 1926 paved the way the following year for Sukarno to form a
federation made up of the remnants of the political parties still in existence
on the sparse Dutch-educated fringes of Indonesian society, modelling it on
the Indonesian Nationalist Party (INP). Sukarno launched his new party on
4 July, in honour of the American Revolution. His goal was *merdeka*
(independence), an aim already taken up by the Indonesian students in the
Netherlands. Mass unrest ensued, partly fuelled by the introduction of a
new version of the *wayang*, or Javanese shadow play, in which the Dutch
were portrayed as a usurping dynasty. All Javanese watch the *wayang*, and
Sukarno's ability to exploit it as a source of mythical metaphor was an
important part of his charisma. When he was imprisoned for two years in
December 1929, like a subtropical Dreyfus he became a *cause célèbre* with
his defence entitled *Indonesia accuses*. In his absence, however, the INP
disintegrated and two rivals emerged who later became his colleagues:
Mohammed Hatta, a Muslim born in 1902 who studied economics at
Rotterdam, and Sutan Sjahir, a former law student at Leyden. Both were
more pro-Western and élitist than Sukarno, and regarded his mysticism and

flights of oratory with a certain amount of irony. However, before joining forces with him their sole achievement had been to organize a society of intellectuals. After establishing his own party, Partindo, Sukarno was deported once again in 1933. Nevertheless, by the end of the period of Dutch rule he had gained a much wider popularity. Hatta became Vice-President of the Republic of Indonesia until his resignation in 1956, while Sjahir became Prime Minister from 1945 to 1947 before being exiled by Sukarno. Sjahir would later comment in his autobiography that he had been too abstract and remote from his people, and too westernized: turned around, this amounted to an acknowledgement of the reasons for Sukarno's own political superiority over his rivals. Between 1922 and 1941, the agglomeration of diverse peoples and cultures which made up the Dutch East Indies became Indonesia in the eyes of the intellectuals. Malay, the former language of business spoken by the Dutch and Chinese, became Indonesian, the 'language of revolution'. Yet until the 1960s, Indonesia continued to be haunted by a certain cultural schizophrenia. Its intellectuals and notables tended to think partly in Dutch (and later American English) even though they continued to speak in Indonesian, while the peasants and many lesser bureaucrats continued to remain Javanese, Moluccan or natives of Aceh, rather than define themselves in terms of the new nationality.

Although they lacked the advantage of such outstanding leaders as Indonesia, the Federated Malay States also experienced nationalism, but in a much more localized form. In this sense, therefore, the British system of segregated schools for Malay, Chinese and Indian pupils bore fruit. Malay nationalism also had Islamic origins, arising out of stays in Cairo or Hejaz (the future Saudi Arabia), and a dual ambition: to reform Islam and to unify the Malay peoples, in other words the inhabitants of present-day Malaysia and Indonesia. The Young Malay Union (founded in 1938) and several other 'young' movements (an epithet derived from Ataturk's influence), often peasant in origin, opposed the British and inspired the ideas of the Indonesian nationalist left. They were also already following Tokyo's lead well before the Second World War. The other nationalist element consisted of Malay civil servants in the administration, who were frequently descended from the aristocracy of the sultans. Their chief aim was to halt the social advancement of the Chinese and Indian immigrants, who in 1930 numbered 31 per cent and 21 per cent of the population respectively. They fought to increase the number of posts available exclusively to themselves and to create additional reserves of land for Malays by banning property ownership by other ethnic groups. Here, too, a future legacy may be found in the economic policy launched by Malaysia in the wake of the 1969 race riots, which was designed to benefit the *bumiputra* (i.e. Malay) economy at the expense of what was seen as excessive Chinese dynamism. However, it is also arguable that the traditional Malay concepts of land and of the *kampong*, or collective village, are not readily compatible with the law of property. As a result, conflict over the very status of the tribal territories and hostility towards the privatization of property swept through the entire Malay–Oceanian world, from Fiji to Vanuatu and New Caledonia. This local feature ultimately made Malay nationalism a staunch ally of the colonial administration, especially in the form of the Malay societies established in 1938. The Chinese once again felt the pull of the mother country, joining overseas branches of the Kuomintang and even the Malay Communist Party. Ironically, Japanese repression later steered them towards a patriotic, pro-British stance. As for the Malays, after a pro-Japanese phase during the war, they formed a nationalist movement, building on existing pre-war foundations. There still remained anti-Chinese hostility (though better controlled since the 1969 pogroms), the Islamic movement (more often than not a rallying cry for nationalist and electoral ends) and even an element of pro-Japanese feeling, as witnessed by the famous slogan 'Look East' coined by Prime Minister Mahathir during the 1980s.

In Burma, too, a local quality, this time Buddhist and anti-Islamic in origin, governed the birth of nationalism. In *Burmese Days*, the young George Orwell, son of an officer in the colonial police among the minorities of the interior, portrayed the unbelievable hierarchy of hypocrisy and envy created by colonial society with all its subtle distinctions. Yet he failed to grasp the importance of the monks and the Buddhist tradition which held the balance of political power in Burma. Religion and xenophobia constituted the two facets of Burmese nationalism during its ascendancy. The international crisis of 1930 dealt a crushing blow to the peasants of the Rangoon Delta. There, too, the British encouraged immigration by South Asian bureaucrats, soldiers and traders who joined the traditional Arab merchants along the coast and in the cities. In Burma, even more so than in Malaysia, the *chettiar*, an Indian caste, vied with the modern banks and the overseas Chinese for loans and interest. In the 1930s many peasants were deprived of their land, and Rangoon was populated mainly by foreigners from South Asia. In addition, the Colonial Office built up its own unique caste consisting of the British and those of the native population who were admitted to their inner sanctum.

The Young Men's Buddhist Association was founded in 1906, in a clear imitation of that epitome of Victorian benevolence, the Young Men's Christian Association (YMCA). In 1920 it became the General Council of Burmese Associations. Extremely British in terms of its prolific, free, English-language publications, it came into being at the same time that the students of Rangoon were beginning their pro-Buddhist agitation and U Ottama, a Buddhist monk newly returned from India, was launching a Gandhi-style movement. This movement spread, and grew in popularity as the result of a peasant revolt in 1930 led by Saya San, a claimant to the throne overturned by the British in 1885. Saya San's disciples, like the Chinese Boxers and the followers of the Ratu Adil in Java, were weakened by their belief in the power of amulets and other magic rituals to defeat the

British. Even so, the royalties from one of Saya San's books served to finance a Marxist library in Rangoon, for Burma's monasteries had made it the most highly-educated country in Asia. Elements of Buddhism and socialism were intertwined in varying proportions in all the anti-British movements. The most important of these, from 1930 onwards, was the 'Our Burma' movement, whose members proudly reclaimed *Thakin*, a term of respect meaning 'master' (analogous to the Hindi *sahib*) which was chiefly reserved for the British. However, the Rangoon Student Association was also a breeding-ground for future political cadres, notably Aung San, the future father of independence, and U Nu, the post-war head of state. Social tensions were now at their height, and even the anglicized Prime Minister Ba Maw established a 'Poor Man's Party'. In 1938 (year 1300 in the Burmese calendar) an uprising was staged by nationalist leaders and workers employed in the fledgling oil industry. Fifty years later, in 1988, crowds protesting against the dictatorship clashed with the army on the same sites, which in the meantime had become almost a Mecca in the collective memory. The movement was suppressed, and with nationalism in decline, the upshot was the formation of a Communist Party in August 1939, which large numbers of nationalists proceeded to join in a striking display of ideological confusion.

Although Buddhism was also a factor in the rebirth of Cambodian nationalism, the latter none the less qualifies as a separate case. As one historian has observed, the word which recurs most often in French descriptions of the Cambodians before 1939 is 'sleep' (Chandler, 1983). Images of indolence, acquiescence and idleness abound, and the Khmer monarchy under Monivong, the grandfather of Norodom Sihanouk, was evidently in steep decline, for the 150th anniversary of the French Revolution was commemorated in Phnom Penh on its very own 'Place de la République'. The awakening of the Cambodian peasants was sometimes violent, as in 1916 when they marched on Phnom Penh in protest against taxes imposed by the monarchy to support the French war effort. Once again, in 1925, it was hostility to taxation which prompted the murder of a colonial official. By this point, no newspapers or literature had been published in Khmer for decades, and the colonial settlers made little effort to pick up the language. Primary education continued to be provided by Buddhist societies and the two monastic orders or *sangha*. On the other hand, there was a boom in road building as well as exports (of rice and rubber), and almost 300,000 Chinese traders settled in the towns, along with Vietnamese immigrants. It was not until 1930 that the first small class of Cambodian students graduated from the Saigon *lycée*, and 1936 in the case of the Sisowath *lycée*. This tiny contingent (numbering fewer than thirty in 1939), together with the royal court, provided the basis for post-war Cambodian politics: for example Thiounn, the pro-French Prime Minister who wielded more influence than King Monivong, fathered many sons who became Khmer Rouge cadres, including Thiounn Mumm, the first Cambodian student to attend the Polytechnique in Paris and later Minister of Education in Democratic Kampuchea after 1970. The Khmer Rouge leader Pol Pot's elder sister was one of King Monivong's concubines, while Norodom Sihanouk himself was well-acquainted with Pol Pot's future wife, who in turn was the sister-in-law of Ieng Sary, the Number Two man in the Khmer Rouge. Other future personalities, such as General Lon Nol, Prime Minister from 1972 to 1975, worked first in the local French administration.

Other seeds of change included a Khmer newspaper, *Nagara Vatta*, founded in 1936, and in particular the Buddhist Institute of Phnom Penh, a school of *pali* (the language of *theravada* Buddhism, closely related to Sanskrit), which was set up under French sponsorship. The two institutions were interlinked and became involved in many activities on the outbreak of war. One of the main consequences both of the colonial order in Cambodia and of the extreme lack of organization on the part of the Cambodians working within and against that order, was the huge cultural divide between rural Cambodia, still dominated by pre-colonial thinking and social structures, and the tiny group of individuals who, chameleon-like, assumed the successive guises of Khmer politics. Admittedly, this upper echelon was far less visible to the population at large than the many Vietnamese and Chinese immigrants who settled in the major administrative centres and urban areas, a situation which provoked feelings of bitterness and enmity. Yet all the leaders of the revolutionary groups of that period had spent at least part of their lives either among the westernized élite or within the Buddhist educational tradition. The latent anger of the peasants was kindled by intellectuals belonging to one or other of these groups, and in many cases was transmitted by rural teachers during the post-war period.

In China, the spirit of reform and westernization was allowed to develop for several decades before the appearance of Leninism, creating a broader political arena which will doubtless open up again in the future after the demise of communism. This was, of course, even more true of Japan, where a successful period of transformation preceded the shift towards militarism in the 1930s. In South-East Asia, on the other hand, the two currents were compressed, evolving almost in unison, while the colonial authorities kept the pre-colonial political institutions artificially alive for their own benefit. Everywhere, communism and nationalism fought tooth and nail. Yet in undergoing reform since 1978, Chinese communism (especially Chinese philosophers and members of the political opposition) has often sought inspiration, consciously or otherwise, in the legacy of the period 1860–1937. Memories of the modernizing mandarins of the imperial Restoration, the Shanghai capitalists of the republican era and the political philosophy of the May Fourth Movement of 1919 have served to irrigate Chinese society, where communist dogma is now as desiccated as a fossil.

In contrast, like their nationalist enemies who largely held sway over maritime Asia in the 1950s, the other communist régimes of Vietnam, Cambodia and Laos, and the post-war guerilla movements across virtually the whole of South-East Asia, enjoyed few of the conditions necessary for the growth of their own political cultures. Vietnam hovered between Peking and Moscow, eventually spawning a crippling bureaucracy. The Khmer Rouge created a bloody pastiche of Maoist violence, blindly obsessed by their unacknowledged kinship with the pro-slavery monarchy of Angkor. In Malaysia and Indonesia the communists remained under the sway of Peking until their demise. Yet apart from the occasional credo functioning as official ideology, such as Indonesia's *pancasila*, the Malay 'Look East' policy and Singapore's Confucianism designed for popular consumption, the régimes and societies of South-East Asia operated without any political capital of their own. The legacy of the colonial institutions, the defence of national security, the development economy of their American mentors and the official cult of harmony, co-operation and consensus bequeathed to the whole of Asia by the Japanese, were all substituted for a political culture.

THE HOUR OF COMMUNISM IN ASIA

The nationalist movements thus predated the arrival of communism by a short period. Culturally diverse and politically disparate, they and their successor movements were all inspired, influenced, challenged or destroyed by the communist tide which enveloped much of the nationalist and anti-colonial unrest. On the other hand, it is also true that many Asian politicians, including the most staunchly conservative and anti-communist among them, were at one time or another fellow travellers of the communist movement. The case of Norodom Sihanouk was not unusual: after having reluctantly become involved in the second Indochina war in order to achieve a reconciliation with North Vietnam which was threatening Cambodia, he then became an unlikely ally of the Khmer Rouge. An even more extreme example was that of Souphanouvong, the so-called 'red prince' of Laos, and his half-brother King Souvanna Phouma. As far as Asia was concerned, the united fronts did not necessarily work in the communists' favour. The prototype for this form of alliance was provided by General Chiang Kai-shek, who succeeded in exploiting the first Chinese united front for his own ends from 1924 until 1927. His own son Chiang Ching-kuo, who was educated in Moscow and married a Soviet citizen, denounced him publicly at the time of the collapse of the united front, before becoming chief of the Kuomintang's secret police and later succeeding his father in Taiwan in 1975. The authoritarian and shrewd leader of Singapore, Lee Kuan Yew, joined forces with the communist unions until 1959, even remaining Vice-President of the Socialist International until he was ousted in 1979. Similar examples occurred in Indonesia, Burma and the Philippines during the Second World War, so much so that at times it has been possible for Asia's conservative leaders to enforce emergency measures suppressing all activity by the communists with the argument that 'they knew them so well'. Asia ultimately avoided a repetition of the Kerensky coup, Lenin's putsch against the short-lived democratic president of the Russian *Duma* in 1917; nor was there any real materialization of the famous 'domino theory', whereby the fall of a single pro-Western régime was supposed to prompt the collapse of all the rest in turn.

And yet no ideology was more instrumental in shaping the face of modern Asia than post-1920 communism, even in those countries opposed to it. It was a European invention which Marx was the first to believe Asia would largely reject: his writings reveal the germ of a theory of 'Oriental despotism' as an explanation for the absence of democracy and a bourgeoisie in Asia. Nevertheless, communism as launched by Lenin, the Third International and the members of the Comintern, met with unprecedented success in Asia. It also underwent considerable modification, often taking on the guise of a peasant guerilla movement. Through contact with traditional Confucian and Buddhist influences, it developed a dimension of spiritual totalitarianism unmatched by Stalinism, which remained much cruder in form. The hour of Asian communism undoubtedly came with the Second World War, the defeat of the old colonial masters and the formation of the national anti-Japanese resistance. Yet the emergence of a generation of individuals and organizations committed to communism may be traced much further back to the Third Communist International in Asia following the Second Congress of July 1920 and the Congress of 'oppressed nationalities' at Baku aimed at the so-called 'Eastern peoples', although admittedly the new Bolshevik government primarily used this term to mean the peoples of Central Asia. Apart from the activities of agents and militants of the International, the spread and expansion of the various movements and parties also owed a great deal to the influence of Chinese communism, transmitted via the overseas Chinese community, which numbered almost three million throughout South-East Asia at the end of the 1920s. This particular aspect later resulted in a twofold rejection. Some of the national communist parties, such as that of Vietnam, eventually spurned Chinese influence, while the indigenous Thai, Malay and Indonesian ethnic groups came to identify the overseas Chinese in a pejorative sense with the threat of subversion, having previously regarded them as accomplices of the colonial powers. The dual parentage of Asian communism is indeed clear, with Moscow and the Comintern on the one side and overseas Chinese agitators on the other.

Socialist, Marxist and anarchist ideas began filtering into Asia at the beginning of the century, especially via Japanese (and later Chinese) translations. The Japanese Socialist Party, for example, was founded in 1906. The influence of Russian nihilism and populist movements, such as *Narodnaya Volya* (The People's Will), with their assassination attempts, was particularly strong in China, where anarchist societies combined Buddhist teachings and their stringent moral code with bloody violence. Sun Yat-sen and the Revolutionary Alliance, a further constituent element in this first revolution, drew inspiration partly from imperial reformist thought and partly from European socialism. His 'Three Principles of the People', which provided the ideological foundation for the Kuomintang and the Chinese nationalists in the twentieth century, strongly advocated the subsistence of the people. Sun Yat-sen himself, a tireless traveller, orator and fundraiser throughout the Pacific prior to 1911, was very much a precursor of the internationalist activity which characterized communism at its height. In Peking in 1918 the example of the Bolshevik Revolution inspired a Marxist study group centred on Li Dazhao, the true founder of the Chinese Communist Party. As of July 1920, it was actually Lenin's theses on the 'national and colonial question', presented to the Second Congress of the Communist International in Moscow, and the debate which ensued which determined the political strategy of the revolutionaries. The great phases of International and later Cominform activity were thus faithfully copied by most of the Asian communist parties: the years of class struggle (1923–4), the united fronts from 1925 onwards, the revolutionary strategy from 1926, the return to the united fronts after the Seventh Congress of the International in 1935 and finally, the order from Stalin to sever these alliances in 1947. The texts often regarded as the most original to come out of the Asian communist movement, such as Mao Zedong's famous *Investigation of the peasant movement in Hunan* of 1926, were published primarily by the Comintern press. The influential role of these Comintern debates is now well established.

Lenin opened up considerable political scope for communism by recommending a 'temporary' alliance with the nationalist (in practice, patriotic) factions within the Asian bourgeoisies in the struggle for independence, and by advocating a 'bourgeois–democratic' phase. Asia's communist movements emerged within this framework, beginning with the Indonesian Communist Party which was formed in Java in 1920. Its real founder was the famous Henrik Sneevliet (alias Maring), a Dutch agent for the International, who nurtured its growth from a Marxist–socialist society dominated by Batavian intellectuals. It was soon followed by the Chinese Communist Party (CCP), which was founded in the French concession of Shanghai in July 1921 by a handful of intellectuals, also aided and abetted by the International. The Japanese Communist Party, founded in July 1922, experienced little of the success enjoyed by its Chinese counterpart. In January 1923 the tiny CCP engineered an alliance with Sun Yat-sen's republican movement, launching its first united front with the Kuomintang in the following year. This political strategy enabled it not only to recruit extremely rapidly under the wing of the fledgling Chinese republic but also to sow its seed abroad in association with the International. In 1923 it recruited among the Chinese in Thailand and in 1925 in Malaysia and Singapore, forming a 'Committee of the South Seas' in 1926.

China was also the birthplace of the Vietnamese communist movement in 1925. It was there that Ho Chi Minh, at the time an interpreter to the Comintern envoy Borodin, came into contact with a group of Vietnamese émigré revolutionaries and founded the League of Revolutionary Youth (Thanh Nien) in Canton in 1925, the first in a long line of communist parties to emerge in Indochina. If Sukarno, the Indonesian leader, was the classic 'man of light', Ho Chi Minh (1872?–1969) was undoubtedly a man of shadows. His very name was a Chinese-Vietnamese alias adopted after 1945, just as Nguyen Ai Quoc (Nguyen the Patriot) was his principal pseudonym prior to that date. According to the official Vietnamese history books he used as many as seventy-two pseudonyms in the course of his career. Even now his date of birth has never been properly established, while the anniversary of his death was brought forward by a day to coincide with the date of the Vietnamese national holiday. Outwardly, 'Uncle Ho' was the epitome of the hardened, moralistic bachelor, yet in 1991, Hanoi sources revealed that he had in fact kept a secret wife. His biography portrays him as the scion of an anti-colonialist Mandarin family who followed in the footsteps of his forebears, but French archive sources reveal that in 1911 he applied for a place at the colonial civil service training college. It was definitely as an idealistic francophile that he travelled to France and sampled the ideas of the constitutionalist Phan Chau Trinh until 1919, the date of the Versailles Conference which clearly did much to arouse nationalist feeling among many Asians. At the Congress of Tours in 1920, like the majority of the SFIO delegates, Nguyen Ai Quoc opted for communism and subsequently spent several years in China under a Chinese alias as an International agent. He was rumoured to have died of tuberculosis in 1932, and although his whereabouts between 1932 and 1938 are unclear, he evidently passed through Moscow on a number of occasions. Ho Chi Minh's political impact, apart from a capacity for guile and deception to outdo even Mao Zedong, lay in the way that he preserved the language and ideas of the French and American revolutions in implementing Marxist–Leninist strategy. In the short term, however, this proved a doctrinal weakness in the eyes of his mentors. The Thanh Nien movement, a pragmatic organization which was even regarded as right wing by the Comintern on account of its many 'bourgeois' followers, was scarcely in a position to counter the VNQDD or 'Quoc Dang'.

The first challenge came with the rapid growth of the CCP and its successes in rural China, where the redistribution of agricultural land worried the landowners and their officer cousins, causing the Kuomintang to turn against its communist ally. The massacre in 1927 was preceded by a number of warning signs which were ignored by most of the leaders of the International, particularly Stalin. The 'tragedy of the Chinese revolution' (Isaacs, 1967) was followed by a series of daring strategic manoeuvres and premature uprisings, including those of Nanchang on 1 August 1927 (the official date of the founding of the Chinese Red Army), 'Autumn Harvest' led by Mao in Hunan province, and the Canton Commune of December 1927. In less than three years, the CCP lost its entire urban party apparatus. In Indonesia, where competition from Islam prevented any alliance strategy in the early years, the PKI, for the first though not the last time in its history, also made a bungled attempt at an uprising which was crushed in

Java in November 1926 and in Sumatra in January 1927. Undaunted, the Chinese militants, aided and abetted by the Comintern, formed a new Communist Party of the South Seas in 1928, which all communists in South-East Asia and Indochina were required to join. As for Ho Chi Minh, he founded the nucleus of the Thai Communist Party in 1928 and was entrusted by Moscow with co-ordinating that international hotchpotch of an organization. The interrelationship between the Indochinese and Thai communist movements, and consequently also the influence of the Vietnamese communists, were both important factors: the latter often subsequently fled to Thailand in order to escape the onslaught of the French security police.

Communism in Thailand, however, was largely identified with the country's considerable Chinese minority. In June 1932, a coalition of army officers and reformist politicians overthrew the absolute monarchy, marking the first in a long series of coups throughout modern Thai history. This actually served to aggravate the tensions between the two communities, as the Thai government attempted to curb the influence of Chinese traders and entrepreneurs and outlawed all communist organizations. The latter reverted to underground operations and the defence of the Chinese community, the mountain tribes and the Vietnamese. Ho Chi Minh's attention was, however, also taken up with internal rifts in the Vietnamese communist movement, which split into three rival factions in 1929, two of them adopting the epithet 'Indochinese' originally coined by the French. In Hong Kong, in February 1930, Ho Chi Minh established the Vietnamese Communist Party (VCP), soon renamed the Indochinese Communist Party by Comintern decree. Headed by the rural Nghe Tinh soviets, which produced many famous cadres, the VCP was at the forefront of the anti-French unrest. These uprisings and their aftermath from 1931 to 1935, characterized, as in China and Indonesia, by improvization and premature insurrection, were later sternly viewed by the International as an 'infantile phase' on the part of Vietnamese communism. However, the International itself clearly played its part, though the apparent disappearance of Ho Chi Minh/Nguyen Ai Quoc in 1932 might be seen as evidence of a purge similar to the one which ousted Li Lisan, Qiu Qiubai and other self-styled 'adventurers' from the CCP. The most important achievement of the Nghe Tinh movement was its accumulation of human capital in the shape of the militants imprisoned in French jails, notably Poulo Condore, where they formed an underground political organization. The survivors of this group subsequently became the movement's future leaders.

As it grew more realistic, Asian communism also became more nationalistic. In China the group of leaders who had links with the International or had been trained in Moscow, later known as the Twenty-eight Bolsheviks, lost ground as a result of their failed attempts at insurrection and clandestine organization in the cities. The rural soviets, in particular those of Jiangxi and Yunnan, allowed independent leaders, including Mao Zedong, to wield their own influence, while the national party leadership was stretched to the limit implementing the ever-changing stream of orders emanating from Moscow. At the end of this phase, during the precipitate retreat of the Long March (1934–5), Mao Zedong, with the help of Zhou Enlai, seized control of the Chinese Communist Party at the Conference of Cunyi in January 1935. The orchestration of the guerilla campaign, the conduct of a people's war and the proceeds of mass mobilization provided a much-needed substitute for the verbose theorizing of the early internationalists on alliance strategies and class fronts. In South-East Asia the PKI, with its international spokesman Tan Malaka, spread to Malaya and the Philippines after its defeat in 1926, but this expansion was one aspect of a pan-Malayan movement which was later taken over by its opponents, rather than forming part of a co-ordinated strategy. In April 1930 the Communist Party of the South Seas quietly disbanded in Singapore and a new Malayan communist party soon came into being. Although it depended heavily on the Chinese rubber-plantation workers and the Chinese business community, it was headed on the eve of the Second World War by Lai Tek, a Vietnamese-Chinese associate of Ho Chi Minh.

The Philippines were already an exception to the rule, with close ties to Latin America which resulted from their hispanicization prior to the 1896 revolution, then from the protectorate exercised by the United States over the independent republic. The Catholic Church was instrumental in promoting a spirit of millenarian populism, and uprisings against the landowners were part of the country's rural tradition. The real founder of Filipino communism consequently bore the name of Crisanto Evangelista: starting out as a militant printing worker in 1906, Evangelista founded the workers' union movement in 1913 and a Workers' Party in 1924. In 1929 the non-communists ousted Evangelista (who then proceeded to establish the Kapitunan, or Society of the Sons of Toil) and in 1930 they proclaimed the establishment of the Communist Party of the Philippines (PCP). This, together with the Association of Farmers and Agricultural Labourers, later formed the nucleus of the Huk guerilla movement during the Second World War. A spontaneous movement with little interest in alliances, the CCP fell victim to repression after 1931 and Evangelista and his comrades were banished to remote islands. Despite these setbacks, the CCP continued to adhere to a hard-line insurrectionist stance until 1935.

As war approached an about turn occurred, in the Philippines and elsewhere, when the Communist International and Moscow adopted a new united front strategy. This reversal of policy was announced at the Seventh Congress of the Communist International in August 1935. The 'class against class' strategy was also rejected in favour of popular fronts and a policy of collaboration with all nationalists against the fascist threat embodied in the newly-formed Berlin–Rome–Tokyo axis.

At this stage, communism had yet to make a decisive impact on Asia. Rural radicalism, premature insurrection, the conflicting barrage of orders emanating from the International and harsh repression by colonial powers and national governments alike meant that the progress achieved by communist unrest, while rather more systematic than that of the peasant revolts and secret societies of the previous century, was scarcely any more fruitful. In 1938, the journalist Harold Isaacs, a critical observer of Chinese Communist Party history, concluded his book with a description of the last remnants of the CCP taking refuge amid the freezing Yenan uplands of Shaanxi province after their flight from the Long March: 'Meanwhile the surviving Communist armies doggedly sustained themselves in far-off Shensi. They were in an impasse...' (Isaacs, 1967: 303). Isaacs' error is understandable, for this was precisely the fate which was to befall the communist guerillas of South-East Asia after the Second World War. The failure of the early 1930s was all the more striking given the fact that owing to the Great Depression and the concomitant slump in the market for all Asian primary industries from mining to hevea plantations, economic conditions were conducive to unrest. Despite that failure, this period marked the emergence throughout Asia of the communist revolutionaries who would step up their struggle during the 1940s and, in some cases, subsequently rise to power at the head of communist states after the war. Mao Zedong, Deng Xiaoping (who had fought alongside the Vietnamese guerillas in Yunnan during the early 1930s), Ho Chi Minh (alias Nguyen Ai Quoc) and virtually all their colleagues up to the 1980s and even the 1990s, owed their origins to this formative period.

SELECTED READING

The theme of the co-operation and competition between nationalism and communism in Asia before the Pacific War has been extensively treated, often through the prism of communism's rise to power. Among the works cited below, Bianco (1987) gives the best perspective on this rivalry as far as China is concerned. Iriye (1965) is essential for its interpretation of the ascendancy of Japanese militarism from a realist international viewpoint. Scott (1976) presents the case for Asian peasant revolts at the forefront of social change.

Anderson, B. (1993) *Imagined communities: reflection on the origin and spread of nationalism*, London: Verso.
Behr, E. (1989) *Hirohito: l'empereur ambigu*, Paris: Robert Laffont.
Bianco, L. (1987) *Les origines de la révolution chinoise, 1915–1949*, Paris: Gallimard.
Carrère d'Encausse, H. and Schram, S. (1965) *Le marxism et l'Asie, 1853–1964*, Paris: Armand Colin.
Cayrac-Blanchard, F. (1973) *Le parti communiste indonésien*, Paris: Armand Colin.
Chandler, D. (1983) *A history of Cambodia*, Boulder: Westview Press.

Dirlik, A. (1978) *Revolution and history: origins of Marxist historiography in China, 1919–1937*, Berkeley: University of California Press.

Hane, M. (1982) *Peasants, rebels and outcasts: the underside of modern Japan*, New York: Pantheon Books.

Iriye, A. (1965) *After imperialism: the search for a new order in the Far East, 1921–1931*, Cambridge, MA: Harvard University Press.

—— (1987) *The origins of the Second World War in the Pacific*, London: Longman.

Isaacs, H. (1967) *La tragédie de la révolution chinoise, 1925–1927*, Paris: Gallimard.

Khanh, H. K. (1982) *Vietnamese communism, 1925–1942*, Ithaca: Cornell University Press.

Lacouture, J. (1967) *Ho Chi Minh*, Paris: Éditions du Seuil.

Lee, C. (1983) *Revolutionary struggle in Manchuria, Chinese communism and Soviet interest, 1922–1945*, Berkeley: University of California Press.

Lewis, J. W. (ed.) *Peasant rebellion and communist revolution in Asia*, Stanford: Stanford University Press.

Marr, D. G. (1971) *Vietnamese anticolonialism, 1885–1925*, Berkeley: University of California Press.

Popkin, S. L. (1979) *The rational peasant: the political economy of rural society in Vietnam*, Berkeley: University of California Press.

Schram, S. (1966) *Mao Tse-tung*, Harmondsworth: Penguin.

Scott, J. C. (1976) *The moral economy of the peasant: rebellion and subsistence in Southeast Asia*, New Haven: Yale University Press.

Skinner, G. W. (1958) *Leadership and power in the Chinese community of Thailand*, Ithaca: Cornell University Press.

Tai, H. H. (1992) *Radicalism and the origins of the Vietnamese revolution*, Cambridge, MA: Harvard University Press.

Van der Kroef, J. M. (1965) *The Communist Party of Indonesia: its history, program and tactics*, Vancouver: University of British Columbia Press.

—— (1981) *Communism in Southeast Asia*, London: Macmillan.

Wyatt, D.K. and Woodside, A. (eds) (1982) *Moral order and the question of change: essays on Southeast Asian thought*, New Haven: Yale University Press.

3 The Second World War

The real paradox about Japan's position in Asia lies in its role as a guest who has outstayed its welcome. Previous occupants of that role include the Hindu civilization, then China with its expansion to the south and the rapid growth in the numbers of overseas Chinese in South-East Asia. The great Western powers themselves built their separate empires there, hindering future Japanese expansion. The forays made by Japanese traders and pirates in the sixteenth and seventeenth centuries as far as the area around the Malay peninsula came to an end as Chinese and Western rivals began to arrive in force. Consequently, between the time of its industrial expansion and modernization and the end of the Meiji era (1868–1912), Japan alternated between the aggressive stance of a belated imperial rival, à la Wilhelmine Germany, and that of peaceful co-operation based on international agreements and treaties with a succession of hegemonic powers, first Britain prior to the First World War, then the United States from 1920 until the deterioration of the 1930s. Psychologically, in determining its own modern cultural identity, Japan scarcely hesitated between anglicization and germanization: it initially chose the model of Victorian England, later shifting gradually towards American-style modernization. The only evidence of a Prussian model was confined to the political institutions established under the Meiji constitution and to the build-up of the defence industries in the immediate pre-war years. In retrospect, the three-quarters of a century separating the birth of Japan's colonial empire from the failure of its crazed bid to conquer Asia in 1941–5 came to be viewed as one and the same march into the abyss, led by an authoritarian military–industrial régime. The official Japanese submission to the Allied verdict on the causes of the Second World War after 1945 and the pacifist response of a people horrified at the adventurism of its leaders gave further credence to this wholesale condemnation. This period left Japan facing the loss of nearly three million lives, economic ruin and total diplomatic isolation within Asia.

Since 1945, a large part of the official activity of the Japanese government, including Emperor Hirohito towards the end of his reign and his successor Akihito as of January 1989, has been devoted to extending symbolic apologies and other, more concrete forms of reparation to Japan's

Asian neighbours in respect of its wartime conduct. These apologies are sincerely meant, particularly when they refer to the period 1931–45, known as the 'valley of darkness' (*kurai tanima*), between the annexation of Manchuria and the Japanese defeat. Japan's diplomacy of repentance has been scrupulously tendered to nearly every one of its neighbours, but within Japan itself it has been accompanied by a desire, voiced by many Japanese historians and certain politicians, to place some of the burden of responsibility for the Pacific War and its causes on the shoulders of the United States. This development is partly linked to the revival of nationalism. Japan has undeniably offered every possible expression of outward contrition to the victors of the Second World War, yet in terms of self-questioning and the rejection of authoritarian political institutions, it has not come nearly as far as present-day Germany. Despite the internments at Sugamo prison and the trial of acknowledged 'war criminals' (the term used by both the Allies and the Japanese to mean not simply those who had committed specific atrocities, but also those chiefly responsible for the war), Japan avoided the equivalent of denazification, beginning with the Emperor himself, who was spared by the terms of the surrender and at the decision of SCAP (Supreme Commander Allied Powers, the post dominated by General MacArthur) and is exonerated from blame in virtually every one of his biographies.

Each year, this ambiguity is illustrated in the debate as to whether members of the Japanese government should take part, whether in a private capacity or otherwise, in the visit to Yasukuni temple, which is dedicated to the 'war dead', including many leaders from the period 1937–45. It is also reflected in the special status held by the national anthem and flag, which, despite having lost their constitutional function in 1945, are being reintroduced in Japanese schools. Yet this revisionist tendency, fuelled by the blows inflicted on Japan's self-esteem in its trade disputes with the United States (and occasionally Europe) is also linked to a more differentiated assessment of the country's imperial past, which in the eyes of many Japanese ought to count for more than just its final escapade. Japan's decisive impact on its Taiwanese and Korean neighbours has by no means been wholly negative, while the foundations for the future industrialization of north-eastern China were laid by Japan during the Manchukuo era. On these questions, and also on the issue of access to the South-East Asian primary products on which their archipelago depended, the Japanese often make a plea to be judged by the same criteria as the other great powers. The conquest of South-East Asia in 1941–2 was initially viewed with extremely divergent attitudes by the colonial powers on the one hand and by most of the indigenous populations on the other. However, there remains the fact of Japan's military atrocities, to which the reaction is normally silent shame, sometimes denial. Yet it is the memory of those deeds which explains the intensity of the pacifist convictions felt by the Japanese, as well as their reluctance to follow the United States into conflict with North Korea, China and Vietnam.

THE BIRTH OF THE JAPANESE COLONIAL EMPIRE

It was the Emperor and the Meiji restoration, with their advances in administration, education and industry, which launched Japan's overseas expansion. The relative balance which had formerly existed between China and Japan was destroyed for two reasons. First, whereas China had largely been colonized by the West, Japan remained largely independent, despite being forced by the Americans to open its doors to trade in 1853 on somewhat unfavourable terms. This, incidentally, also helps to explain its subsequent protectionist leanings. Japan was able to catch up in terms of industrial and scientific development, despite Western jealousy. Second, similar ideas and in many cases similar slogans were adopted both by the Japanese Meiji restoration and the concurrent Tongzhi restoration movement in China, which officially lasted from 1861 to 1875, although Empress Cixi continued to preside over the reform debate until her death in 1908. These slogans included *ti-yong* ('Take Western knowledge as the instrument and Eastern wisdom as the foundation') and what the Japanese called *fukoku kyohei* (*fuquiang* in Chinese) – 'national wealth and power' by way of opposition to the West. China and Japan both suffered some of the same constraints: in 1911, the unequal treaties concluded with the West debarred Japan from setting customs duties, while the administration of China's customs and excise as well as its control over foreign trade were transferred into Western hands. The difference was that the Meiji restoration was successful, founded on the creation of protected industries, with officialdom and private capital coming together in the new *zaibatsu* (financial coteries turned giant conglomerates). The Chinese restoration, on the other hand, was a failure, due partly to Western intervention and partly to the fragmentation and decline of the Chinese élites, as seen, for example, in the near-total collapse of the *guandu shangban* (privately-managed firms under state control), which might have been the Chinese equivalent of the *zaibatsu*. Fifty years later, during the Nanjing decade (1928–37), Chiang Kaishek and his colleagues made a further attempt to construct what Mao Zedong called 'bureaucratic capitalism', with a similar lack of success.

Japan's internal progress immediately led to overseas expansion by a series of phases. In 1874, as one warmongering clan called for military action (partly to give the *samurai* a new role abroad after reform had made them redundant at home), a punitive expedition was launched against the island of Taiwan, culminating in the annexation of the Ryukyu Islands by Japan in 1879. In 1876, Japan forced Korea to open its doors to free trade, just as the West had done earlier. Sino-Japanese rivalry for control of the Korean peninsula led to a war in 1894, which was soon won by Japan, much to the astonishment of Western governments. By the Treaty of Shimonoseki of 1895, China ceded to Japan the island of Taiwan (which initially rebelled against the decision), the Diaoyutai Islands (known to the Japanese as the Senkaku Islands) and the whole southern part of Manchuria consisting of the Kwantung peninsula. Within China itself, Japan was granted the same extortionate privileges as the European powers, who none the less forced it to relinquish its hold over Manchuria, partly to the benefit of the Russians. Confronted with these circumstances, Japan forged its first foreign alliance in 1902 with the British. In February 1904, it attacked Russia without prior declaration of war, driving its troops out of Manchuria, and in 1905, in Tsushima Strait separating Japan from Korea, it sank the Russian imperial fleet which had been dispatched from the Baltic. This signalled a Japanese victory, abetted by Britain and the United States and ratified by the Treaty of Portsmouth, concluded under American auspices. Japan thus resumed its lease on southern Manchuria, won recognition for its protectorate over the kingdom of Korea, and acquired half of the large island of Sakhalin, off the coast of Siberia. The full annexation of Korea followed in 1910.

By this stage Japan had drawn level with the other major world powers in Asia and gained a proper colonial empire of its own. It extended this as a result of the First World War, when it seized Germany's Asian colonies, consisting of the Chinese port of Qingdao, the Shandong peninsula and the Marianas, Caroline and Marshall archipelagos in the North Pacific. The Peace of Brest-Litovsk, signed between Bolshevik Russia and Germany, prompted a joint expedition by Western and Japanese forces in July 1918 to take aid to the White Russians in eastern Siberia. Their landing at Vladivostok proved to no avail, but it was clearly viewed by Japan as a chance for expansion. The Treaty of Versailles of 1919 affirmed the transfer of all German territorial possessions into Japanese hands, contrary to Chinese nationalist expectations. This collusion between Japan and the old colonial powers provoked the great Chinese patriotic movement of May Fourth 1919, an episode of cultural unrest which lies at the root of present-day political currents in China. In Korea, a similar anti-Japanese protest movement led to a heavy crackdown on 12 March 1919, a date which remains one of the two major national holidays in Korea, the other being the anniversary of 15 August 1945.

Korea and Taiwan: towards assimilation

Korea, with a population in 1938 of 22 million, and Taiwan with close on 10 million, did not so much expand the *Lebensraum* of the Japanese (whose population at that time stood at 69 million) as increase their labour force. Both became fully-fledged Japanese provinces, sending their own members to the Diet and supplying recruits for the Japanese army during the Pacific War. Yet Japan treated the two colonies very differently according to the way in which it perceived its relationship with the Koreans and the Chinese. In the case of the former, the relationship was both one of over-identification and an extension of the oppressive hierarchy imposed by traditional Japanese social divisions.

Some Japanese ideologists and historians developed the notion that the Korean and Japanese ethnic groups possessed a common origin, a view partly justified by the fact that Japan was progressively populated over thousands of years by migrants who came 'on horseback' from Korea, Manchuria and Mongolia. However, they sometimes also exaggerated or invented historic periods of Japanese domination over Korea in order to 'prove' that the latter had always belonged to Japan. Whatever the case, the Koreans were completely subjugated and their identity suppressed. Their partly-expropriated lands were used to accommodate the overflowing Japanese rural population, while the Koreans themselves were resettled in Manchuria. In fact, the former 'hermit kingdom' had made considerable attempts to modernize itself, just as Japan had done during the Meiji era, and China during the reign of the Tongzhi. Its patriot leader, Taewon Gun (1864–73), had similarly endeavoured to resist external pressure: the treaty of 1876 which had opened Korea's doors to foreign trade was followed in 1882 by a further treaty with the United States. This move was made on the advice of Chinese diplomats and Li Hongzhang in order to avoid Korea becoming a Russian or Japanese protectorate so that, up to 1939, the Americans were obliged to maintain considerable economic interests there, including gold mining and railways. This policy failed, however, and Korea was unable to trust the United States, which was quite willing to trade its own protectorate in the Philippines in exchange for Japan's hold over Korea. In 1905, in his correspondence, the father of George Kennan, as an ambassador to Korea, had expressed his contempt for Koreans. His son was to become the chief architect of the Department of State policy which made Europe the priority between 1947 and 1950. The 'Europe first' policy would lead to a neglect of the Korean peninsula, and the outbreak of the Korean War thus took United States diplomats by surprise. The continuity of American behaviour towards Korea helps to explain why, despite the fact that the US Army literally saved South Korea in 1950–3, there is such an undercurrent of anti-Americanism in Korean political culture.

Following the annexation of Korea in 1910, Japanese colonization got off to a violent start under the iron hand of General Terauchi. After a more liberal interlude, it worsened again with the prospect of the creation of a 'Greater East Asia Co-prosperity Sphere' from 1936 onwards, while Korea was prepared as a supply base for the Japanese war effort. It was at this time that the Japanese imperial Shinto cult became compulsory. This provoked a major conflict with Korea's 500,000 Christians, who built up their moral and political influence during this period and played a key political role after the Second World War. More damaging was the fact that despite the efforts made to improve education, the Korean language was banned in schools in favour of Japanese, and monosyllabic Korean family names were replaced by polysyllabic Japanese ones. Nevertheless, whereas in 1933 a quarter of Korea's children were attending school, by 1940 this proportion had doubled. In 1939, all Korean-language newspapers were banned, despite the fact that their readership had risen dramatically in previous years. Mobilization was stepped up with the onset of the Pacific War. In 1945, over 2 million Koreans were forced to enlist for what was generally hard labour in Japan, Sakhalin and the Pacific, while 300,000 Korean women were drafted to 'service' Japanese soldiers, a measure which affected one in two Korean households. It was this, as much as the wartime food shortages, which was responsible for the eventual force of resentment that built up in Korea, belying the imperial rescript ordering the annexation of Korea, which had formulated the concept of a 'spirit of equality' with metropolitan Japan. Yet the historical and cultural differences between the two countries were exacerbated over an even longer period by their cultural, linguistic and geographic closeness. This affinity was exaggerated by the Japanese and at the same time refuted by their overwhelmingly contemptuous attitude to the Koreans, who were regarded, especially by poorer Japanese citizens, as an underclass at their beck and call. As far as the Koreans were concerned, mass hatred and the colonial legacy made a difficult combination. None the less, ex-officials, traders and assorted collaborators from the days of Japanese colonization later formed an influential group in South Korea, especially after the downfall of President Syngman Rhee in 1960, while some were to play a part in the normalization of Japanese–Korean relations.

Although the colonization of Taiwan did involve some conflict, its outcome was very different. It is certainly true that Formosa's traditional independence and role as a refuge of heterodoxy *vis à vis* Chinese central government made it fundamentally predisposed to accept its detachment from the rest of China. Neither a brief attempt at an independent republic nor a fairly heavy siege of Taipei in 1895 averted radical colonization. Admittedly, this was based on a military government until 1919, but at that point Japan took a lesson from its problems in Korea and placed Taiwan under a civilian administration. The island was forced to become a major rice supplier to Japan, which ordered land reform in 1905, facilitating the emergence of a class of small independent landowners. This precedent partly explains the smooth passage of the subsequent 1948 land reform which was decreed by the Kuomintang against the interests of Taiwan's major landowners, who had regrouped in the meantime. Though the people were bound by a system of surveillance and mutual denunciation whose origins were as much Chinese (the *baojia*) as Japanese, they benefited from considerable investment in social welfare and modern infrastructure, including a major university in Taipei. In 1936, 40 per cent of Taiwanese male children were attending school, a much higher proportion than in any of the Western colonies, in Asia or elsewhere (Myers and Peattie, 1984). In any discussion of the Taiwanese post-war economic 'miracle', it should perhaps be remembered that it was the system of mass education introduced by the Japanese colonists (and overlooked by their Western counterparts), as well as a common Confucian heritage, which formed one of the cornerstones of Taiwan's future economic expansion. Conversely, by extending its existing industrial and commercial monopolies into Taiwan, as well as by using a few local families as exclusive intermediaries, Japan reoriented all Taiwanese trade towards the metropolis, of which the colony became a mere extension: furthermore, this was the same model of economic management which it was to apply in South-East Asia from 1942, starting with Singapore. From 1919 onwards, ethnic assimilation, which the Japanese colonists had previously refused to the people of Taiwan, became official government policy, and thousands of Taiwanese subsequently trained as doctors, engineers and teachers. They were also granted the hitherto forbidden right to set up their own businesses. Even before the Japanese language became compulsory, it was already a means of social advancement. Between 1896 and 1936, the island's GNP rose by 260 per cent, while the standard of its education and infrastructure was higher than that of the rest of China. Its agricultural research on rice, which enabled it to become an exporter of rice to Japan, paved the way for the famous 'green revolution' pioneered by the Rice Institute in Manila in the early 1960s. After 1936, as Japan stepped up preparations for its conquest, Taiwan was put back under military government and absorbed as a province of Japan. Taiwanese entrepreneurs and Japanese commercial firms joined in the pursuit of economic penetration of mainland China and South-East Asia. With the outbreak of the Pacific War, the whole island rallied to the Japanese cause, with Taiwanese males serving in the imperial army, even in occupied China. During the war, resistance within Taiwan was non-existent: in 1945, Japanese soldiers stationed on the island were dutifully obliged to await the landing of tattered Chinese units from the mainland to find out who they should surrender to. The island was restored to the Chinese nationalist government by the United States in October 1945.

On a linguistic and cultural level, Japan made its mark on Taiwan, reviving the island's special status *vis à vis* the rest of China and by setting in place the infrastructure to support its future economic expansion, giving it the second-highest standard of living in Asia. There is no mistaking the nostalgia that emanates from the work of the well-known Taiwanese film-maker Hou Hsiao-hsen. His *City of Sadness*, portraying the massacre inflicted on the island by Kuomintang troops in February 1947, marks the turning-point between the Japanese era and the nationalist régime, and in so doing shows itself far more in favour of the first. The Taiwanese people have hesitated between Peking and Tokyo on more than one occasion.

The invasion of China

With the First World War, Japan strengthened its special relationship with China and began imposing on it semi-protectorate status. In January 1915, it tried to force the Chinese government to agree to the famous 'Twenty-one Demands', designed to grant Japan the same privileges as the Western powers and which the Chinese saw as extortionate. In some cases, Japan also used the lure of economic diplomacy to win local allies, as in the case of the Nishihara loans which bolstered the Duan Qirui government in 1917–18. In the long term, Japan acted in accordance with what it perceived as competition with the West for influence. After 1928, for example, it regarded Chiang Kai-shek as a United States puppet, just as the West saw Wang Jingwei, the former leader of the left wing of the Kuomintang and pro-Japanese head of the Nanjing government after 1938, as being manipulated by the Japanese. None the less, these early moves were made, if not with the approval of every Western power (Japan subsequently disassociated itself from Britain, with which it was in too direct competition), then at least with the assent of the United States, whose anti-imperialism failed to outlast the Woodrow Wilson presidency. After the First World War, the United States and eight other powers, including Japan, took part in negotiations which, thanks to the efforts of the Japanese Prime Minister Keihara, led in February 1922 to the Treaty of Washington. This marked a crucial gain for the Americans, as the treaty established an upper threshold for the capacity of war fleets stationed in the Pacific, limiting the Japanese imperial navy to 60 per cent of the size of the American and British fleets. In return, the United States agreed to abandon the expansion of its naval bases west of Hawaii, thus creating a geographical division of naval power. However, in practice, in the course of negotiations, Japan managed to limit the challenge to its monopoly of influence in Manchuria and protect such schemes as the South Manchuria railway. In connection with the latter, Japan founded a major institute for economic, social and political research and surveys on China which was without equal in the Western colonies. Japan thus gained unrivalled knowledge of Chinese terrain and was able to plan a far more advanced programme of colonization. Researchers from the Manchurian Railway Institute also went on to form a political and technocratic élite that was instrumental in rebuilding the Japanese economy after the Second World War.

This balance was only temporary. In attempting to unite China, partly at least, under its control with the Northern Expedition (1925–7), Chiang Kai-shek's republican government inevitably clashed with its powerful neighbours to the north. In 1928, the Japanese Kwantung Army took on the task of assassinating General Zhang Zuolin, a Manchurian warlord who had failed to prove sufficiently compliant. His son Zhang Xueliang, dubbed 'The Young Marshal', later became one of the main instigators behind the formation of an anti-Japanese united front in December 1936. The incident was significant as it provoked a constitutional challenge within Japan, resulting in a shift of power away from the civilian government towards the imperial army. In future, the army would be directly answerable to the Emperor, although he himself would have preferred to have seen the government interposed between himself and the military. In 1929, a confrontation arose with Russia over the ownership of the Eastern railway in which the Soviet army easily overwhelmed the Chinese forces, thus indirectly prompting concern among the Japanese army stationed close to the Kwantung peninsula. Back in Tokyo, this incident lent credence to army theories about a Soviet threat to the north, whereas up to that point the diplomats had endeavoured to protect Japan's special national interests through compromise with the West. In any case, a total ban on Japanese immigration by the United States in 1924 (the Chinese, for their part, having been banned from entering since 1886) had already provoked a wave of anti-Americanism, a mood that was only exacerbated by the Great Depression of 1929, which hit Japanese exports and brought poverty to the rural masses. From that point on, any diplomats and politicians who called for entente with the West, the society which they had once wanted to join, found their position weakened.

The Showa reign of Emperor Hirohito, which commenced in practice in 1921, but officially in 1926, affirmed a desire for peaceful relations with the West and witnessed the last days of the 'Taisho democracy', named after the reign of Emperor Yoshihito (1912–26). However, it soon underwent a shift towards militarism. The pressure from officers in the army, many of whom came from working-class, ultra-nationalist backgrounds, was admittedly very intense, with a large number of propaganda associations and other, more secret societies such as the famous Sakurakai (Cherry Blossom Society). In 1931, police arrested hundreds of left-wing militants and intellectuals. Internal political stability was threatened by two military plots in 1931, two more in 1932 (resulting in the assassination of the Prime Minister and the Finance Minister) and further attempts in 1933 and 1934, as well as a general climate of opinion which hailed the courage of the right-wing conspirators in contrast to the corruption in political circles. The democratization of Japan, which had led to the introduction of universal male suffrage in 1925 and representation for opposition parties (even left-wing ones) in the Diet, came to a halt. It gave way to a fragmentation of the official élites, which split up into the traditional oligarchies of the Meiji era and the bureaucrats in the various ministries and army services, and to pressure from young activist officers.

On 18 September 1931, having fabricated an incident out of thin air, the Kwantung Army occupied the whole of Manchuria, establishing the puppet state of Manchukuo in 1932 with Puyi, China's last emperor, at its head. This proved economically and industrially successful: by encouraging large-scale immigration by impoverished peasants from north-western China at a rate of over a million a year during the early 1930s, by using the railways to commercialize wheat and by laying the foundations for a mechanical engineering industry, Japan mapped out the course of future economic development, just as it had done in neighbouring northern Korea. Between 1900 and 1940, the Manchurian population rose from 14 million to 44.5 million. However, Japan did not stop there. In January 1932, following an anti-Japanese boycott and a series of incidents in the industrial suburb of

Chabei, Shanghai was bombed and the Japanese navy landed three troop divisions which occupied the conurbation with some difficulty. In the hope of appeasing Japan and in order to conserve its manpower for deployment against the communist guerillas, the Chinese government, based in Nanjing, none the less issued a muted response and agreed to a zone being drawn around Shanghai from which Chinese troops were excluded.

These episodes marked the first steps along the road to war. When challenged, Japan resigned from the League of Nations in March 1933. The Kwantung Army overran the province of Jehol and forced the Chinese army to withdraw from the region bounded by the Great Wall, Peking and Tianjin. By now the dominant power in northern China, and having absorbed Manchukuo, Japan paused while its civilian government defended a common line with China against the Westerners, their unequal treaties and their concessions. This marked the official birth of pan-Asianism, jointly advocated by Japan's two main army factions. The Control faction (*Toseiha*) took the view that Japan, by pursuing pan-Asianism and forming a bloc together with Manchukuo and China, should manoeuvre the Western powers in order to combat the Soviet Union. In contrast, the Imperial Way faction (*Kodoha*), which regained the upper hand after 1934, thought that Japan should take an independent line, seek a non-aggression pact with the Soviet Union and, above all, consolidate its forces. Both factions, admittedly, were in favour of direct action in China and shielded any officers who committed acts of provocation. Thus, in December 1934, the pro-expansionists (who, incidentally, were not confined solely to army personnel) imposed their view on the reduced Cabinet, insisting that Japan should continue to wear down the Chinese republican government in northern China. General Doihara skilfully used persuasion and corruption to subjugate Chahar, demilitarize Hebei and punish anti-Japanese intrigue. In fact, it was Wang Jingwei's republican administration in Nanjing which staged a bloody crackdown against anti-Japanese student protests in the major cities in July 1935. In November the Japanese split off part of Hebei province and officially announced plans for an 'independent' government for the five northern Chinese provinces bordering Manchukuo. In November 1936, Japan and Germany signed the anti-Comintern pact, the first stage in the formation of the Axis.

In an attempt to save face, the Chinese republican government continued to compromise with the Japanese until December 1936. However, public opinion was fermented with patriotism and the communists proposed a united front. In December 1936, Chiang Kai-shek himself was kidnapped in Xian by communist agents with the help of General Zhang Xueliang, and was only released on a guarantee of joint action against Japan. In Tokyo, the methodically-minded General Ishiwara, a veteran of the Kwantung Army and the instigator of the Manchuria campaign, drafted a five-year plan to prepare Japan, industrially and militarily, for a war which would reach far beyond its borders. Although he may have anticipated a future conflict with the United States, the General initially planned for what he saw as an inevitable war with the Soviet Union, convinced that in military terms it was still highly superior to Japan. The same man who had instigated the invasion of China also led the last ditch attempt to persuade his government to make a few concessions to the Chinese republican government and thus ensure that Japan left itself a way out during the coming conflict. He was backed by Prime Minister Konoe but opposed by a number of his own subordinates as well as Admiral Tojo, who advocated a straight re-enactment of the Manchuria campaign of 1931. The Marco Polo Bridge incident which occurred near Peking in July 1937 opened hostilities between the two countries, escalating into a full-scale war throughout the Chinese continent in January 1938, when Japan broke off diplomatic relations.

THE RUN-UP TO THE PACIFIC WAR

In some respects, Japan's invasion of China appears to have been a rash move. All arguments in favour of caution were countered by an incremental logic: first Japan sought new *Lebensraum* in Korea, then flanked it with a buffer state in Manchuria; but then north China had to be turned into a buffer zone and brought under the Japanese yoke, which in turn created a need for further expansion. 'War breeds war' was the watchword of the Kwantung Army generals, for whom war did indeed seem an end in itself. Japan also believed that as far as China and its Western rivals were concerned, it was simply carrying out a policy befitting a great power belatedly taking the international stage. This on its own was not enough to trigger a global conflict, the boundaries of the Japanese rationale being confined to the Asian region alone. However, it was in pursuit of this very logic that Japan became drawn, contrary to all rational argument, into an unequal conflict with the United States for the total domination of the Asia–Pacific region.

In October 1937, Roosevelt decided to 'quarantine' Japan indefinitely. The State Department then waited until the following year before condemning Japan for its violation of the Open Door principle laid down by the United States at the end of the nineteenth century. Japan's response was that 'the rules had changed', and in November 1938 Prime Minister Konoe, converted to the expansionist viewpoint, announced a 'new order in East Asia'. In June 1939, the United States then announced a break-off in trade relations for the following year, thus gradually substantiating its threat to deprive Japan of essential oil and steel resources. In August 1939, Japan and Germany signed a non-aggression pact and, in September 1940, the Triple Alliance was officially launched, based on the Berlin–Rome–Tokyo Axis. This deterioration in external affairs coincided with a transformation in the domestic political order. In February 1936, a further military conspiracy eliminated several members of the government and posed a direct threat to the Emperor. This time, the more conservative officers in the Control Faction regained the upper hand, but the army as a whole eluded civilian control. Surprisingly, political debate continued during 1936–7, and the political parties within the Diet, including several socialist members, still retained their freedom. However, they no longer retained much influence over the course of events and eventually all the civilian politicians acquiesced, including Prince Konoe, who remained as Prime Minister until July 1939 and returned to this office in July 1940. All the parties were then temporarily dissolved and the people, reorganized into administrative units, were forced to join the Imperial Rule Assistance Association. When the Chief of Staff, Admiral Tojo, was named Prime Minister in October 1941, the military takeover was complete. The *kokutai*, or national ideology, was proclaimed throughout the empire, composed of strands of myth surrounding Japanese nationhood together with an anti-Western outlook. Yet this switch to dictatorship took place within the framework of the core institutions established under the Meiji constitution, and all political and military decisions were taken 'in the name of the Emperor's will'. The Emperor himself, a traditional, even retiring character, was unquestionably the object of deification and adulation, yet in the 1942 elections over a third of the Japanese population failed to vote for the official candidates, a feature which distinguishes Japan from the fascist régimes of Europe.

The Pacific War properly began in July 1937, when the Japanese army overran the whole of China, seizing the entire central coastal region (including Shanghai) in September, Nanjing in December and the southern cities of Hankou and Canton in 1938. The nationalist government found itself driven back into the interior and set up a capital at Chungking, in the Sichuan basin. The imperial army installed a puppet government in northern China and took advantage of a collaborationist government in Nanjing, headed by Wang Jingwei. However, hostilities were by no means confined to the nationalist government alone, while the communist guerilla forces fanned out from their bases in Yenan, in north-western China. Japan emerged victorious, but its position remained precarious as it faced several threats, including that of a northern front with the Soviet Union and, in particular, a potential Anglo-American blockade of strategic resources, including oil, tin and rubber. Today, a number of Japanese historians continue to stress the part played by fears of a blockade, foreshadowed in the retaliatory trade measures which the United States announced in 1939. At that time, Japan was even more vulnerable in terms of supplies of resources than it is today. Yet in effect it was Japan's rash military action in conquering South-East Asia to guarantee reliable supplies that led to the blockade being imposed. This in turn 'necessitated' the destruction of American naval power, thereby triggering the Second World War in the Pacific. Throughout this process, the rivalry between the Japanese army and navy only served to whet the appetite for war, and particularly explains why the Japanese navy put forward the unrealistic aim of eliminating the United States from the Pacific.

In extending their grip to Indochina in 1940, the Japanese still did not unleash the ultimate chain of events. To a certain extent, this delay stemmed from their problems in China, where the republican government was continuing to receive supplies of weapons and raw materials via three routes, the most important of these being the French railway in Yunnan. French guarantees failed to reassure Japan, and on France's rapid defeat in May–June 1940 the moment had come to seize its colonies, as had happened to Germany's possessions during the First World War. In July 1940, Japan demanded the right of passage for its troops, a ploy which it repeated with similar success in 1942 in relation to the kingdom of Thailand. General Catroux, followed by the Vichy government and its representative, Admiral Decoux, then took the 'realist' decision to comply with Japan's demands and henceforth accept Japanese supremacy. However, the Japanese troops advanced irrespective of any agreement. Meanwhile, French Indochina also found itself trapped in a pincer movement by the Thais, who took advantage of the situation to recapture by force the north-eastern provinces which had been annexed to French Indochina in 1907. Admittedly, the Americans refused to respond directly to the pleas for help issued by Admiral Decoux and the Vichy government, waiting until 1941 before enforcing a full blockade against Japan. By this time matters had already come to a head. Vichy France signed a treaty with Japan and Germany which actually made reference to a 'common defence', and Japan reoriented the whole Indochinese economy, including mines and trade, in its own favour while extending its military presence into the south of the peninsula. In Tokyo, the concept of a 'Greater East Asia Co-prosperity Sphere' was officially launched. At that point, the United States, the Netherlands (including the Dutch East Indies) and Britain (together with Malaya, Singapore and Burma) announced a total oil blockade.

THE CONQUEST OF SOUTH-EAST ASIA AND THE IMPACT OF THE JAPANESE OCCUPATION

This move placed Japan in an immediate dilemma: whether to withdraw, particularly from China, thereby securing a compromise, or whether to advance. Misjudging its own capability, Japan decided to attack. It launched a surprise raid on Pearl Harbor on 7 December 1941, re-enacting its 1904 offensive against Russia without prior declaration of war. In the process it destroyed most of the United States' battleships (excluding its aircraft carriers) as well as two British battleships off the coast of Malaya. This was the necessary prelude to its *blitzkrieg* on South-East Asia: between February and May 1942, Singapore, the Dutch East Indies, Malaya, the Philippines and Burma were conquered, while Thailand maintained an independence that was more nominal than real, in exchange for an equally nominal declaration of war on the Allies and an all too real agreement to grant Japanese troops access across its territory. By the end of 1942, the imperial army had reached the absolute limits of its expansion, close to the north-east coast of Australia and the northern coast of New Guinea. At Midway, Hawaii and Guadalcanal in the Solomon Islands it had already come up against the US Navy, which on both occasions put up its toughest battles.

The effect of Japanese occupation on Asia as a whole was immense. Furthermore, it should not be seen as confined to the suffering endured in the occupied areas, real though this was. As with its earlier colonization of Korea and Thailand in 1937, Japan's impact was diverse and varied considerably according to local circumstances and the state of its relations with the existing cultures. Initially it was the former Western colonists who suffered the greatest loss. With its prisoners-of-war, immortalized in the film *Bridge on the River Kwai*, and its humiliation of the old colonial masters in the eyes of the colonized population by showing their defeat at the hands of other Asians, Japanese propaganda took every opportunity to highlight the implementation of the principle of 'Asia for the Asians', one of Greater Japan's key slogans in the late 1930s. In many colonies, the Japanese were received either with indifference or with open arms. The latter was especially true of Malaya and Indonesia, where the indigenous populations began to demonstrate a new national pride that was targeted against the British and Dutch colonists; it was also true, in many ways, of Indochina, where the tiny gallicized, educated élite of fewer than 10,000 people had been forced to accept inferior positions, as was also the case in Burma.

If Asian nationalism came into being in the 1920s, it underwent rapid growth during the Japanese occupation, which initially encouraged its opposition to the old colonial rulers. Later, especially in the final months of the war, as the bitterness engendered by the realities of occupation began to set in, the nationalists began to turn against Japan, whereupon the Japanese encouraged nationalists in several Asian countries to obtain independence. In early 1943, following their defeat at Guadalcanal, the military (i.e. the navy as distinct from the army) proposed a plan of independence linked to Japan. This was formally declared in Burma in August 1943 and in the Philippines in October of the same year, at the same time as a provisional government and national army came together in Malaya to 'liberate' India, together with the Indian nationalist Subhaj Chandra Bose, a former associate of Gandhi. In Malaya, whose vital importance for supplies of raw materials was a major concern for Japan, this form of independence was finally contemplated by Japanese diplomats in February 1945. In Vietnam, in a unique move, Japan abolished the competitive entrance examination for the French colonial administration. However, from the outset it encouraged the local nationalist movements and declared independence, as in Cambodia and Laos, in March 1945, after ousting the colonists who had become a liability following the Allied victory in metropolitan France. It was thanks to the tacit agreement of Japan that Ho Chi Minh and his partisans were able to seize control of the entire country in August 1945, proclaiming the Independent Republic of Vietnam on 2 September, the date of the Japanese surrender aboard the battleship *Missouri*.

While the course of events differed from country to country, and although the massive scale of collaboration with Japan often became taboo in Asia after 1945, it constituted an overwhelming fact, as fundamental as the memory of the atrocities committed by the imperial army. In the Dutch East Indies, for example, it had an enormous impact. There, racial hostility was rife and Dutch officials were swiftly replaced by new Indonesian officials. The nationalist leaders – Sukarno, Hatta and Subardjo – actively collaborated with the Japanese, albeit with some reservations. In turn, Japan distributed their propaganda and also helped to shape their ideology. The Japanese encouraged Malay Islamic feeling so far as to unify the education system, which had been segregated along ethnic lines during the Dutch era, and also to impose the use of the Indonesian language for the first time. In his autobiography of 1965, Sukarno expressed his gratitude to the Japanese military for having spread not only his name, but also his face throughout the archipelago (Sukarno, 1965). Most of the Indonesian officers who liberated their country after the Dutch withdrawal had passed through the *Peta* (patriotic defence forces) and the *Giyu-gun* (volunteer army), two Japanese paramilitary organizations which were operational throughout South-East Asia. This was the route followed, for example, by General Suharto, who became Sukarno's successor from 1965–6. Mohammed Yanin, the future cultural commissar in Sukarno's 'guided democracy', began his career producing Japanese propaganda in Java. In 1945, it was General Terauchi who held a formal meeting with some Indonesian agents in Dalat (Vietnam) to offer them a guarantee of independence. The declaration of August 1945 was drafted by Sukarno and a number of others in the residence of Admiral Maeda. Its underlying ideology, which would later serve as a bible for modern Indonesia, was deeply permeated with the Japanese dogma of the time: it stressed the idea of community (*kerakyatan*) and the role of consensus and wise men, rather than democracy, and affirmed a rejection of individualism. Indonesia's military caste would remain characterized by the warlike mentality and voluntarism inspired by the *seishin*, the famous Japanese cult of energy.

In Vietnam, most members of the Cao Dai and Hoa Hao sects gave direct support to the Japanese in an attempt to bypass the colonial powers. Ngo Dinh Diem, the future South Vietnamese head of state from 1954 to 1963, Catholic and friend of the Japanese consul in Hué, was consulted by Admiral Decoux on the issue of relations with Japan and was considered for a time to head the 'independent' government of 1945. There was also a certain resemblance between Vichy propaganda, which was modified in Vietnam under the auspices of Bao Dai to point out a link between Pétain and Confucius, and the Japanese system. The Vichy youth movements represented even less of a contradiction of the true master, as Japan had wisely assigned the three Vietnamese states the same kind of indirect protectorate status as the Thai kingdom.

In Cambodia, the Japanese occupation had an even more rapid polarizing effect. Once installed as king by Admiral Decoux in April 1941, the young, impressionable Norodom Sihanouk had to contend not only with his French advisers but also with the presence of 8,000 Japanese soldiers, who in July 1942 allowed a Buddhist-inspired pro-independence demonstration to take place, led by a monk named Hem Chieu, whom the French promptly arrested. After several further incidents, a number of Cambodian nationalists sought refuge in Tokyo, where they were clearly kept in reserve for the future. However, it was Sihanouk himself, guided by his Japanese adviser Tadakame, who took up Japan's offer of independence in March 1945. He then annulled the agreements with France, restored Khmer as the official language and renamed his country Kampuchea after the Angkor monarchy which had reigned between the eighth and fifteenth centuries. In August 1945, Sihanouk surrendered to a nationalist coup which installed the pro-Japanese Son Ngoc Thanh as Prime Minister. In October 1945, the French retook control and, in 1946, they negotiated a compromise with King Sihanouk, but not with Son Ngoc Thanh, the short-lived Prime Minister of independent Kampuchea, who was immediately put under arrest. Thanh, a Vietnamese-born Khmer educated in France but also in Japan, was imprisoned and later put under house arrest in Poitiers until 1952, becoming the most famous of all the Khmer nationalists. As late as 1948, Pol Pot and his allies in the Association of Khmer Students in France were still closer to the anti-monarchist, nationalist Thanh than to the newly-formed Cambodian Communist Party, founded under the auspices of the Vietminh. The events of summer 1945 thus had a decisive impact on Cambodia. Between 1945 and 1953 the French once again replaced the Japanese, but this time as a hangover from the colonial order rather than as a new foundation.

In Burma, the collapse of British rule brought into play the pre-war nationalist élite, the young Thakins, who were none the less divided into pro-Japanese and pro-British factions. The main group centred on Aung San, the anglicized former President of the Rangoon student movement and future father of Burmese independence in 1948. He and twenty-nine officers switched their allegiance from China (albeit under occupation at that stage) to Japan. The Japanese provided them with military training and established the 23,000-strong Burma Independence Army, which took part in the struggle against the British in January 1942. Notable among its ranks was General Ne Win, who became the strongman of Burma from 1962 onwards. However, it was Dr Ba Maw, the Prime Minister who had dominated Burmese politics under British rule, whom the Japanese installed as leader in 1943. The left wing of the Thakin nationalist movement, headed by Soe Gyi, also relaunched the Burmese Communist Party in 1943. From 1943 onwards, Aung San, who was Defence Minister in the pro-Japanese government, prepared the resistance together with his associates. In May 1944, they united with the Anti-Fascist League for the Freedom of the People, an anti-Japanese united front which co-ordinated its own attacks with those of the Allies. As for the British, they succeeded in forming special guerilla units, codenamed Forces 136 and 137, made up of Karens and Kachins, many of whom were Christian converts. Later, during the Vietnam War, the United States found that it could mobilize some of the region's ethnic minorities to combat Vietnamese infiltration. Thus, in Burma's case at any rate, all post-war military and ethnic movements date from the period 1942–5.

In the Philippines, it was the élites formed within the system of large landownership and senatorial oligarchy which collaborated with the Japanese, sometimes with underlying patriotic motives. The change of master came almost naturally to a country which had seen the United States succeed the Spanish in 1898. Consequently, most of the leading families were involved with the Japanese, including the Aquino de Tarlac clan, the Laurel family (José P. Laurel becoming President of the pro-Japanese government in 1943) and the father of Ferdinand Marcos who himself was to present a highly embroidered account of his own anti-Japanese exploits. The Japanese encouraged the revival of both the national language, or *tagalog*, and a sense of Malay pride which did much to fuel anti-American feeling after the war. Yet anti-Japanese resistance also ran high in a country where the American influence on education was much stronger than that of Europeans in their own colonies. Great numbers of Filipino partisans fought alongside the American GIs, and the Filipino communists led by Luis Taruc formed, alongside the Hukbalahap, South-East Asia's largest guerilla movement. It was a force which resumed action after the end of the war. The post-war political scene in the Philippines was just as marked by the ambiguous behaviour demonstrated by the élites of 1941–5. Sergio Muneco, who had been the right-hand man of former President Manuel Quezon, as well as being a fellow refugee with him in the United States, returned with General MacArthur in 1945 as the prosecutor in charge of purges. Despite his moderate stance, he lost to Manuel Roxas in the presidential elections of 1946. Roxas, the former head of the agency in charge of rice shipments to Japan during the war and a member of the drafting committee for the 1943 constitution, had acquiesced in the declaration of war against the United States while limiting its practical implications. He was reinstated as well as backed in the elections by MacArthur himself. José Laurel, who was charged with treason but later pardoned, was a candidate in the 1949 presidential elections, and his official portrait still hangs in the presidential palace at Malacanang. When called on to negotiate the details of reparations to the Philippines in 1954, Japan simply despatched its former wartime ambassador to Manila. Although anti-Japanese patriotism was a vital factor in the politics of the archipelago after 1945, the war left behind the image of a corrupt élite, justifying recourse to rebellion.

In Singapore and the British colonial entity which was to form Malaya in 1948, the Japanese occupation was even more fraught with conflict from the outset, owing to racial factors. The overseas Chinese were indeed clearly in the majority in Singapore, and even in the Malay peninsula. Their patriotism posed a problem for the Japanese, whether it was focused on the Kuomintang or the communists, or whether it turned them into anglicized 'King's Chinese'. For example, Lee Kuan Yew, who has dominated Singaporean politics since 1959, acknowledges that as a young lawyer he was a translator for the Japanese Domei agency, yet he still maintained the best possible relations with the British after 1945, suggesting that he may have remained in close contact. Local conditions were also affected by hostility between Chinese and Malay, which the Japanese generally helped to fuel. In 1938, the Malays, influenced by the Indonesian nationalists, formed a pro-independence movement called the Young Malay Union, which already had contact with Tokyo and certainly gave the Japanese a favourable welcome. For example, Tunku (to use his noble title) Abdul Rahman, a former Cambridge student and subsequently post-war Malaya's leading political figure, 'saved' his father, the sultan of Kedah, whom the British wanted to take with them on their defeat in January 1942. The Japanese occupying forces played on existing ethnic divisions, awarding a number of scholarships to Malay students, who admittedly had not been overwhelmed by British generosity in this respect. They retained the British primary education system with its system of ethnic segregation and built up the Indian National Army around a nucleus of Malay Hindus, to counter the anti-Japanese activities of the Tamil rubber-plantation workers. The propaganda issued in favour of racial harmony was based on a well-known saying of Jinmu, the first Japanese Emperor: 'Eight pillars under one roof' (*hakko ichiu*). This mantra, advocating world peace but at the same time hinting at the role of Japan, was echoed throughout Asia after 1940.

However, as far as the Chinese were concerned, the Japanese attitude was quite different. It undoubtedly involved an element of calculation, playing Malay nationalism off against the influential minority of the international business community, and also a fear of patriotic loyalty to China, where Japan was continuing to get bogged down. The imperial army corps which occupied northern Malaya and Singapore in 1942 had come direct from southern China, where it had encountered bitter opposition. On their arrival, the Japanese arrested and deported large numbers of Singaporeans, among them David Marshall, who became Prime Minister on the city's independence in 1956, but above all 70,000 Chinese. Singapore was renamed Syonan, the 'Light of the South'. In Malaya, as part of an elimination procedure, Japan opened a number of camps, where 50–60,000 Chinese were notably executed in March 1943. It is true that the Japanese occupation of Malaya had some mitigating effects: by creating mass population movements that drew the Malays out of their traditional *kampong* (villages) and by drafting the women into service, Japan unwittingly paved the way for post-war nationalist unrest. However, other aspects of their policy prompted the people to rise up against them: for example, by way of reparations to Thailand, they split off four of the most traditional northern provinces from the Federated Malay States. The Malays found themselves in the minority in what was left of the Malay peninsula, and a Muslim secessionist element was to cause unrest in southern Thailand throughout the modern period. By reorienting all prosperous Malaya's exports towards Japan, the occupying forces also destroyed the basis of the local economy. More than anything else, however, Japan's anti-Chinese policy fuelled nationalist feeling among the Chinese community, most of whom joined the resistance under the aegis of the Malay Communist Party (MCP). Admittedly, it was the young Chinese rather than the wealthy *tokays* (businessmen) who took part in this struggle. As in Burma, the British were just as capable as the Japanese of exploiting ethnic rivalry. Thus, in December 1941, they introduced into Singapore the guerillas belonging to the MCP, which was to be their ally throughout the war. Conversely, the Japanese encouraged the anti-Chinese xenophobia of the Malays, leading to riots prompted by competition over agricultural land. The period of the Japanese occupation was thus instrumental in deepening the ethnic rivalry between Malaya's two main communities that has been the linchpin of its politics since 1945.

Finally, Thailand – the only nominally independent country left in the region – entered Japan's orbit with relative ease. There were various contributory factors, including the historic links forged between the Siamese nationalists and the Japanese following the overthrow of the absolute monarchy in June 1932 and Siamese hostility towards the wealthy, influential Chinese minority (all of whose newspapers had been banned in 1942). There was also the factor of Thai irredentism with regard to the provinces ceded to French Indochina in 1907. These were reclaimed in 1941 with the decline in French power, and Thailand in turn expanded at the expense of the Federated Malay States. In Bangkok, territorial issues of this nature incited considerably more passion than the Second World War. In January 1942, General Phibun, the nationalist leader who had come to power in 1939, became Burma's 'Guide' and declared war on the Allies in what was a purely formal gesture (the Thai ambassador in Washington failed to inform the US Government of the fact). In September 1944, Phibun was forced to resign under pressure from the United States. An 80,000-strong army was then formed in defence of a free Thailand by Pridi Phanomyong, who became Minister of Foreign Affairs. However, Phibun himself was returned to power by a military coup in November 1947. It was therefore the same military clique which dominated national politics from 1932 onwards, with Thai foreign policy merely tacking pragmatically before the changing winds of external events. In contrast, the Thai Communist Party was formed in December 1942, in total symbiosis with the Chinese communists, and would bear the mark of its political and ethnic origin throughout its life.

As in Korea, where mutual hatred and contempt prevailed despite the closeness of the two cultures, Japan's occupation of China was unique in both its scale and its violence. The capture of Nanjing in 1938 involved the massacre of over 100,000 Chinese civilians who were, literally, put to the sword. However, it is important to avoid the kind of retrospective myth-making which extrapolates from these atrocities in order to credit the anti-Japanese resistance with unanimous support. There was not one, but at least two occupation régimes, and a great variety of Chinese reactions to them. In fact, the collaborationist government of Wang Jingwei, based in Nanjing and Shanghai, subsequently proved far less of a problem than the northern part of the country, the scene of direct clashes between the Japanese and the communist guerillas.

In 1938, the Japanese army 'cleansed' the countryside of northern China. However, as the guerilla war began to escalate, particularly after the notorious Hundred Regiments offensive launched by the Red Army in August 1940, Japan's obsessive occupation turned into a massacre. The CCP had originally tried to provoke the Japanese army in order to galvanize a flagging Chinese united front. A cycle of resistance and repression was set in motion, with the peasant population of northern China rallying to the side likely to offer the best protection, i.e. the Red Army. There then came the phase of the war which was inspired by the famous order to 'kill, burn, destroy!' (*sanko-seisaku*) supposedly issued by General Okamura in May 1942. In fact, Okamura had thought that he would be able to use far more sophisticated anti-guerilla tactics, but within a few months this interpretation of his command had become a reality. In the process, the Japanese also invented modern techniques of counter-guerrilla warfare which the French, Dutch, British and especially the Americans were obliged to study in their archives after 1945. The main features included the forced rounding-up of populations, the defence of transit routes and strategic positions, blockades of turbulent zones, the use of electrified barrages (including one of 140 kilometres around Suzhou in central China) and the creation of vast empty corridors. The results included millions of deaths, the flight of tens of millions of refugees away from the war zones, the ruin of the country's economic capacity (including the network of irrigation systems and dykes) and the extraordinary mobilization of Chinese manpower. Not only did this upsurge of nationalism embodied by the CCP pave the way to power for the communists, as all commentators now agree; like Tito in Yugoslavia and Castro in Cuba, Chinese communism had fulfilled its claim to national legitimacy. It was also in the course of this all-out effort that the communists developed their cast-iron discipline, their organizational structure and the egalitarian, pragmatic techniques used to mobilize the Chinese peasantry, which later formed the backbone of the People's Republic of China. Yenan and its generation were thus replicated throughout northern and central China, largely as a result of the blind brutality of the Japanese army.

As for the guerillas' tactics, they would prove the mainstay of the revolutionary conflicts and wars of liberation which came after 1945. They included withdrawing as the enemy advanced, building tunnels, accumulating grain reserves, vanishing into the countryside and breaking through surrounding enemy lines, utilizing village militias, assassinating village chiefs and letting people keep 'white faces and red hearts', in other words collaborate with the Japanese by day and support the guerilla forces by night. The catechism recited by Mao's soldiers, for which much of the inspiration came from the nineteenth-century Taiping movement, strengthened the intense bonds of personal allegiance which existed in that clan-based, feudalistic society. The republican government, which had retreated as far as Chungking in Sichuan, was unable to compete in this struggle, despite financial and military aid from both the United States and the Soviet Union. Not only was Chiang Kai-shek, so often the victim of Western arrogance, persuaded to sign a separate peace treaty in 1940, even more importantly, his organization was also more liberal, disorganized, corrupt and, above all, more inefficient than the CCP. Republican patriotism was of little use in the occupied zones; furthermore, by mimicking the slogans and institutions of the Kuomintang from which it had itself originated, the collaborationist government in Nanjing left behind a whiff of treachery which the CCP was able to exploit.

In 1937, at the start of what it referred to as the 'China Incident', the Japanese army heaped scorn on the 'communist bandits'. From 1942 it began to show increasing respect in its dealings with the famous Eighth Route Army, as the main component of the communist guerilla forces was called. In August 1945, Mao boasted of 'harvesting the fruits of victory'. The region which he described as being within his reach comprised, so he claimed, 95 million Chinese, 900,000 soldiers and 2 million members of village militias – the critical mass which he judged sufficient to seize power in China within five years.

The greatest upheaval initiated by the Japanese thrust across Asia was the consequent rise of Chinese communism. Taken together, however, the countries of South-East Asia were far more cautious in choosing between Japan and the Allies than was generally acknowledged after the war. The Greater East Asia Co-prosperity Sphere, celebrated with a meeting in Tokyo in November 1943, not only forcibly reoriented all regional trade towards Japan, it also had an added political dimension, which admittedly was based to some extent on anti-colonial hostility and ethnic rivalry. Though initially welcomed in many cases, the Japanese often came to be hated either because of the behaviour of their troops or as a result of the economic collapse resulting from their presence, following the forced mobilization of millions of peasants across South-East Asia. From Calcutta to Vietnam and from Batavia to northern China, the Second World War ended with one of the most disastrous famines in history, due to the total disruption of the food trade and also, in some cases, to the hostilities themselves and the use of scorched-earth tactics. However, this did not prevent a great many of Japan's former local partners from maintaining or resuming leading political and economic positions in their respective countries after 1945.

Thus, the independence movement in Asia frequently stemmed from this period of suspension of colonial power between 1941 and 1945. Ho Chi Minh and the Vietminh were supported by the American Office of Strategic Survey (OSS); the Sino-Malay communist leader Chin Peng was decorated by Queen Elizabeth II; the Huks in the Philippines were armed by the Americans; and the famous 'Dixie mission' went to the aid of the Chinese communists in Yenan. The nationalist rationale employed by the Japanese backfired, though not without the Allies helping to legitimize the nationalist, revolutionary forces. In these circumstances, as the Singaporean Prime Minister Lee Kuan Yew was to say of his own region in 1961, 'there was never a chance of the old type of British colonial system ever being repeated' (Chew and Lee, 1991: 110), nor would the authority of the other powers hold firm for much longer.

SELECTED READING

Japan's relations with Asia during the Pacific War, although the subject of much questioning, have not been a major area of research by Western historians. Among the works listed below, McCoy (1980) is essential to understanding South-East Asian reactions to Japanese conquest, while Myers and Peattie (1984) is an in-depth study of Japan's presence in Korea and Taiwan during the colonial era. Kataoka (1974) presents an updated interpretation of the Chinese communists' success during the war with Japan, which places less emphasis on nationalism than the classic work by Chalmers Johnson (1962). Olson (1970) is a factual enquiry into the crucial topic of how Japan patched up its relations after 1945 with the countries it had conquered.

Boyle, J. H. (1972) *China and Japan at war: the politics of collaboration, 1937–1945*, Stanford: Stanford University Press.

Chew, E.C.T. and Lee, E. (1991) *A history of Singapore*, Singapore: Oxford University Press.

Guillain, R. (1990) *J'ai vu brûler Tokyo*, Nîmes: Arléa.

Johnson, C. A. (1969) *Nationalisme paysan et pouvoir communiste: les débuts de la révolution chinoise*, Paris: Payot.

Kataoka, T. (1974) *Resistance and revolution in China: the communists and the second united front*, Berkeley: University of California Press.

Lee, C. (1983) *Revolutionary struggle in Manchuria: Chinese communism and Soviet interest*, Berkeley: University of California Press.

——(1985) *Japan and Korea: the political dimension*, Stanford: Hoover Institution.

Lintner, B. (1990) *The rise and fall of the Communist Party of Burma*, Ithaca: Cornell University Press.

McCoy, A. W. (ed.) (1980) *Southeast Asia under Japanese occupation*, New Haven: Yale University Press.

Myers, R. A. and Peattie, M. R. (eds) (1984) *The Japanese colonial empire, 1895–1945*, Princeton: Princeton University Press.

Olson, L. (1970) *Japan in postwar Asia*, New York: Council on Foreign Relations.

Schaller, M. (1979) *The US crusade in China, 1938–1945*, New York: Columbia University Press.

Tuchman, B. W. (1971) *Stilwell and the American experience in China, 1911–1945*, New York: Macmillan.

4   From decolonization to the Cold War (1945–54)

Between the Japanese surrender on 15 August 1945 and the outbreak of the Korean War on 25 June 1950, most of the Western colonies in Asia were resurrected briefly, only to disappear again through negotiation or by force. At the same time, rivalry set in between the new nationalist governments, some of which included a progressive element (in Indonesia and Burma, for example), and their rivals in the communist movements and régimes, which also had their own share of nationalist aspirations.

The course of events ran as follows. First there came the creation *ex nihilo* of two rival Koreas in July 1945. This was followed in Vietnam by the revolution of August 1945 and a declaration of independence that was thwarted by the return of the French, leading to the first Indochina War (December 1946 to September 1954). In 1946, the United States agreed to grant the Philippines their independence, but this was followed in 1948 by the revival of the Huk guerilla movement. Independence was negotiated by the British in Burma in 1947 (the same year as in India, Pakistan and Ceylon), but against a background of civil and ethnic strife which still continues over forty years later. Indonesia wrested its independence from the Dutch between 1945 and 1949, while the new Republic quelled a communist uprising and unified the entire East Indies archipelago, partly by force. In Malaya, the Union formed within the Commonwealth remained suspended, owing to the alliance between the British and the Malay sultans, but a state of emergency was declared in March 1948 because of an uprising by the Malayan Communist Party. After some delay, mainly on security grounds, full independence finally came to Malaya in 1957 and Singapore in 1959–60.

In China, the Red Army and the communists with their united front initially managed to negotiate with the nationalists, thanks to the good offices of the Americans. From 1946 onwards, however, hostilities resumed and the communists gained the upper hand throughout continental China during 1948–9. By thus winning the civil war, they forced Chiang Kai-shek's republican government to retreat onto the island of Taiwan, which became a nationalist refuge. Finally, the offensive launched by North Korea in June 1950 marked the outbreak of full-scale war right across the Korean peninsula, lasting until 1953. The war not only brought the Chinese and the Americans head to head, but above all served to reinforce the demarcation line between the two major international blocs. The 'loss of China' and the Korean War came in the wake of the Berlin blockade, the erection of the Wall between the two Germanies and the first Soviet nuclear explosion. At that stage the United States abandoned the reformist aims which it had held during and after the Second World War, concentrating instead on support- ing all anti-communist governments, including throughout the French war in Indochina, which was lost in 1954. Up until the diplomatic and political failure of the United States in the Vietnam War in 1975, the front line between the two superpowers in Asia remained where it had been drawn, if necessary by war, in 1953 at the Korean Armistice and in 1954 at the Geneva Conference on Indochina.

THE TWO SUPERPOWERS AND DECOLONIZATION

By 1954, the only parts of Asia still under colonial rule were New Guinea, Borneo, Timor and Hong Kong. A third of the Asian population was ruled by communist governments which, despite not having been democrat- ically elected, generally possessed far greater legitimacy than the people's republics established in Eastern and Central Europe at the same period. In Asia, with the exception of the future North Korean capital of Pyongyang, it was not Soviet tanks which carried in the victors. Nor was it a 'new generation' which came to power in most cases, but rather the veterans of the previous decades' struggles, from Mao Zedong and Ho Chi Minh to Sukarno, or occasionally a successor generation which had been groomed for the part through contact with the colonists, as in Malaya and the Philippines. Yet the immediate post-war period saw the establishment of most of the present-day Asian régimes and their fundamental political orientations for many years to come. It was also a period of extraordinary ambiguity for several reasons: the relative balance between the nationalists and the communists was often determined, or unwittingly influenced, by the uncertainty of the British, Dutch and French colonial policies. Although they remained in the background until 1949, the two superpowers, the United States and the Soviet Union, still influenced events, whether directly, by virtue of their military might and the effects of the measures taken in 1945 with regard to Asia, or indirectly, through their slowly emerging plans for the region. Between the last months of Roosevelt's presidency and the Truman administration, which was primarily influenced by the develop- ment of the Cold War in Europe, there occurred a shift away from a desire for rapid decolonization towards support for a more gradual transition to nationalist, anti-communist governments. The dilemma faced by the Soviet Union was even more complex: on the one hand, it was torn between support for the independent nationalist governments of Asia and a return to seizing power 'from below' through class conflict; but on the other hand, it also faced a choice between the strategy of united fronts, linking the progressive bourgeoisie with democratic protest, and supporting the armed struggle which was being directly launched by several communist movements in South-East Asia, for example in the Philippines, Malaya and Burma.

Both superpowers also acted in accordance with their respective alliances, as well as their own leading priorities. In the United States, the Roosevelt era was marked by a return to the anti-colonialism of Woodrow Wilson. Roosevelt was particularly suspicious of French collusion with the Japanese in Indochina, a factor which influenced the initial United States stance towards Vietnam. However, as the Cold War escalated, American diplomacy shifted towards closer support for its main European allies, i.e. Britain and France. The 'Europe first' policy championed by George Kennan in the State Department primarily meant making European reconstruction the chief economic priority in order to combat Soviet communism. On the other hand, the growing intensity of the Cold War meant that communist activity in Asia was increasingly seen as a direct challenge, and American policy in the region became based on the same confrontation.

As for the Soviet Union, its Far East strategy led to the outbreak of the Korean War in June 1950. However, the theory that the Soviet Union embarked on a policy of revolutionary conquest in Asia, as had happened in the early days of the Third International, has by no means been proven. Admittedly, in this key debate to explain the origins of the Cold War, the main archives on the communist side are still unavailable, whereas in the United States they are largely accessible due to the extremely short delays in releasing documents. From the unauthorized release of the Pentagon Papers during the Vietnam War in 1972 to more recent studies on the Korean War, the most important confidential American directives (and, in particular, all the presidential directives issued by the National Security Council) and subsequent testimonies compared alongside the contemporary correspondence of the leading protagonists have all entered the public domain. To cite just one example, we now know the views of leading American officials and advisers on the potential use of the atomic bomb during the Korean War and against China in order to defend the outposts of Taiwan. The same is by no means true of the Soviet, Chinese, North Korean and Vietnamese governments, still less of guerilla movements which were defeated. While the strategy of the Cominform (the successor to the Third International) is now relatively well known regarding continental Europe due to the testimony of former West European participants, it is still unclear as far as Asia is concerned. What is certain is that, on the whole, it was much less influential there than in continental Europe.

Following the collapse of Soviet communism in 1991, it only remains to await the release of archives before a definitive choice can be made between the two main conflicting theories. The first discoveries have concerned Stalin's involvement in the North Korean invasion of June 1950, and confirm the standard Western thesis. But other areas still remain untouched and open to different interpretations. On the one hand, there is the view put forward by historians of the Cold War and the era of anti-communist containment, claiming that it was the orders and deliberate policy of Moscow that kindled the post-war revolutionary movements in Asia, at any rate after September 1947 and the establishment of the Cominform. Then there are the theories of the so-called 'revisionist' school, which command little credibility when they suggest, for example, that it was the United States which started the Korean War; yet, in other respects, these theories closely coincide with the views of many liberal historians, for whom the wrongs of colonialism, the ambiguity of American policy and, above all, the revolutionary potential inherent in various Asian societies are generally enough to explain events, without any need to invoke the hand of Moscow.

The United States and Asia

America's Asian policy after the end of the Second World War might be described as ambiguous, evolutive and subject to variation depending on its practitioners. The Allied victory had clearly required a concentration of material resources and political alliances to the exclusion of all other objectives. Even in the closing days of the war, between July and August 1945, the preparations for a landing in Japan overtook more long-term, strategic considerations. Thus, at Potsdam in July 1945, the American Chief of Staff disclosed in passing to his Soviet counterparts that the United States did not yet have any concrete plans for the occupation of Korea, meaning that the occupation would be carried out jointly by Allied military units. Stalin, however, inferred that he was being presented with an opportunity, and within a few days he had launched a land offensive in Manchuria and an air attack on North Korea. At the same time, he made a short-lived bid to occupy the north of the Japanese island of Hokkaido which was immediately turned down by President Truman. Considerable numbers of Japanese troops were stationed in Singapore, Malaya, the Dutch East Indies and, on an even larger scale still, Indochina. The local pro-independence partisans rushed to fill the vacuum created by Japan's eleventh-hour diplomacy of encouragement. The Allied troops – first British, then Dutch and finally French – took nearly all of 1945 to get into position, so great was the priority which the American command gave to concentrating resources on Japan and the Pacific. The French observer Paul Mus, describing the power vacuum which existed in Vietnam in 1945, commented that the peasants appeared to have lived through a century in nine months.

Furthermore, from Kunming to Chungking in China and from Luzon and Singapore to the Golden Triangle and northern Tonkin, the Allied forces which had infiltrated the occupied territories, namely Forces 136 and 137 of the British Special Operations Executive (SOE) and the United States Office of Strategic Survey ((OSS), the forerunner of the CIA), as well as the liaison officers on the ground, had developed close collaborative links with the Asian nationalist forces, often including the political or ethnic guerillas. This led to some extraordinary scenes: for example Chin Peng, the leader of the Chinese-Malay communist guerillas, held negotiations with the British aboard a submarine off Perak, and Ho Chi Minh, the former number one Comintern agent in South-East Asia, where he was fabled for his chameleon-like persona, was in contact with the OSS, writing to Washington on eight occasions between Autumn 1945 and February 1946 to obtain American support. Zhou Enlai and his English-speaking journalists at the Communist Liaison Bureau in Chungking, who were to form the core of the Chinese diplomatic service after their final victory, succeeded in winning the sympathy of even the most hard-headed American diplomats, while Luis Taruc and his comrades in the Huk resistance movement were the beneficiaries of parachute drops organized by General MacArthur.

In some cases, Roosevelt adopted a stance which did not bode well for the future of the former colonies. This was particularly true of French Indochina, where official collaboration with Japan galled the American President. In January 1944 he wrote: 'For a hundred years now, France has bled this country white' (Roosevelt, 1952: 493). Meanwhile, political relations with Ho Chi Minh, who had returned from Moscow to the caves of northern Tonkin after a period in the Yenan province of China, were set fair. At the Cairo conference in 1943, Roosevelt had set out a plan for tripartite rule in Taiwan, Korea, Manchuria and Indochina, involving China, the Soviet Union and the United States. In the Philippines, America itself had guaranteed to see through the transition to independence scheduled for 1946, and it was this model which guided Roosevelt. At the Tehran conference of November 1943, he spoke of 'fifty years of international trusteeship' for Korea, a similar timescale to that which the Philippines were following. Although the official Dutch attitude to Japan was not open to the same criticism as the French, Roosevelt was equally convinced that colonialism should also be brought to an end in the Dutch East Indies. This was far less true of the British, both under Churchill and under the Labour Party which succeeded him after the 1946 General Election. In March 1946, Churchill coined the famous term 'iron curtain' in condemnation of the Soviet takeover in Eastern Europe, while the British Labour Party came to an agreement with the French authorities over Indochina.

Wartime stances and the advance presence of American elements in close contact with local movements were the reasons why, from Batavia (Jakarta) to Cochinchina (southern Vietnam), the Allies were received with cheers and placards in English heralding freedom and independence. In Vietnam, the officers of the OSS did not exactly rush to free Admiral Decoux's officials, who had been held by the Vietnamese following their internment by Japan during the last days of the war. In contrast, the British troops, who were the first to arrive in both Indochina and Java, acted much more favourably towards their European allies, paving the way for their return.

Under the terms of an agreement between the British and their Chinese allies, the former occupied the land south of the 16th parallel (one degree from where the demarcation line would be drawn between North and South Vietnam in 1954) while the latter took the territory to the north. As might be expected, the British troops were better disposed towards the French than were the Chinese Kuomintang troops.

In Korea, the United States rallied swiftly after its initial lapse in the early summer of 1945. In August, it drew a demarcation line along the 38th parallel just to the north of Seoul and, after a swift landing to the south of it, was able to receive the Japanese surrender, while the Soviet Union occupied the north. Korea's division into provisional occupation zones was intended to give way to a system of joint international trusteeship, for the Potsdam Declaration of the previous month only referred to Korean independence as taking place 'in due course'. The United States government clearly failed to anticipate the strength of the Korean reaction on all sides to a delay in receiving independence. Washington even planned to prevent independent Korea's spokesman in the United States, Syngman Rhee, from returning to Korea on account of his opposition to the trusteeship plan. Meanwhile, the United States refused to allow the Soviet Union to occupy the north of the Japanese island of Hokkaido, which, had it succeeded, would have meant dividing up Japan along the same lines as Germany. Stalin failed on that score, but he immediately exploited the existence of the demarcation line along the 38th parallel to create a satellite state in North Korea. Although the Koreans were, in theory, liberated at the end of the war, they found themselves as firmly divided as if they had been defeated.

In October 1945, the US Air Force organized an airlift into northern China for the benefit of the republican army to curb the spread of communism and prevent Mao Zedong from joining forces with the Russians in Manchuria. American efforts then focused on the negotiations between the CCP and the Kuomintang to try to maintain the united front of the war years. The negotiations failed to prevent the outbreak of civil war in July 1946. In January 1947, the chief American negotiator, George Marshall, admitted failure in this regard, thus leading to the first toughening of America's stance.

Although President Roosevelt and the Democrats inspired by the New Deal had initially opposed a return to colonialism, this phase soon passed. In 1946 the United States' Asian policy was one of overt neutrality rather than of scrupulous non-intervention. It was thus possible for weapons destined for Second World War allies (the Free French and the Dutch) within the framework of the Lend-Lease plan to be shipped to Asia, even if Washington frequently insisted on their identification marks being removed. The Pentagon Papers revealed that in 1946 the United States granted US$160 million to France for 'vehicles and other supplies earmarked for Indochina'. On the death of Roosevelt and his replacement by former Vice-President Truman (who subsequently won a sweeping election victory in his own right) America's involvement in the Cold War gradually deepened. In 1947 the Marshall Plan of economic aid for European reconstruction and the 'Truman doctrine', aimed at the containment of communism, together banished all remaining traces of anti-colonialism. The United States none the less continued to put more pressure on the Dutch than on the French. France was, after all, a permanent member of the United Nations Security Council and therefore had the right to veto any resolution; furthermore, the Vietminh was merely a front for the Indochinese Communist Party, which had only appeared to dissolve itself in 1945–6. By contrast, in Indonesia, after a phase dominated by a progressive government allied with a number of communist factions, the nationalist leaders Sukarno and Hatta crushed a communist uprising at Madiun (Java) in October 1948, and were therefore much more acceptable to American policymakers than Uncle Ho.

American neutrality certainly ceased to apply to China after the failure of the Chungking negotiations between the communists and the Kuomintang. Yet the United States continued to waver over the question of firm engagement. It was mainly to appease the pro-Chiang Kai-shek lobby in Congress, made up of republicans opposed to public spending among other things, that George Marshall, by then Secretary of State, added to America's aid for Europe a major package of $4 billion earmarked for China. However, its use was poorly monitored, and no specific steps were taken to prevent victory by the communists in 1949. In 1945, the ambassador to Chungking, John Hurley, had considered the latter merely as agrarian reformers, George Marshall regarded them as immune to the influence of foreign communists, and Truman himself described them as so-called communists. In December 1948, George Kennan, the celebrated architect of anti-Soviet containment, had viewed the loss of China as both inevitable and of minor significance. This underestimation gave grounds for attacks on the State Department and the Democrats by the Republicans and the extremist Senator Joe McCarthy. In retrospect, it seems highly probable that it was the importance of Asia (apart from Japan) that was underestimated, rather than communism.

In 1947, admittedly, the United States concentrated on Japan as a reliable partner in Asia, just as in Europe it revised its attitude towards Germany. In May 1947, Secretary of State Dean Acheson described these countries as two of the largest workshops in Europe and Asia. The rest was seen as underdeveloped and of little significance: indeed, the first economic advisers to South Korea recommended that it should principally be turned into a vast grain-producing economy. After the victory by Mao Zedong's forces in 1949, the United States initially decided not to contribute to the defence of Taiwan. Secretary of State Dean Acheson, somewhat prematurely, predicted a Sino-Soviet rift. He took the view that a policy of non-intervention would be likely to turn Mao into another Tito, in other words a progressive nationalist independent of Moscow. When, in January 1950, Dean Acheson

drew a United States 'defensive perimeter' in Asia, both the Korean penin-
sula and Taiwan were excluded. The widespread, immediate reaction in the
United States to the North Korean offensive of 25 June 1950 proved Dean
Acheson's formula wrong. It is possible that a certain mistrust of the
unpredictable, rash moves made by the South Korean President Syngman
Rhee and General Chiang Kai-shek may also have been a factor in this.
However, Joseph Stalin appears to have charged headlong into this ambigu-
ous situation, just as he had done in the summer of 1945.

Thus, up until the signing of the Sino-Soviet Friendship Treaty in February 1950, the United States was reluctant to guarantee the defence of
Formosa, leaving its international future open, along with that of the other
former Japanese colonies. Yet on 14 June 1950, General MacArthur referred to Formosa as an 'unsinkable aircraft carrier', whereupon the young
Yasuhiro Nakasone, a member of the Japanese Diet, challenged MacArthur
to try and persuade the United States to fully guarantee Japan's security. In
1982, having become Prime Minister, Nakasone would use MacArthur's
exact words from 1950 to describe his own country.

The North Korean offensive did much to galvanize America's stance. In
the following weeks, while the US Army prepared for a landing at Inchon in
Korea, the Seventh Fleet 'neutralized' the Strait of Formosa and Truman
quarantined China behind a so-called 'bamboo curtain'. All of a sudden,
Dean Acheson suspected a communist attack on the whole of Asia. Following a successful landing by MacArthur's troops in September, an order was
given to pursue the aggressors beyond the 38th parallel, in other words to
enter North Korea. This marked the 'roll back' of communism, the sequel
to containment, resulting in the entry of the People's Republic of China into
the war in October 1950. During his first few months in office following
election, President Eisenhower contemplated the use of the atomic bomb in
the Korean War. It was also he who, in April 1954, formulated the famous
'domino theory', whereby the downfall of one government allied to the 'free
world' would trigger the defeat of its neighbours one by one.

This new American stance transformed the whole of Asia, as it led to the
systematic signing of a number of security agreements, first with the Philippines in August 1951, then with Australia, New Zealand and Japan in
September 1951, Korea in October 1953 and Taiwan in December 1954. It
also resulted, in September 1954, in an attempt to create an Asian NATO in
the shape of SEATO (South-East Asian Treaty Organization). Worried at
this development, Mao Zedong cabled to Zhou Enlai, on his way to the
Geneva Conference, that they had been wrong not to resume the liberation
of Taiwan immediately after the Korean ceasefire. From September 1954
onwards, China began bombarding the small, heavily-fortified islands just
off the mainland which still belonged to Formosa. In March 1955, Allen
Dulles, head of the CIA and Chief of Staff at the Pentagon, called for the
nuclear bombardment of China. In the same month, this threat was publicly
echoed by Eisenhower and Vice-President Richard Nixon, targets were

identified by General Curtis LeMay and a test flight was carried out over China. The crisis was resolved in April, when Zhou Enlai, following the conference at Bandung, announced that China wished to be 'the friend of the United States'. Meanwhile, however, in order to defend the Quemoy and Matsu Islands (the base for a quarter of Formosa's armed forces) following China's attack on the small Dachen Islands, Eisenhower 'successfully went to the brink of the abyss', as United States Secretary of State John Foster Dulles was to put it some months later.

Between 1945 and 1949, mainly due to its preoccupation with Europe, the United States had gradually allowed its Asian policy to become based on the struggle against communism. From 1950 to 1955, the Korean War and a deep-seated confrontation with 'Red China' made Asia the Cold War's main theatre of operations. Moreover, the very expression 'Cold War' is quite inappropriate, since the Korean War was the bloodiest conflict to take place since 1945, and the use of the atomic bomb was also contemplated. Whereas up to 1950 some members of the State Department saw in Mao a nationalist who might break with the Soviet Union at any moment, from 1950 onwards it was the Cold War warriors who counted on a rift. Thus, from John Foster Dulles' point of view, the Russians might cease to support Mao. The United States gave strong backing to anti-communist governments throughout Asia. This confrontational attitude towards China persisted, with the Kennedy administration in the early 1960s being particularly intransigent. In 1955, the same year as the clash with Eisenhower over the Strait of Formosa, the Chinese government in turn began building its own nuclear weapon. From this period onwards, Mao Zedong began furnishing himself with the means for a strategy independent of the Soviet Union.

The Soviet Union and Asia

In Washington adminstrations came and went, but in Moscow Stalin ruled up to his death in February 1953. It was he who determined Soviet policy, assisted by a small number of lieutenants such as V. Molotov and A. Zhdanov. Yet the continuity of this dictatorship was not necessarily reflected in its Asian policy: even before the war, Stalin had already shown himself to be particularly hesitant in forming perceptions and making choices. His mistrust of the Chinese communists, and Mao Zedong especially, also went back a long way. While Stalin had been the one really responsible for the CCP débâcle in 1926–30, stemming from a series of conflicting decisions relayed by the International, he had never accepted Mao's subsequent rise to power, for Mao was one of the few communist leaders not controlled directly by the Soviet party apparatus. Nor did Stalin abandon his policy of recognition and aid for the Chinese nationalist government, which remained a priority throughout the Second World War. He adopted a purely defensive position *vis à vis* Japan regarding Russian interests threatened by various Japanese military incursions, first in Manchuria, then in Eastern Siberia. The outcome of this cautious manoeuvring was the mutual non-aggression pact signed between Japan and the Soviet Union in April 1941, which distracted the attention of the Japanese army away towards other targets in southern Asia, forming an Eastern counterpart to the German–Soviet Pact.

As far as both Stalin and America were concerned, once the Second World War ended, the main contest was fought very much in Europe. The great Allied conferences at Tehran, Yalta and Potsdam produced fewer results as far as Asia was concerned, and only Korea's future was initially planned there: its independence was to be restored, but accompanied by a transitional system of international trusteeship. Yet in December 1944, Stalin confided to United States diplomats his concern 'to re-establish Russia's position as it had been before the Russo-Japanese war of 1905', in other words to include not only Sakhalin and the Northern Kuriles, but also the full right to intervene in northern Manchuria and guaranteed access to the warm-water port of Dalian (formerly Port Arthur). No mention was made of Korea, yet in Siberia the Soviet Union had amassed two divisions of Korean partisans, among them Kim Il Sung, who had joined the Soviet forces at Khabarovsk.

The Soviet Union's demands were accepted at Yalta in exchange for a guarantee that it would, in turn, go to war with Japan. The Russians proceeded to sign the Anglo-American Potsdam Declaration of 26 July 1945, which called for the surrender of Japan and a gradual transition towards Korean independence. On 8 August, just one week away from the end of hostilities, they broke their non-aggression pact by declaring war on the Japanese. At the cost of surprisingly limited losses in the Far East, Stalin had recouped all that Russia had lost since 1905. He systematically held onto these gains: for example when Mao, in Moscow in December 1949, called on him to return the port of Dalian, Stalin used the Sino-Soviet Friendship Treaty of 1950 to make the restitution conditional on the restoration of peace in the region. In fact, this was to be delayed until 1955 due to the Korean War. Stalin likewise ordered the ransacking of the industrial capacity of Manchuria, which he knew he could not keep, but spared that of North Korea, which was destined to become a satellite state. In Xinjiang and Mongolia he introduced mixed enterprises in mining, the success of which infuriated Mao. Stalin eventually secured the allegiance of Gao Gang, the Chinese communist leader of Manchuria, who attempted to challenge Mao's power in 1953 and was duly eliminated. In every move he made, Stalin did not so much oppose American imperialism as resume a traditional stance, banking on the new Chinese government's need for aid. Mao described his negotiations for Soviet aid with Stalin and his colleagues in Moscow from December 1949 to February 1950 as being 'like snatching a piece of meat from the jaws of a tiger'.

This attitude on the part of Stalin, conservative and at the same time defensive towards his spoils, was no isolated case. Until the eleventh hour, Moscow continued its diplomatic recognition of Chiang Kai-shek's government, even relocating its embassy to follow the nationalist troops in their retreat across the continent. In Vietnam, Ho Chi Minh issued a formal declaration of independence on 2 September 1945, and also benefited from the abdication of Emperor Bao Dai. However, although Vietnam had temporarily conquered most of the territory and the regional capitals in 1945, Moscow waited until January 1950, two weeks after the Vietnamese revolutionaries had issued an international appeal for recognition, before deciding to grant them diplomatic recognition. More recently, the USSR maintained diplomatic relations with the Lon Nol régime in Cambodia (1970–5) up until its last days in April 1975, when Soviet diplomats, like their Western counterparts, were driven out by the Khmer Rouge. After the fall of the Marcos régime in the Philippines in 1986, Moscow was among the last to transfer diplomatic recognition to President Cory Aquino. The ultra-conservative continuity of the Soviet position, at least, belies the image of a power intent on exporting revolution to Asia.

So far, in the temporary absence of archives, there is no satisfactory explanation for the behaviour of the Soviet Union. However, it is possible to formulate some hypotheses. From 1920 onwards, the Soviet government operated a dual policy, embracing both the official diplomacy of Bolshevik Russia and the low-profile or underground activities of the International and its successor, the Cominform. It also wavered between the 'defence of socialism in a single country', the key slogan of Stalinism, and the expansion of the socialist camp, which was carried out opportunistically, by diplomatic and military means, rather than in conjunction with revolutionary movements. From 1956 onwards, Khrushchev's policy of peaceful coexistence and the Soviet Union's willingness to open an exclusive dialogue with the United States clashed with the interests of many satellite régimes and communist parties: the GDR of Walter Ulbricht, the French Communist Party under Maurice Thorez and Maoist China after Albania felt betrayed by Khrushchev's new-found moderation.

Prior to this period, Stalin had never been able to stop himself gambling on several possibilities, covering his tracks and acting equivocally. This was true of the famous toughening in the Soviet Union's international stance announced by Zhdanov in September 1947, at the time of the formation of the Cominform in Poland. Although Soviet arguments subsequently reverted to the condemnation of the peaceful means being used in the West and called for class struggle in Asia, they only mentioned that part of the world in passing, and then it was in order to criticize directly the whole strategy of national alliances within the framework of the united fronts, which would, none the less, bring the Chinese and Vietnamese communist parties to power. In February 1948, the World Federation of Democratic Youth, under Soviet control, organized a conference in Calcutta attended

by representatives from nearly all Asian countries. Because it took place
shortly before communist uprisings in Burma, the Philippines, Indonesia
and particularly Malaya, and also because of the anti-American tenor of its
speeches, the conference has often been seen as a Soviet plot to ignite Asia.
However, unlike the crucial meetings between the Cominform and the West
European communist parties at the same period, the Calcutta conference,
which had, moreover, been planned and then delayed for nearly two years,
was a public event bringing together nearly 900 delegates. Admittedly, they
included many progressives and fellow travellers as well as a significant
delegation of Chinese communists. However, virtually no other Asian communist leaders attended, apart from Than Tun of Burma. In other words, if
Moscow ever did issue a call for a rebellion, the Calcutta conference is
hardly likely to have been the place.

The causes of the post-1945 revolutions in Asia must be sought elsewhere.
They were originally inspired by local political and social conditions, amid a
colonial system discredited by war and a climate of nationalist ferment that
was by no means confined to the communist parties alone. The latter were
dominated by men who had received their training in the revolutionary
skirmishes after 1920 and in guerilla operations during the Second World
War. Despite their Marxist–Leninist political rhetoric, they did not need
orders from Moscow to move into action. This can largely be explained by
local circumstances, whether ethnic (as in Malaya) or political (as in Indonesia), whether characterized by factional rivalry (as in Burma) or by deep-
rooted social unrest (as in the Philippines). The example of the Chinese
revolution, poised for victory, gave an irresistible impetus; moreover, from
1949 onwards, the People's Republic of China represented a massive rearguard for the communists of Indochina, making the French defeat inevitable. On a broader level, an international community was crystallizing that
was chiefly opposed to the Dutch and French colonial powers: in January
1950, Pandit Nehru convened an Afro-Asian Conference in New Delhi to
defend the new Indonesian Republic against the Dutch. This was the forerunner of the 1955 Bandung Conference and the historical beginning of the
non-aligned movement. Up to 1950, the Vietminh openly operated an arms
supply bureau in Thailand, a country which was little suspected of conniv-
ing with communism.

THE END OF THE BRITISH, DUTCH AND FRENCH COLONIAL EMPIRES

There was a striking unity about the aims, if not the methods, of the British,
Dutch and French on their return to Asia in 1945. All three were, admittedly, obliged to comply with the agreements reached within the framework
of the Western Alliance, notably the Atlantic Charter, and with the declaration of the rights of peoples put forward by the United Nations. Initially,
therefore, the three colonial powers formulated proposals for a form of

autonomy or independence within the framework of a union or federation, designed to preserve most of what had gone before. In each case, this solution met with opposition from the Asian nationalists, resulting in negotiations and short-term solutions of varying durability.

The Indochina War

In the case of France, this took the form of a plan in March 1945 for an Indo-Chinese Federation within the framework of the French Union. The text of the plan was vague as to the freedoms to be granted, while in having five Indochinese states it preserved the colonial division of Vietnam into Tonkin, Annam and Cochinchina. What it granted with one hand, it took away with the other, as it persisted in the use of the traditional term 'Governor-General'. The plan was immediately overtaken by events. Between August and October 1945, Ho Chi Minh and his partisans held control of the entire country, owing to a tactical alliance with the Chinese troops of the Kuomintang to the north and the indifference or assistance of the Japanese troops. After the arrival of the 'soldier monk', High Commissioner Thierry d'Argenlieu, from Free France, negotiations in March 1946 between the French envoy Sainteny and Ho Chi Minh went much further, recognizing a 'Vietnamese government' within the French Union, although the boundaries of its jurisdiction were unclear. Ho Chi Minh, who a few months earlier had been quoting the American Declaration of Independence, now declared a 'peace of Brest-Litovsk', referring to the separate peace treaty concluded by Lenin with Germany in 1918. Meanwhile, France had paid the high price of abandoning all its former rights in China, particularly in Yunnan, in return for the withdrawal of 160,000 extremely troublesome Chinese troops. However, some on the French side, notably d'Argenlieu, played on existing divisions, just as the Dutch were to do in Indonesia with an equal lack of success: as a result, a state of Cochinchina was created in June, but its first leader committed suicide some months later. Until October, Ho Chi Minh carried on negotiations in France, while the situation on the ground deteriorated with the increasing grip on power by the Vietminh and the violence perpetrated by the colonists, especially in Cochinchina. At the end of 1946, as Léon Blum, the President of the French Council of Ministers, declared himself willing to grant Vietnamese independence, colonial war broke out. An uprising led by Vo Nguyen Giap was countered by the bombing of Haiphong by Thierry d'Argenlieu's forces, and the French swiftly recaptured Hanoi.

By contrast, in Cambodia and Laos, the 'French solution' prevailed throughout the duration of the war in Vietnam. In Cambodia's case, the influence of the indigenous administrative élite, centred on Norodom Sihanouk, made it possible for the formula of autonomy (and in 1949 the formula of associate state) to be implemented without any major opposition. All that was necessary was for Sihanouk to suspend the Assembly with its recalcitrant majority. A largely insignificant movement known as 'Khmer Issarak' (Free Khmer) also joined forces with Vietnam, forming the nucleus of what would one day be called the Khmer Rouge. Things were much more problematic in Laos, where the French encountered hostility from certain members of the royal family, namely Prince Souvanna Phouma and Prince Souphanouvong. Having fled to Thailand, they formed a government of the Pathet Lao, or Lao Nation. The guerilla movement only took hold in the provinces of Laos on the Annamite mountain range on the border with Vietnam, which were former Vietnamese possessions. They were the scene of the famous 'Ho Chi Minh Route', a network of jungle tracks which until 1975 enabled Vietnamese fighters to penetrate the whole of Indochina. In 1949, only Souphanouvong continued the struggle alongside the communists, following them until his death in 1987. However, some members of the Laotian royal élite, many of whom had ties of kinship with Vietnam, chose to play the neutralist card, first against France and later against the United States.

In Vietnam, Ho Chi Minh's movement found itself hard up against the Bac Bo, a mountainous area north of Tonkin, resisting bombardment and a total blockade by the French army. In the south, the guerilla army, though initially thin on the ground, began to expand. In the early stages, the colonial war was small in scale, French mobilization being limited to professional soldiers, including many from the Foreign Legion and French Africa. As a result, it was conveniently hidden from the gaze of French public opinion, which immediately after the Second World War was hardly in favour of military action. Furthermore, even the French Communist Party, a partner in the Paris government, had little time for anti-colonialism: Minister Maurice Thorez's admonition to Thierry d'Argenlieu was: 'If you must hit, hit hard!' (Dalloz 1987: 95). As for the Vietminh, it mobilized the rural population in support of aims that were both patriotic and socially conscious, one example being its literacy campaign. Although each communist programme differed in its implementation, collaborators generally had their land confiscated, but the French, by contrast, handed over their spoils in Cochinchina to the leading landowners whose land had been expropriated by the communists in August 1945. Even more so than Mao, Ho Chi Minh was a past master of the art of gradualism and tactical moderation, winning the war outright in the rural heartland. These experiences are fundamental to any understanding of present-day Vietnam. The intellectual mandarins, many of whom had received a French education (for example Vo Nguyen Giap, who was a professor of history, and Phan van Dong), the veterans of the zones liberated by the Maoist guerillas in China (including the most dogmatic of them all, Truong Chinh, whose Vietnamese *nom de guerre* meant 'Long March') together with Ho Chi Minh, one of Asia's most versatile strategists, led the rural masses first to independence, then to social revolution. Iron-fisted methods, Maoist brainwashing and political assassinations, followed by the internment of opponents, coexisted alongside the revolutionary morale, a curious amalgam of Vietnamese romanticism and an egalitarianism worthy of nineteenth-century social utopian Gracchus Baboeuf. The movement clearly held the population in its grip, although as Phan van Dong occasionally suggested in the late 1970s, the élites remained untouched by it. The French, and the Americans after them, were consequently left with the impression of a faceless war, and often struck blindly, thus radicalizing the population against them even further. It was only after 1975 and the final defeat of the United States that bureaucratic domination by a few family groups, endemic corruption and ideological bankruptcy began to overtake the nationalist–communist government, which had the strongest tradition of legitimacy in the whole of Asia.

The escalation of the Cold War in 1949–50 did little to change the situation, despite bringing considerable American military support for France. At the same time, the Vietminh had acquired a powerful rearguard in the shape of the People's Republic of China. Much later, after the Sino-Vietnamese rift of 1979, the Chinese government revealed precise details of the extent of China's involvement during the final phase of the war with France, including the provision of equipment, munitions, weapons, troops and even generals. Meanwhile, the 'dirty war', with its succession of atrocities and acts of torture, had a heavy impact on French public opinion, whose priorities were very different from those of the colonists and the army. However, this unfavourable climate would not have been enough to set events in motion, had the French army not been defeated on the ground. This happened for the first time in October 1950 at Caobang and Langson, in the mountains to the north, where two French élite units were annihilated in retreat. An even more emphatic defeat came at Dien Bien Phu in May 1954, with the triumph of Vo Nguyen Giap, the Vietnamese sappers and porters and, less obviously, the huge Chinese artillery which the French command had virtually discounted when setting up camp in that famous basin. At the last moment a vacillating United States refused French pleas to take a firmer lead in a conflict which it considered dubious despite the Cold War. Although hostilities dragged on, France's political will was broken. Following the fall of Dien Bien Phu, the international conference on Indochina opened in Geneva, bringing together the great powers and the regional actors.

The birth of Indonesia

In Vietnam, state and nation had been swept away by colonization, but they were a sufficiently recent memory for Ho Chi Minh and his Leninist organization to be able to draw on them successfully. In the Dutch East Indies, on the other hand, decolonization coincided with the birth of a totally new nation. As a whole, the movement showed many similarities to events in Indochina. In both cases there figured: the expansionist nationalism of a core group, on the one hand the Vietnamese of Tonkin, on the other the

Javanese; a nationalist (and in many cases communist) old guard, which had grown stronger in Indonesia under the Japanese occupation than in Indochina; the sudden power vacuum of August 1945, prompting an immediate declaration of independence and a mass uprising that was better controlled by the Vietnamese communists than by the Indonesian nationalists; the fraught return of colonial power and the tortuous negotiations over a possible form of union within the framework of independence; the attempt by the Dutch and the French to play off peripheral states against the nationalist centre, by setting up a federation against the centralizing influence of the republics declared in August 1945; and, lastly, the utter failure of this dilatory policy, notwithstanding two Dutch attempts to regain control in 1947 and 1948 and a colonial war fought by the French. The international setting and the historical context of Vietnamese and Indonesian independence clearly had much in common, and this would leave a legacy. At the time of the Vietnamese occupation of Cambodia in 1979, the anti-communist military in Jakarta constituted the faction within ASEAN that showed most support for Hanoi, as well as being the one most hostile to China. Indonesia's founding fathers saw a parallel between their conquest of the East Indies archipelago after 1945, often by force, and the attempt by the Vietnamese in 1979 to create an Indochina under their own control.

The political forces at work in the two countries were, however, very different. In Indonesia there were three such forces – nationalism, Islam and communism – each made up of a host of small political parties and mass movements. This state of affairs immediately led to violent mass conflict that was partly inter-ethnic. Yet such violence, which included political assassination on a scale similar to that seen in Vietnam, failed to prevent this triangular interplay of forces. In Vietnam, on the other hand, Ho Chi Minh and his followers soon came to dominate the masses and simplified the political equation in their own favour. Accordingly, when Sukarno and Mohammed Hatta proclaimed an Indonesian Republic in September 1945, there followed a widespread uprising which they had neither organized nor intended. It was presented as a rebellion by the vigorous forces of youth, and the term 'young' came to signify mass patriotism, just as it had previously served to cement the semi-articulated mood of Malay nationalism prior to the Second World War. However, it also coincided with an upsurge of Islamic and ethnic feeling, resulting in a spate of massacres which made victims of all the minorities. Armed gangs emerged with charismatic leaders, while many of the militias which had disbanded during the pro-Japanese era reassembled to take part in the uprising. The army derived its strength and ideology from these popular, violent origins, far removed from the Republic's nationalist leaders based in Jakarta. The latter adopted the *Pancasila*, Sukarno's five principles of nationalism, internationalism, representative government, social justice and faith in one God.

The movement was sufficiently strong to drive the Dutch back into a few coastal enclaves and dissuade the British army from playing anything more than a symbolic role. However, its violence led to a revival of the scheme proposed by the Dutch, who in 1945–6 had initially found themselves in a stranglehold. This involved creating a patchwork of states within a federation linked to the new Republic of Indonesia, and was thus dependent on the traditional chiefs of the other regions and the outer islands. In fact, these chiefs, who thus gained reputations as pro-Dutch collaborators, had good reason to worry at the violent way in which the Javanese were asserting central power. As for the republican governments which succeeded one another amid the shifting political coalitions in Jakarta, they none the less exhibited a certain measure of continuity. For example, Sukarno and Hatta were continuously key actors, while several small, left-wing groups, including some communists, played a part. Whatever the shade of the government, it found itself constrained by the realism needed to negotiate with the Dutch.

In November 1946, the Dutch had conceded diplomatic ground, granting recognition to the new Republic and accepting the idea of a United States of Indonesia. However, as in the French case, the composition of the latter was not fixed and the whole plan was accompanied by a cumbersome union with the Netherlands. At about the same time, the Dutch established new states throughout the whole eastern end of the archipelago and subjected the central islands to a draconian blockade. Between July 1947 and January 1948, they recaptured part of the islands of Java and Sumatra by force, and this move, which met with strong disapproval from the international community, prompted United States intervention. This resulted in a new agreement, signed in January 1948 on board the American battleship *Renville*. This brought events to exactly the same stage reached in Indochina with the second attempt at the formation of a French Union, the difference being that in the former case it was the Indonesians who were forced to make all the concessions. Spurred on, the Dutch accelerated moves towards separatism by the myriad islands and powers in the archipelago. As for the government of the Indonesian Republic, it suffered a decisive rift. In the summer of 1948, a left-wing group, headed by the reconstituted PKI, condemned the agreement with the Dutch and called for armed struggle. One militant, Musso, who had suddenly returned from Moscow after a ten-year absence, immediately took command of the resistance front. This divergence split the coalition government, which still included a few more moderate socialists, as well as Sukarno and Hatta who advocated negotiation with the Dutch. They were joined by a faction within the communist movement led by Tan Malaka, who had formerly been a member of the Comintern in the 1920s.

This split once again blew the lid off Java's socio-political cauldron, precipitating a crisis which echoed the first communist uprising in 1926, as well as foreshadowing the tragedy of 1965. Those army regiments and paramilitary units which sympathized with the communists refused government orders to disband and launched a rebellion in Madiun in September

1948, abetted by pro-communist trade unionists. This forced Musso and the other politicians advocating armed struggle to put their words into action. However, although the movement relied on mass support from the most deprived peasants and from officer sympathizers, it was not based on any pre-existing political campaign or any broader alliance. Ranged against it were the local societies or *santri* and the Islamic youth movements, which once again raised the alarm. Some, like the paramilitary Hizbollahs (the warriors of the faith) called for a holy war. In Jakarta, the Indonesian Nationalist Party, led by Sukarno and Mohammed Hatta, united its forces with the Islamic Masjumis against the rebels. This made a favourable impression on the Americans, who from then on backed the supporters of Indonesian independence. The suppression of the Madiun rebellion ended in several thousand deaths, including those of Musso and the socialist leaders who had rallied behind the PKI. However, it only temporarily removed the communist threat, for in the early 1950s the PKI rose from the ashes with its social base still intact. Madiun was a turning-point. The Dutch, perceiving it as a sign of weakening in the republican camp, invaded the whole of Java. In December 1948, they seized the leaders of the Indonesian nationalist movement at Jogjakarta, mirroring a similar, unsuccessful French operation against the Vietminh in early 1947. The Dutch operation turned into an international fiasco, for the nationalists, having won their anti-communist spurs at Madiun, were now receiving American support. The United Nations, prompted by heavy agitation from India and the emerging Afro-Asian movement, intervened with renewed vigour. In November 1949, the Dutch were forced to agree to independence, and the Republic of Indonesia (as opposed to the previously intended United States of Indonesia) was established at the end of the year.

The nationalists thus fought on several fronts at once. The first was against the Netherlands, but economic realism forced Indonesia to come to terms with both the Batavian planters and the Chinese business community in its early years. The second was against the communists, although some members of the nationalist leadership were themselves pro-socialist, while the PKI also regrouped in the overpopulated rural areas. Lastly, Indonesia's founders were also struggling to build a single, centralized nation, in which the Javanese clearly predominated, a problem which was to confront the Indonesian Republic incessantly from 1949 onwards. Numerous rebellions broke out, some backed by local army commanders: an Islamic movement arose in western Java, where an Islamic state was proclaimed in August 1949 (this movement was to re-emerge in 1961–2), and also in the outer islands in 1958–61, in Sulawesi (Celebes, or the Republic of the Moluccas) and in Aceh, part of north-eastern Sumatra, which demanded independence until the 1990s. The Indonesian army unified the archipelago by force. The United Nations prevented it from seizing Western Guinea when the latter declared its independence in 1957, but the sudden departure of the Portuguese from Timor in 1975 prompted General

Suharto to seize control of the island. This led to a new and bloody struggle against the Timor Liberation Front (FRETILIM), backed by Moscow and Cuba, and part of the Timorese Catholic Church. The Indonesian army was in fact only partly centralized, composed of the three territorial divisions into which Java has been split since 1945, as well as outposts on the other islands, where the commanders were often a law unto themselves. The federalism pushed for by the Dutch had certainly been aimed at breaking the mould of nascent Indonesian nationalism, but it also contained a good deal of anthropological and religious realism.

Malaya and Singapore

The former Straits Settlements and the Malay states also witnessed the same compound clash of colonial power, nationalism and communism, but in their case the resulting rifts were much less pronounced. Admittedly, the British failed with their first plan, namely the creation in 1946 of a Malayan Union, excluding Singapore which was to remain a separate colony. This scheme for direct rule, with limited powers for the Malay sultans, was virtually identical to the French and the Dutch plans of the same period. It was in opposition to this scheme that modern Malaya's leading political party, UMNO (the United Malay National Organization), was founded, following a meeting of a pan-Malayan congress which, with the backing of the hereditary sultans, launched a boycott of the British plan. The nationalists saw the British as once again wanting to 'divide and rule', and were particularly worried at the links forged between the British army and the Chinese and Tamil communities during the Second World War. Pogroms were launched in 1945 against the Chinese 'squatters' – ex-plantation workers who had settled on vacant ground and thus contravened the policy by which land was set aside for Malay farmers. The whole of modern Malay politics would be based on the idea of the *bumiputra* (sons of the soil), in contradistinction to the ethnic groups introduced under colonial rule. Moreover, a similar antagonism is also apparent throughout the Malay–Oceanian world, in the New Hebrides (Vanuatu), Fiji and New Caledonia for example. However, Malays were in the minority in the Malay peninsula, and consequently, from 1946 up to the present day, Malay politicians have had to form alliances with other ethnic groups or parties in order to win elections. Onn bin Jaafar, one of the early presidents of UMNO, attempted this against the advice of his comrades and failed in his bid to form a Malay independence party. This would later prove possible with the help of Chinese notables and businessmen, many of whom were opposed to communism. They originally came together in the Federation of Chambers of Commerce, and later in the Malay Chinese Association (MCA), founded in February 1949 with the blessing of the British. The Indian Congress Party of Malaya was also open to an agreement. The cardinal rule of Malay politics is summed up by Mauzy and Milne (1980): 'Communal divisions in

Malaysia were so deep that it was impossible to form successfully a single non-communal party; but they were not too deep to *destroy* an alliance of communal parties'. This strategy was initially rejected by UMNO, although it later adopted it for its own.

In 1948 the British, like the Dutch and French, revised their political plans for the remaining colonies. They proposed an agreement to establish a federation, a plan which was more generous to the Malays and therefore more restrictive towards the other ethnic communities. Although it perpetuated the system of direct British rule, it made provision for a consultative Legislative Council or 'Legco', a body which had full responsibility for the transition process throughout Britain's colonies, from Kenya to Hong Kong. The plan gave power to the sultans in matters pertaining to Islam and Malay custom, and thus came very close to envisaging a religious state. Above all, it guaranteed to restrict the level of naturalizations, in particular imposing an upper limit of one-fifth of the Chinese resident in Malaya, thus excluding potential voters. Doubtless because of ethnic division and the dominance of the sultans, this compromise worked. Within UMNO there emerged the moderate, aristocratic figure of Tunku Abdul Rahman, the Cambridge-educated brother of the sultan of Kedah. He succeeded in bringing together UMNO, the MCA and the Indian Congress Party in a federation known as the Alliance, which emerged as the majority party in the first elections, held in 1955. As Chief Minister, the Tunku led his country to independence, and the coalition which he headed is still in power today. Independence was declared in August 1957, accompanied by a constitution founded to a large extent on the British and Indian models, with an impartial civil service, an independent judiciary, a bicameral parliament and an honorary head of state who was elected every five years by the nine hereditary sultans. However, Article 150 of the constitution, which made provision for the possible declaration of a state of emergency, was soon invoked. Islam became the state religion and the Malays found themselves guaranteed jobs and land set aside for their own use.

Since 1948 this pact between the British and the Malays had driven a section of the Chinese community into armed resistance, while the Malay Communist Party declared an uprising throughout the colonial territories (including Singapore and North Borneo), based on an initial core group of former anti-Japanese resistance fighters. This tough, skilled guerilla force was backed simultaneously by the Chinese 'squatters' and the plantation workers. It was initially heavily dependent on Chinese support, but this was limited due to the lack of common borders and to the early problems faced by the People's Republic of China, for instance having to rely on Malaya itself for rubber supplies between 1949 and 1951. In the enemy camp, after a brief phase of all-out war (including air raids), the British army, commanded by General Temple, began to explore a more prudent strategy which constituted a classic example of counter-guerilla operations. In February 1952, Temple declared the need to win 'hearts and minds', a phrase later echoed by General Westmoreland, the commander of the United States forces in South Vietnam in 1965. The cornerstone of Temple's strategy was the forced migration of 500,000 Chinese villagers, mostly 'squatters', aimed at depriving the guerillas of support in what was known, literally, as 'Operation Famine'. In Indochina, Colonels Trinquier and Bigeard claimed a counter-guerilla strategy which involved transporting the rural population to fortified villages; they would suffocate the fish (e.g. the guerilla) by emptying the fishbowl, reversing Mao's famous precept to be among the people like a fish swimming in water. The Americans later revived this strategy under the name of 'strategic hamlets', and it is noteworthy that similar methods were used by the new communist régime in Cambodia and its Vietnamese allies against the remaining Khmer Rouge forces along the Thai–Cambodian border. Meanwhile, the MCP practised terrorism, in particular assassinating defectors and any individuals who displayed a lack of zeal. In parallel with this, after 1951, it developed by broadening its base beyond the Chinese community and carrying out underground urban operations. From 1953 onwards, however, the British managed to lift the siege in many areas and the MCP was soon confined to the neighbouring jungle regions of Thailand. The rebellion had clearly been a failure, as well as being instrumental in damaging relations with China (which claimed to support the MCP) until the late 1980s. The state of emergency was lifted in 1960, but the official anti-communist line continues, together with constraints on legal and practical freedoms. These constraints have also affected the more peaceful debate which characterizes Malay parliamentary affairs, and have particularly served to curb freedom of expression and the emergence of an opposition press.

Ethnic factors also complicated matters in Singapore, a British colony where the Chinese form the great majority. There, over a period of fourteen months beginning in 1955, the transition to independence was managed by David Marshall. A socialist, Jewish lawyer of Iraqi origin, interned by the Japanese during the Second World War, Marshall cut a highly flamboyant figure. However, a new political party emerged in the form of the Political Action Party (PAP), led by Lee Kuan Yew. He forged a united front with the pro-communist forces and trade unions, enabling him to score a resounding victory in the 1959 elections. He then turned against his fellow travellers, thus repeating, as it were, the Kerensky-coup-in-reverse which Chiang Kai-shek had already managed to carry out in China in 1927. Lee Kuan Yew (who actually stayed a member of the Socialist International until 1979) was just thirty-six years old at the time. He was a Hakka Chinese from Singapore, but some credited him with Chinese–Indonesian ancestry, others with origins in Saigon. In any event, brought up in the midst of the colonial system, he studied at Cambridge, where he rivalled the young Tunku Abdul Rahman with his oratory and acquired his lieutenants Goh Keng Swee, the first technocrat of modern Singapore, and Rajeratnam, who became Minister for Foreign Affairs. On returning to

Singapore as a qualified lawyer, he vigorously defended the postal unions and socialist associations against the British government, only to imprison or banish several of their leaders after 1959. Although Lee was allied with the communists and the socialists, he came to a rapprochement with the British government in 1955, at the expense of David Marshall, who was proving tiresome in his requirement for justice and due process of law. Yet when Lee Kuan Yew swept to power in the 1959 elections, he none the less did so on a populist platform and in alliance with the communist-affiliated unions. This power was never to be relinquished. In puritanical style, without political scruple, yet ultimately without bloodshed either, Lee Kuan Yew, through method, authoritarianism and panache, was to build a city-state that is now the wealthiest nation in South-East Asia.

Burma and the Philippines after independence: the communist challenge

In many respects the situation in the Philippines resembled Malaya's. In both cases, revolt stemmed not so much from colonial rule, whether direct or indirect, but from the local social and political order as a whole. This was also true of Burma, where the rebellion by the Red Flag faction of the Burmese communist movement came after the declaration of independence of 1948, rather than before it. Ethnic factors also played a major part. During the Second World War, Burma's mountain-dwelling minorities had in many cases been organized into small embryo states by their British mentors, and in some cases by Thailand: the latter was particularly responsible for introducing plans for a Shan state. The tribal minorities were unable to accept the centralization of political power into the hands of the plains-dwelling Burmese. In the Philippines, as well as the old antagonism between the peasants, who possessed a long Malay heritage while being widely Christianized, and the landowners and westernized urban élites, there was also hostility on the part of the Muslims in the south (the Moros) to the Filipino state as a whole.

American vacillation in the Philippines (which none the less confirmed their independence in July 1946) encouraged recourse to armed struggle. Following a period of fairly severe purges against those who had collaborated with Japan, General MacArthur reinstated Manuel Roxas by way of a compromise with conservative forces. Roxas scored a triumphant victory in the presidential elections of April 1946, and the oligarchs and ruling classes of the war years returned with him. The US army, which had been trying to disarm the Huks and imprison their leaders for some time, criticized the National Party's alliance with them. Ultimately, although the Americans did not attempt to maintain a political union with the Philippines, the US Congress none the less paved the way for a form of economic neo-colonialism, admitting free imports of American goods into the archipelago and extending property rights for Americans without any reciprocal rights for Filipinos in the United States. In March 1947, the United States acquired a ninety-nine year lease on the vast military bases of Clark Field and Subic Bay. Two months later, members of the Filipino Congress allied to the Huks, including Luis Taruc, were excluded on charges of fraud. In the heart of the island of Luzon, a cycle of repression and insurrection began, involving the landowners backed by Roxas and the farmers' unions affiliated to the Huks. This feature of vendetta following on from wartime events was as important a factor as social unrest in triggering the rebellion. In September 1947, Taruc rejoined the armed struggle, which the Philippines Communist Party itself only endorsed in 1948. As far as it was concerned, land reform, purging collaborators and rooting out corruption were equally important rallying issues.

Taruc and his friends were, however, wrong to believe in the political fragility of a government compromised by its own past. In the face of escalating guerilla warfare, the United States introduced a political plan drafted jointly by Colonel Edwin Lonsdale of the CIA, who later provided the inspiration behind American counter-guerilla operations in Vietnam, and Filipino politician Ramon Magsaysay. As Defence Minister, Magsaysay formulated a programme covering rural and social aid, the redistribution of land to political supporters and an amnesty. At the same time and, as many witnesses testified, as a matter of priority, the peasants were worn down by psychological warfare, consisting of assassinations and the use of terrifying 'magic', with sacred masks and 'vampirized' Huk corpses left lying along the roadsides. The PCP was demolished in Manila in 1950 and Taruc surrendered in 1954. Meanwhile, despite the relative lack of any real reforms to his credit, Ramon Magsaysay became a charismatic figure, winning a resounding victory in the presidential elections of 1953.

Guerilla warfare was never to disappear from the Philippines. In some cases it merged into banditry, social or otherwise, while it was a former Huk guerilla, Commander Dante, who revived the New People's Army at the end of the 1960s. As for official government policy, it fluctuated between one extreme dominated by the United States and another of nationalist reaction influenced by the leading local families.

The causes of the Korean War

The war in Indochina, the Indonesian challenge and the uprisings in Malaya, the Philippines and Burma are readily explained by the fact that the old systems under colonial rule were out of step with the new political realities. Equally clearly, the Korean peninsula marked the scene of the first international conflict to be triggered directly by the Cold War. The Korean War was started in June 1950 by North Korea and sustained by the Soviet Union. Liberal historians such as Horowitz (1967) and Stone (1952), and later 'revisionists' such as Gabriel Kolko (Kolko and Kolko 1972) lacked solid arguments when, against the background of the Vietnam War in the 1970s, they attributed responsibility for the Korean War to the United States or South Korea.

Admittedly, the new South Korean President Syngman Rhee, who had been the leader of the republic-in-exile since 1919, was just as hungry for war as his neighbours to the north: he adopted the slogan 'March North' and called on the United States for military support, which the Americans formally refused to give in the case of a forced reunification. The year 1949 was punctuated with military incidents along the 38th parallel, responsibility for which has never been fully established. Furthermore, the fact that the United States government failed to give any clear signal of military support for Korea (Eisenhower later showed similar hesitation in 1954 over the question of the islands in the Strait of Formosa) meant that North Korea and the Soviet Union were able to misconstrue Washington's true intentions. Yet this vacillation by the United States does not mean that it invited a North Korean invasion, nor does it mitigate Stalin's and Kim Il Sung's primary responsibility: in 1990 a similar argument would be used by those who thought that Saddam Hussein's Iraq had actually fallen into an American trap in invading Kuwait. Finally, it is true that Soviet troops were officially withdrawn from North Korea in December 1948. The US army would also leave the following year.

However, the new North Korean régime was totally dependent on the Soviet Union for a number of reasons. First, the Korean communists were, by force of circumstance, split into several groups: the resistance in the interior, led by Pak Hon Yong, which lost ground in South Korea after 1945; the Chinese-controlled Yenan faction (the old 'Shanghai faction' of the 1920s) which recruited heavily among the Korean population of Manchuria; and the Soviet faction (the old 'Irkutsk faction' of the 1920s), many of whose members held Soviet passports, and which included Kim Il Sung. However, Kim Il Sung also belonged to a subsidiary group, the 'Kapsan faction', which had fled from Manchuria into Siberia, and this appears to have enabled him to carry out the physical elimination of the Soviet faction proper during the 1950s. When General Romanenko's troops landed at Pyongyang in August 1945, they found a provisional national council made up of eighteen nationalist veterans, including the Catholic Cho Mansik, and two communists from the interior, to whom the Japanese governor had handed over his powers. Opposite this body the Russians installed Kim Il Sung, who was known only very slightly via tales of his supposed military exploits.

Kim Il Sung, who remained in power continuously from 1945 to 1994, was even more of an enigma than Ho Chi Minh or Saloth Sar (Pol Pot), whose own life stories are riddled with gaps. Some of his enemies, in exile in Moscow or Tokyo, even claimed that the real Kim Il Sung had died in 1937 and that his name had been assumed by the existing holder. His fulsome official profile portrayed him as the son of poor yet patriotic parents who had fled to Manchuria to escape the Japanese and looked after the needy in hospital. His own grandfather was supposedly responsible for the sinking of the United States cargo ship *General Sherman* in 1866, and most of his forebears are virtually venerated as 'revolutionaries'. In fact, although his family did indeed leave Korea shortly after the Japanese annexation, they did so as traders, and the young Kim was unusual in having the benefit of a full school education. He joined the guerillas in 1932 at the age of twenty and took command of a small unit under Chinese control. Many of his comrades from this period took up important military posts in North Korea during the 1950s and 1960s. The guerillas were increasingly threatened with elimination after 1937 and fled to Siberia in 1942, a fact unmentioned in Kim Il Sung's official biography, which tells of 10,000 battles against the Japanese. Having joined the Soviet border guard (the troops belonging to the MVD (Ministry of Interior Affairs), the forerunner of the KGB) Kim entered Pyongyang in August 1945 in Soviet uniform, and remained there incognito for one month before appearing in public.

Kim Il Sung's first priority was to eliminate his rivals, communist and non-communist, initially in conjunction with his Soviet mentors and later in opposition to them. The assassinations began in September 1945, accompanied by clandestine infiltration of all organizations. The leader of the resistance in the interior, Cho Mansik, vanished into Soviet hands in 1946. This incident prompted the flight to the South of many Korean nationalists and Catholics, who had initially been rallied by a policy of deception. Over a period of several months, Kim Il Sung replaced them in the thankless role of fellow travellers by a religious sect called 'Heaven's Gate': in the 1980s, the régime would even act out the illusion of a 'social democratic party' under anonymous leaders and welcomed the Reverend Moon's sect with great ceremony. Moreover, after the Soviet troops had withdrawn, Kim Il Sung had more room for manoeuvre. In October 1950, he purged General Mu Chong, the leader of the Yenan faction. The most difficult point for the North Korean régime came in 1951, when it was threatened by Allied troops and abandoned by the Soviet Union, which was now keen to negotiate. Kim Il Sung none the less embarked on the first of his purges against the 'Soviet faction' with the arrest of its leader, Ho Ka-I, who 'committed suicide' in March 1953. Some months after the armistice of Panmunjon in November 1953, Kim Il Sung eliminated Pak Hon Yong and the other leading 'communists of the interior' who had fled north across the 38th parallel, on the grounds that they had acted as agents of United States imperialism. As far as the first generation of communist militants was concerned, the tally was now complete.

Admittedly, the Chinese communists also instigated a number of internal purges, both in Yenan in 1942–3 and after 1949, while Ho Chi Minh had his Trotskyist, religious and nationalist rivals assassinated from September 1945. Yet the hallmark of Kim Il Sung's leadership, from the outset until at least the 1980s, was the way in which, systematically and successively, he murdered all potential rivals and all communists who failed to side with him personally. Unlike Stalin, the North Korean dictator did not wait to consolidate his power before taking these steps, but initially relied on the Soviet party apparatus to instigate the purges. He also appears to have behaved more rationally than the Khmer Rouge did when in power in Cambodia from 1975 to 1979, always acting with the backing of a tightly-controlled police force and eliminating his targets at opportune moments. Until his death in 1994, Kim Il Sung was the longest-ruling leader of any communist country, indeed the most durable head of state anywhere in the world.

The invasion of South Korea also appears to have been a logical extension of this 'terror machine' set in motion in 1945. Not least of the advantages for Kim Il Sung in starting the war was the fact that it enabled him to rally all the Southern communists to his side before destroying them. At the same time, he maintained that the North (the People's Democratic Republic of Korea, founded officially in November 1948) would provide a 'democratic base' from which to liberate the South. In terms of this justification, through propaganda, of a conflict which remained 'internal', the Korean War followed in a direct line from the anti-Japanese resistance. This then raises the question of whether Kim Il Sung forced the hand of Stalin and the Soviet Union, as Nikita Khrushchev suggested in his otherwise unreliable memoirs. It is undoubtedly true that differences emerged between the two governments during the war, especially after 1951. Yet Khrushchev also claimed that the theory of Korea's self-liberation in itself had certain diplomatic advantages from Stalin's point of view. The huge shipments of arms supplied by the Soviet Union from July 1949 onwards exceeded the stocks left behind in the South under the guard of 500 American advisers. All the volunteers (over 50,000 in number) who had served in the ranks of the Soviet and Chinese armies were amassed under the North Korean flag. Finally, secret telegrams recently unearthed from the Kremlin archives have since proved beyond the slightest doubt that Stalin participated in the planning of the invasion, and that Mao Zedong was informed in advance of this move, which he himself approved: China's position in this respect remains more ambiguous, for it was probably unable to afford to challenge Stalin's decision at that time.

The determination of the Northern side (and of the Southerners too, albeit only vocally) to unify Korea by force was one of the major factors in the war. Indifference or vacillation on the part of the United States seems undeniable in view of the defeat of the South: between 25 June and 1 August 1950, Syngman Rhee's army was swept away, retaining only a small refuge around the port of Pusan, while all stocks of American weapons were seized.

The idea that Stalin saw himself as exploiting a mere local opportunity created by the supposed weakness of the United States is a more likely hypothesis than that of a grand strategy. As for the new communist government in China, any part in starting the war, let alone any enthusiasm for doing so, is very much open to question. It is doubtful whether it was in any position to isolate itself from its partners just one year after coming to power, with the country emerging exhausted from civil war. Following tough negotiations for aid from Stalin, Mao and his colleagues feared a Soviet invasion of north-eastern China. For them, the Korean War represented a heavy burden in human, economic and political terms. Furthermore, the Yenan faction within the Korean communist movement was already being targeted by Kim Il Sung, and China could scarcely hope to wield much influence over someone whom Moscow had set in power.

It was the speed and success of the counter-attack by United States troops, fighting under the United Nations flag, which led to the involvement of China in the war. Soon after a massive landing at Inchon, Pyongyang, the capital of the North, was seized by General MacArthur's troops on 19 October 1950, and on 26 October a South Korean detachment reached the Yalu River dividing Korea from China. There then followed sporadic attacks by the Chinese which one month later had become a spate. Zhou Enlai had already notified the United States, via the Indian ambassador in Peking, that if the Americans were to penetrate North Korea, China would enter the war.

Korea: the Cold War's hottest conflict

For the first time since 1945 public opinion in the West was shaken by the Korean War, especially as a result of the peace campaigns by the communist parties of Europe: General Ridgway, who succeeded General MacArthur in April 1951, was accused, without proof, of using biological warfare. However, the dimensions of the war were little appreciated, even though it was fought on a much broader scale than the Indochina War. The military contingents – from Britain, Australia, New Zealand and France – grouped together under the UN flag had little impact compared to the United States troops. Tales of virtuoso pilots like Chuck Yeager, the future astronaut portrayed by the novelist Tom Wolfe, and the inimitable army folklore immortalized by the film *M.A.S.H.*, disguise the true horrors of the conflict, which contained elements of both civil and international warfare. Seoul was seized twice by the communists, who on both occasions indulged in a massacre of their opponents. Pyongyang was captured once by the Allied troops, then bombarded by massive air-raids, with 1,403 sorties on 29 August 1951 alone. While from a distance the communists appeared to outnumber the enemy, their equipment was vastly inferior to that of the Americans. The deployment of jet fighters superior to MiGs, the transportation of troops by helicopter and the use of napalm further revolutionized modern warfare. This wrecked the 'human waves' strategy of the Chinese People's Liberation Army: the fact that 54,000 Americans and 400,000 South Koreans were killed in 1950–3, but that 600,000 North Korean soldiers and nearly a million Chinese lost their lives illustrates the Allies' disproportionate strength. There were also heavy repercussions across

China: the campaign to 'Aid Korea, resist America' marked a crucial stage in the process of mobilization and the toughening of the régime in the newly-conquered Chinese towns. Fully re-equipped and reorganized along Soviet lines after that bitter experience, the Chinese army saw the passing-out of a new generation of officers, the Korean War veterans, who had commenced their training before 1949: thus, with its twelve marshalls, its colours and a new emphasis on technology, it broke away from its civil war, guerilla mould.

SELECTED READING

Alperovitz, G. (1967) *Atomic diplomacy: Hiroshima and Potsdam*, New York: Vintage Books.

Bundy, M. (1988) *Danger and survival: choices about the bomb in the first fifty years*, New York: Random House.

Buszynski, L. (1983) *SEATO: the failure of an alliance strategy*, Singapore: Singapore University Press.

Chang, G. H. (1990) *Friends and enemies: the United States, China and the Soviet Union, 1948–1972*, Stanford: Stanford University Press.

Chen, J. (1994) *China's road to the Korean War: the making of the Sino-American confrontation*, New York: Columbia University Press.

Chin, A. *The Communist party of Malaysia: the inside story*, Kuala Lumpur: Vinpress.

Cohen W. I. and Iriye, A. (1990) *The great powers in East Asia, 1953–60*, New York: Columbia University Press.

Colbert, E. S. (1977) *Southeast Asia in international politics, 1941–1956*, Ithaca: Cornell University Press.

Dalloz, J. (1987) *La guerre d'Indochine, 1945–1954*, Paris: Editions du Seuil.

Devillers, P. (1952) *Histoire du Vietnam de 1940 à 1952*, Paris: Editions du Seuil.

Fitzgerald, F. (1973) *Fire in the lake: the Vietnamese and the Americans in Vietnam*, New York: Vintage Books.

Godement, F. (ed.) (1990) *Le désarmement nucléaire en Asie: l'autre volet de l'accord FNI*, Paris: Masson.

Goncharov, S., Lewis, J. W. and Litai, X. (1993) *Uncertain partners: Stalin, Mao and the Korean War*, Stanford: Stanford University Press.

Jeshurun, C. (ed.) (1985) *Governments and rebellions in Southeast Asia*, Singapore: Singapore University Press.

Joyaux, F. (1979) *La Chine et le règlement du premier conflit d'Indochine*, Paris: Publications de la Sorbonne.

— (1985 and 1988) *La nouvelle question d'Extrême-Orient*, 2 vols, Paris: Pavot.

Keerkvliet, B. J. (1977) *The Huk rebellion: a study of peasant revolt in the Philippines*, Berkeley: University of California Press.

Khrushchev, N. (1970) *Khrushchev remembers*, Boston: Little, Brown & Co.

Kim, H. (1978) *Unification policies of South and North Korea: a comparative study*, Seoul: Seoul National University Press.

Kolko, J. and Kolko, G. (1972) *The limits of power: the world and United States foreign policy, 1945–1954*, New York: Harper & Row.

Langer, P. F. and Zasloff, J. J. (1970) *North Vietnam and the Pathet Lao: partners in the struggle for Laos*, Cambridge, MA: Harvard University Press.

Lewis, J. W. and Xue, L. (1988) *China builds the bomb*, Stanford: Stanford University Press.

Lowe, P. (1986) *The origins of the Korean War*, London: Longman.

McKahin, G. (1952) *Nationalism and revolution in Indonesia*, New Haven: Cornell University Press.

Mayers, D. (1988) *George Kennan and the dilemmas of U.S. foreign policy*, New York: Oxford University Press.

Murti, B. S. N. (1964) *Vietnam divided: the unfinished struggle*, London: Asia Publishing House.

Nagai, Y. and Iriye, A. (1977) *The origins of the Cold War in Asia*, Toyko: University of Tokyo Press.

Nam, K. (1974) *The North Korean communist leadership, 1945–1965: a study of factionalism and political consolidation*, Alabama: University of Alabama Press.

Pike, D. (ed.) (1990) *The Bunker papers: reports to the President from Vietnam, 1967–1973*, Berkeley: Institute of Asian Studies.

Pluvier, J. (1974) *Southeast Asia from colonialism to independence*, Kuala Lumpur: Oxford University Press.

Richer, P. (1981) *L'Asie du Sud-Est*, Paris: Imprimerie Nationale.

Sainteny, J. (1967) *Histoire d'une paix manquée*, Paris: Fayard.

Scalapino, R. A. and Kim, D. (eds) (1989) *Asian communism: continuity and transition*, Berkeley: University of California Press.

Segal, G. (ed.) (1982) *The China factor: Peking and the superpowers*, London: Croom Helm.

Sherwin, M. (1975) *A world destroyed: the atomic bomb and the grand alliance*, New York: Vintage Books.

Tsou, T. (1963) *America's failure in China*, Chicago: Chicago University Press.

Whiting, A. S. (1960) *China crosses the Yalu: the decision to enter the Korean War*, Stanford: Stanford University Press.

Yahuda, M. (1996) *The international politics of Asia-Pacific, 1945–1995*, London: Routledge.

Yergin, D. (1977) *Shattered peace: the origins of the Cold War*, Boston: Houghton & Mifflin.

Zagoria, D. P. (1962) *The Sino-Soviet conflict*, Princeton: Princeton University Press.

— (ed.) (1982) *Soviet policy in East Asia*, New Haven: Yale University Press.

5   The apogee of Asian communism (1949–75)

After 1948, the political map of Europe remained fixed for forty years: with the division of the continent into blocs, an insurmountable demarcation line sprang up between East and West. In Latin America, the only communist victory was that of the Cuban revolution of 1956, following many years of ideological vacillation on the part of its leader. In Africa, the Mediterranean and South Asia, Moscow found allies, many of them fickle, and gave rise to a number of military-progressive régimes, ranging from Algeria, through the states at war in the Horn of Africa during the 1970s, to South Yemen, although most of them were clan-based, even feudal, rather than Marxist–Leninist. It was only Asia, without either the backing or the coercion of Russian tanks, which witnessed the spectacular, enduring rise of communism, not only as an ideology, but also as a system of political power. China from 1949 onwards, North Korea since 1945–8, North Vietnam since 1945–54, as well as unified Vietnam, Cambodia and Laos on the withdrawal of the Americans in 1975, all established governments based on the dictatorship of the proletariat and the supremacy of the Communist Party. As demonstrated by long periods of guerilla warfare elsewhere in South-East Asia, communism wielded major influence and threatened to sweep away established authority over a much wider area still. The above list does not include certain other Asian communist régimes which constitute special cases, such as Outer Mongolia, which became a Soviet satellite, or Afghanistan, whose occupation by Soviet troops in 1979 was the end result of a conflict between two local clans inspired by Marxism–Leninism.

This communist upsurge really had two successive culminations, in 1955–6 and 1975, both very different in nature. In the first, the Soviet Union made its mark on Asia while giving free reign to the dynamism of the Chinese communists and the more amorphous, occasionally baroque progressivism of other developing countries. China managed to stabilize its economy following the civil war, launching a programme of industrialization, the model and finance for which were provided by the Soviet Union. Both China and Vietnam saw considerable progress in literacy and in the distribution of agricultural production among the peasantry. When the Afro-Asian Conference met at Bandung (Indonesia) in the spring of 1955, the Chinese Prime Minister Zhou Enlai skilfully gave the impression of a policy of progressive neutrality in the name of the principles of peaceful coexistence. There he met Jawarharlal Nehru, the Prime Minister of India, the Soviet Union's other major ally. One year earlier, at the Geneva Conference in 1954, Ho Chi Minh had obtained the north of Vietnam for his own people, for want of a better deal and because of pressure from the Soviet Union and its Chinese allies. He did not, however, make any concessions on the principle of the permanent division of the country. Kim Il Sung, who in the same year had launched the slogan of self-sufficiency (*Juche*) for his country, also established genuine North Korean independence within the communist world, notably by carrying out a policy of liquidating all supporters of Moscow and Peking identified within his own government. Sukarno's Indonesia, in alliance with Moscow and Peking, was the home of the world's largest opposition communist party. Even Norodom Sihanouk's Cambodia and U Nu's Burma, with their 'Buddhic socialism' and their pursuit of a 'third way' between capitalism and communism, took the platform at the Bandung Conference. In 1956, de-Stalinization in the Soviet Union and the revolts in Eastern Europe, as well as the breakdown in the unity imposed by Moscow on the communist world, had not yet weakened the international influence of communist ideology. It is true that diplomats from Japan and other anti-communist countries, notably Ceylon, also attended the Afro-Asian Conference. History has focused less on the role of the moderates at Bandung and more on the fact that it represented the formation of a new, Third World International, officially neutral yet progressivist and communist in its inspiration.

Conversely, 1975 marked the absolute high point of the communist world in geopolitical terms, albeit amid total disunity. A few years later, certain observers still believed it to be expanding, even though all the signs of internal systemic failure were already present. However, 1975 saw the collapse of three régimes in Indochina that were backed by the United States, marking the first defeat in America's history (politically rather than militarily, though this is still open to debate). This handed communism a region it had been eyeing for thirty years, and to many Third World countries, as well as to most Western public opinion, it symbolized victory for what was often seen as a people's war against imperialism. Furthermore, since 1969 there had been a significant Soviet military thrust towards Asia, involving the reinforcement of the Soviet Pacific fleet and the army divisions and nuclear missiles on the Chinese border and in the Far East. This regional arms race, in contrast to the 'low profile' announced by the United States in 1969 and particularly to the withdrawal of American land forces in 1975, was a regional manifestation of the strategic conflict taking place on a global scale, rather than an attempt to 'thrust towards warm waters', as some have interpreted it. Yet under the sway of 'Brezhnev the African, builder of an extra-European empire' (Carrère d'Encausse, 1986: 12), Asia also became the scene of military bases, quasi-colonial intervention troops and diplomatic treaties. The culmination of this era came with the Soviet escapade in Afghanistan in December 1979. Decreed by Leonid Brezhnev, backed by the anti-Chinese Stalinist V. Suslov and Admiral Gorschkov, commander of the Pacific fleet, the occupation was to prove the graveyard of the Soviet colonial dream. In Asia, too, the rot had set in, and the Sino-Soviet rift of 1959–63 brought about a fratricidal power struggle between Moscow and a Peking exhausted by the Cultural Revolution and the zigzags of Mao's tyranny. China was teetering on the brink of chaos. North Korea, fossilized under Stalinism and an unprecedented personality cult, had already been largely overtaken in the economic stakes by South Korea, despite the fact that the South had initially been far less industrialized. In Vietnam, the communists toppled Saigon and the South Vietnamese régime in April 1975. Contrary to the idealized portrayal of their capture of the United States Embassy, they entered the city amid pervasive gloom, had little success at mobilizing the population and started to become worn down in the face of passive resistance from the population in the South. In Cambodia, in a sinister parody of Mao's anti-urban theses, the Khmer Rouge seized Phnom Penh, only to deport its population forthwith, heralding the dawn of the glorious future with an immediate descent into hell.

CHINA: THE MAOIST ERA

From 1949 until his death in 1976, Mao exerted a unique influence on his country, as well as on the international communist movement and the Third World. Even before 1949 he had developed a Chinese version of Marxism, moulding Maoist ideology through a series of alterations. His attempts to chart a Chinese route to socialism from 1955 onwards initially ended in disaster with the Great Leap Forward of 1958–61, then in an impasse with the Cultural Revolution of 1966–71. However, this did not lessen their impact on Chinese society and institutions, while they also inspired numerous revolutionary movements which were either detached from Moscow, or independent of it. In addition, the unique tendency of Chinese communism (also imitated to a lesser extent by Vietnam) to alternate short phases of debate and increased freedom of protest with brutal crackdowns, serves to alleviate the purely bureaucratic features of its history.

From Yenan to Peking

The victory of Chinese communism in 1949 was the result not of a classic revolution like that of 1917 in Petrograd, nor of an international power struggle, as with the people's democracies of Europe in 1946–7. Instead, it marked the outcome of two decades of civil war, when the Red Army took control of growing swathes of the population. The mechanisms and methods applied to the whole of China in 1949 were thus already tried and tested to a large extent. However, this victory was not absolute: communist militants and their revolutionary ideology were virtually non-existent in the cities, having been wiped out by Chiang Kai-shek in 1927. Two-thirds of China had been conquered in a classic, swift military offensive in 1949 and had almost no experience of the communist movement, which in turn suffered from a shortage of cadres and often aroused distrust. Beyond 'Liberation', which the new régime was to celebrate symbolically on 1 October, the main priority of the Chinese revolutionaries was to establish their political order on a national scale, even before embarking on the transformation to socialism. This primary objective was to be pursued through mass campaigns on a vast scale, while the rallying of the peasantry, the rebuilding of the economic infrastructure and the concentration of financial assets into state hands all took precedence over collectivization. From Peking to Canton, over a distance of 2,300 kilometres in less than six months, the last phase of an apparently interminable civil war was played out. Poverty-stricken and bloodied by war, China longed for order above all else, and in this respect the Red Army had a good reputation for fair dealing. Many of China's bourgeoisie, workers and intellectuals welcomed the communist victory with relief. Of those still opposed, more than two million left for Hong Kong and Taiwan, thus lessening the task facing the Communist Party. Mao Zedong and his followers chose to enforce, in their own words, a robust dictatorship, while limiting the extent of the repression to certain well-defined socio-political targets. On the one hand, the moderation which characterized the period of the war with Japan was still very much in evidence, especially in the united front, with its eight democratic parties and its illustrious group of 'independent' figures, who were given the token distinction of helping to create the government's definitive political institutions, notably a Council of Affairs of State and a host of centralized ministries structured along Soviet lines. However, what actually took place was the imposition, unchallenged, of a dictatorship of the proletariat, which was not declared until July 1949. The takeover was largely the work of the Red Army, whose officers generally took control of the main levers of power. The early upheavals in Chinese society also stemmed to a great extent from the activities of the Red bases prior to 1949. As for the new political hierarchy, it involved keeping the ruling structure of the Yenan period unchanged until the Cultural Revolution of 1966. If this was true of the ordinary Red Army soldier and his family, who saw first land reform, then rural collectivization guarantee material security and sometimes even a choice of employment, it was even more true of the country's leaders: the Yenan generation provided the People's Republic of China with its political and administrative framework.

The mass campaigns

Between 1949 and 1952, the Communist Party instigated a number of unprecedented large-scale 'mass campaigns', designed to persuade and constrain, terrorize and educate, transform and control. This duality of aims and methods underlay all the movements launched by Mao Zedong, the most important of which, at national level, were the marriage law and the law on land reform of 1950. The first, by favouring the freedom of individuals to choose their spouse, ushered in a spate of divorces, marking a break with the traditional oppression of Chinese women, particularly among the peasantry. Yet it also acted as a weapon against notables and reluctant revolutionaries of all classes by destroying one of the many family bonds which had characterized Chinese society in the past. Land reform, which had begun in the liberated zones in 1946, continued until 1951. It was not an original idea on the communists' part, but had already been advocated by many reformists during the republican era. Similar reforms had also been declared in Japan in 1946, in Taiwan in 1948, in the Philippines (with less success) and, of course, by Ho Chi Minh in Vietnam, albeit accompanied by considerable tactical restraint. However, in China (as in Vietnam) the move to create a small class of peasants, living in freedom on their own plots of land, and the abolition of the tyranny of the landlords were accompanied by tighter political control over the peasantry. As well as being extremely violent, including cases of 'excesses' being unleashed by the peasantry against the former wealthy members of the rural population, the land reform campaign also helped to establish local political networks which, a few years later, would form the basis for collectivization. The activists who agitated for land reform, the associations of poor peasants which were set up and the rural cadres recruited at this stage gave the government the leverage it still needed in many regions. Some of the other mass campaigns were even more overtly repressive. The hunt for 'counter-revolutionaries' in 1951 ensnared intellectuals, clergy of various denominations (particularly Catholic priests), members of secret societies and all the supporters of the old régime who had made the mistake of remaining on the mainland. The Three-Anti campaign of 1951, against corruption, waste and bureaucratism, purged the party ranks of those who had let themselves become corrupted after victory, while the Five-Anti campaign of 1952, focused on financial corruption, brought China's urban bourgeoisie to heel. The real power within enterprises changed hands, although in theory they remained in the private sector. Together these mass movements created the Communist Party apparatus (still relatively limited in size with six million members in the early 1950s) as well as that of the trade unions and mass organizations such as the Women's League and the Youth League.

These movements also gave rise to a new social dynamic. Meetings for confrontation, accusation and mutual self-criticism, the 'tales of bitterness' about the years prior to 1949 and the key role of repentance and 'thought reform' for individuals helped to sever bonds of solidarity and patronage as well as all the loyalties of the past. The mass campaigns yielded a new generation of political activists which supplied the communist cadres of the future, recruited especially from the Communist Youth League. The voluntary contributions, fines and confiscations occasioned by these movements provided the initial funds for the planned economy which was launched in 1953. The population was accordingly divided into sixty social classes, many of them very narrowly defined. In February 1957, Mao estimated the death toll resulting solely from the campaign for the suppression of counter-revolutionaries at 700,000, adding, by way of an epitaph, that 'those executed were shackles on the forces of production'(MacFarquhar et al. 1989: 142). In 1958, however, he put the number of victims of the founding phase of the People's Republic of China at two to three million, in other words approximately 3 to 5 per cent of the Chinese population.

The Soviet model challenged

After the upheavals of the communist takeover, the years covered by the first Five Year Plan (1953–7) ushered in a period of steadier growth. On a political level, the government completed the establishment of its institutions, particularly via the Constitution of 1954, and although thought reform campaigns were launched periodically against intellectuals, more extreme initiatives were avoided. The implementation of the first plan (the aims of which were not fully declared until 1955) and the long-drawn-out process of transforming the Chinese countryside (co-operatives for manual labour set up from 1952 and state control over the sale, purchase, transportation and storage of grain introduced from 1953) paved the way for the gradual construction of communism, closely modelled on the Soviet example as far as industry was concerned, yet better organized and more progressive than Stalinism in the countryside. In retrospect, the plan represents the absolute classical period in the history of Chinese socialism. It was particularly marked by financial success, since from 1953 onwards, the funds available for public investment equalled more than 25 per cent of China's GNP. From 1950 to 1959, industrial and mining schemes, supported by vast amounts of Soviet aid, went from strength to strength, with the rate of industrial growth reaching over 18 per cent per annum in the period of the first plan. The standard of living rose, sometimes very rapidly indeed for those who benefited from newly-created jobs in industry and government. The sections of society which made up the 'national bourgeoisie' – engineers, workers and intellectuals as well as business owners – experienced a renewed calm after the trials and tribulations of the early years. Mao himself estimated the number of executions during this period at 70,000, carried out in the course of a campaign against 'hidden counter-revolutionaries' which marked its bloodiest episode.

This relative calm was fragile, however. At the top, Mao Zedong's goal was to speed up the construction of communism, attacking anyone and everyone who stood in his way. In July 1955, contrary to the warnings of his advisers on economic and rural affairs, he decided to carry out a rapid collectivization of agriculture. From December 1955, all Chinese peasants were grouped into co-operatives, which, although they remained modelled along the lines of the existing villages and were based on individual private property ownership, still marked a radical break with the past. This process of collectivization, carried out with the help of large numbers of rural cadres and the support of the impoverished peasants, was relatively success-ful despite sporadic episodes of passive resistance from the peasantry. This experience taught Mao that his intuition could prove right, contrary to the advice of experts and the lessons of Soviet precedent. Before long, Khrush-chev's de-Stalinization policy and his revelations before the Twentieth Soviet Party Congress in February 1956 discredited the Soviet path and the Soviet model once and for all. Mao immediately began working to pre-empt any possible upheavals in China: he personally took the initiative to intro-duce a programme of internal liberalization, aimed at allowing expressions of discontent and criticisms of weaknesses in the communist apparatus. However, from this point on, he also granted himself much greater freedom to make decisions concerning the transformation of the country.

From January 1956, encouraged by the rapid progress of rural collectivi-zation, Mao launched a number of initiatives. On the one hand, he attempted to speed up agricultural growth by fully mobilizing China's human resources, an effort which immediately failed, but none the less prefigured the Great Leap Forward. Urban industry and trade were also collectivized within two months. Mao challenged the economic planning and bureaucratic methods of the cadres. In January 1956, Zhou Enlai launched an appeal for the collaboration of all patriotic intellectuals, recog-nizing in doing so that most were non-communist. In April, Mao criticized the application of the 'Soviet path' to China and gave his backing to the reformists' arguments: this new pragmatism was also, admittedly, an echo of Khrushchev's reforms, which were at their height in Moscow at that time. In May 1956, there emerged the liberal slogan of the 'Hundred Flow-ers' – 'May a hundred flowers bloom, may a hundred schools of thought contend!' – a Chinese variation on the thaw taking place under Khrushchev in the Soviet Union. However, behind this slogan, Mao and his associates hesitated long and hard over their response to de-Stalinization. China's leaders initially reacted reasonably favourably to the latter in April 1956, viewing the Polish Spring and events in Hungary with equanimity. Eventually, however, they ended up inciting the Soviet army to intervene in Budapest, and in December 1956 they defended Stalin against the bar-rage of criticism being levelled against him by Moscow. Although Mao acknowledged all the arguments put forward by the advocates of de-Stalin-ization in Moscow, criticizing the planning and the unwieldiness of the communist system, he actually envisaged speeding up and radicalizing progress towards communism. This change of pace caused considerable misunderstanding and self-delusion on the part of those who dared criticize the Communist Party, under the impression that Mao had authorized them to do so.

The Hundred Flowers

During the winter of 1956–7, Mao experienced difficulties with the launch of a campaign for the rectification of the communist system announced at the Eighth Party Congress of September 1956. He therefore decided to draw even more closely on the discontent prevailing at all levels of Chinese society, sounding a warning in February 1957, for the first time under a communist government, against the presence of 'contradictions among the people'. Had the Chinese people been able to read the actual text of the speech given by Mao on this occasion, they would have remained on their guard. However, the text distributed within the Party was more liberal than the original, which had, moreover, been incoherent and riddled with long-winded observations on the advantages and disadvantages of brutal repression. Between April and June 1957, these exhortations finally culminated in the Hundred Flowers campaign – seven weeks of considerable freedom of expression, when tongues were loosened and reviews, wall posters and meetings proliferated, including within the communist organs. Not only students and intellectuals, but also workers and peasants living near the major cities, threw themselves into a protest which soon turned into a challenge to the Communist Party. They received a rude awakening. On 7 June 1957, the Communist Party caused an upheaval in the political climate with the launch of a major 'anti-rightist campaign' against all those holding heterodox views. It lasted seven months, touching nearly 400,000 people, particularly city-dwellers, students, intellectuals and workers, and crushing every hint of criticism and any form of expression that deviated, however slightly, from the official slogans. A new, third version of Mao's February 1957 speech on 'contradictions among the people' was officially published, retrospectively condemning the excesses committed in the name of the earlier version. Yet this repression of all critical elements did not signify defeat for Mao: on the contrary, communist cadres who opposed his ambitious goals were also forced to toe the line. All opposition, whether from liberals or from within the party apparatus, was silenced by purging and slimming down the ranks of central government and by transferring large numbers of cadres down into production. Within a few months, Mao launched several mass movements which began causing economic and social upheaval. Following the launch of the first Soviet *sputnik*, he also attempted, unsuccessfully, to secure the rapid transfer of Soviet nuclear and space technology. Relations with Nikita Khrushchev began to deteriorate, and from then on Mao would steer China without paying any heed to the warnings of Soviet advisers.

The tragedy of the Great Leap Forward

From the end of 1957 onwards, the mass campaigns and production targets spun out of control. This frenzy followed in a direct line from the anti-rightist campaign and led on to the Great Leap Forward, which was officially announced in May 1958. The 'hydraulization' of rural China within a few months, through vast public works to construct canals, dykes and reservoirs; reforestation carried out by means of peasant labour; literacy campaigns; the immediate introduction of universal primary education: all were implemented without central finance, for local schemes such as these did not put a stop to efforts by central organs such as the economic plan and the ministries to promote heavy industry. There was one watchword, 'Walk on two legs', one being heavy industry, the other being the Chinese countryside: indeed this became the key slogan of the Great Leap Forward, which was based above all on the frantic mobilization of labour thought to have been under-utilized in the past. The authorities also launched a race to expand the collective co-operatives, which grew in six months from the modest size of fifteen to twenty farms to the vast scale of the first people's communes, such as *Weixing* (Sputnik) Commune in Henan province.

In the summer of 1958, this frenzy reached its zenith. In a matter of weeks, all agriculture was reorganized into people's communes, grouping together in some cases between 200,000 and 400,000 inhabitants. The Politburo only published legislation regulating these retrospectively and, in the short term, encouraged free access to basic resources such as food, canteens, education and medical care. However, the population was harrassed and forced to hand over to the people's communes their small plots of land, farming implements and, in some cases, their kitchen utensils for melting down, to feed the small rural furnaces. The work was carried out by collective labour squads: in December 1958, an official circular instructed the cadres to allow the peasants eight hours of freedom per day.

At its peak, the movement was accompanied by growing ambitions for China, which was supposed to 'catch up with Britain' and achieve a rapid twofold increase in the harvest yield and in steel production. Decentralization marked the end of central planning and statistical collection. For many months, China's leaders were carried away by the effect of their own propaganda for the Great Leap Forward and had trouble discerning the truth behind their own speeches. The year 1958, which was extremely favourable as far as weather was concerned, compounded their self-delusion. Yet the first tours of inspection by the leadership beginning in autumn 1958 revealed an imminent crisis in the making, with exaggerated statistics, harvests lying neglected in the fields by peasants drafted into rural industry, the terror of a population forced into producing ever-increasing amounts of grain, and fear of what was to come. In the spring of 1959, a number of retrenchment measures were adopted.

However, the political struggle within the Communist Party led to the Great Leap Forward being prolonged. In July 1959, at Lushan, the Defence Minister, Marshal Peng Dehuai, directly questioned the excesses of the Great Leap Forward and the propaganda cult surrounding Mao Zedong. Mao turned what had been a restricted meeting into a plenary session of the

Central Committee. There he isolated Peng, and after a virtuoso self-criticism he was once again given *carte blanche* by his colleagues. Peng Dehuai was ousted (he later died during the Cultural Revolution) and was replaced by Marshal Lin Biao, Mao's future heir-apparent. Doubtless in order to justify himself, Mao, rather than tempering the Great Leap Forward, as he had already begun to do, instead relaunched it.

The death toll of the Great Leap Forward reached horrific proportions with the sudden cut-off in Soviet aid in June 1960. The grain harvest had benefited from the favourable weather of 1958, while rural industry had achieved a modicum of growth at the cost of chaos elsewhere in the economy. In 1959, 15 million displaced peasants swelled the urban population, harvests failed from 1959 onwards and the food crisis worsened in 1960, while disposable income per capita for the same year was 20 per cent less than in 1957. After reaching an artificial peak, industrial production fell by 43 per cent in 1961. Many of the major public works begun during the Great Leap Forward had been hastily carried out and were soon written off. Famine set in during the 'three black years' of 1959–61, including in the major cities, where the usual death announcements and black armbands were banned in order to avoid alerting visitors. In the work camps and prison farms alone, the death toll for 1959–62 may be estimated at 4 million. The total fall in the population was over 50 million, while the number of deaths directly attributable to the movement is estimated at between 13 and 30 million. The Great Leap Forward thus proved to be the greatest disaster in twentieth-century Chinese history.

Mao challenged

The failure of the Great Leap Forward crystallized the struggle at the top. In 1961, Mao was preoccupied by the incipient Sino-Soviet rift and, largely retrospectively, ratified internal measures adopted to mitigate the disaster. In the same year, China's leaders, particularly Liu Shaoqui and Deng Xiaoping, annulled most of the innovations instituted by the Great Leap Forward and agreed to an immediate return by the peasants to individual farming on a province-wide scale, while others launched into thinly-disguised attacks on Mao Zedong, who was held responsible for the failure. The spearhead of the latter group was Peng Zhen, Mayor of Peking. It was under his patronage that the historian and dramatist Wu Han published a classical play in February 1961 entitled *Hai Rui dismissed from office*, criticizing the removal of Peng Dehuai. In the *Peking Daily*, poison pen letters appeared from the hand of the polemical historian Deng Tuo, which satirized Mao in undecidedly unmetaphorical terms. According to sources dating from the Cultural Revolution, it was also Peng Zhen who was reputed to have gathered together in a Peking park a group charged with the task of assembling an act of political impeachment against Mao. In January 1962, in front of an audience of 7,000 leaders, Mao was forced to give a devastating self-criticism, admitting incompetence particularly in economic affairs, while Liu Shaoqui declared the failure of the Great Leap Forward to be largely due to human error. Mao's prestige reached a nadir and voices soon spoke out in defence of Peng Dehuai, who was venerated, so to speak, as a 'prophet outcast', to borrow a term used of Trotsky by the historian Isaac Deutscher (1963). However, Chinese propaganda kept most of these actions out of the public eye and continued to sing the praises both of the Great Leap Forward and of Chairman Mao.

The aftermath of the Great Leap Forward was likewise a mere interlude. On the one hand, economic growth and foreign trade picked up as a result of the implementation of orthodox communist policies while China's leaders, headed by Zhou Enlai, set about reinstating professionals and intellectuals. It was in the early 1960s, in the most prosperous agricultural areas, that the yields of the two (or in some cases three) annual harvests and the system of collective labour reached the highest levels in the history of collectivization. State-run industry also seemed to have stabilized and the government, keen to assert its independence, quickly repaid its debts to the Soviet Union while opening its doors to the first significant volume of Western trade. The Chinese government appeared totally united over the issue of the Sino-Indian war of October–November 1962, fought in the mountains of Kashmir and Ladakh. It also appeared unanimous in its hostility to the Soviet Union, and the rift between the two finally came in July 1963. Mao none the less actively plotted his revenge, launching several movements based on his pet themes. These included the purging by his wife Jiang Qing, from 1963 onwards, of the Chinese theatre, which Mao considered feudal and decadent, and the renewed indoctrination of the People's Liberation Army with the publication of the 'Little Red Book', *Quotations of Chairman Mao*, in 1964, which was destined to achieve a world publishing record two years later. Above all, in September 1962, Mao caused a major upheaval in the countryside with the Movement for Socialist Education, designed to purge the peasants of individualistic, capitalist and 'feudalistic' tendencies. During the débâcle of the Great Leap Forward many 'spontaneous tendencies' had actually re-emerged: gambling, superstitious thinking, moonlighting, usury, arranged marriages and the dereliction of collective duty had increased, while many rural cadres had resigned, cornered by the political convulsions that had taken place since 1955. Mao's angry response was 'Never forget class struggle!' The Movement for Socialist Education became the battleground for rivalry between China's principal leaders: Mao's enemies initially tried to contain the political impact of the movement, then tightened the pressure on local cadres in 1964 in order to deprive the Great Helmsman of his pretext. Mao promptly mustered all the pragmatism of which he was capable in order to restrain the severity of his colleagues, for his desire was not so much to disgrace the lower cadres as to change the line-up at the top. In January 1965, he declared an extension of the movement to all areas of politics, in order to combat the 'capitalist path': from then on, the touch paper was in place, ready to ignite the flames of the Cultural Revolution.

The Cultural Revolution

The 'Great Proletarian and Cultural Revolution', described as a 'flight into utopia' (Bergère, 1989: 117) and a 'struggle for power at the top among a clutch of individuals' (Leys, 1971: 23), marked both the height of Mao Zedong's power and an episode of untold chaos. A whole generation of Chinese youth, exhorted by their leaders to re-enact the era of the Long March, gave it their all: for countless Chinese intellectuals, professionals and cadres it proved a deadly tragedy. It was a revolution in name only, for a small group of leaders close to Mao, which soon became known by the cryptic name of the 'Centre', were the constant moving spirit behind the political decisions of the Red Guards. The Guards judiciously obtained confessions and documents incriminating the enemies of the Great Helmsman, although their zeal was thwarted on several famous occasions. Political manipulation none the less proved difficult, given the total lack of any political education or historical knowledge among the younger generation, the considerable fragmentation of rival groups, and the conflicts at the top, sometimes violent, sometimes muted, which soon ended in total disaster. It soon became a three-way interplay as the army of Marshal and Defence Minister Lin Biao began to establish itself as a key actor. At times during the early stages (1966–8), the Red Guards believed themselves to be leading a largely spontaneous movement, thus re-enacting the Chinese Revolution and exposing their differences. Their downward transfer of nearly 19 million young Chinese city-dwellers to the countryside and manual labour from December 1968 onwards put paid to that illusion. From then on, the Cultural Revolution was reduced to the scale of an internal dispute, with the ultra-radical Maoists gradually losing the struggle.

The Cultural Revolution began as an internal Party conflict. As in the case of the Hundred Flowers correction campaign, the cadre structure initially hampered Mao's attempt to extend the Movement for Socialist Education to other spheres. In November 1965, Mao published a pamphlet in the Shanghai press attacking the dramatist Wu Han, who had mocked him in the theatre, while in February 1966, the army Chief of Staff was arrested: thus, from the moment of its conception, the Cultural Revolution combined public polemic and mass appeal with an organizational conflict based on military power. In May 1966, Mao created the core group of the Cultural Revolution, notably including his wife, Jiang Qing, and his former private secretary, Chen Boda. The first wall poster of the Cultural Revolution, attacking the University of Peking and the city authorities, was soon produced by a philosophy teacher, Nie Yuanzi, thus drawing the entire school-age population into the movement. Schools closed for several years from July 1966, while students and pupils were urged to turn themselves into Red Guards: they immediately split into rival factions, with the children of cadres and soldiers pitted against the offspring of the former bourgeoisie and also against the intellectuals. In August 1966, the Central Committee reassembled, but a number of delegates were prevented from taking part and their places in the chamber were taken by soldiers. Mao summoned China's youth to Peking, where they gathered in their millions, blocking trains, railway stations and public places as they thronged toTiananmen Square for vast meetings held in front of impassive leaders. It was at this point that the short-lived Red Guard press came into being, with its fanatical Maoist cult and its tendency to disputes between its various factions. The hunt for 'revisionists' was on, and would prove fatal not only for many cadres but also especially for virtually all China's intellectuals, painters and other creative artists, who suffered beatings, deportation and massacre in the name of the struggle against 'poisonous weeds'. This revolution also had its precautions: it was not supposed to affect production greatly, especially in military-related areas of industry and research. Yet before the end of the year, Peng Dehuai, Liu Shaoqui, Peng Zhen and Deng Xiaoping were arrested along with thousands of civilian and military leaders. One of the differences between Maoism and Stalinism was that although Liu Shaoqui and other less prominent figures were executed, the lives of many others were spared.

In early 1967, the Cultural Revolution began to follow a new logic, namely the introduction of a 'revolutionary' order inspired by mass action. There was a utopian quality to certain programmes, for example when the Red Guards, inspired by Chen Boda, set up the Shanghai Commune and declared free availability of goods and the freedom to dismiss leaders. This conjunction of Maoism and an anarcho-syndicalism reminiscent of the Paris Commune was short-lived and Mao disowned his imitators for the first time. The major event was the appointment of regional governments, with participation being introduced in principle for members of the army, alongside party members and activists. At times, the Red Guards clashed increasingly violently with the authorities and with their colleagues, and the army was forced to intervene as mediator. In Sichuan (south-eastern China) and Wuhan, full-scale pitched battles ensued, complete with cannon, and army convoys destined for Vietnam were frequently plundered. The army tightened its control at this stage, but it was divided. While Lin Biao had already been chosen as Mao's successor, some regional commanders took up the cudgels on behalf of local party leaders against the Cultural Revolution and its activists. As a result, at Wuhan in July 1967, the army seized a key envoy from the Maoist Centre and achieved a certain toning down of the Cultural Revolution. This date marked a decisive turning-point. The Red Guards were radicalized in vain: in Peking the Foreign Ministry was stormed, while in the provinces an increasing number of independent anti-government movements emerged. However, the Cultural Revolution group had already given in: at a famous meeting, Jiang

Qing delivered a eulogy to Zhou Enlai, while Chen Boda faded into the background.

After the trial of strength which took place in the summer of 1967, provincial revolutionary committees were set up at an increasing rate to replace the pre-1966 party organs. While the Centre issued calls for unity, the Red Guards were disbanded and sent down to the countryside. The local struggles, the revolutionary rhetoric, the excessive cult of Chairman Mao and the penal institutions established under the name of 'May 7 Schools' were to continue for several years. However, the Communist Party did restructure its organization. The Ninth Party Congress of April 1969 constituted both a Maoist litany, with Lin Biao lauding the Great Helmsman as a 'genius', and a check on the radicals. The factional strife at the top continued, with Zhou Enlai, Jiang Qing and Lin Biao as the chief protagonists. In September 1971, the outside world learned of Lin Biao's death, two years after he had been chosen as Mao's successor: following an unsuccessful coup attempt, his plane reportedly crashed in Outer Mongolia. His death was accompanied by the departure from the political scene of a number of military commanders, while the press praised the virtues of army compliance and democratic centralism, in other words restored supremacy for the Communist Party. The latter curbed the seemingly unstoppable rise of the army, which, though it made up 46 per cent of the Central Committee in 1969, had been reduced to 23 per cent by 1973.

The reduction in the role of the military opened the way for the reinstatement of large numbers of cadres, orchestrated by Zhou Enlai. 'Leftist' excesses were condemned, especially those perpetrated against individual initiatives in the countryside, and the use of economic statistics was soon reintroduced, while China's imports of technology increased. However, those leaders who had owed their own advancement to the Cultural Revolution fought to save their positions and prevent the return of the former cadres. The latter still had their victories, and criticism of 'leftism' grew stronger. In April 1973, Deng Xiaoping, who had been the Cultural Revolution's number two target after Liu Shaoqi, was reinstated and unofficially awarded the post of Deputy Prime Minister. However, the backlash was not long in coming. At the Eleventh Party Congress, Wang Hongwei, a radical Shanghai cadre whose advancement had taken place under Jiang Qing's patronage, became number three in the Party. He was joined at the Politburo by activists such as Chen Yonggui, a former peasant who had been responsible for the rural model of Maoism in Dazhai, and Hua Guofeng, a former cadre from Mao's native region. The radicals launched a new movement and from then on the campaign against Lin Biao was linked to the denunciation of none other than Confucius himself. Its aim was to denounce the conservatism of the 'intellectuals', in other words Zhou Enlai, and to pay tribute to Mao Zedong in the guise of Qin Shihuang, the brutal dynastic founder responsible for eliminating similar 'odious intellectuals'. This offensive reached its height during the spring of 1974. Propaganda, which in the main continued to be produced by Cultural Revolution activists, was targeted especially against a film by Italian director Antonioni, who had been invited to China by Zhou Enlai, as well as against classical music, economic 'revisionism', inequality in education and 'bourgeois law'.

However, in contrast to the enormous upsurge of 1966, the leading radicals encountered apathy from a population weary of repressive and often obscure campaigns. Zhou Enlai proceeded to gain a reputation as the ultimate defence against arbitrary action, while intellectuals and artists found themselves allied with the traditional communist leadership. In July 1973, Zhou Enlai went into hospital, as much for protection against his critics as for cancer treatment. The ailing Mao no longer appeared in public and generally communicated through his closest followers as intermediaries. The competition for the succession had begun. In 1975, a study campaign focused on the dictatorship of the proletariat relaunched the offensive by the radicals and differences arose between their followers and those of the moderates in China's industrial centres. As with the onset of the Cultural Revolution, each faction built up a social base of supporters, while the army once again resumed the role of arbiter.

In January 1976, Zhou Enlai died in the middle of a radical offensive. The fate of his successors appeared sealed, while Deng Xiaoping, who was suddenly nowhere to be seen, became the target of repeated attacks. Suddenly, however, a certain forgotten protagonist came back on the scene, when, in April, a popular demonstration in Tiananmen Square in memory of Zhou Enlai became transformed into a public attack on the Maoist radicals. The Chinese people feared a new Cultural Revolution and the protesters denounced autocracy in poems and readings from the imperial era. This expression of the will of the people proved short-lived, and the resulting crackdown was heavy. One of the gains made by the radicals in the wake of this was the dismissal of Deng Xiaoping. The Tiananmen Square incident none the less marked the point of origin for all the popular dissent and the great opposition movements of post-Maoist China. In the meantime, the incident worked in favour of the Interior Minister, Hua Guofeng. However, the Party once again found itself split into two camps and discontent mounted across the country. The real power shifted onto a regional footing, and Deng Xiaoping lay in wait in the south, under the protection of General Xu Shiyou, commander of the military district of Canton. For many Chinese, the end of the régime was marked by the Tangshan earthquake of July 1976, with an official death toll of 250,000. On 9 September, Mao died and a month of mourning was declared, during which all the factions mobilized. In October, Hua Guofeng switched sides, putting the Gang of Four under arrest and accusing Mao's widow, Jiang Qing, of fomenting a coup. This date, which today is officially regarded as a 'Second Liberation', marked the end of the Maoist era. Jubilant crowds took to the streets in communist China's last great mass campaign, this time targeted against Maoism itself.

No-one knows the human toll of the decade 1966–76, but it was, by any standards, less deadly than the Great Leap Forward. In general, rural China retained its administrative and economic structures, even though productivity suffered as a consequence. On the basis of a figure of 40,000 victims originally cited in an internal document for Guangdong province, and later on the basis of comparable figures for several other provinces, it is sometimes calculated that fatalities across the country as a whole totalled one million. This number does not take account of the suffering endured by all those who were deprived of their jobs, subjected to ill-treatment or deported, nor the collapse of moral values. The interruption of higher education for at least five years, China's isolation from the outside world, the advancement of large numbers of activists whose main talent was to be able to speak the current jargon, and the suffering and bitterness of those who took part, likewise represented a lasting deficit.

The ruling group which governed China after the purging of the Gang of Four faced a number of insoluble difficulties. On the one hand, the denunciation of the Maoist radicals necessitated a purge of the administrative machinery and met with a great deal of enthusiasm from the people. At times, the winter of 1976–7 seemed like a bloody Thermidor, for instance in Sichuan, where entire revolutionary committees were executed. On the other hand, however, Mao's successors were forced to contend with considerable pressures, both from the cadres who were calling for reinstatement, starting with Deng Xiaoping, and from the military which in many cases supported them. Part of the population saw the downfall of the extreme Maoists as the end of a dynasty. The campaign against the Gang of Four (or Gang of Five, as many Chinese referred to it, thus including Mao himself) was strongly reminiscent of the litany of persecutions and other atrocities of the Cultural Revolution. Private activities, ranging from trade to the Peking Opera, resumed spontaneously. Hua Guofeng, the chance unifier of a Maoist centre who considered himself a moderate, initially attempted to put the brakes on the process of de-Maoization. As the denunciation of Deng Xiaoping continued, he prepared a final volume of Mao's *Selected Works*, began building a mausoleum in Peking and devoted himself to restoring the classical order, reintroducing examinations and a wage hierarchy and bringing about an end to mass labour mobilization in rural China.

This moderate Maoism – a contradiction in terms – failed to last. Between February and March 1977, several of China's military commanders and provincial leaders exerted pressure, sometimes violently, to secure Deng's reinstatement. In May 1977, the most open of all Mao's texts, *On the Ten Major Relationships*, written in April 1956, was published for the first time, not so much to honour Mao's memory as to exploit it in order to lend legitimacy to the changes underway. In July 1977, Deng Xiaoping was reinstated to number three in the government hierarchy. As Vice-President of the Central Committee his followers included army moderates and seasoned administrators. In his speech to the Congress, Deng launched what was to become his slogan against his rivals: 'Less empty talk and more hard work!'

The divided factions of 1973–6 thus became reunited at the top. This time, however, Mao's successors had the more difficult task. The régime's mass mobilizations had been discredited and the people were above all awaiting a period of liberalization and a rise in living standards. Communist political power had always used ideological mobilization as a weapon, but its successors recycled old ideas and showed little skill at manipulating the masses. Pitted against them, Deng Xiaoping enjoyed the loyalty both of Party veterans, especially the cadres who had suffered under the Cultural Revolution, and of a population still prepared to trust leaders who might save them from disaster. Deng thus capitalized both on the legacy of Zhou Enlai and on the daring of the protesters. A consummate tactician, he started placing his own men in key positions, for instance putting Hu Yaobang in charge of the Party's Organization Department which controlled cadre promotion.

Hua Guofeng made one last attempt to rekindle the flames. In the spring of 1977, a highly ambitious programme of industrial development was announced, based on large-scale imports of technology and also exploiting old Maoist methods of mobilization. This 'little Great Leap', as it gradually became known, soon created a dual imbalance: too many goods were imported from abroad, while industrial production went out of control and was squandered on useless and low-quality goods. From the summer of 1978, criticism of this deliberate policy was joined by challenges to the Maoist legacy. In Peking, the Democracy Wall of Xidan, which had already served the Hundred Flowers campaign in 1957, became the focus for attacks on Hua Guofeng's supporters, who were arraigned in public. Within the Party, Deng Xiaoping organized an economic and social critique of Maoism and set up an experiment on the scale of Anhui province which developed into land reform in the following year.

MAOISM: THE MOULD FOR ASIAN COMMUNISM?

Did Maoism act as a staging-post along the road to Marxism–Leninism for the communist movements of Asia, or was it an alternative road in its own right? This question has been avoided by experts on the national communist movements, who rarely approach their subject from a comparative perspective. The followers of these movements have been even less keen to address the issue, being primarily concerned with preserving a semblance of independence. And in truth, beyond the internationalist links of the communist world and its ideology, national rivalry and feeling equally influenced relations between the communist parties: the Sino-Vietnamese dispute, for example, became evident in 1954 in the wake of the Geneva Conference, as the result of a struggle for power in Indochina.

Yet history compels us to question the influence of the Chinese model: was it exerted consciously, via the influence of pro-Chinese factions, or indirectly, by virtue of the dominant cultural role China has always played in relation to certain neighbours, such as Korea and Vietnam? Its historic exports of Confucianism, imperial bureaucracy and the mandarinate, together with the long-threatened national identity of the Koreans and Vietnamese, who drew on Chinese nationalism in order to drive out the colonists, have created a legacy that is still alive today. Moreover, the Maoist model of military and political warfare (whose cardinal rule was to fuse the two) proved a powerful magnet for other communist movements in Asia and even beyond. In China specifically, the People's Liberation Army and the application of the Maoist 'mass line' theory formed the twin pillars of political legitimacy. China's two neighbours admittedly had difficulty keeping track of the political about-turns of the Great Leap Forward and particularly the Cultural Revolution. In foreign policy, too, they always maintained a clear vision of their own national interests. However, some of their institutions and methods were based on the Chinese model, which appeared to be more highly developed than the Stalinist system.

Kim Il Sung's Korea post-1953

North Korean communism was built on foundations which owed more to Russian than to Chinese influences and was brought to power by the Soviet army, rather than by a civil war or a war of independence. Moreover, during the mid-fifties, Kim Il Sung pursued a policy of systematically eliminating members of the Chinese and Soviet factions within his own party, taking advantage of the veiled struggle for power in which both were engrossed. Following the Panmunjon armistice of 1953, Kim launched a campaign of systematic criticism against party cadres which resulted in 70 per cent of them being punished. Kim forced them to become the scapegoats for all the unpopularity of the war and for the suffering endured during that period. His policies were inspired by both Peking and Moscow in equal measure. Like Mao, Kim adopted a system of Soviet-style economic planning, with a Three-Year Plan lasting from 1953 to 1955, followed by a Five-Year Plan, which accentuated heavy industry, contrary to the wishes of Korea's large lobby in support of light industry and the consumer industries. This did not stop him embarking on a gradual programme for agricultural collectivization from 1953 to 1958 which was closely modelled on the Chinese system, although unlike Mao, Kim did not force a rapid pace.

Yet for Kim Il Sung, as for his counterparts in China and Vietnam, the most glittering prize of all was independence. This included independence from China, which in other respects often gave him his inspiration. Thus, in 1955, without ever quoting Mao, he declared the basis of his régime to be self-sufficiency, which corresponded exactly to the Maoist principle of 'relying on one's own strength' (*zili gengsheng*). When Khrushchev caused tremors in 1956 with the denunciation of the personality cult in Moscow, Kim briefly put his own cult under wraps. However, at the same time, at the Third Congress of the Korean Communist Party in April 1956, he reaffirmed the membership of the Central Committee, of which thirty-nine members out of a total of sixty-nine had disappeared since 1948, a figure of Stalinist proportions. This was followed by a joint alliance between the pro-Soviet and pro-Chinese factions against Kim's monopoly, but its leaders were put under arrest. In September 1956, in an unprecedented joint move, Anastas Mikoyan (on behalf of Moscow) and Peng Dehuai (on behalf of Peking) went to Pyongyang to try and dissuade Kim Il Sung from eliminating the two groups, but he simply postponed this new purge by one year. In the summer of 1957, while China was engrossed in the 'anti-rightist' campaign and Moscow was being forced to confront many internal problems, Kim Il Sung struck again, eliminating both factions.

At the same time, in August 1957, Kim Il Sung held national elections, in which 99.92 per cent of the population cast their vote and an identical percentage voted for the official candidates. In March 1958, he was able to declare, without fear of contradiction, that his party 'had been completely purged of the hateful historical phenomenon of factionalism' and that his authority would never again be subject to criticism. However, while this was taking place, China continued, up until 1958, to maintain significant numbers of troops on North Korean soil. China had evidently turned down the chance to intervene in North Korea's internal party affairs and Moscow sided with this position from 1957 onwards, notably putting an end to dual nationality for members of the pro-Soviet faction. Kim Il Sung had won, and managed to keep this game of ping-pong going between Peking and Moscow until the collapse of Soviet communism in 1991.

In other respects, Kim continued to take inspiration from Maoism and from Stalinism. Although unlike China he maintained the Five-Year Plan, in June 1958 he nevertheless launched a movement reminiscent of the Great Leap Forward, called the *Chollima undong* (Flying Horse Movement) after a mythical winged horse whose leap spanned 10,000 *li*. Several of its features – the sending down of large numbers of cadres into production, the adoption of a new charter for industrial management, the promotion of the three 'revolutions' (ideological, scientific and technological, recalling the 'three red banners of Maoism') – were straight replicas of Maoism. When Mao boasted in 1958 of 'catching up with Britain' within ten years, Kim announced that North Korean production per capita for the mining and industrial sector would reach Japanese levels by the following year – a more technocratic, but equally presumptuous echo of one and the same ambition.

However, compared to the Great Leap Forward, the *Chollima undong* does not appear to have caused the same degree of dislocation. Kim created 'great socialist villages', banning private ownership of small plots of land. Yet he did not attempt the same total collectivization, the reorganization into vast communes and the frantic pursuit of rural industry which had characterized China's Great Leap Forward. He attempted to steer clear of the deepening Sino-Soviet rift, signing mutual security treaties with both Peking and Moscow in July 1961. This failed to prevent a drastic reduction, if not complete cut-off, in Soviet aid between 1962 and 1965, just as China had suffered two years before. In some cases Kim Il Sung even appeared to be influencing the shape of Chinese Maoism, rather than vice versa: for instance, the term 'Red Guards' was used in North Korea to denote reservist militias before it appeared in China, while in the early 1970s, Mao used the expression 'flying leap' to describe a mass movement in production. While North Korea's foreign policy steered a middle course between Peking and Moscow, the fundamental nature of the Chinese and North Korean régimes often served to bring them together.

Kim Il Sung completely preserved North Korea from the influence of the Cultural Revolution, although he entered a totally new dimension with his own personality cult, which had become fanatical since the early 1960s. At the beginning of the 1970s, Kim Il Sung had a museum built in his honour, covering an area of 240,000 square metres, which was visited by many Westerners. He appears to have taken the almost simultaneous outbreak of the Vietnamese War and the Cultural Revolution as a favourable omen for his own attempts to reunify Korea by force. A successful raid by a North Korean commando unit on the South Korean President's Seoul residence in January 1968 and the capture of the United States surveillance ship, the *Pueblo*, two days later showed evidence of this upsurge in the temperature in North Korea. From 1967 onwards, the proportion of national expenditure allocated to the army regularly exceeded 30 per cent.

Between 1964 and 1969, each North Korean citizen was automatically registered with the public security service under one of fifty-one designated political and social categories, which together formed the three main social classes: the privileged 'masses of the central core', in which former students of the School for Orphans of the Revolution were to play an increasingly dominant role; the 'masses outside the core', made up of elements, such as workers and peasants, who, while socially acceptable, were not especially politically committed; and the 'miscellaneous masses', former members of the bourgeoisie, dissenters and victims of all types and their offspring, as well as those whose families had migrated to the South in 1950–3. The latter were particularly denied access to higher education and were punished especially harshly in cases of political differences. North Korea's concentration camps also comprised several levels of punishment, including one which involved indirectly condemning victims to a lingering death by giving them minimal food rations, while execution by flogging was commonplace. All in all, North Korea comes across as the fanatical systematization of the worst traits of Stalinism and Maoism combined.

However, North Korea's economic performance prior to this turning-point can be seen in a positive light. At any rate, official South Korean sources and foreign specialists quote the figures claimed by the Kim Il Sung régime. North Korea had, admittedly, started from a much more favourable industrial base in 1945 than the South, producing 95 per cent of the country's steel output, 85 per cent of its chemical production, and 80 per cent of its coal. This partly explains the success of the Stalinist system of industrial planning which enabled North Korea to become the Oriental equivalent of East Germany. However, agricultural resources and education, including university education, expanded considerably. Alone of all the other Asian communist capitals, Pyongyang presented the image of a fully-developed urban centre whose inhabitants, hand-picked by the régime, enjoyed a wide range of social services. There was an unmistakeable element of propaganda in this success-story and a hint of the 'Potemkin village', reminiscent of the painted wooden frontages which Catherine the Great's minister had erected along her route. Later on, the régime readily committed the crudest possible acts of fabrication, for example building a *trompe l'oeil* village opposite the Panmunjon demarcation line. Similarly, a model hospital in Pyongyang, frequently visited by prestigious foreign guests during the 1980s, was actually peopled by actors and extras playing the part of doctors, nurses and patients.

Yet at the end of the 1960s, North Korea remained a respected nation by virtue of its industrial dynamism, which South Korea had yet to catch up with. The independence which Kim Il Sung had managed to achieve by violent means, within a communist system that was on the road to collapse, won him many friends throughout the world, from Ceaucescu's Romania to the Cambodia of Norodom Sihanouk and the French Communist Party of Georges Marchais, to name but a few. In this respect, the system of Kim Il Sung was quite distinct from both its major sponsors, the Soviet Union and China.

North Vietnam between two wars

All anthropologists and sociologists who study Vietnam have stressed the importance of the village system, the bamboo perimeter fence creating a symbolic enclosure for the communal space within. Vietnamese communism was shaped in this image, far more decentralized and more collective in nature, even though rivalry and banishment occurred there too. It was in many ways pragmatic, yet it ultimately proved resistant to successive foreign attempts to influence it. Vietnam is also the only country in Asia to have experienced almost uninterrupted war since 1945, apart from a few years of relative respite after 1954 and a reduction in the immediate threat since 1989, when Vietnamese troops withdrew from Cambodia. While China and Korea used mass mobilization in pursuit of economic and political goals (and while North Korea remains the most highly militarized country in the world), only Vietnam has had uninterrupted experience of communism at war.

Even more so than in neighbouring régimes, this collective leadership was very close-knit. At its centre stood Ho Chi Minh, or 'Uncle Ho', the only leader to enjoy a permanent place in Vietnamese propaganda until his death in 1969. Surrounding him were clustered Le Duan (1908–86), Phan van Dong (1906–92), Truong Chinh (1907–88), Pham Hung (1913–88) and Le Duc Tho (1910–90). All remained in power until their last gasp, and together they attained a political longevity unrivalled in modern times, giving Vietnamese communism a degree of continuity which Maoism, for example, failed to achieve. It was only in 1960 that a Politburo was formed, but its small central group had in fact been in existence ever since the beginnings of Vietnamese communism and held together throughout the course of the century, with a cohesion ultimately unparalleled by other communist systems. There were, admittedly, signs of doctrinal differences in 1954–5, for example when Truong Chinh, an advocate of rapid agricultural collectivization, emerged as a supporter of the Maoist path, although he lacked support from Peking. Phan van Dong, on the other hand, was often regarded, rightly or wrongly, as being more liberal and tolerant of intellectuals and progressive allies, but at the same time he was the faithful lieutenant of General Secretary Le Duan, who succeeded Ho in 1969. Pham Hung appeared to act as the bridge between political control of the army and the security apparatus, particularly during the final phase of the conquest of South Vietnam. As for Le Duc Tho, who negotiated the Paris Agreements of 1973 and consequently won the Nobel Peace Prize, he exemplified the politico-military successes of Vietnam at war, as well as the post-1978 impasse over Cambodia.

The only Chinese influence which this group was willing to acknowledge was a totally negative one, namely factionalism, an old scourge which the Vietnamese deemed to be Chinese and which, during the era of communism at war, they believed could be overcome by unparalleled bonds of collectivism. It is interesting to note the resemblance between this and the situation in South Vietnam. In retrospect, the confidential telegrams of Ellsworth Bunker, the American ambassador in Saigon between 1967 and 1973, suggest that he was haunted by a similar vision of Chinese-style factionalism hindering his efforts to build a viable régime in Saigon.

Yet post-1954 Vietnam was very much inspired by China in earlier days, in terms of accelerated land reform and collectivization, marked by the revolt of the Nghe-Anh peasants who had been the first to organize Rural Soviets in 1930. The revolt was brutally suppressed, casting a shadow over the future of North Vietnam, yet it pales into relative insignificance in comparison with the toll of violence which occurred in China between 1949 and 1952, and also, a fortiori, the Great Leap Forward. In 1956–7, the Vietnamese government also announced a 'Hundred Flowers' policy of liberalization which soon incurred hostility from intellectuals and writers. As in China, this newfound openness subsequently came to an end and most of the country's leading talents were silenced, even imprisoned in many cases. In 1958, Vietnam did not follow the Great Leap Forward, but instead formed 'great co-operatives' throughout the Red Basin delta of Tonkin, which bore the hallmark of the Chinese model. The political rise of General Vo Nguyen Giap, the victor of Dien Bien Phu, began with an open refusal to follow Chinese policy. Before he emerged as a possible source of liberalization after 1975, Giap long gave the impression, rightly or wrongly, of being very close to the Soviet Union. The army was, admittedly, becoming increasingly dependent on Soviet aid, and with its officer class it constituted Vietnam's most modern institution.

Institutions and official ideology were well suited as vehicles for Chinese thinking. It was via these means that Truong Chinh introduced Mao's 'new democracy' in the 1940s, while in 1980, the Vietnamese constitution championed 'three revolutions' which echoed the famous red banners of Maoism, albeit couched in the scientific terms often favoured by the Vietnamese. From 1958, the peasants were deprived of their small private plots of land, which they would regain in 1964. On this level, one of the major contrasts between Vietnam and China was the forceful protest by the Vietnamese communist intellectuals in 1963. However, the Vietnamese communists were torn between dreams of Soviet-style modernization and the waging of a new war which drained all their energies in the early 1960s. It is that policy, as well as the popular legitimacy it conferred on the Communist Party, which serves to explain an organization that was apparently indestructible, yet which also proved resistant to subsequent changes.

How far did Asian communism follow in the footsteps of its Stalinist or Soviet master? Or did Asia, as a peasant society rather than a proletarian one, witness an Asian form of communism with highly specific characteristics? The uniqueness of Maoism as distinct from Leninism has been greatly exaggerated. There is a very precise historical relationship linking Mao's theses and the stance of the International during the 1920s, particularly the Farmers' International (the *Krestintern*) under the influence of the Bolshevik leader Bukharin. It is none the less true to say that Bukharin was not Stalin, and that, on the contrary, his theses were rejected by Stalin in Moscow. Instead, Mao was supposedly inspired by a minority tendency within the Communist International, which happened to be in charge of rural affairs. A number of very diverse elements lend their weight to a second hypothesis, which is that Asian communism was responsible for ideological and systemic innovations to its Soviet mould. On the one hand, China's and even more so Vietnam's concern with the tactical adaptation of land reform programmes represented a major contrast with Stalinist policy. In Asia, a gradual strategy which enabled the survival of a measure of individualism among the rural population often conflicted with the 'Great Change' of collectivization in Moscow in 1929. The political, or at least the physical survival of most of the original communist leaders was yet another feature of both China and Vietnam (though not Korea), whereas Stalin eliminated the former Bolsheviks between 1930 and 1938. This is one of the reasons for the durability of Asian communism, with its endemic system of clan-based patronage, its factional disputes (which in China particularly were of Byzantine complexity) and a struggle over party line which has never really ended, either in China or in Vietnam. There has traditionally existed a vast gulf in Asia between the intellectuals and the masses, which explains why communism has been able to maintain political vigour at the top despite the tragedies it has brought upon the people. By contrast, after 1956, the communist régimes in the Soviet Union and East Europe appeared to relax as far as the people were concerned, but became more firmly entrenched at the top.

East Asia's neo-Confucian ideology resurfaces, sometimes unwittingily, in the movements and structures for political, psychological and moral indoctrination, although it was clearly Lenin who was really responsible for inventing the revolution's mass campaigns and rectification campaigns. Stalinist 'brainwashing' has been described by Arthur Koestler and many others, but the term is none the less Chinese, and the 'thought control' enforced during innumerable study sessions and campaigns of correction and self-criticism was developed on a scale unknown in the Soviet Union. Not even in the Soviet Gulag were these movements driven with so much zeal as they were against Chinese detainees in the prisons and work camps. Other extreme characteristics distinguish Asian communism from its Soviet predecessor. The manner in which Mao and Kim Il Sung were venerated was different from the cult of Stalin. Stalin wished to create a false impression of himself as a man of vision, yet benevolent and straightforward, or calm, wise, humane, sincere, as his own propaganda described the Father of the Peoples. He remained a man, even though he was respected and feared: '*Venga il baffone!*' ('The man with the moustache is coming!') the peasants of Sicily cried in 1947. In contrast, the cults of Mao and Kim Il Sung portrayed them first and foremost as miracle workers and prophets. Although the Great Helmsman and Kim Il Sung were seen as supernatural and remote, they supposedly had the power to reveal themselves to mere mortals, like the Buddha himself. A wave of their hands could cause storms, as Mao effectively did in the summer of 1958, when he launched the Great Leap Forward with tours of the countryside. On Kim Il Sung's eightieth birthday in 1992, propaganda sources revealed that tens of thousands of sparrows had been slaughtered to make him a feather quilt. This touching vignette of rustic well-being was also a disturbing metaphor for a holocaust of another kind which facilitated the irresistible rise of Kim. These often Byzantine personality cults in China and Korea had a more ascetic counterpart in Indochina, as in the austerity-tinged mystique surrounding the whole personality of 'Uncle Ho' as the embodiment of a rural god, but also in the hermetism, the penchant for pseudonyms and the anonymity of the Vietnamese Communist Party, which often changed its name, seemed to disappear periodically, yet guarded its arguments and disputes from any popular participation. In Cambodia, the Khmer Communist Party even hid behind the name of *Angkar* ('The Organization') for most of its brief period in power, while its militants cultivated pseudonyms and misappropriated the term 'brother' for use between themselves, including in the records of torture sessions.

The corollary of this tendency to assume religious transcendence is the frequent recurrence of utopian programmes and convulsive phases in Asia's communist régimes. In China, these took the form of the Great Leap Forward and the Cultural Revolution. In fact, specialists in Chinese political sociology have identified in its economy a strong political cycle of voluntary impulses and forced retreats, which still continues today in times of de-Maoization and reform. North Korea has experienced the mania of stunt-pulling, as seen for example in 1988, at the time of the Seoul Olympics, when it built large numbers of empty skyscrapers in order to affirm its superiority. One of these, the highest man-made structure ever built, is now closed because the mixture of concrete and sand used in its construction made the whole building too dangerous. Lastly, in Cambodia, the whole of the Khmer Rouge programme represented a truly deadly brand of millenarianism. Its attempt to create an independent, autarkic Cambodia on the basis of the empire of Angkor, as well as its genocide and its vast public works based on deportation, culminated in self-destruction.

Once again it is true to say that the North Korean régime defies all attempts at categorization, combining Stalinism, Maoism and elements of the old Korean monarchy. Thus it features a Soviet-style *nomenklatura* and a system, inspired by Maoism, which divides the population into fifty-one classes. However, the hierarchy in North Korea is more openly political in nature and creates a distinct social apartheid. The absolute inflexibility of these boundaries and the degree of privilege accorded to the highest class, that is the revolutionary cadres and their families, clearly evoke the *yangban* aristocracy of the old hermit kingdom. In contrast, the physical elimination of victims of dwarfism by the government, one of its many brutal acts, is an example of eugenic killing that is without parallel in any other communist régime and is a direct echo of Nazism. Any comparative study of Asia's communist systems must consequently pay more attention to the power of spiritual traditions than was the case during the Soviet freeze. The rejection of these traditions by communism has not stopped them being reused by subsequent régimes in a perverted form. Added to this, there is the magnetic attraction of the eschatology offered to the rural population: the abolition of the property-owning classes and the glorification of 'the people' have inspired many successive generations of Chinese youth, even though there is more sympathy for the persecuted former élites, especially intellectuals, than might generally be expected. Following successive waves of mobilization and their failure (in Vietnam, the wars and the eventual crisis after 1979 had the same effect), society drifted back towards the imitative reflexes of the traditional clan system and, more generally, to the patronage on which the communist movement has always based its own organization.

SELECTED READING

Barnett, A. D. (1967) *Cadres, bureaucracy and political power in Communist China*, New York: Columbia University Press.

Bergère, M. (1989) *The golden age of the Chinese bourgeoisie*, Cambridge: Cambridge University Press.

Boudarel, G. (1991) *Cent fleurs écloses dans la nuit du Vietnam: communisme et dissidence, 1954–1956*, Paris: Jacques Bertoin.

Chandler, D. P. (1991) *The tragedy of Cambodian history: politics, war and revolution since 1945*, New Haven: Yale University Press.

Chang, P. H. (1978) *Power and policy in China*, Philadelphia: Pennsylvania University Press.

Dittmer, L. (1974) *Liu Shao-ch'i and the Chinese Cultural Revolution: the politics of mass criticism*, Berkeley: University of California Press.

Domenach, J. L. (1982) *Aux origines du Grand bond en avant: le cas d'une province chinoise, 1956–1958*, Paris: Éditions de l'École des Hautes Études en Sciences Sociales et de la FNSP.

——(1992) *Chine, l'archipel oublié*, Paris: Fayard.

Domes, J. (1980) *Socialism in the Chinese countryside*, London: C. Hurst.

Dreyer, J. T. (1976) *China's forty millions: minority nationalities and national integration in the People's Republic of China*, Cambridge, MA: Harvard University Press.

Duiker, W. J. (1983) *Vietnam: nation in revolution*, Boulder: Westview Press.

Ellison, H. J. (1982) *The Sino-Soviet conflict: a global perspective*, Seattle: University of Washington Press.

Feray, P. (1984) *Le Viet-nam*, Paris: Presses Universitaires de France.

Fitzgerald, F. (1972) *Fire in the lake*, New York: Little, Brown & Co.

Goldman, M. (1967) *Literary dissent in Communist China*, Cambridge, MA: Harvard University Press.

Guillermaz, J. (1979) *Le Parti communiste chinois au pouvoir*, Paris: Payot.

Harrison, S. S. (1978) *The widening gulf: Asian nationalism and American policy*, New York: The Free Press.

Howe, C. (1978) *China's economy: a basic guide*, Cambridge: Paul Elek.

Lardy, N. (1978) *Economic growth and distribution in China*, Cambridge, MA: Cambridge University Press.

Leys, S. (1974) *Ombres chinoises*, Paris: 10/18.

Lifton, R. J. (1961) *Thought reform and the psychology of totalism: a study of brainwashing in China*, New York: W. Norton.

MacFarquhar, R. (1974 and 1983) *The origins of the Cultural Revolution*, 2 vols, London: Oxford University Press and Columbia University Press.

——et al. (eds) (1989) *The secret speeches of Chairman Mao: from the Hundred Flowers to the Great Leap Forward*, Cambridge, MA: Harvard University Press.

Mandares, H. et al. (eds) (1974) *Revo cul dans la Chine pop: anthologie de la presse des Gardes rouges*, Paris: 10/18.

Parish, W. L. and Whyte, M. K. (1978) *Village and family in contemporary China*, Chicago: Chicago University Press.

Pasqualini, J. (1975) *Prisonnier de Mao: sept ans dans un camp de travail en Chine*, Paris: Gallimard.

Rice, E. E. (1972) *Mao's way*, Berkeley: University of California Press.

Roux, A. (1983) *La Chine populaire*, 2 vols, Paris: Éditions sociales.

Sah, D. (1984) *Korean communism and the rise of Kim*, Ann Arbor: University Microfilms.

Salisbury, H. E. (1992) *The new emperors: China in the era of Mao and Deng*, New York: Avon Books.

Schram, S. (ed.) (1977) *Mao parle au pouvoir, 1956–1971*, Paris: Presses Universitaires de France.

Schurmann, F. (1971) *Ideology and organization in Communist China*, Berkeley: University of California Press.

Soeya, Y. (1987) *Japan's postwar diplomacy with China: three decades of non-governmental experience*, Ann Arbor: University Microfilms.

Solomon, R. H. (1971) *Mao's revolution and the Chinese political culture*, Berkeley: University of California Press.

——(ed.) (1981) *The China factor*, New York: Spectrum.

Teiwes, F. C. (1979) *Politics and purges in China: rectification and the decline of Party norms, 1950–1965*, Armonk: M. E. Sharpe.

Zafanolli, W. (1981) *Le Président clairvoyant contre la veuve du timonier*, Paris: Payot.

6 Japan and democracy (1945–74)

Japan lay in ruins when, on 15 August 1945, Emperor Hirohito addressed his subjects in a radio broadcast. In courtly language which few of his listeners understood, Hirohito shielded himself by reference to the precedent of the Emperor Meiji surrendering to Western pressure in 1895; yet he also clearly evoked the danger of 'seeing the nation reduced to ashes' (Horsley and Buckley 1990:1). The Japanese economy, locked in a stranglehold by an air and sea blockade from the summer of 1944 onwards, had been devastated by bombings which had razed all the main cities apart from Kyoto. Millions of Japanese soldiers and settlers scattered throughout Asia found themselves trapped by the Pacific War and either drifted home or were taken prisoner. Food shortages began to take hold across the archipelago and, in the closing days of the war, many factories and government stockpiles were moved or ransacked, sometimes out of a concern to safeguard equipment, but more usually in order to fuel the black market. The imperial army had prepared a fortified hideout for Hirohito in the mountains at the heart of the archipelago and planned to resist any invasion hand-to-hand, but the United States, basing its plans on the course of events of the previous months, counted on invading first Kyushu, then the main island of Japan, without any expectation of heavy losses on their own side. Throughout the Pacific War, Japanese losses were over ten times higher than those of the United States. The tradition of the *bushido* (the 'way of the warrior' or samurai code of honour), elevated to mythical status by General Tojo, prevented Prime Minister Kantaro Suzuki from responding directly to the Allied ultimatum issued at Potsdam on 25 July 1945. In particular, he hoped to secure a guarantee that the Emperor would not be removed, but without success. Although the imperial government had received a broad indication that a terrible weapon was about to be used, it continued the hostilities, thereby exposing its people to the nuclear bombing of Hiroshima and Nagasaki. It was Hirohito himself who took the decision to surrender on 15 August. Japan was immediately occupied and lost its independence. This it did not regain until the ratification of the San Francisco Peace Treaty with the United States in April 1952, a peace which it did not sign with the communist states, and has still not signed with the former Soviet Union in 1996.

Japan's subsequent renaissance is still the subject of much enquiry on the part of historians. How was the American desire to graft certain democratic reforms onto the practices and character of Japanese political life as it stood before militarism actually achieved? Above all, how did Japan manage to rise to the number one position among the leading industrial countries?

Between the Japan of the period immediately following 1945, whose people survived by selling bamboo knick-knacks, Christmas decorations and china figurines to the United States, and the Japan of the early 1970s, which was already then making its mark as the world's leading producer of optics, electronics and motorcycles, there were, none the less, a number of common features, which domestic prosperity was slow to remove. The most important of these was indubitably the way in which the Japanese maintained a sense of their own uniqueness and vulnerability. Although the post-war years had Americanized Japan's outward face, the physical and political isolation caused both by the odium of its neighbours and by the Cold War in Asia accentuated its singularity. Above all, it may be the fact that the Japanese are so painfully aware of their own separateness and vulnerability that makes them the world's best translators, adapters, explorers and, all in all, the best connoisseurs. Their thirst for knowledge, which was later to contribute to the economic and technological strategies of their firms, originally stemmed from the collector's ability to accumulate knowledge about human beings, societies, art forms which they admire for being so different. It is this which enables them to produce the best documentaries on the ethnic groups of the South Pacific and amass information on the wines of Bordeaux and the villas of Tuscany, just as they possessed the best social science experts during the colonial era, and just as the style-watchers in the major car manufacturers understand better than anyone else the needs and aspirations of American consumers.

Pre-war colonial and imperial policies had caused millions of Japanese to intermingle, and in some cases become assimilated, with other Asian nationals, a process which was suspended in the post-war era. Instead, the economic and political crucible of Japan was to become a prototype that would ultimately be an inspiration to its neighbours and, in certain respects, the envy of the rest of the world.

THE IMPACT OF THE OCCUPATION (1945–52)

MacArthur and SCAP

Japan at the time of its defeat and occupation has been immortalized in *The street of shame* and other post-war realist films, although they never depict the Americans: they portray better than any long verbal description the dislocation caused by the rejection of traditional values. The demoralized population burst the psychological and political bonds which conditioned them in the past. This resulted in a powerful surge towards socialism and communism, creating the worst period of political instability in Japanese history. Added to this there was the impact of the United States Occupation by SCAP (Supreme Command of Allied Powers). During the brief closing phase of the Roosevelt administration, Japan's new course was determined by a combination of Democrat political advisers, many of them advocates of the New Deal, and army officers, led by a Republican administrator, General MacArthur. The Americans had started preparing for a military government back in early 1942, before the Battle of Midway. Admittedly, the Morgenthau plan's vision of 'pasteurizing' German and Japanese society had already been abandoned. However, the original occupation plan directly attacked the Japanese spirit, its feudalism and the overwhelming dominance of the *zaibatsu*, Japan's large industrial–financial conglomerates. MacArthur spoke of establishing 'democracy and Christianity' in Japan, and it was United States army officers who conducted journalists to the prisons where Japanese communists still languished in October 1945, an episode which provided the pretext for the dismantling of the Home Ministry and the political police, which still stood intact (Guillain, 1986). The effects of this policy soon resulted in the purging of 200,000 individuals for their wartime responsibilities and the abolition of the Meiji constitution, to be replaced by a text largely drafted in MacArthur's office. The famous Article 9 of this document prohibited Japan from possessing an army and from taking part in any war. These restrictions prompted a parliamentary debate, and even the Japanese communists in the Diet stressed the country's right to legitimate defence. In order to secure the adoption of Article 9, Prime Minister Shigeru Yoshida favoured a restrictive interpretation permitting the formation in 1950, if not of an army, then at least a 150,000-strong self-defence force. However, Yoshida continued to rely on the United States' initial hesitation as a way of limiting military expenditure, particularly in the face of later American pressure to increase it. SCAP policies also led to the dismantling of the major industrial groups, land reform leading to the confiscation of landlords' estates, the liberalization of education and the granting of freedom of action to all political and trade union organizations. Overseas, especially in the United Kingdom, Australia and New Zealand, where many soldiers had endured horrific conditions in the Japanese prisoner-of-war camps, there was pressure to try Emperor Hirohito for war crimes, just as was about to happen to the Nazi leaders at Nuremberg.

This purging and revolution from above which took place in Japanese institutions and society enabled the re-emergence, within a few years, of a political, economic and social life that was ultimately much closer to its pre-war form than had been anticipated in 1945. One of the most prominent examples of this was the political survival both of Hirohito himself and of the respect, if not the cult, which surrounded him. Similarly, there was a rapid reinstatement of pre-war political and administrative personnel and a parallel purge of 'Reds' from government and business in 1950–51. The very limited use, in effect, of anti-trust legislation was abandoned completely over time. On an economic level, the institutions, methods of oversight and management which had been set up during wartime were reintroduced, leading to an extremely rapid industrial and financial renaissance. Lastly, the onset of rearmament, followed by moves to bring education back under partial political control and the adoption of national security legislation also harked back to the pre-war political system, albeit in a more limited way.

The chrysanthemum school versus history

There has long been an avoidance of debate over these issues. The best-known works on the period, by Edwin Reischauer (1987), who as US ambassador was also a key player in the events which he later analysed, and Ruth Benedict (1946), both portrayed the new Japan as following a royal road towards democratization and westernization. In so doing, they avoided the responsibility of SCAP itself which, from 1948 onwards, because of its obsession with anti-communism and anti-Sovietism, was largely to blame for jeopardizing the reforms declared in 1946–7: this is the whole crux of the second occupation phase, when the 'reverse course' succeeded an abortive reform programme inspired by the New Deal. Furthermore, these authors perceived as great friends of the United States individuals who, as many archives and memoirs published have since shown, were pragmatic yet nationalistic Japanese politicians. The most striking example was Shigeru Yoshida himself, the Prime Minister who dominated the post-war period up to 1954, and who came across as a Japanese Adenauer. Through courtesy, flattery and evasion, he continually isolated the keenest advocates of reform within SCAP in order to capitalize on the fear of the 'Reds'. Extremists on right and left alike often accused him of being an 'American lackey', yet in 1950 he wrote in his memoirs: 'Just as the United States was a British colony but is now the more powerful, so Japan will become the stronger of the two partners' (Yoshida, 1962). Reischauer frequently underestimated the skill and effort with which Japanese politicians and civil servants strove to minimize the harsh effects of American decisions. The American school known as 'the chrysanthemum and the sword', after the title of Benedict's famous book, found it hard to reconcile, on the one hand, its westernized vision of the new Japan as the friend of the United States, supposedly witnessed by the fact of entente and friendly negotiations with Japan, and, on the other, its own culturalism regarding Japanese society itself. In the name of this culturalism, they recommended placing strong emphasis on the immutable nature of Japan's own individual characteristics and not treating it as an ordinary partner. As a historian, Reischauer, who in his official capacity as ambassador had represented the strong arm of American domination, adopted a somewhat vindicatory view of Japan, often concealing the dubious past of some of his interviewees. Later on, the irremovable former Democratic senator Mike

Mansfield was accused by some of acting as a Japanese ambassador to Washington, rather than vice versa, in the cause of maintaining Japanese–American relations.

The revisionists and the theory of Japanese uniqueness

In reaction against this highly westernized view of post-war Japan and in response to the frustrations the United States encountered as it found itself increasingly challenged for economic supremacy, a revisionist school was formed in the 1970s, represented by Chalmers Johnson (1982) and Karel van Wolferen (1990). Becoming increasingly widespread and ever more controversial, the revisionist school simultaneously posited a considerable measure of continuity between the pre- and post-war periods, the unique and irreducible nature of Japanese culture and society and the total inability of criteria based on the Western democracies to describe Japanese political and economic affairs. This view was not restricted to any particular political persuasion: as well as traditional conservatives opposed to Japanese nationalism, it also included progressives eager to create a social revolution that would finally bring the work of the Occupation to an end. The ethnocentric attitude shared by these Westerners towards Japan ironically coincided with the view of many Japanese, for whom westernization was never anything other than a necessary evil, particularly in the political and intellectual spheres, or who, conversely, denounced what was perceived as the inadequate, even hollow nature of the democratization process. Once again, the first of these groups included Shigeru Yoshida himself, who was quick to deposit the peace protocol to the San Francisco Treaty at the foot of Mount Ise, the imperial Shinto shrine, before presenting himself to Hirohito as his 'loyal servant Shigeru'. This very careful wording in itself totally contradicted the separation of Emperor and state and the principle of government accountability to the country, which the authors of the 1946 constitution had aimed to instil. Yet the Japanese left, socialists and communists alike, also persistently attacked the United States and criticized any form of compliance with it, especially the security treaty. It is worth recalling that while the Japanese communists were the only constant opposition force working against Japanese militarism prior to 1945, the socialists, then renamed the Social Masses Party, often collaborated in the building of an indigenous brand of national socialism. As with the German Greens, the anti-Americanism of the Japanese left was fuelled by a variety of more or less conscious influences.

This debate was followed with avid interest by the Japanese themselves. In the final analysis, the dilemma was not so much between the different schools of interpretation, but rather lay at the very heart of the matter, for the Japanese remained extremely unsure as to their own status between Asia and the West, and even as to the very form their institutions should take: the dispute over the revision of the 1946 constitution lasted until at least

1950. The Marxist schools of thought which have left such an indelible mark on Japanese academics and intellectuals also came together shortly after the war, resurrecting arguments from the 1920s. More important still, the process of reconciliation – between victors and vanquished, between democracy and the preservation of the imperial system (*tenno*) and national identity (*kokutai*), between democratization and the protection of existing positions, and between freedom and fears of communist-inspired movements – called for considerable pragmatism and compromise. This was sometimes achieved at the cost of rhetorical contortions and the habitual use of ambiguous, provisional clauses, which later came to burden political discourse. The greatest quality of Japan's post-war politicians was that they tried to reconcile the irreconcilable, just as Hirohito, in his capitulation speech, had spoken of 'enduring the unendurable' – rejecting militarism yet restoring institutions similar to those of the Taisho period, establishing democracy yet reinstating personnel from the pre-war parties, limiting semi-monopolies in the economy yet maintaining industrial efficiency, surrendering to the dictates of the United States yet holding on to a measure of autonomy for the future.

They were assisted in this by the policy of the Occupation, which from the outset was limited to governing Japan indirectly, unlike Germany in 1945. Imperial officials therefore played a key part in the chaotic transition which took place in 1945–6, especially since the Americans were in a poor position to grasp the intricate workings of Japanese society. In particular, SCAP laid down very clear guidelines for the purges, which were gradually relaxed as the Cold War developed. Once again, Yoshida may serve as an example. When one of his collaborators was targeted by the 1948 purges, Yoshida exhorted him to 'think of himself as having been bitten by a mad dog'. Yet Japanese historians strongly suspect Yoshida of having contributed, with MacArthur, to the sacking of his main conservative rival, Ichiro Hatoyama. Yoshida, a diplomat (like both the other post-war conservative prime ministers) as well as an anglophile and advocate of a Pax Americana which would renew the entente with England that had prevailed at the beginning of the century, was a genuine admirer of capitalism. In the final days of the war he was imprisoned for his involvement in a group which, along with Prince Konoe, accused General Tojo and his faction of preparing for the introduction of communism by finally taking control over the economy. Yet it was the United States the superpower which he admired, not the United States the democracy. 'Whilst we have much to learn from the West in terms of abstract logic, I remain convinced that Chinese literature and poetry are infinitely more valuable for their ability to grasp human relationships.' (Yoshida 1962: 221) This distinction echoed the perpetual slogan which had accompanied Asian restorations since the nineteenth century, setting Western methods in contradistinction to the Oriental soul. It was reinforced by certain archetypal tensions inherent in the Japanese psyche: the pairing of *omote–ura* (revealed appearance–concealed interior) and the contrast between *tatemae* (declared principle) and *honne* (actual practice). These collective mental traits, derived from the submissiveness of the past and the traditional code of conduct, resurfaced in the relationship between occupied Japan and its Western masters and appeared to persist. Over and above the influence of Japan's own traditions, the constraints imposed during the Occupation era were instrumental in creating this split personality. Thus, as far as their political institutions were concerned, the Japanese often explicitly sought to adopt the British system as their inspiration (rather than the American one, thus reviving one of two pre-war traditions, the other being an admiration for Prussia). Yet the heart of the country's political life – its *jinmyaku*, or 'personal links' which, even more so than in the West, place a premium on loyalty, the mutual exchange of services rendered, and the role of the clan – remained very much Japanese. The psychological and cultural tensions which stemmed from this illustrate a fundamental ambiguity underlying the task of adapting the modern age to Japan.

THE TRANSITION TOWARDS A NEO-CLASSICAL SYSTEM

These signs of psychological and social continuity clearly show that any attempt to divide the post-war period into periods has its limitations. It is, of course, necessary to distinguish between, first, the initial occupation and the lead-up to it (September 1945 to February 1947) and, second, the 'reverse course' launched by the Americans following the threat of strikes in February 1947, then the period of the Korean War (June 1950 to July 1953), which Shigeru Yoshida described as a 'gift from the gods' for the Japanese economy. This marked the starting-point for what was very much a neo-classical era in Japanese history: the United States provided the alliance which had formerly been anticipated with Great Britain, while a parliamentary system resurrected from the 1920s proved little obstacle to an economic dirigisme left over from 1930–40. The era began with the signing of the San Francisco Peace Treaty and the US–Japan security treaty in September 1951. In November 1954, Yoshida was ousted by his old enemy Ichiro Hatoyama, who rebuilt a grand conservative coalition by merging the post-war parties into the Liberal Democratic Party (LDP) in November 1955. The economy was put at the top of the agenda until the period of the Nobusuke Kishi cabinet (February 1957 to July 1960), when the renegotiation of the security treaty caused heated debate nationwide. After Kishi, the era of economism returned in the shape of Prime Minister Hayato Ikeda, who in 1960 made his famous promise to 'double the income' of the Japanese. He was succeeded in November 1964 by Eisaku Sato, who set a record for political longevity until his departure in November 1972. Then came Kakuei Tanaka, champion electioneer in his Niigata constituency as well as in the Diet. As a former Finance Minister, his own ambitious plan to 'reconstruct the Japanese archipelago' through major public works and the launch of the high-speed train (*shinkansen*) to iron out regional inequalities, echoed Ikeda's promises to the Japanese. Despite successes abroad, notably the diplomatic recognition of China, the Tanaka era ended in November 1974 with the Lockheed affair, the biggest political and financial scandal since 1945. Tanaka's own blundering and the part played by the US Congress were crucial to this episode, which laid bare the corruption in Japanese politics. The pillars of the temple had finally cracked, and the role of money in Japanese politics would in future periodically undermine the power of the Liberal Democratic Party. From then on, Japanese politics would be exposed to the microphones and spotlights of the international press. Foreign efforts to achieve a greater opening-up of the country also affected the authority of the conservative party. None the less, the opposition parties failed to make any long-term inroads into LDP supremacy until 1993.

Politicians and the personal continuity of conservatism

Yet if we discount the influence of international events and American policy, this period displays considerable continuity from a Japanese point of view, particularly as far as personalities are concerned. During the war, Yoshida, formerly a diplomat under Shidehara, the most able of all the pre-war Foreign Ministers, had likewise followed Prince Konoe, the former Prime Minister, whose procrastination had helped push the country down the road to war. Unlike the ruling military, both men believed in a need for caution. In 1945, they mobilized to save the imperial system. Subsequently, however, Konoe was accused of 'war crimes' and committed suicide, whereupon Yoshida went so far as to buy Konoe's house and move into his bedroom. There was nothing to distinguish him from his rival Hatoyama, who was targeted in the 1946 purges on account of his greater prominence prior to 1941, but later returned to the political stage, succeeding Yoshida in 1954. While in office, Yoshida formed a clan which dominated the Diet, appointing seventy-nine ministers who thus owed him their careers. His two right-hand men were Ikeda and Sato, in other words the same men who were to lead Japan from the demise of the Kishi cabinet until 1972. The politician who, at sixty-eight years of age in 1946, owed his rise to the top to a combination of circumstances, ultimately notched up more than twenty-five years of political history. Kishi himself, who held office in 1957–60 but then continued to wield considerable influence within the LDP, had co-signed the declaration of war in 1941. A close relative of the general manager of the pre-war Nissan *zaibatsu*, at the age of forty-six he was the youngest-ever head of the Ministry of Commerce and Industry, the forerunner of the post-war MITI – a key post which explains the three years he spent in prison after 1945. Moreover, he was also the half-brother of future Prime Minister Eisaku Sato.

This continuity at the top was also mirrored in the principal institutions, as well as in the political parties themselves. With the exception of the Co-operative Party founded by Takeo Miki in 1947, all were a direct continuation of the pre-war period. Miki, who was undoubtedly the first 'outsider' to figure in Japanese politics, took on the military following his election to the Diet in 1937. It took the Tanaka scandal for the LDP party bosses to nominate him Prime Minister for a brief period from 1974–6. While in office, he made a vain attempt at some political reforms, which notably included putting an end to the way that the factions operated with the LDP. Yet it was also Miki who made a symbolic gesture designed to mark continuity: for the first time, albeit in a private capacity, he visited Yasukuni Temple on 15 August for the annual ceremony to commemorate the war dead. Among the plaques dedicated to great numbers of soldiers at Yakasuni (where 2,400,000 names are inscribed), there also figured those chiefly responsible for the Pacific War, including the Prime Minister and General Tojo. By going there one month after his San Francisco trip to sign the peace treaty, Yoshida had created an ambiguity. Yasuhiro Nakasone, that most dynamic and nationalistic of all the Japanese post-war prime ministers, took it one stage further by making a similar visit in an official capacity for the August 1985 ceremony. Protests from several Asian countries, including China and South Korea, forced subsequent leaders to abandon this innovation until Kiichi Miyazawa resurrected it in 1992, this time in a personal capacity.

This action and policy on the part of Nakasone, who had only been a young officer in 1945, showed that it was not by any means necessary to have belonged to the pre-war political or bureaucratic classes to carry on the tradition, even at the cost of public controversy. However he was the exception, and continuity still appeared to be the rule. Thus, until 1976, all successive deputy ministers at MITI had belonged to its predecessor organizations: the Ministry of Commerce, founded in 1925 and renamed the Ministry of Munitions in 1943, resumed its former appellation shortly before the Japanese defeat and in 1949 became the Ministry of International Trade and Industry (MITI). This continuity of personnel was, as we will see, equally great in economic organizations such as the two main employers' organizations, the Keidanren and the Keizai Doyukai, in other government bodies, notably the Home Ministry, renamed the Ministry of 'Self-Management', and among the surviving members of the class of young officers which had graduated from military academy after 1941, and who were reclaimed by the self-defence forces from 1954. In his memoirs, Yoshida himself presented as his second triumph (after that of saving the imperial throne) the fact that he had secured the right for the leading Japanese *zaibatsu*, even in cases where they had been dismantled, to retain their highly prestigious names (Mitsui, Mitsubishi, etc.) for their parent companies. From 1947 these names remained in abeyance until the relaxation of Japanese anti-trust legislation in 1952.

The driving forces behind the Liberal Democratic Party

From the beginning of the Meiji era up until 1993, a conservative majority has only once been voted out of office, and that was between May 1947 and March 1948, when the socialist Tetsu Katayama held power. Nevertheless, this merely meant a coalition, with the left remaining in the minority within the Diet and in the country at large. This did not prevent factional splits forming in the conservative ranks: before the war the two main parliamentary parties, the Minseito and the Seiyukai, were backed by Mitsubishi and Mitsui respectively. The clans uniting politicians and civil servants (*hanbatsu*) were a tradition dating back to the Meiji era. In 1955, several smaller movements came together under the aegis of the LDP. Despite several subsequent rifts, and cycles when its popularity waxed and waned, the party's domination of Japanese politics indubitably justified the ironic term 'one-party democracy' applied to the Japanese system (Ike, 1972: 76). This domination has resulted in parties staying permanently in opposition, their strategies rarely aimed at bringing about a change of government, but more often realistically designed to head off competition from the other minority parties. The Japanese Socialist Party (JSP) has succeeded in doing this better than the rest, but by hiding behind a front of doctrinaire utopianism – a solid tradition of granting political favours to rural voters and trade unions which rivals that of the LDP. Again, like the LDP, each opposition party is dependent on the organizations which finance it and its interests, including the permanent trade unions of the Sohyo, the rural leagues, the North Korean and Soviet sponsors who fund the JSP, the reformist trade unions which back the social democrats, and a Buddhist sect which finances the Komeito. Only the LDP, in one sense, manages to avoid such constraints, since, by spreading its need for support across a range of client groups, it can ultimately control and manipulate them within its orbit. What is seen in Japan is therefore what Robert Scalapino has called a 'one-and-a-half party democracy' (Hrebenar, 1986: 6), rather than a genuine multi-party system. Among the opposition, particularly in the Socialist Party and above all the LDP, factions or *habatsu* formed once again, bringing together the members of the Diet themselves, but not the bureaucracy. Though initially numerous and characterized by intense personal loyalty to their leaders, they were rationalized in the early 1970s, becoming in many cases more depersonalized, yet they never developed into tendencies or movements between which a political, ideological or even a policy debate could spring up.

How far did the LDP's aims and methods ensure this dominance? In 1947, the number of socialist and communist voters had risen to 30 per cent of the electorate, the highest ever attained by the left. The LDP vote has been remarkably stable ever since, at 45 to 50 per cent of the electorate, the variation being due to independent conservative candidates crossing over to the LPD after elections and to extremely moderate opposition forces such as the Social Democratic Party, the Buddhists of the Komeito and, later, the New Liberal Club. The relationship between the latter and the leaders of the LDP factions was often more marked than the effort which it put into bringing about political alternation. Apart from local elections, particularly in the major cities, the opposition parties never succeeded in ousting the LDP, although the latter did lose its absolute majority in the Diet for a time during the early 1970s.

Political supporters and electoral districts

The structural causes of the LDP's near-monopoly are now well known, and indeed have not changed a great deal since the 1950s. The LDP is not set up as a centralized party or a mass party, but instead rests on two pillars: its factions and the personal supporters of each member of the Diet. Within the factions a strict discipline is imposed, ensuring semi-automatic access to the most coveted posts, particularly the ministries, according to seniority. Within each individual constituency, members form a *koenkai*, or network of supporters, consisting of other local Diet members, activists and political sympathizers. This extensive network – which in the case of an efficient politician may include up to a third of the local electorate – forms both a channel for services rendered to voters and a propaganda network, and is also extremely expensive to finance, as are the different headquarters for each Diet member. The emphasis is on services rendered to the elector- ate, rather than ideology. This system means that the members of the Japanese Diet are primarily 'grassroots politicians', close to their electorate, and even lobbyists, while minimizing their interest in nationwide issues. This may also be attributed to the notorious idiosyncrasies of the Japanese electoral system: in one and the same constituency, several members were elected simultanously in a single round of majority voting, and yet each voter only had one choice; therefore, in order to maintain a majority in the Diet, a large party like the LDP had to pick several candidates for the same constituency, who would inevitably compete with one another and try to build up their own personal body of supporters, displaying only a notional allegiance to their political party. Conversely, the smaller opposition parties with a more pronounced ideological base, like the socialists and the communists, had to limit the number of their candidates, because if they allowed their vote to be split across several candidates within the same constituency, they ran the risk of seeing none elected whatsoever. It was therefore extremely difficult for them to up their representation quickly, even when public opinion shifted in their favour. Furthermore, their Diet members are tied to their local electorate by the same bonds of patronage. Seats are transferred and handed down, giving Japanese politicians a dimension of patronage, nepotism and sometimes even dynastic ties.

The division of power at the top

Though decentralized, the LDP is still based on a highly codified system of relationships at the top. Its principal leaders are nominated by agreement between the factions, whether in the majority or not, and the main rival factions are brought together in the formation of ministerial teams. The duration of ministerial posts is very short in order to satisfy those waiting in the wings. This is the key to the considerable power which senior civil servants wield over decisions, since the politicians themselves rarely have the time to build up the necessary expertise or set up technical teams. While the majority system of politics seems remarkably stable on the whole, this stability is achieved through the permanent redistribution of posts between factions and politicians, according to the alliances between the former and the seniority of the latter. Individual security and politics are thus merged, although this inevitably makes government decisions unpredictable and susceptible to influence. However, in this respect the Japanese model of public affairs is not nearly as monolithic as the overall lack of political alternation might suggest.

The prototype 'catch-all party'

It is these factors which have given the LDP its flexibility and pragmatism. The party is an amalgam of interests and client groups drawn from a very wide range of spheres, yet the opposition resembles it in many ways. A number of members of the Diet are also representatives for trade unions, farmers, teachers, the professions and assorted trade federations run on a sectoral basis. From the outset the LDP has always participated in friendship visits to an extremely diverse range of foreign countries, including China and North Korea. At the same time, a system of 'tribes' (*zoku*) of Diet members has evolved, based on the activity of each ministry or major administrative body, from the prestigious MITI to the postal administration. These play a crucial part in channelling public money into their constituencies and, in terms of power, they have taken over from the all-powerful bureaucrats of the immediate post-war period. Thus Kakuei Tanaka, the undisputed champion of political electioneering before he himself became the victim of it, managed to arrange for a special branch of the Japanese high-speed rail link, the Shinkansen, to be laid to his rural, isolated mountain constituency of Niigata, on the Sea of Japan. A feature of the Japanese economy, also linked to this form of pressure on politicians, is the increasingly large deficit run up by government bodies and public concerns (though not the central state budget). The Diet rarely intervenes openly in the preparation of the budget, but the civil servants – who draw up the expenditure plans prior to receiving the corresponding income – make up for this. The ministries which appear to be the most powerful, such as the Finance Ministry, MITI or the Ministry of Foreign Affairs, in fact have access to fewer funds than ministries such as Agriculture, Construction or Home Ministries, which, though less prestigious, are deeply involved in local expenditure.

The best example of this is undoubtedly the persistent influence of the Agriculture Ministry, which epitomizes the alliance between political conservatism and the small independent farmers. In physical terms, the Ministry occupies one of the four corners of the large Kasumigaseki office block in Tokyo, a prime location which it shares with Foreign Affairs, MITI and the Finance Ministry. Since the war, an authentic social contract has bound the conservatives to the farming community. In 1941, a policy to subsidize purchase prices for small farmers and agricultural workers (but not landlords) transformed the social hierarchy of rural Japan. The 1947 land reform, though tolerated rather than welcomed by conservatives, improved the lot of farming families and, later, of households which combined part-time farm work with employment in other sectors. Because the rural regions, particularly of the interior and the north of the country, have been over-represented in parliament during the post-war period, rural support has become an important base for the LDP, which in turn has kept farm prices high, to the detriment of urban consumers. Full and part-time farmers, who comprise 20 per cent of the population, elect 30 per cent of Diet members. Furthermore, as competition for votes within the urban constituencies is more open and more ideologically-based, many minority votes are lost, helping to enhance the value of the 'tactical' rural vote. At the time of its sharpest decline in 1973, the LDP still held nearly 50 per cent of the seats in the Diet with barely more than 20 per cent of the vote in the major cities. This example gives a clearer illustration of the populist and sometimes old-fashioned roots of Japanese conservatism and the powerful obstacles which exist to any change.

Money and politics

Yet another feature of the system is the barely-concealed way in which Japanese firms increasingly finance not only the LDP but also many other politicians and organizations. This form of funding, which had already been a tradition before the Second World War, increased continuously until the scandals of the 1970s, 1980s and even the 1990s. The post-war period was marked by numerous sensational incidents such as the Showa Denko affair of 1948 and the naval shipyards affair of 1954 which helped to bring down Yoshida: his principal lieutenants, Ikeda and Sato, were only saved from arrest because of intervention by the Minister of Justice. Recent decades have shed more light on the way political funding and corruption operate in Japan. Following the revelations of bribery in the 1974 Lockheed affair, pressure from abroad (particularly the United States) and promises of a clean-up gave added weight to the revelations of some quarters of the Japanese press. In a system which closely combines *dirigisme*, or state control, at all levels of the economy with patronage seen as the ultimate form of electioneering, scandals are inevitable and scarcely punished. Furthermore, voters and politicians alike frequently deplore the consequences. Once charged, and in some cases sentenced, the politicians concerned seek *misogi* (ritual purification) from their voters at the next election, thus cleansing themselves of the taint of corruption. Before Tanaka, Sato and above all Kishi were implicated in financial scandals on a number of occasions without sustaining any major damage to their careers.

Democracy challenged

The continuity with the pre-war era in terms of political personnel, the resurgence of nationalism and the dominance of the LDP and the bureaucracy resulted in two successive challenges to the Japanese political system. The first, echoing the frustration felt by the Americans during the Occupation, highlighted the intimidatory effect, sometimes even verging on blackmail, that extreme right-wing ideas and groups could have on Japanese society. A whole host of examples were cited as proof of this, ranging from the campaign for the revision of the constitution led by one wing of the LDP, to gradual moves to restore political control of education and school textbooks, and the existence of right-wing organizations as fanatical as they were aggressive. In particular, right-wing groups were responsible for an assassination attempt on former Prime Minister Kishi, accused of 'treason', then for the assassination of the President of the Japanese Socialist Party in October 1960 and a number of more recent fatal attacks on officials and ordinary citizens who dared to question Hirohito's part in the lead-up to the war. In 1970, the suicide of famous Japanese novelist Yukio Mishima was partly ridiculed, partly elevated to symbolic status by critics of this constantly-recurring extreme right-wing movement: after breaking into the headquarters of the Japanese self-defence forces, he committed *harakiri* on live television.

All in all, however, it was generally a new breed of political violence which flourished in post-war Japanese society, with demonstrations by the trade unions and left-wing political groups in 1947 and the row over the US–Japan security treaty in 1957–60. At the beginning of the 1970s, the Zengakuren, an extra-parliamentary student league founded in 1948, stirred up a number of violent street riots, rather than assassination attempts. Their subsequent decline into factionalism as well as the growth of an underground Red Army, produced more dangerous results. Often, however, protest and even violence were transformed into ritualized confrontation worthy of *kabuki* theatre, as in the long-drawn-out battle over the very existence of Tokyo's Narita airport which arose between the police and the student leagues allied with the local farmers. This interminable dispute followed on in a direct line from the struggle in the 1950s by the rural community and the left against the setting up of American bases and the consequent expropriation of land.

To combat these albeit relatively few risks, and particularly to maintain the traditional docility of the urban population, the post-war governments quickly reasserted authority in many forms. The police force was large and closely involved in neighbourhood life. Local residents' networks acted as its eyes and ears, harking back both to the Imperial Association of the war years and the systems of mutual surveillance present in all neo-Confucian societies (China, Korea, Taiwan and Japan). The procedures for judicial and police investigation did not incorporate due hearing for all parties, and relied on confession rather than proof. Wrongdoers were punished with social ostracism, a distant echo of the total deprivation of all human contact which produced the *hinin*, or untouchables, stripped of all human identity. This form of social sanction was more common than imprisonment: fewer than 3 per cent of criminals received custodial sentences, and 87 per cent of those were for periods shorter than three years. Discreet yet regular use of the death penalty completed the picture, and this was not suspended until November 1989 (without any formal decision), only to be reintroduced in 1993. It has often been observed that the Japanese systems of justice and civil order are highly authoritarian compared to those of the West, and this must be viewed alongside the almost non-existent rate of individual crime (though not financial corruption and organized crime). It is not clear whether this is due to deliberate conservative policy, or the outcome of a system of social eugenics supported by the great majority of the population.

In a further aspect of public order, Japan holds the record, with nearly 400,000 people confined to psychiatric institutions. Social pressures and rigid norms governing personal conduct are the reason for this degree of exclusion from normal society. The presence of nearly three million Japanese 'outcastes', the Burakumin, who are often employed in 'unclean' jobs, such as the leather and fur trades, gives a further indication of the force of these exclusion mechanisms. Furthermore, the Burakumin are organized into a pressure group like any other. Strict official rules governing aliens, for instance the obligatory filing of fingerprints, tight immigration controls and the almost total refusal to admit political refugees or 'boat people', are a further aspect of this climate. It is easy to emphasize the contrast between this rigidity and the highly tolerant attitude shown towards the activities of the Japanese underworld, which is prosperous and highly-respected, and since the war has played an active part in shareholders' annual general meetings in order to ensure, for a price, the successful rubber-stamping of decisions taken by the company directors. The control exercised by the Japanese underworld is not limited to its involvement with business and the LDP. Neither the Soka Gakkai, the Buddhist sect which supports the Komeito party, nor the Korean communities in Japan who provide frequent financial aid to North Korea to improve the lot of their relatives at home, nor even the Japanese Socialist Party with its notorious dependency on the owners of the ubiquitous *pachinko* (gambling machine) parlours, are by any means immune to dubious influences.

Yet none of these shady activities can match the vast quantities of money handled by the LDP party bosses in their dealings with officials and companies: in 1973, for example, Kakuei Tanaka allegedly bought US$425 million worth of shares. The key to political power lies in the LDP's extraordinary ability to mobilize special interest groups.

THE ECONOMIC MIRACLE: THE ROOTS OF GROWTH

There is currently no shortage of works on the Japanese economic miracle, but there is little agreement between them. The analyses put forward frequently deal with very different chronological phases of this miracle, which partly explains their diversity. They identify different components to the phenomenon which are actually complementary, rather than mutually exclusive. All the various schools of thought contain an element of truth: the culturalist school, represented by Chie Nakane (1974), which accentuates the unique features of the Japanese civilization; the economist school, represented by Edward Denison (1975), with its emphasis on the part played by Japan's post-war transition and its attempt to catch up; the managerialist school, accentuating the 'zero defect', 'zero inventory' and 'just in time' principles of William Ouchi (1982) and others; and the institutionalist school, centred on the controlling hand of the state and the economic bureaucracy, represented by Chalmers Johnson (1982), who influenced the majority of those writing during the 1980s. Other complementary variants stress the part played by unique social phenomena such as the trading companies (*sogo sosha*) and economic cartels (*keiretsu*), while educational and human capital (the famous 'factor X' identified by the economist Harvey Liebenstein, who influenced Ronald Dore, for example) and the sociology of work (Ezra Vogel, 1983) fill the remaining gaps in the Grail-like quest to explain Japan's economic miracle. Over time, with the boom in the Korean and Taiwanese economies and now other Asian countries too, similar arguments are being revived in relation to Japan's neighbours. The Confucian factor is now taking the place of the old cultural explanations, but the argument of comparative advantage in world trade and the theory of the dirigiste state still continue to be the other dominant approaches.

Is this to say that the miracle was no such thing? This is by no means true, for the continuity and scale of the Japanese economic boom remain unique. However, a fault line did emerge in 1973–4, at the time of the energy crisis which hit Japan, with its overdependence on external supplies, more severely than other industrialized economies. This coincided both with the progressive revaluation of the yen and with growing international pressure on Japan to harmonize its economic practices. Although many institutions and customs survived beyond 1974–5, the Japanese economy changed – and at precisely the moment when the policies and tools of the post-war era were becoming widely known to its overseas competitors.

Facts and myths

Japan's rise between 1945 and 1973 may be illustrated by several points. In 1945, the occupying powers estimated national income at approximately US$15 per capita. A quarter of Japan's productivity had been lost, reducing its production capacity in theory to 1937 levels, and even less in reality. In 1973, Japan, with 3 per cent of the world's population occupying 0.3 per cent of its land surface, accounted for 10 per cent of the global economy. After an initial recovery period the Japanese economy steadily gained momentum from 1950 onwards and was fully reconstructed to maximum pre-war levels by 1953, achieving a real growth rate of approximately 10 per cent per annum between 1950 and 1973. This growth was so phenomenal that it consistently outstripped the forecasts of economists and official planners, and expansion was accompanied by a transfer of growth from the primary sector (agriculture) and the light consumer industries (textiles) to heavy industry, particularly chemicals, and later the engineering and electrical industries, so that in engineering, for example, production was multiplied by 65 per cent between 1950 and 1973. During this period, several successive growth cycles stand out, including the Korean War boom, the Jinmu boom (1956–7), the Iwato boom (1959–60) and the Izanami boom (1967–9) – the last three named after mythical emperors and Japanese ancestral gods. The corresponding slumps of 1954, 1957, 1961 and 1965 barely qualify as recessions, but merely as voluntary cooling-off periods engineered by the government by means of credit restrictions which were aimed at restoring a balance of payments threatened by an over-rapid rise in imports. Indeed, up until the early 1960s, Japan's domestic growth was still quite dependent on vital imports, including energy and raw materials as well as capital goods and technology, and therefore also on foreign currency earnings. These originally came from the money spent by the occupation forces in connection with the Korean War, but later on, export earnings gradually took over, producing a balance of payments surplus from the early 1960s onwards. The growing prestige attached to Japanese products, from cheap knick-knacks to high-tech goods, greatly reduced the relative cost of importing raw materials needed for production, thus paving the way for domestic growth.

Yet old myths die hard, and it is almost as vital to remind ourselves what this economic miracle was not. It was not solely the result of economic liberalism, because dirigisme in many forms regulated the competition intensified by the major oligopolistic groupings reassembled in the early 1950s. Nor was it entirely based on exports, since they did not grow any more rapidly than the domestic economy: in 1965, Japan had not yet recovered the share of world exports which it had held back in 1938; in

1975, it accounted for only 7 per cent of international trade, while its overseas trade represented little more than 10 per cent of GNP, a level below those of other industrialized countries. Nor was it by any means solely due to picking specialized industrial niches, because Japanese firms, especially the major trading companies, competed with each other as they all simultaneously tried to gain a foothold across the whole spectrum of industrial products. In order to reduce its dependency on imports, the Japanese economy operated 'full set production' for all consumer goods, often at the expense of consumer interests. Finally, the Japanese miracle was by no means based on a monetarist (that is, restrictive or merely balanced) financial policy, but instead on the aggressive dynamism of its firms, which were encouraged to run up heavy debts, underwritten by the state financial institutions. Only constant parity between the dollar and the yen between 1949 and 1971 (at $US1 to 360 yen), which ultimately led to an undervaluation of the Japanese currency, together with the doctrine of balancing the central state budget (but not any of its other investments) acted as constraints on economic policy. Put simply, growth was orthodox in budgetary terms but financially inflationary, with considerable allocations of credit either by public bodies or with state backing. Lastly, at a social level, hierarchical stratification and even industrial authoritarianism remained the norm during the early decades and, in the major industrial groups, signs of a Japanese model of innovatory social relationships were only visible to a limited degree, and were more noticeable in the newer firms. As for the pursuit of 'zero defect' and the quality circles which have since become a common feature of Japanese-style management, they were merely popularized in Japan by the American W. E. Deming, although they admittedly found greater success there than in Detroit. On a technological level, despite the very high standard of Japanese engineering, most technological innovations during the early decades were imported. The earliest example of this, as well as one of the most famous, was shipbuilding, with Japanese yards assembling vessels from welded prefabricated units, a method which had been copied from the American construction of the famous freighters of the Second World War known as Liberty Ships.

It is nevertheless true to say that the pupil eagerly drew inspiration from its master, sometimes surpassing the latter with lightning speed. In most sectors, however, Japanese products remained synonymous with low prices and uneven quality into the mid-1960s. This also explains General De Gaulle's uncomplimentary remark when he once described Prime Minister Ikeda as a 'transistor salesman'.

Breaks and continuities

It is just as easy to attribute Japan's economic achievement to the success with which new methods and policies were established after 1945 – the market and competition, capital and openness to the outside world, imported technologies, social and trade union democracy – as it is to exaggerate the revival of the bureaucratic, corporatist, authoritarian capitalism of the pre-war era. In fact, in this sphere, as in politics, the same pre-war personnel, the same traditional institutions and the same handed-down methods came back into play, albeit with very different objectives and a new frame of mind. The essence of the Japanese model clearly lies not in some miracle formula, but rather in the juxtaposition of sometimes contradictory influences. It is the equivalent, on a socio-economic level, of the talent for organizing, combining and adapting technologies which was to make Japanese industry the world leader, without even putting the effort into core research and higher education which characterized both the German and American models.

Yet for all that, the way that Japan's pre-war economy had been organized had never enjoyed unanimous support, something which was even more true of the state mobilization declared from 1943 onwards, amid what the more astute already realized was an atmosphere of defeat. The post-war period carried on with some of this framework, but, amid an atmosphere of freedom, it also allowed different interests to be clearly articulated, thus even contributing to overall dynamism. To give some examples of this, the great pre-war *zaibatsu* were holding companies, tightly controlled by the families who founded them and specializing to a fairly large extent in a given branch of the economy. These great dynasties could not condone either the increasing control of the economy, nor could they accept the separation of ownership and management advocated both by General Tojo and the official planners in the Ministry of Commerce and Industry. During the war years, as in fascist Italy, a conservative opposition group was therefore launched, including some diplomats. Like Shidehara and Yoshida, they were opposed to central planning, the takeover of concerns by the state and a state-controlled economy, which they saw as an ominous prelude to Soviet-style collectivization. However, these vacillating moderates failed to constitute a genuine political force. Entrepreneurs frequently balked at attempts to convert the entire economy to the war effort, and from 1944 onwards, they even condemned Japan's warmongering as suicidal. Not all *zaibatsu* were equally involved in the war industry. The great houses of the Kansai region around Osaka and Kyoto, for example C. Itoh and Marubeni, focused on textiles and other consumer goods, while Mitsubishi and Mitsui were biased towards mechanical engineering and the arms industries. In the immediate post-war period, those groups involved in more peaceful activities and less tied to the bureaucracy temporarily moved into the forefront of Japanese firms. As has already been pointed out, Yoshida had no qualms about pointing the American purges in the direction of some of his enemies in the bureaucracy from time to time – although the total number of officials purged in the Ministry of Commerce and Industry remained extremely low, at less than sixty. Until 1956, diplomats seconded from the Ministry of Foreign Affairs (where Yoshida and a good many politicians in the American Occupation came from) thus kept an eye on their colleagues in MITI.

Conversely, Yoshida and his supporters were deeply hostile to the dismantling of the *zaibatsu*, while some members of the industrial bureaucracy saw the demise of these large industrial dynasties as the chance to start moving once again towards state control of the economy. These democratic interests dovetailed with the ideals espoused by the American Occupation, which was mainly concerned to 'defeudalize' Japan and believed it was implementing the dirigiste techniques of the New Deal and Rooseveltian mobilization, whereas the Japanese civil servants were actually pursuing none other than their traditional policy of increased state control over the economy. The history of this period has long revealed a considerable divergence of views within the American Occupation, yet it is only just beginning to shed light on the ideological differences and conflicts of interest which were present among the Japanese at the same period.

Dynamic financing of the economy and overloaning

In the monetary and financial sphere, continuity prevailed even more strongly, even taking into account the considerable demands imposed by the United States. The Japanese government initially attempted to continue the payments which it still owed to firms for war supplies, which represented an enormous financial burden. As there was no supply of goods in return, these payments drove inflation up and in February 1946 the Americans put a ban on the pursuit of any further indemnity. This ban coincided with the foundation of Japan's post-war institutions and, most importantly, financing mechanisms. In future, instead of reimbursing money owed to firms, the government and the Bank of Japan actually loaned them the necessary capital via the intermediary of a Reconstruction Finance Bank, established one month later.

This was a crucial measure. It resumed the practice of financial disequilibrium adopted by the state during the Meiji era and revived in 1943 in order to meet the needs of the war economy. As the central bank, the Bank of Japan was therefore a net lender to commercial banks and firms. The post-war Finance Minister Tanzan Ishibashi thus followed in the footsteps of his predecessor from 1932 to 1935, Korekiyo Takahashi. Like Takahashi, he adopted a bold Keynesian-type policy involving the allocation of state loans for pump-priming purposes. This measure prompted a controversy among Japanese economists and SCAP alike over the potential risks of continuing inflation. Yet it also had the effect of making firms closely dependent on loans granted by state institutions. This tradition was perpetuated by several later developments, for example the launch of the Eximbank (Import-Export Bank of Japan), the blueprint for which had been drawn up in 1950, and the Japan Development Bank in March 1951. As they were heavily indebted after the war, firms were encouraged to take risks which were very large in theory, but in practice were guaranteed by the state: indeed all the Japanese commercial banks followed the lending guidelines laid down by the state. Firms which were undercapitalized ran up debts far in excess of the value of their assets. Their shareholders had little control over the decision-making process, while the main backers – the state itself, hiding behind the banks – were able to dictate their moves. This form of indirect control was introduced at the time of the most severe capital short-age in 1946 and survived until the early 1970s. It is possible to see an indication of this unique, high-risk aspect of the Japanese model by com-paring the reserves and loans of the Banque de France in 1972 with those of the Bank of Japan: the Banque de France held commercial bank deposits to a value of four times that of its own loans, whereas the reserves held by the Bank of Japan were seven times less than its loans to other financial institutions (Suzuki, 1980).

Keynesianist without Keynes, dirigiste without a plan (although a num-ber of guidelines were adopted), state controlled without nationalization – this was the style of Japanese financial policy, with major implications for the future. The whole system was based on heavy debts incurred in anticipa-tion of future profits and rendered viable by state backing. Each time the economy slowed down, the issue of whether the loans were approved or refused by the state became a matter of life and death for the firms con-cerned. Furthermore, Tanzan Ishibashi was forced to resign in 1952 after announcing to the Diet at the time of one such mini-recession that he 'was not overly concerned about the suicides of a few businessmen'. The Finance Minister, rather than the Central Bank, fixed the level of interest rates and routed credit allocation through a complex financial network, boosting or slowing the economy and its various sectors. Furthermore, from 1946 to 1949, the Yoshida government circumvented the American ban on long-term state debt through the annual issue of one-year bonds which were bought by the public. By requiring Japan to carry out its own reconstruc-tion, the Americans encouraged wage-earners, in the absence of disposable assets, to channel a high proportion of their income into savings, themselves strictly controlled by the state. The stringency of Occupation policy rein-forced the wartime tradition of compulsory saving, based on patriotism and corporate loyalty. The vast system of postal savings accounts, which syphoned off up to a third of overall savings in the 1970s, perpetuated this form of state control, although in that case it was based on financial terms (interest rates and tax exemptions) which were favourable to the small investor.

Conversely, the traditional lack of financial accountability on the part of the major firms, both with regard to their shareholders and in terms of the risks they took, continued up to the 1990s. The banking supervisory bodies, the Finance Ministry and the Bank of Japan, gave their backing to bail-out plans, and to any financial support arrangements which helped to stabilize the economy. It was this tradition which enabled the leading firms to undertake long-term investments without fear of risk, instead of relying on short-term gains supported by their shareholders. An echo of this was still visible, in a different context, at the time of the 1991 scandal involving the top securities houses, such as Nomura and Yamaichi. After the 1987 stock-market crash, these firms perpetuated the old practice of compensating preferred customers – essentially the 200 leading Japanese companies (but not small shareholders). The large stockmarket and real estate profits of 1985–7 had made it possible to finance the biggest wave of industrial investment in Japanese history: for the major firms, speculatory risk was limited by the usual clauses covering compensation for losses by securities firms. This conduct was in fact directly inspired by the overall financial and credit policy established after the war. However, once the Japanese financial markets were liberalized and opened up to international markets in the 1980s, it became totally unacceptable in the light of the new Anglo-Saxon regulations which then came into force. The extraordinary financial risks taken on the Japanese capital markets between 1985 and 1987, like the financing of huge investments through profits from the speculative bubble in the Japanese securities and real estate markets, was in fact a replay of the post-war situation on a massive scale. In both cases, the Japanese counted on their collective unity to build up a supply of capital which would be invested in industrial growth over the long term. The difference between the two is that in the second case, overspeculation and the global scale of the phenomenon alarmed the government, which decided a deflation that caused a market collapse.

Finally, owing to a combination of constitutional restrictions, the climate of pacifism and above all the presence of the United States security umbrella, Japan was able to reduce its military expenditure considerably. While a major share of both research and state funding in America, Britain and France (not to mention the Soviet Union) was devoted to arms, and whereas army-related investment and operational expenses syphoned off between 3 and 6 per cent of those countries' GNP, Japan consistently kept its military spending at under 1 per cent of GNP. This limit has never been significantly exceeded, even by the equipment programmes of 1980 and 1990, because Japan's GNP has itself grown even faster than military expenditure. At the beginning of the 1990s, each Japanese citizen was required to pay approximately US$200 towards the defence effort, compared with US$600 in France and US$1,200 in the United States.

Physical control of the economy

The other pillar of this indirect dirigisme was the controlled distribution of raw materials, which were of crucial importance both during the war and afterwards – a policy which was continued into the 1950s by means of import quotas. Here, the wishes of the United States dovetailed with the traditions of the past, particularly in the shape of the Cabinet Planning

Board which began operation in 1937. Reinstated during the emergency of 1946, state allocation of coal, oil and other imports which were gradually approved (and partly funded) by the United States led to the continuation of the pre-war cartels, though by transferring their management to the state at the expense of private capitalists. The ministerial bureaucracies grouped firms together by sector, taking on the powers of the corporatist Supervisory Associations of the war years. By means of the Bureau of Foreign Trade (set up by order of SCAP in October 1945), the Economic Stabilization Board and later the Economic Planning Agency, the state pulled the levers which made industrial production possible.

The birth of the 'industrial cocoon'

In February 1949 the United States government, represented by Joseph Dodge (who masterminded monetary deflation in Germany in 1946), acted as the arbiter in the Japanese dispute between the advocates of Keynesian-style growth and those opposed to inflation. Dodge enforced stringent deflation, which soon led to a dramatic rise in unemployment, while simultaneously fixing yen–dollar parity at a rate that was initially detrimental to Japanese exports. The Dodge plan, which was generally detested by Japanese politicians and economists, nevertheless had consequences which neither its authors nor its opponents had envisaged. The resulting redundancies which it caused in both the public and the private sector permitted a purge of left-wing militants, who had formerly been protected by SCAP. At the same time, since the United States administration no longer wished to bear the financial burden of Japanese inflation, it handed over the control of the economy to the Japanese government, which thus inherited most of the extended powers previously wielded by SCAP. By allowing private companies to borrow extensively through the intermediary of the commercial banks and the Bank of Japan, the authorities partly cancelled out the deflationary effects of the Dodge plan and made firms even more dependent on a leading bank: this marked the birth of the *keiretsu*, the links between finance and industry which followed on from the pre-war *zaibatsu*, except that the former were more flexible. Six major banks became the orchestrators of networks of businesses and trading companies which reunited the pre-war groupings. The first to be reconstituted was Mitsui, in 1952, and the last Mitsubishi, in 1959. Furthermore, by enforcing budgetary orthodoxy and the inviolability of exchange rates, the Americans obliged the Japanese to devote more energy to exports as the only way of financing imports and therefore of ensuring growth: MITI's main role from the outset was, in fact, to promote exports.

The means for this interventionist promotion were thus in place. MITI's stringent regulation of exchange rates and capital in December 1949 allowed the identification of export priorities – and bans: for example,

Japan was to be closed to foreign cars until 1960, although during the same period, Renault and the British company Rootes were helping Japanese motor manufacturers to restore their production facilities. Petrol allocations placed the subsidiaries of foreign firms in Japan at a disadvantage. At the same time, imports of technology, in the form of machinery, patents, licences, etc., were both encouraged and strictly controlled by MITI, which could thereby determine industrial policy targets and hold down the cost of granting foreign patents, due to the lack of open competition between Japanese purchasers.

Overall fiscal policy was also revamped in favour of firms and their investments, while MITI perfected a policy of selective support and protection for fledgling industries. In the course of the 1950s, this policy initially benefited the steel and electricity generating industries, shipbuilding and chemical fertilizers, and later man-made textiles, plastics, petrochemicals and car manufacture, the last one being the electronics industry in 1957 (Johnson, 1982). With the help of JETRO (Japanese External Trade Organization), MITI also created a world network for economic information, foreshadowing the revival of the international information resources of the *sogo sosha*, or major trading companies. Admittedly, MITI's prescience should not be exaggerated. It also made several errors, as in 1953 when it prevented newcomer Akio Morita (the founder of Sony) from buying the patent for the transistor from the United States. However, this mistake was ultimately remedied when the patent was later purchased at rock-bottom price, because of the failure by the Americans to foresee the transistor's potential as a mass consumer product. And so Japan's and the modern world's leading industry was born, initially to the benefit of Matsushita. MITI likewise delayed the entry into the car manufacturing arena of Soichiro Honda, a brilliant engineer who had converted from the war industry to mopeds and motorcycles. These measures, supposedly adopted to protect what were seen as the more mature industries, proved that the main talent of the industrial bureaucracy at that time lay in organization, rather than in innovation.

From *zaibatsu* to *keiretsu*

The post-war period brought with it the fragmentation of private economic power. The political purges affected the *zaibatsu* families who were the main directors of the concerns and paved the way for the rise of newcomers. Economic devastation brought unemployment, exacerbated by the enforced return of millions of soldiers and settlers. The black market, salvage work and the dealings which went on in the vicinity of the United States troops gave enterprising individuals the chance to make money and placed the underworld in a powerful position. Furthermore, some of the clauses governing the Occupation favoured small business and competition for the first time since the Meiji era, for example the Fair Trade Commission, an institution which was inspired by America's New Deal and has survived to this day.

However, the general challenging of institutions triggered defensive reactions from Japanese society, reflecting the stratification which had begun to develop during the war. One case in point was the famous custom of lifetime employment, by which employees of the major firms were guaranteed absolute security of employment (though not of any given post, as that could vary considerably) without any contract or statutory conditions. This social institution actually owed its origins to the shortage of industrial labour during the First World War, which in Asia was a period of enormous industrial growth. The system was reinforced during the Second World War, when Japanese employees reacted against the competition created by the forced introduction of Korean and Chinese workers, and was consolidated immediately after the war in the major firms with the help of SCAP measures which restricted companies' freedom to lay off employees. A dual labour market was thus created in which large firms with their stable workforces coexisted with small businesses, particularly in the shaky and poorly-paid service sector. This system did, admittedly, allow unemployment to be consistently limited to 2 per cent of the active population throughout the modern period. The unproductive, marginal jobs carried out by women, the elderly and the potentially unemployed form a reservoir for the economy, while promotion by seniority also reduces poaching and wage battles between major firms.

Similarly, the unionization advocated by SCAP generally took place in the confines of individual organizations, often following the precedent of the patriotic associations which had existed during the war. It was an in-house form of unionism which took hold, although the communist and left-wing socialist federation of the Sohyo initially vied with the reformist social democrats of the Domei. Within the firm, unionism remained corporate in nature, although it sometimes led to violent disputes with management. The purge of the Reds in 1950 reduced communist and left-wing influence to a few federations of civil servants and public employees, as well as the influential teachers' body. Union activism was thus limited to the annual spring offensive of the Shunto, the chance to weigh up the opposition and make some concessions at a general level without challenging the social environment of the firm.

However, the most important response to the process of economic and social liberalization in the post-war period was, quite simply, the painstaking effort made to reconstitute the financial, industrial and commercial groups. The anti-trust law of 1947 was undermined from the day it came into force. Originally 325 concerns came into the category of *zaibatsu*, and were initially supposed to disband completely. The law was eventually made to apply to just eighteen of them, particularly the leading names in the military and financial industries. What is more, this dismantling still only affected the main links with the holding companies of parent organizations.

After the 1951 San Francisco Peace Treaty, the government began planning to review these measures. The first opportunity came in the form of an economic recession which caused it to place authoritarian restrictions on the production of textile firms. In 1953 this precedent led to a total revision of the 1947 anti-trust law which cancelled out most of its effects. The business cartels were once again allowed to restructure a particular sector of activity in the case of economic downturn, or as otherwise necessary. Further parallel measures were taken to legalize cross-holdings, which today constitute a central feature of the stability enjoyed by the 'hard core' of Japanese capitalism.

Within a few years, the concerns which give the Japanese economy its particularly strong collective structure were reconstituted under the name of *keiretsu*. This term encompasses several different levels of relationship: indeed it was not so much the strict ties of capital ownership which were re-established, but rather the allegiances cemented by a small amount of cross-holding in terms of capital, a handful of commercial and financial ties reinforced over time, and the personal friendships of the directors. Unlike the pre-war era, the latter were no longer the owners of the businesses they ran; having been promoted from the rank of executive, they were balanced by the entry of senior civil servants into firms in a process literally known as *amakudari* or 'descent from heaven'. These highly informal relationships do not rule out disputes and internal rivalry, even when the names of the major firms are imposed on many of their affiliated companies. The prestige of the parent companies lingers on: Nissan executives, for example, will tend to look down on those of Prince, which is a member of the same *keiretsu*, while those of Nomura, in the securities industry, consider themselves highly superior to those of Kokusai Securities, the second-largest securities firm in the Nomura group.

At a more mundane level, the term *keiretsu* also denotes a synergy between the activities of sister firms. This is nowhere more clearly demonstrated than in the nine large trading companies or *sosha*, whose global network permits the exchange of information, products and processes between all the parent companies. Focused on trade in basic products such as energy, steel, textiles, domestic distribution and the captive markets of the Third World, they accounted for 50 per cent of Japan's overseas trade up until the end of the 1960s. Their influence declined when the car manufacturing and electronics giants appeared, wanting to take control of their own commercial distribution. Other links were duly forged, for example between each of the major car firms and their respective networks of subcontractors, as well as a preferred bank. Some of these subcontractors, such as Nippon Denso which is affiliated to the Nissan group, would also in turn become international giants in the car equipment market.

Sosha and *keiretsu* do not exist throughout the Japanese economy. Some of the newer and generally most innovatory firms, such as National, Sony,

Honda and later Kyocera, which specialized in industrial ceramics, were originally much more monolithic than the major groups. Though still dominated by the personalities of their founders, they initially offered their staff greater internal mobility. Furthermore, the presence of the *keiretsu* did not mean that the whole of industry shared a common strategy, still less took part in the united economic conspiracy which filled the nightmares of many of Japan's rivals. On the contrary, competition between the major groups was overwhelming, especially in cases where the products and services on offer were identical. It was a clear case of oligopolistic competition, as was true of the leading washing powder and tyre manufacturers at a global level. Until the influence of MITI and the Bank of Japan eventually declined in the 1970s, one of their central roles was to limit this competition, for instance by staggering major plans to invest in firms competing within the same sector.

Post-war Japan was split into two layers, one corresponding to the period before defeat, which bequeathed a culture, bureaucratic instruments and continuity of most personnel, and the other corresponding to Americanization, including the take-up of democracy and the rise of opposition groups, including also the large, double-edged anti-nuclear movement, which signified both the horrors suffered at Hiroshima and Nagasaki and a rejection of militarism. Although, in ideology and in fiction, the Japanese are often viewed in terms of one or other side of this split, the reality is different as far as most Japanese are concerned, for they themselves embody both of these layers. The dual identity – Asian and Western combined – which had existed at the beginning of the century was thus revived, setting the Japanese apart from most other Asians.

During this period, Japan was not completely isolated from the rest of Asia: it was back in 1945 that the first boats unloaded raw materials imported from Korea in defiance of the United States embargo. The 1950s and 1960s were devoted to a painstaking strategy of reparations in relation to the occupied countries. Either unofficially or via the more discreet channels, Japan resumed trade with the People's Republic of China, even supplying a small amount of aid at the beginning of the 1960s by providing a fishing-fleet on a credit basis. Only the Soviet Union's determination to reject any Japanese–American alliance in 1959 destroyed the compromise negotiated with Nikita Khrushchev in 1956 over the Northern Territories, the four islands in the Kuriles archipelago occupied by the Soviet Union, two of which were due to be handed back on the signing of a peace treaty. Washington showed clearer foresight when it ceded the island of Okinawa back to Japan.

Japan also benefited from the economic and financial terms extended by Washington to its new ally in the Cold War in Asia. Yet it was the hard work of the Japanese people, the expansion of the domestic market, state control and the willingness of its financiers to undertake risks which produced Japan's 'economic miracle': indeed, viewed in this light, it is anything but miraculous.

SELECTED READING

Abe, H., Shindo, M. and Kawato, S. (1994) *The government and politics of Japan*, Tokyo: University of Tokyo Press.

Abegglen, J. C. (1958) *The Japanese factory*, Glencoe: Free Press.

——and Stalk, G. (1985) *Kaisha: the Japanese corporation*, New York: Harper & Row.

Adams, T. F. S. and Hoshii, I. (1972) *A financial history of the New Japan*, Tokyo: Kodansha International.

Beasley, G. W. (1990) *The modern history of Japan*, Tokyo: Charles E. Tuttle.

Benedict, R. (1946) *The chrysanthemum and the sword*, Boston: Houghton & Mifflin.

Bouissou, J. (1992) *Le Japon depuis 1945*, Paris: Armand Colin.

Denison, E. E. (1975) *How Japan's economy grew so fast*, Washington: Brookings Institution.

Dore, R. P. (1958) *Land reform in Japan*, London: Oxford University Press.

Dower, J. W. (1988) *Empire and aftermath: Yoshida Shigeru and the Japanese experience, 1878–1954*, Cambridge, MA: Harvard University Press.

Duus, P. (ed.) (1988) *The Cambridge history of Japan, vol. 6: the twentieth century*, Cambridge: Cambridge University Press.

Fukui, H. (1971) *Party in power: the Japanese Liberal-Democrats and policy-making*, Berkeley: University of California Press.

Garon, S. (1987) *The state and labour in modern Japan*, Berkeley: University of California Press.

Gravereau, J. (1989) *Le Japon: l'ère de Hirohito*, Paris: Imprimerie nationale.

Herail, F. (1986) *Manuel d'histoire du Japon*, Paris: Publications orientalistes de France.

Hidika, R. (1984) *The price of affluence*, Tokyo: Kodansha International.

Horsley, W. and Buckley, R. (1990) *Nippon, new superpower: Japan since 1945*, London: BBC Books.

Johnson, C. (1982) *MITI and the Japanese miracle: the growth of industrial policy, 1925–1975*, Stanford: Stanford University Press.

Kataoka, T. (1991) *The price of a constitution: the origin of Japan's postwar politics*, New York: Francis & Taylor.

Katzenstein, P. (1978) *Between plenty and power*, Madison: University of Wisconsin Press.

Kosaka, M. (1982) *A history of postwar Japan*, Tokyo: Kodansha International.

Langdon, F. C. (1966) *Japan's foreign policy*, Vancouver: University of British Columbia Press.

Lehmann, J. (1982) *The roots of modern Japan*, London: Macmillan.

McCormack, G. and Sugimoto, Y. (eds) (1986) *Democracy in contemporary Japan*, Armonk: M. E. Sharpe.

Morris, I. (ed.) (1969) *Thought and behaviour in modern Japanese politics*, New York: Oxford University Press.

Nakamura, T. (1995) *The postwar Japanese economy – its development and structure, 1937–1994*, Tokyo: University of Tokyo Press.

Nakane, C. (1974) *La société japonaise*, Paris: Armand Colin.

Ouchi, W. (1982) *Théorie Z*, Paris : Interéditions.

Pinguet, M. (1984) *La mort volontaire au Japon*, Paris: Gallimard.

Reischauer, E. O. (1987) *Japan: the story of a nation*, 3rd ed., Tokyo: Charles E. Tuttle Co.

Sabouret, J. (1983) *L'Autre Japon: les burakumin*, Paris: La Découverte.

Sato, S. (1990) *Postwar politician: the life of former Prime Minister Masayoshi Ohira*, Tokyo: Kodansha International.

Scalapino, R. E. (1955) *The beginnings of political democracy in Japan*, Berkeley: University of California Press.

——(ed.) (1977) *The foreign policy of Japan*, Berkeley: University of California Press.

Schaller, M. (1985) *The American occupation of Japan: the origins of the Cold War in Asia*, New York: Oxford University Press.

Seizelet, É. (1990) *Monarchie et démocratie dans le Japon d'après-guerre*, Paris: Maisonneuve & Larose.

Suzuki, Y. (1980) *Money and banking in contemporary Japan*, New Haven: Yale University Press.

Thayer, N. B. (1969) *How the conservatives rule Japan*, Princeton: Princeton University Press.

Upham, F. K. (1987) *Law and social change in postwar Japan*, Cambridge: Harvard University Press.

Van Wolferen, K. (1990) *L'Énigme de la puissance japonaise*, Paris: Robert Laffont.

Ward, R. E. and Sakamoto, Y. (eds) (1987) *Democratizing Japan: the Allied occupation*, Honolulu: University of Hawaii Press.

Yoshida, S. (1962) *The Yoshida memoirs*, New York: Houghton & Mifflin.

Yoshihara, K. (1982) *Sogo sosha: the vanguard of the Japanese economy*, Tokyo: Oxford University Press.

Yoshino, M. (1986) *The invisible link: Japan's sogo sosha and the organization of trade*, Cambridge, MA: MIT Press.

7 Japan: leading world power?

The end of the post-war period may be dated to Japan's Tanaka era, a name which denotes both a dynamic Prime Minister, who held office from July 1972 to November 1974, and the first Japanese public scandal to have truly international repercussions, namely the Lockheed affair, with which he was associated. Admittedly, these dates do not coincide with Japan's real revival as an economic power. A decade earlier, in 1964, Japan had joined the OECD, the club for the most highly-developed countries, and had become the twenty-fifth member of the International Monetary Fund to abandon foreign exchange controls. In the same year, the Olympic Games were held in Tokyo, in a futuristic stadium built by the architect Kenzo Tange, while the world's first high-speed train, the Shinkansen, ran between Tokyo and Osaka for the first time. Also in 1964, for the second time since 1945, the overall economic growth rate surpassed 13 per cent. In the following year, 1965, the balance of foreign trade began to show an underlying surplus, and in 1967 Japan rose to become the number two world economic power, overtaking West Germany in terms of GNP. This did not signify any drastic change, but was simply the result of the hard work put in by the post-war generation. This upward trend continued, for by 1991 the Japanese economy was two-thirds the size of the United States economy. In April 1995, at the height of the revaluation of the yen, the Japanese economy surpassed that of the United States in size. This development, alongside the simultaneous decline of the United Kingdom, was the biggest upheaval so far in the hierarchy of the main industrialized countries, which had remained unchanged since the end of the nineteenth century.

Conversely, the lengthy reign of Emperor Hirohito, which only came to an end in January 1989, represented a psychological continuity going back to the tragic events in Japan's history since the 1920s. Although Hirohito's presence hampered full reconciliation between Japan and its principal Asian neighbours, as Emperor he stood for the Japanese state and Japanese diplomacy to the last, interspersing his expressions of regret at Japan's part in the Second World War with audiences which were much sought-after by overseas politicians. In 1971, he paid his first visit to Europe since the war, and in 1975 he travelled to the United States. At the end of the 1980s, he received a visit from China's Deng Xiaoping as well as the South Korean President Roh Tae-woo. Even Emperor Akihito's accession to the throne in 1989, marked by a ceremony attended by many Asian heads of state, failed to put a final end to this period of ambiguity, for some months afterwards the Mayor of Nagasaki became the victim of an assassination attempt for having criticized Hirohito's part in the war. Conversely, in one case, the subject of Japan's duty to tender apologies created a minor controversy in December 1991, at the time of the fiftieth anniversary of the attack on Pearl Harbor: Prime Minister Kiichi Miyazawa expressed his 'regrets' at the fact that the war had been started, but the issue of the nuclear bombing of Hiroshima and Nagasaki by the Americans was widely seen by Japanese puplic opinion as reciprocal. A few months later, the fate of the Korean 'comfort women' who had been deported during the Pacific War led Japanese officials to apologize to Korea.

THE POLITICAL SYSTEM: CRISIS AND CHANGE

The Tanaka phenomenon

The Tanaka era marked the most significant watershed in Japan's post-war history. The United States had recently ceded back Okinawa, finally bringing an end to the American Occupation, and Japan once again became a major player. The American withdrawal from the Vietnam War following the Paris agreements of 1973 was a clear indication of this development in Asia. At the international level, Kakuei Tanaka was the architect of China's diplomatic recognition, a few months after taking up office. Japan thus forged ahead of the United States in normalizing its relations with the People's Republic. As a result, there quickly developed an embryonic form of economic co-operation between China and Japan, though economic grievances and mutual suspicion precluded the establishment of a Peking–Tokyo axis. Like Richard Nixon after the Watergate scandal, Tanaka continued to be a welcome guest of the Chinese government after his downfall. Yet, above all, it was in terms of domestic politics that Kakuei Tanaka's rule proved decisive. Tanaka, the poorly-educated son of a cowman, was a newcomer who emerged from among the ruins of war. In 1945, finding himself in possession of a sum of public money which he had been granted to set up a piston factory in Korea, he embarked on a political career. In 1947, he became the member for Niigata, an isolated, underdeveloped mountain region on the Sea of Japan, and was a people's politician with a finely-honed common touch. Tanaka rewrote the rules of Japanese politics by openly exposing the patronage on which it was based. The Yoshida school, made up of former top officials like Sato and Ikeda, gave way to a politician who would dominate the ministries, creating a new generation of politicians which would form the biggest political group in the Diet. Within the LDP, in government organizations and even for members belonging to other political parties, he built up vast slush funds over which he exercised ultimate control. However, he dealt more with local businessmen desperate for public contracts, rather than with the major conglomerates.

By the time the Japanese press began reporting Tanaka's activities they were already common knowledge in political circles. However, in 1973 the Watergate affair which led to the downfall of President Nixon was in full swing in the United States. In its wake, the international press and American Congressional commissions of enquiry attempted to outdo each other in their zeal. The circumstances surrounding the sale of civil aircraft by Lockheed to Japan (and Italy too) were to land Tanaka in the eye of the storm. The dubious, albeit commonplace practices collectively referred to as 'structural corruption' were subjected for the first time to the scrutiny of the world's press, at the same time as a shift appeared to take place in Japanese public perceptions. Once exposed, the bizarre details of the way in which Lockheed had paid its commission – in cash, in a suitcase handed over to Tanaka's secretary out in the street – led to loss of face and downfall for the Prime Minister. Tanaka had already been to prison for misappropriation of public funds, and returned there for several days in July 1976, but the hearing dragged on until he suffered a brain haemorrhage, which appeared to incapacitate him. It was therefore a surprise to see him taking off on another private visit to China in August 1992, after more than fifteen years of seclusion. One might add that other members of various Japanese governments have also been found guilty and imprisoned from time to time since 1945 without any international repercussions, but the fact was that the Tanaka affair marked a new international interest in Japanese politics. This exposure in turn both worried and irritated the Japanese media. However, Tanaka was, and continued to be after his downfall, a popular man whose legendary generosity, particularly in the eyes of his voters, more than made up for its illegality. It was his independence, as much as the extent of his finances, which irked his fellow politicians. In order to dispel the whiff of scandal, they chose as his successor Takeo Miki, a man ever on the conservative sidelines, in a public effort to stage a clean-up. As a result, Miki became the first post-war leader to promise a radical reform of the electoral system and the dissolution of the factions within the LDP, these being the two immediate causes of political corruption. However, this endeavour, like the Miki interregnum itself, was short-lived. Miki, a pacifist with slight neutralist tendencies and sympathies towards the Arab world, made his mark on politics by further reinforcing the taboos surrounding Japanese defence. In 1976, he laid down the Three Non-Nuclear Principles: not to produce nuclear weapons, not to possess them, and not to allow them onto Japanese soil. He also induced the Diet to agree to put a ceiling on Japan's defence expenditure of 1 per cent of its GNP, a restriction which continued in principle up until 1986.

The chronological thread

The failure of reform and factional struggle within the LDP caused a significant decline, with a succession of prime ministers failing to exceed the customary two-year mandate agreed between the faction leaders. The LDP vote had been crumbling since the early 1970s, and the former 'single party' of Japanese democracy lost its absolute majority in the Diet in the 1976 and 1979 elections. In the upper house (which has fewer constitutional powers) its dominance was constantly under threat. A group known as the New Liberal Club defected in 1976, and there was a high price to pay in order to lure them back over to the majority. Tanaka had taken charge of the Eisaku Sato faction, one of his initial moves being to set up an internal study group. After Miki came Takeo Fukuda, leader of the main faction to rival the vast Tanaka clan, who held power until December 1978. Masayoshi Ohira, who took over as his successor until a fatal heart-attack in June 1980, was an ally of Tanaka. Like the two prime ministers who came after him, he failed to introduce a Japanese equivalent of VAT when this routine measure met with opposition from the sales lobby. When Noburu Takeshita finally introduced it in 1988, it became one of the major causes of the LDP's electoral decline. The Tanaka and Fukuda factions fought continuously throughout the Ohira administration, and it was a pale shadow of Ohira, Zenko Suzuki, who succeeded him in June 1980, following a resounding defeat at the polls. Suzuki, finding himself outshone in international meetings with the flamboyant Ronald Reagan, was forced to hand over to Yasuhiro Nakasone in November 1982.

Nakasone proved the most powerful post-war Japanese prime minister and stayed in office for five years, until November 1987. However, like his predecessors, he was dependent first and foremost on Kakuei Tanaka and his clan, whose leading members he appointed onto his government. Nakasone put a stop to nepotism in the factions of the LDP by introducing a permanent government team, while also ably coming to terms with Noburu Takeshita, Tanaka's former right-hand man, who had formed his own sub-group, subtly orchestrating colleagues on all sides of the Diet. It was eventually Takeshita to whom Nakasone handed over office in November 1987. However, although the LDP returned to dominance following an electoral triumph in 1983, its power was again eroded by the reforms introducing VAT, which incurred opposition from businessmen and housewives. As in South Korea and Taiwan, farmers, including the large number who farmed part-time, were alienated from the conservative party by the announcement that the food market was to be opened up to foreign imports. Above all scandal continued in the shape of the famous Recruit affair. Japan's foremost employment agency, which had additional interests in telecommunications, had corrupted almost the entire political class (the Communist Party excepted) through cash payments and by the manipulation of its share prices. The first to be affected was the Finance Minister Kiichi Miyazawa, one of the blundering ones who had already picked up their donations. The climate of uncertainty was exacerbated by Takeshita's resignation in May 1987, although he still remained the most influential politician in the Diet.

The political cycle set in motion by the Tanaka affair then repeated itself. A prime minister was chosen from within a minor faction, owing to its lack of involvement in the Recruit scandal. Sousuke Uno, the most short-lived of all Japan's post-war leaders, was ousted in August 1989 following an extremely trivial sex scandal. The fact that this incident, which had the effect of mobilizing Japanese women for the very first time, was in itself so mundane, highlighted above all the depths to which the public perception of politicians had plunged. The LDP lost support in the elections to the upper house, held in July 1989, which resulted in a boost for the Japanese socialists with their female leader, Takako Doi. However, Mrs Doi's vote was largely poached from her communist and social democrat rivals, rather than from conservatives. Hopes of reform were equally strong in both camps. Toshiki Kaifu, the unknown who was pushed to the fore by the principal faction leaders, was appointed in August 1989 due to his unblemished reputation. A young man with, as he admitted himself, a penchant for spotted ties, he none the less appeared to be of unusually low political standing. Yet with his American-style election campaign Kaifu succeeded in restoring the LDP's image, scoring victory in the Diet elections of February 1990. The phenomenon initiated by Mrs Doi proceeded to fade away, owing to failure of the Japanese socialists to agree on a realistic programme. However, Kaifu was the prisoner of the factional strongmen, notably Noburu Takeshita, who had ambitions to return to centre-stage, and Shin Kanemaru, the LDP veteran who conducted his own private diplomatic relations with Moscow, Washington and Pyongyang. In a total game of fools, these shadow leaders allowed Kaifu to embark on a bold programme of electoral reform, just like Takeo Miki in 1975. Because Kaifu posed a threat particularly to sinecures and personal fiefdoms, he was rejected outright by opposition and government supporters alike. The younger generation of members in the Diet failed to win out against the faction leaders. The classic case of this was when the forty-year-old General Secretary of the LDP, Ichiro Ozawa, was beaten in the Tokyo elections by the outgoing mayor, even though his opponent was over eighty years of age and handicapped by criticism, especially over the construction of the new Tokyo city hall, a costly forty-eight storey skyscraper, where the private mayoral suite was rumoured to be fitted with gold taps.

Having proven genuine reform to be impossible, the council of LDP elders proceeded to bring about the downfall of Kaifu, who was accused of mishandling the Japanese role in the Gulf War and of failing to obtain the restitution of the Northern Territories by Gorbachev. However, unable to agree among themselves, the elders entrusted the premiership to the weakest of their number, Kiichi Miyazawa. Miyazawa, who became elected in November 1991, was a protégé of Ikeda. A former Finance Minister with acknowledged technocratic abilities, Miyazawa was an internationalist who had long experience of dealing with the United States especially. It could even be argued that he was the 'ultimate disciple of the Yoshida school' to emerge during the post-war period (Kataoka, 1991: 2, 129). None the less, he was permanently second in line for the LDP succession, seventy-one years old and almost as dependent as Kaifu on factions beyond his control. Within a few months, he was hit by several financial scandals involving his associates and was forced to abandon all his plans for electoral reform, which foundered on the perpetual issue of constitutional amendments concerning national defence.

All in all, the atmosphere of political and institutional crisis, introduced by the Tanaka affair in 1974 and dispelled by the strong government of Nakasone, was revived and exacerbated in the early 1990s, with no prospect of any alternative to an LDP majority. While the LDP's internal affairs at that time may have appeared to be manipulated by a group of geriatrics, like the Chinese Communist Party or the Taiwanese Kuomintang, a handover to a new generation was nevertheless inevitable. It was possibly due to his very seniority that Miyazawa was so widely supported on his nomination. For the time being, Japanese politics seemed caught in a dilemma between structural corruption in the majority party (and even outside it) and the impossibility of a changeover due to the fossilized state of the opposition. In March 1992, over 80 per cent of Japanese public opinion saw any political reform as impossible. The country which had often acted as an alternative to the Western model for other Asian governments in transition was itself not immune to democratic crisis. When the LDP finally scored a victory in the elections to the upper house in July 1992, despite failing to win a majority of seats, it owed its success to the incompetence of the opposition. Many Japanese had abstained, while a new party had formed as an offshoot of the LDP, modelled on the New Liberal Club of 1979. This time its inspiration came from none other than the grandson of Prince Konoe, the subtle but unreliable statesman who had dominated Japanese politics prior to 1945.

The distribution of powers

Plagued with financial corruption, Japanese politics was increasingly proving dominated by factionalism and even nepotism. In the Diet, one in four members had inherited his position from his father, this number rising to one in three in the case of the LDP (only 5 per cent of seats were held by women). Exposure to the international political scene often proved uncomfortable for politicians accustomed to a closed, ritualistic world. Noburu Takeshita, for example, a sharp-witted former teacher of English, could not even speak the language, while during a visit to Washington former fisheries expert Zenko Suzuki appeared unaware of the existence of the US–Japan security treaty. Japanese politics was strewn with spectacular gaffes of this nature. What is more, from that point on, Western microphones would pick up the stereotyped, often chauvinistic comments addressed by political leaders to their supporters, as in August 1986, when Nakasone attributed Japan's economic superiority over the United States to its ethnic homogeneity, or when the President of the Diet referred to American workers in January 1992 as being 'fat and lazy'. Both attitudes were common in post-war Japanese society, but their international repercussions were something new. Moreover, the transient nature of political power, totally subordinate to brokering between the clans and to ministerial consensus, became much more noticeable once Japan became, economically at least, a major power. At the time of the first trade disputes between Japan and America, during the textiles negotiations of 1968–71, Henry Kissinger had already discovered that a Japanese prime minister could not offer a firm decision, but only his goodwill. The numerous official promises to open up Japanese markets and to implement 'structural adjustment' (that is, to bring Japan's economic and in particular administrative practices into line with the liberal economics championed by the United States) were very slow in taking effect. On the one hand, the Japanese government frequently made a show of announcing such measures in order to fend off American pressure, while on the other hand neither the Prime Minister nor the Foreign Minister were able to force the hands of MITI, the Agricultural Ministry or Japan's powerful companies, professional lobbies and distribution channels.

For these reasons, Japanese political power found itself facing a crisis, amplified by the current moral standards, by the resonance-box effect of the Japanese and international media, and by growing dissatisfaction on the part of voters weary of what they perceived as an excessively flawed democracy. Yet this crisis was relative, and cannot compare with Italy's *malgoverno* or the dark days of the Fourth Republic in France. It was the 'one-party democracy', not the party system, which proved ill-adapted to the era of renewed power. The influence of a largely uncorrupt civil service remained considerable, although senior civil servants became increasingly conscious of their limited prestige compared with that of high-ranking industrialists.

The end of the LDP monopoly

In the end, the LDP was to lose its political monopoly, not because of any strengthening of the opposition, but as a result of defections from its own ranks: one wing of the party, consisting in many cases of younger politicians, adopted a more reformist line and was in some cases also more prepared to readopt nationalism, split away in 1993 to form several new political parties. The Renewal Party, led by former LDP strongman Ichiro Ozawa, and Morihiro Hosokawa's New Party were more typical of this shift, while the Sakigake Party of Masayoshi Takemura marked itself out rather as representing an Italian-style radicalism, wooing the voters by adopting a moralistic stance: it was Takemura who, as Minister of Finance in 1995, travelled to Tahiti to demonstrate against French nuclear testing.

In June 1993, for the first time in the history of Japanese democracy, a grand coalition formed in opposition to what was left of the LDP: it revived hopes of real political reform, particularly as the personality of its leader Prime Minister Hosokawa, a former actor, dynamic politician and individualist, unencumbered by the clanship ties of the LDP from which he had split, captured the imagination of the Japanese electorate. Less than one year later, in April 1994, Hosokawa in turn met his downfall in a classic political corruption scandal: like so many others, he had in the past financed his electoral campaigns through the support of haulage and delivery firms, which were also known to have underworld connections. Meanwhile, Hosokawa had initiated fundamental changes: acknowledgement of Japan's responsibility for the Pacific War (instead of the contrition without explanation which constituted the traditional response), the opening up of the rice market to imports (an electoral taboo for the LDP, as well as for the Japanese socialists) and, above all, political reform. It was Hosokawa who steered electoral reform legislation through the Diet, even though it was not fully adopted until December 1994, under the next government. By adopting one round of single-member voting in the constituencies for Diet members, the highly variable majority backing Hosokawa cut the Gordian knot of Japanese politics. Admittedly, the system was completed by a high degree of proportional voting for the regions (200 seats out of 500), which favoured the large parties, or at least so they thought, particularly the Socialist Party which called for this concession.

When Hosokawa announced his resignation – at the end of a parliamentary guerilla campaign conducted against his plan to raise VAT, and in the shadow of a scandal which affected him in turn – the Japanese people's feelings of disenchantment with their politicians were at their height. The Hosokawa government, made up of disparate forces, with pacifist socialists alongside active nationalists who advocated the notion of Japan becoming a 'normal state', was hardly distinguished by its bold approach as far as Japan's external commitments were concerned, despite the quality of its advisers. The resulting coalition was so improbable that it initially beggared belief: the LDP allied with the socialists in order to regain power, pushing an ageing member of the socialist left wing, Tomiichi Murayama, to the fore. The Murayama government launched in June 1994, then regarded as ephemeral, lasted until January 1996: in classic style, when going through a bad patch, the LDP pushed a politician to the fore to act as a screen, before staging a comeback itself. After the election of the enterprising Minister of MITI, Ryutaro Hashimoto, to head the LDP in late 1995, the time came to push Murayama off the stage.

However, whereas other politicians who have performed this role of LDP stuntman – Takeo Miki after the Tanaka scandal, or Kaifu after the downfall of Takeshita – had been popular figures, the Murayama government prompted the Japanese to reject politics. In the local elections in Tokyo and Osaka, the electorate appointed new men as leaders of Japan's two largest cities, both well-known actors whose declared moralism and individualism made them non-conformist heroes in the eyes of the ordinary 'salaryman'. Murayama paid for his political survival with the collapse of the socialists, who, furthermore, were forced to abandon their ideological convictions. A new opposition coalition centred on a New Frontier Party (Shinseito) had little success in attracting voters. The LDP governed by default.

In 1995, Japan was shaken by three violent shocks which rocked its self-confidence and its economic performance. An earthquake at Kobe, Japan's leading port, claimed 5,000 lives and exposed a contradiction between Japan's resilient, close-knit society and the political and administrative authorities which became tangled up in knots in their management of the emergency services. Some weeks later, there came the crazed plot of a Buddhist sect which carried out a mass act of terrorism, letting off poison gas in the underground station in the Kasumigaseki district of Tokyo (the hub of Japanese state power) and several other locations, and later killing the head of the Japanese police: not only was it a rude awakening for a people convinced of enjoying total public security, but the investigation above all revealed that the sect concerned was far from a purely fringe phenomenon. Attracting many students, and especially scientists, as recruits, well-supported financially, and well-established in Russia owing to its funding, it epitomizes the drift towards extremism of a religious tendency that serves as a refuge for many Japanese. Lastly, in April 1995, Japan underwent its third *endaka*, or yen hike. Admittedly, it was the level of its trade surplus with the United States which prompted the rise, but this time the Japanese economy had been in a state of internal stagnation for eighteen months. Gaining more than 20 per cent against the dollar, the yen nipped hopes of economic recovery in the bud. Lagging behind as far as relocation is concerned, Japanese firms are showing a new, albeit paradox-ical vulnerability: after all, a reduction in exports would be enough for the currency to drop. However, the three shocks of 1995 also hit the Japanese stockmarket, and ultimately undermined the viability of the banks and other financial institutions. These were sitting on a mountain of debts inherited from the days of the speculative bubble. Japanese consumers, heavily overindebted through having purchased houses at that time, and hit by the fall in the property market, no longer responded to financial stimuli. In September 1995, the Bank of Japan's basic rate of interest was reduced to 0.8 per cent per annum, in the hope of reducing the cost of debt and setting the economy moving again. An eighth government plan for reflation released the equivalent of nearly 140 billion dollars, half of which was for public works.

At the same time, this crisis has been greatly exaggerated by the way in which it has been perceived in Western eyes: Japan remains a formidable industrial machine, whose economic links with the rest of Asia are expanding, as they have done with every revaluation of the yen. While it is not yet approaching the 'normal state' hoped for by certain nationalist politicians, Japan is well on the way to becoming a normal society. Just like the West, it is being swept by a political crisis, and its financial supremacy has been undermined. As several banks failed in 1995, the tale of a Japanese broker at Daiwa Bank in the United States, who accumulated total losses of US$1.1 billion over eleven years of secret deals, highlighted the international vulnerability of the Japanese financial edifice.

The Nakasone exception

Amid this crisis in the executive, the Nakasone administration seems like an aberration, while laying the guidelines for the likely future course of Japan's international strategy. Like Yoshida and the bureaucrat ministers of the post-war period, Nakasone's roots lay deep in the imperial, militarist era. Yet the strength of his early involvement in the revival of Japanese nationalism places him apart from the 1950s consensus viewpoint. Like Tanaka, he embodied the politician's desire for power over the bureaucrat, rather than vice versa. After receiving a degree in law from the prestigious Todai University and serving as a naval officer prior to 1945, he was elected to the Diet in 1947. The young Nakasone immediately took issue with the new constitution and its restrictions on national defence, petitioning MacArthur for a mutual defence treaty and demanding an end to the United States Occupation. In 1966, when the chaos of the Cultural Revolution in China was causing considerable concern in Japan, Nakasone called for a tripling of the defence budget. A shrewd manipulator of factions, he aligned himself with Prime Minister Sato and in 1970 became Director-General (Minister, to all intents and purposes) at the *Boecho*, or Defence Agency. Nakasone re-emerged as Minister for MITI under Tanaka at the time of the 1973 oil crisis and remained minister after the downfall of the premier. Ultimately, it was the Tanaka faction which elevated him to power in November 1982.

Nakasone's long mandate was not totally devoid of political incident, featuring in particular the judicial revival of the Tanaka affair in 1983. Yet Nakasone maintained solidarity with the accused and governed with the support of the lesser conservative and centre parties before winning a majority. Like Japan's pre-war leaders, he was dependent on a circle of personal advisers from outside the government, and was therefore able to impose his will in several spheres. In particular, under the banner of administrative reform, he tackled Japan's huge budget deficits, which had risen to 6–7 per cent of GNP since the early 1970s, by hacking through some of the most corrupt branches of government. In the process, he carved up the national railways on a regional basis as a prelude to privatization. The railways were the cause of a colossal deficit, which stemmed as much from local political pressure as from their own low productivity. Nakasone likewise paved the way for the privatization of the postal service, thus diligently copying the Thatcherite model in a very different setting. Above all, he weathered the trade crisis with the United States by acting out the issue for the benefit of Japanese citizens: his media stunt of 1985, when he bought an imported tie in a department store, made just as much of an impact on public opinion as the highly official Maekawa Report, calling for an opening-up of Japan's domestic market. In a conformist society where consumer individualism is seen as a 'protruding nail', the ultra-nationalistic Nakasone's gesture in support of imported goods was taken as a green light. The yen then appreciated considerably against the dollar in 1985, at which point the fall in prices for imports gave him slightly more credibility. Nevertheless, Japan's trade surplus showed no sign of reducing: on the contrary, the value added to goods 'made in Japan' for export and the famous 'J curve' (i.e. the delay in the reaction of international trade to monetary fluctuations, disrupting the market adjustment process) forced the balance of payments surplus up to an unprecedented high of US$87 billion in 1987 compared with US$10 billion in 1980. This figure dropped back at the end of the 1980s, before climbing to a similar level again in 1991–2.

A tall man with an arrogant tone of voice, who could even be flamboyant at times, Yasuhiro Nakasone personalized his post. With President Reagan in particular he formed a flattering 'Ron and Yasu' relationship which won him general admiration in a country still suffering from an inferiority complex regarding the United States. Yet the same impulse led him to make controversial, symbolic gestures. In August 1985, for example, he became the first leader to visit Yasukuni Temple, dedicated to the war dead, for the annual commemoration ceremony. The resulting furore, particularly in the rest of Asia, was repeated when Nakasone's Education Minister stated that the Japanese annexation of Korea in 1910 had been carried out with Korean consent. These remarks led to the sacking of the minister concerned, but the Nakasone era was still undoubtedly typified by the plan to rewrite history textbooks from a conservative, nationalistic standpoint and by the attempt to restore the official status of the Japanese flag and national anthem in schools, all options which Nakasone had advocated since his youth.

And yet, as with the Reagan era at the same point, it might be argued that this revival of the past had more to do with appearance than reality. The conservatives' plans failed in the face of the opposition they encountered and, if the Marxist schools of thought seemed to be close to extinction as far as intellectuals were concerned, this was for global reasons unconnected with official policy. Nakasone, a lifelong advocate of constitutional reform, had not even broached the issue publicly. On the contrary, the modernization of Japanese society seemed to be taking effect during the same period, including the parody of a leisured consumer society represented by a wealthy minority.

A Japanese Gaullist?

Ultimately, it was in the realm of Japan's international standing and its defence that the Nakasone era appears to have been most significant. The label 'Gaullist' has been applied to several post-war politicians in different senses. Ichiro Hatoyama, Yoshida's hapless rival, and Nobusuke Kishi, the Prime Minister who signed the revised mutual security treaty in June 1960, also deserve the same label, as both were determined to place Japanese relations with the United States on an equal footing. Far from advocating a greater degree of separation from the United States, they attempted, not without nationalistic motives, to transfer its entire role in the alliance to Japan. It was also in 1968 that a commission of official experts envisaged the defence role of the Japanese navy as being to defend the seaways as far as the Strait of Malacca in South-East Asia. Japan was so wary of depriving itself of any possible future status as a nuclear power that the ratification of the Nuclear Non-Proliferation Treaty, which Japan had signed in 1970, was preceded by several years of parliamentary debate. Nakasone thus formed part of a tradition which had been revived before his mandate commenced.

The results achieved appear to have been extremely meagre. Although the Nakasone government displayed considerable unity, it totally failed to make any amendment to Article 9 of the constitution. It was in the area of education that Nakasone attempted to challenge the status quo by appointing a National Board and hiring former members of the pre-war police force to combat trade unionism within the teaching community. Yasuhiro Nakasone clearly belonged to that group of politicians who would have liked to restore the spirit if not the letter of the famous imperial rescript on education of 1890, which was seen by liberals and the left as a major cause of Japanese authoritarianism. In fact, apart from the desire and the ability to establish a stronger executive, Nakasone's 'Gaullism' was chiefly visible in his diplomacy within the Western alliance. It was helped by a rise in international tension following the occupation of Cambodia by the Vietnamese army in January 1979, the Soviet occupation of Afghanistan in the following December, the new doctrine of rearmament and confrontation announced by the Reagan administration, and even isolated yet symbolic incidents, as in September 1983, when a Soviet fighter shot down a South Korean Boeing 747 off Sakhalin, killing 269 people. Although the Japanese military kept quiet as to their real capacity for monitoring and pursuit in this dangerous region, the affair came at just the right moment to vindicate Nakasone's policy. The installation of 162 SS–20s in the Far East in 1979, as well as the presence of Soviet medium-range missiles in Europe, gave Nakasone the chance to demonstrate Japan's role in the Western alliance.

Anchoring Japan within the Western alliance

This could well be seen as the moment when Japan truly became part of the Western alliance. Nakasone used his own standing, as well as the summits between the heads of state of the seven leading industrialized nations, to drive home this point. At the G7 Versailles summit in June 1982, this move was resisted by reservations on the part of the French. In the final communiqué to the Williamsburg summit of May 1983, Nakasone obtained the first official statement of multi-lateral solidarity to incorporate Japan, something which the anglophiles at the start of the century had always sought but never achieved. Nakasone similarly succeeded in blocking a solution to the problem of the SS–20s, which involved shifting them to the east of the Urals, in other words in the direction of Asia. Even after having raised the question of the stationing of 100 United States missiles in Alaska at the Venice summit in June 1987, his own insistence enabled the Reagan administration to secure the so-called 'zero-option', i.e. the total destruction of the SS–20s. This step was announced by Gorbachev in July 1987 and led to a treaty with the United States the following autumn. For the first time Japan had made her presence felt in global strategic negotiations between the two superpowers. During this period, Nakasone clearly wished to protect Japan's maritime access routes, and not simply the 1,000 nautical miles offshore defined by his predecessor. He embarked upon a programme of military expenditure, putting an end to the old limit of 1 per cent of GNP. In 1983, a law was passed allowing the export of technology with potential military applications to the United States. This particularly meant Japanese electronic components, some of which had become irreplaceable for the Pentagon. Japan also made considerable amounts of military purchases, which certainly helped to absorb its trade surplus. In parallel with this, Japan's civilian nuclear programme was expanded and a space launcher was also built. Japan promptly backed Reagan's strategic defence initiative (the famous 'Star Wars'), to which Japanese optical, electronic and information technologies were well adapted. In 1987, Mitsubishi, the former manufacturer of the Zero fighter, the most advanced model of its day, broke its usual silence and officially declared the existence of its military production arm.

In Asia, these new developments provoked questioning and, in some cases, concern. However, Nakasone had inaugurated his term of office with a surprise visit to Seoul, during which he promised US$4 billion in aid for South Korea. While a firm supporter of the Western alliance, Nakasone made simultaneous efforts to establish full relations with all Japan's Asian neighbours in order to strengthen its regional influence. There was no question of any neutralist tendency, nor even a revival of the concept of a Greater Asia: in fact, Japanese aid took over in Asia from American aid, which it supplemented in the name of Japan's regional role. It is true that this shift of power in favour of Tokyo certainly could have implied an enhanced political role, but the Japanese government and Japanese business wished to maintain an anchor in the West and freedom of access to global markets at all costs.

THE ECONOMY: FROM WORLD NUMBER TWO TO WORLD NUMBER ONE?

When the oil crisis broke in October 1973, one anonymous senior official, appointed by MITI to oversee Japanese supplies, informed the horrified Kakuei Tanaka and Yasuhiro Nakasone that the country had little more than a fortnight's oil supplies in stock. Tanaka furiously demanded to know how this could have happened, foreseeing above all the collapse of the Japanese economy. In the resulting pandemonium, while Japanese *sogo sosha* tracked even the smallest oil cargo across the globe, the shops were raided by Japanese housewives still conditioned by a reflex instilled in times of shortages. The impact of the *shokku* of 1973 on a country which was virtually the prisoner of its own supply system cannot be underestimated. What is more, there were in fact two *shokku*: in August 1971, by suspending the convertibility of the dollar into gold, the United States had triggered a monetary whirlwind which left the yen considerably revalued, just like the currencies of other export economies such as the Deutschmark. For the first time, Japanese exports faced a considerable rise in their sale prices. Since then the yen has continued its revaluation. Its rise between 1978 and 1985 initially coincided with a fall in the dollar: in 1970, the dollar was worth ¥360 and DM3.6, while in 1980 it equalled ¥226 and DM1.82. In 1985, a further revaluation took place, and in 1991 the dollar still equalled DM1.78 marks but only ¥140. In 1992, it dropped to DM1.46 and ¥128. While the big Japanese motor manufacturers regarded themselves as competitive with the dollar standing at ¥100, other sectors, such as consumer electronics, were forced to relocate their production overseas.

For Japan, as for other industrialized economies like France and Italy, 1973 thus marked the end of an era of rapid growth at an average of over 10 per cent per annum from 1952 to 1973. From then on, the average remained between 4 and 5 per cent per annum for five years, with a plunge in 1974 and a peak in 1989–90, considerably higher than the growth rate of the other major industrialized countries. However, this did not stop Japan having to prop up or diversify troubled industries and stimulate domestic consumption. Furthermore, Japan was no longer catching up with the more advanced economies and profiting from their technological experience, but was itself innovating in turn. It was also more overtly cautious in its industrial policy, while economic expansion reduced the dominance of the state *vis à vis* private enterprise. With a GNP per capita of nearly US$24,000 in 1990, and ranking as the world's second-largest exporter after Germany (albeit with a much larger trade surplus), Japan has become an international giant. And yet the Heisei boom (the longest of the post-war period, lasting 58 months from November 1986 to September 1991) was founded on Japanese domestic demand to a much greater extent than in the past. The remarkable rise in exports only accounted for 1 per cent of the country's annual growth between 1980 and 1985, while from 1985 to 1990 this figure even sank as low as zero or a negative contribution.

The dynamics of public spending

From 1973, however, domestic demand was heavily stimulated by the efforts of the state. Two pressures combined to bring this about: first, the increasing importance of socio-economic lobbies within the LDP, and second, the efforts by conservative politicians to supply an extremely diverse range of subsidies to their voters. In 1972, Tanaka had inaugurated an impressive programme of public works and public spending with a plan for a high-speed train that would run the length of the country. A major share of public subsidy went to sectors in difficulty. As a result, Japan's budgetary and financial management underwent a new cycle: since the beginning of the 1950s, the traditional practice of overloaning had gradually given way to orthodox monetarism, making Japan in 1973 one of two major countries (alongside France) whose national debt accounted for the lowest proportion of GNP, at 12 per cent. From 1973 onwards, the state contracted debts by issuing bonds, while greatly expanding its fiscal investment and loan programme (FILP), which acted, so to speak, as a kind of second budget, just as large as the first. This policy, launched in 1953 and the Japanese equivalent of the French Caisse des Depôts, was larger than the central budget itself. The level of state debt in relation to annual GNP thus rose to 39 per cent in 1980 and passed the 50 per cent mark in 1985, a rate only exceeded by the United States and Italy. A Keynesian budget was then adopted in order to sustain economic activity, marked by a notable rise in public spending. Between 1978 and 1983, Japan was the only one out of all the industrialized countries to maintain and even increase the level of public spending as a proportion of its GNP, which was itself also undergoing considerable growth.

Despite the increase in public spending as a proportion of GNP, the Japanese state administration remains by far the most frugal in this respect, with the exception of the United States. In 1988 for example, the state budget proper was little more than US$480 billion, barely 20 per cent higher than the total French budget, for an economy three times as large. This frugality is due to several factors. First, Japanese operational expenses are extremely low. Education absorbs less than 10 per cent, and defence less than 5 per cent of the Japanese central budget. Military expenditure (the third highest in the world in absolute terms) thus remains below 1 per cent of GNP, no longer due to any prohibitions, but to economic dynamism. Nevertheless, Japan's total expenditure on health and social welfare rose from 2 per cent to 18 per cent of GNP between 1970 and 1982. In 1990, state spending on pensions accounted for less than 5 per cent of public expenditure. Public spending on research is likewise extremely low, with private enterprise putting up the bulk of the resources. One area in which there has been a consistent increase since 1973 is the budget for investment in infrastructure and support for the hardest-hit groups and sectors such as farmers, shopkeepers, construction and SMEs (small and medium enterprises), providing a considerable cushion against the effects of the global economic crisis and helping to reduce income differences. Although this is the antithesis of a European-style welfare state, it is still not a purely industrial policy. Most government subsidies go to farmers, the construction industry, the energy sector, small businesses and railways. The ministries responsible (with the exception of MITI and the Finance Ministry) have effectively become cash dispensers for the LDP. In return, sectors and regions in difficulty contribute to the coffers of LDP Diet members, either via professional associations (such as the farmers' leagues or the associations of SMEs) or, in the case of companies, on the basis of public contracts secured.

The state withdraws

From 1983, however, the state ceased to be a net lender, and central administrative costs were reduced even further in percentage terms. The repayment of old debts then absorbed more than 20 per cent of budgetary expenditure. Each year, the Japanese government produces a primary surplus, which is reinvested on the capital markets in repayment of previous borrowing. The Thatcherite model, which was also visible in the form of denationalization, was more strictly applied here than in the UK, yet by directly supplying firms with subsidies and markets during the years of oil-supply adjustment (1973–83) the state thus helped to fuel the vast supply of cheap capital available in the mid-1980s, enabling large-scale technological and financial investment by the major firms. In particular, the latter increasingly became involved in self-financing by means of direct appeals to the financial markets. Thus, between 1974 and the end of the 1980s, the Japanese government's financial policy underwent considerable change, first undergoing a Keynesian, inflationary phase of anti-cyclical adaptation to the crisis, then adopting orthodox monetarism, paving the way for the full liberalization of the financial markets.

Income distribution and savings

Given a state that plays a minimal role and at the same time is largely concerned with supporting the private-sector economy, including its unprofitable areas, it is hardly surprising that the broad lines of income distribution are different in Japan compared to elsewhere. The role of wages in the national income remains low: it rose from less than 50 per cent in 1973 to 53 per cent in 1989, whereas in the other industrialized countries it currently accounts for 70 per cent. Yet social security contributions as a proportion of wage income are also distinctly low, due to the virtual absence of unemployment and the still limited level of personal contributions to social security. The steep rise in the number of pensioners after 1995 is bound to place a heavy burden on the national income. Over the same period, Japanese families made an enormous saving effort, squirreling away 21 per cent of their net disposable income between 1974 and 1976. These years of slump and diversification marked the culmination of post-war economic mobilization. The savings rate gradually declined to a nadir of 14 per cent in 1989, only slightly higher than current French and German levels, but far in excess of individual saving in the United States, where it accounts for 3–4 per cent of net income. It is certainly true that the Japanese wage-earner will traditionally save up in advance in order to buy a house or car, whereas their American counterpart will incur debt in order to achieve the same goal. All in all, the total value of assets held on average by American households is still three times higher than that of Japanese households (on 1986 figures) but it is mostly tied up in real estate. Other factors are put forward to justify this relatively high level, for example the fact that in Japan retirement is financed through capitalization, widespread private education, steep medical costs, and the fact that wage bonuses are paid twice per annum. Yet Japanese wage-earners still lag behind their South Korean and Taiwanese counterparts, whose savings in 1990 alone were equivalent to Japanese levels for the period 1974–6. As for Singapore, where each wage-earner voluntarily pays 34 per cent of his or her income into a government savings fund via capitalization, the individual savings rate is over 50 per cent.

Today, therefore, the bulk of Japan's productive investments – what economists call 'gross fixed capital formation', or GFCF – are less closely dependent on net household savings. Since 1973 this GFCF has reached, and in some cases even exceeded, 30 per cent of GNP, a third more than in the EC countries or the Asian NICs, and double that in the United States. More than half of this GFCF comes from the business sector. Japan's vast trade surplus, the extremely high profit margins created by the cartel-dominated, protectionist distribution channels, and the continuing rise in productivity help to explain the considerable level of corporate self-financing. As a result, they require much less recourse to indirect financing by the banks than they did prior to 1973, and are therefore less dependent on state regulation of credit. On the one hand, this investment margin is self-perpetuating: the extremely rapid replacement of plant and machinery (within less than five years on average) absorbs investment without saturating the markets, thus boosting productivity and, consequently, profitability.

One further source of financing comes from the system of *keiretsu*, the interrelationships between major companies, their subsidiaries, banks and other financial institutions such as pension funds and major securities houses. This form of mutual control, which first appeared in the mid-1950s, has grown in importance. The percentage of shares held by private individuals has fallen by half since the end of the 1960s, while the 'stable core' accounts for over two-thirds of company shares. The resulting stability and the close personal links which exist between company directors, the chairmen of the major banks and their civil service mentors encourage risk-free speculation. In the wake of the 1973 oil crisis, Japanese stockmarket assets held up much better than the economy at large. From the beginning of the 1980s, the market voluntarily continued its unstoppable expansion, with a resurgence in stockmarket speculation corresponding with a boom in land prices. Japan's extraordinarily high share prices (often more than 80 times the annual dividend) seemed totally detached from the rest of the world, and land and property prices, which are the highest in the world due to legislation penalizing new building, appeared to be risk-free, since the majority of the shares were unlikely to be offered for sale, and a land shortage seemed inevitable. These phenomena, coupled with a vast balance of payments surplus, led to a flood of cheap capital, unleashing a frenzy of speculation.

In 1986–9, the Japanese capital markets seemed to have become detached from the rest of the planet. Incredibly low interest rates, combined with a revaluation of the yen, allowed massive financial investment overseas, the most striking examples being the acquisition of New York's Rockefeller Center and CBS in Hollywood, and the manic collecting of Impressionist paintings, which in 1990 was enough in itself to balance trade between France and Japan. The widespread opening of factories in the United States by Japanese firms, including subcontractors of the major Japanese car manufacturers, was a further result of this proliferation of wealth. It was ultimately Japan's savings surplus which financed the United States budget deficit, because until 1989 the Japanese were buying up American government bonds on a massive scale.

The race for high technologies

Japan is the only country in the world where 97 per cent of exports consist of manufactured goods. Conversely, if Japan has become less dependent on the outside world for its energy, this is due to the expansion of its nuclear industry and an intensive, ongoing programme of energy conservation. Raw materials as a share of Japan's total imports fell from 78 per cent to 50 per cent from 1980 to 1990, while its purchases of consumer and capital goods reflected the new openness of the market. Yet in addition to its own domestic market, Japan continues to be a vast processing platform, with industry occupying a place unequalled in other major industrialized countries. While highly dependent on United States patents and licences, and heavily focused on low-technology areas of production such as textiles, timber and light engineering during the post-war period, it has since performed a number of technological leaps, the most spectacular of which came after 1973. The main exports of the 1960s (steel, textiles, shipbuilding, televisions and radios) consequently declined very rapidly under the impact of competition from the newly industrialized countries and, in some cases, from increasing relocation. Government intervention in industrial financing and state control of private-sector decision making lessened as firms became rich. The budgets set aside for most of MITI's high-technology projects were comparable with, and sometimes smaller than, those allocated to similar projects in other advanced countries. The total Japanese state R&D (research and development) budget (including loans) over a ten-year period was thus no more than US$2.3 billion (Okimoto, 1989). These sums are far lower than those committed by the French government to R&D in the electronics industry alone since 1981. The Japanese government's share in the financing of industrial investment (not just research) in the electronics industry does little to enhance the picture, amounting to less than 0.8 per cent of the national total at the end of the 1970s. Overall, the fiscal programme of industrial investment and loans, which accounted for over 30 per cent of industrial capital in the early 1950s, fell below 10 per cent in the 1980s.

Despite this, Japanese industry has emerged the winner. With the exception of a few less fortunate sectors, such as biotechnology and computer programming, its long-term forecasts, a series of more concrete three- and five-year plans and the international strategic choices made by MITI built up a first-rate industrial policy. This contrasts sharply with the policies of countries like France, for example, which failed in the realm of high technology (electronics and data processing) despite being similar in form, and in some cases also more expensive to finance. How was this miracle achieved? First and foremost, MITI's interventions were geared to two precise points in the technological cycle, namely the moment when key innovations emerge and the moment when they become obsolete. In the former case, it produced a technological renaissance and provided venture capital, often in order to amalgamate leading firms which had a tendency to compete. This government funding was useful in encouraging projects which were non-viable in the short term. This was true at the end of the 1980s in nuclear energy, marine resources, the space industry, biotechnology and computer programming. In the case of technological obsolescence, MITI intervened to aid diversification. Although the 'reorganization cartels' responsible for forcing the closure of some plants and firms are less common than in the 1950s, they still exist, enabling firms to avoid maintaining unnecessary surplus production capacity. Recent examples of this include coal mining, textiles, and the chemical and non-ferrous metals industries. However, MITI no longer funds or supports mature industries capable of being sustained by the market, for example computers, integrated circuits, car manufacture, machine tools, consumer electronics, steel and oil (Okimoto, 1989). This list gives an indication of those sectors where MITI intervened during the 1970s, but does not do so any longer.

One further aspect of the success of Japan's industrial policy is that of easy and frequent communication, based on personal networks (*jinmyaku*) linking civil servants, industrial executives, researchers and financiers.

Despite the cut-throat competition which can arise between firms, a sense of team spirit, instilled from the cradle onwards, enables a number of highly diverse players to collaborate on a technological project and then split up again for the application and dissemination stages. Examples to the contrary also exist, for instance the extremely costly war which Sony fought in defence of the Betamax standard against Mitsubishi and other overseas competitors, but these generally feature those rare firms, like Sony, where individualism forms part of the corporate culture. Likewise, negotiation is generally the preferred course of action rather than resorting to courts or tribunals, although plaintiffs may, admittedly, be deterred from the alternatives by the weight of tradition and by the use of thinly-veiled threats. The same is true of the powers theoretically held by shareholders, yet which rarely have any effect. Co-operation and flexibility are both features of MITI's *modus operandi*, where decisions are often taken collectively, way below political level, in other words by civil servants in the light of their own experience. Other factors put forward include the political stability guaranteed by the LDP, which, by adopting a consistently favourable stance towards firms, protects them from political crises, while social submissiveness ensures that strikes and other forms of open confrontation are avoided. Certain areas of government susceptible to the use of patronage, for instance the Ministries of Agriculture, Forestries, Construction and Education, nominate a large number of members to the Diet, organized into groups (*zoku*) which remain loyal to their collective interests. As for MITI, it has long been able to ignore the Diet and its members, allowing its civil servants the chance to concentrate their energies on changing jobs from the public sector to the major firms. In 1988, MITI only had eight former members of staff in the Diet and was the only ministry, apart from the Gaimusho (Foreign Affairs), to avoid the factional atmosphere and managed to preserve its professional and corporate links with Japan's most dynamic firms.

With the liberalization and opening up of the financial markets during the 1980s, the Finance Ministry frequently stole a march on MITI, something which became even more true after 1989. Indeed, together with the Bank of Japan, the financial authorities set about deflating the giant speculative bubble which had formed over the stock and real estate markets. The United States added its own pressure to the worries besetting Japan's economic masters. The Finance Ministry offered a breeding-ground for senior politicians profiting from their past fiscal relationships with business: neither side escaped the flood of revelations about enormous financial scandals.

Japan: between protectionism and free trade

The breakthrough achieved by Japanese overseas trade at international level has been accompanied by controversy over its causes. First and foremost, Japan's overseas trade continues to form a smaller proportion of GNP (14.6 per cent in 1995) than in countries like France and Germany. There has been undeniably a liberalization of imports by the government since the days of the 'cocoon state': in 1960, 59 per cent of all Japanese imports were subject to quotas, but only 12 per cent by 1993. Since the early 1980s, Japanese customs duties and import restrictions on industrial products have been lower than in other industrialized countries: tariff barriers and quotas have largely been phased out, while a similar plan was introduced at the end of the 1980s for certain special categories of goods, such as alcohol and some agricultural products (such as plywood, beef and citrus fruits). Only rice, the prime focus of the farmers' lobby in Japan, as in Korea and Taiwan, remains a lost cause, despite pressure from the United States government. Lastly, public contracts are only being opened up to foreign firms with great difficulty.

Yet this trade liberalism, which is now adhered to as a principle, does not prevent Japanese overseas trade from being both specialized and unbalanced. In the first place, its exports are focused on a few specific niches, from cars to audiovisual equipment. In other spheres, Japanese industry performs less well, although it still represents the bulk of the domestic market, the consequence of a post-war industrial policy which diversified as much as possible in order to avoid reliance on imports. Less than 4 per cent of the production capacity of Japanese companies was located overseas in 1986, compared with 15–20 per cent in the case of other industrialized countries. Also in 1986, imports of manufactured goods only accounted for 3.7 per cent of GNP, compared with 7.2 per cent for the United States and 15–20 per cent for almost all West European countries. Overall, intra-industrial trade (that is trade with other countries within a common industrial sector) is much lower than in any other industrialized country, proving that Japanese industry relies very little on foreign suppliers and also that consumers have little choice of foreign products in those sectors where the home-produced goods on offer are of inferior quality. For example, Japanese housewives typically continued to use noisy, non-automatic washing-machines until the early 1980s, because they were unable to purchase more sophisticated American or especially European models.

Furthermore, the very high costs of penetrating Japanese distribution channels, not least in terms of rent costs, have served to penalize more recent newcomers, both Japanese and foreign. There is a strong temptation for a European or American producer to rely on a Japanese trading company to sell a small number of products at a high price, yielding a considerable profit margin without actually penetrating the market. Foreign imports may adorn the shelves of the most prestigious department stores, but it is not clear whether they have really impinged on the fundamental purchasing habits of the Japanese. A law restricting department store opening-hours protects small retailers and their high profit margins. It has taken nearly three years of negotiations for the American toy giant Toys 'R' Us to be able to open its first store in Japan with a huge commercial success, however. Informal barriers, such as the allegiances which exist between Japanese firms or simply the reluctance of many consumers to buy less familiar products, continue to be very important. In the absence of a policy of state support for exports, the leading Japanese companies, on the basis of their own funds and considerable profit margins, frequently fix their sales prices in accordance with a long-term commercial strategy for market penetration, rather than in terms of their immediate profitability. It is this which leads to their being accused in Europe and America of dumping, a charge heard much less often from other markets such as those of Asia and the Pacific, because there Japan occupies a position of strength and charges higher prices. On the one hand, such accusations are founded on a misunderstanding: Japanese companies operate on a much longer timescale than their European and especially their American counterparts. Every year, sometimes quarterly, European and American firms are required to show profits in order to keep up their share prices. Where possible, they compensate for this through captive markets or markets restricted by external factors. For example, the same car sold in Los Angeles at a price not much higher than that which it would fetch in Japan, would be worth a third more in Germany where an unofficial quota still limits Japanese vehicles to 15 per cent of the market, and 50 per cent more in France, where the import quota is set to a mere 3 per cent of the market. Production and sales volumes are therefore achieved in the United States, while profits are reaped in Europe, especially in the protectionist markets which claim to want to safeguard their own industry. This multi-national strategy does not signify the rejection of economic liberalism but rather its very culmination, forcing the actors involved to face the challenge either of resorting to protectionism or of seeing whole swathes of home-grown industry disintegrate.

The LDP: invisible cement or outmoded structure?

Any attempt to enquire into the source or sources of the success of the Japanese economy, and particularly its technological advances, eventually reaches a dead end. State control of the economy has been weak since 1973, even though the stockmarket upheavals of 1990–1 restored the regulatory role of the Finance Ministry and the major banks – when they themselves were not implicated in the same scandals, that is. MITI itself appears to have been much less dirigiste than in the immediate post-war period as Chalmers Johnson saw it (Okimoto, 1989: 1–3). If there is an industrial policy, it is neither better financed nor any more restrictive than that of any other industrialized country, apart from the United States. Japan's monetary, financial and budgetary policies between 1973 and 1980 appear to have been bold, not to say high-risk – opposed in every way to the monetarism and budgetary orthodoxy currently preached throughout the European Union. Whole swathes of Japanese society are neither particularly productive nor subject to market forces: public utilities and monopoly services, such as gas, electricity, telephones, railways, small businesses, directors of public works, farmers, doctors and dentists who enjoy extremely high guaranteed incomes. What is more, because of the way in which the pricing structure operates, it is the Japanese consumer who picks up the bill for these inefficiencies and subsidies.

Yet in fact, such malfunctioning contributes to Japanese social equilibrium by sustaining rural areas, small towns and non-wage-earners. It also serves to explain the minimal unemployment rate (running at 2.1 per cent in 1990) and the uniformity of Japanese lifestyles from one end of the archipelago to the other. Government subsidies also round out the development of the archipelago's infrastructure, which is still very backward in comparison with the more established industrialized countries. One third of major and minor roads in Japan are unsurfaced, 55 per cent of homes lack mains drainage, and the housing stock is still notoriously inadequate and often of abysmal quality. The LDP, which was undermined by a decline at the polls in the early 1970s, has tackled these deficiencies and regained electoral support in the process. It acts as a mechanism for income redistribution by virtue of the influence of pressure groups, which balance the political power wielded by the major firms. Pressure group resistance to the destabilizing effect of imports – from rice to public works to trade in general – often fuels the wider international trade disputes, which hit the major firms the hardest.

This policy of harmonizing diverse interests and client groups naturally has various side-effects. Even more so than in the past, the LDP is the archetypal catch-all party, acting as a magnet for an extremely wide range of aspirations and occasionally embracing highly contradictory lobbies, just as on an international level it has managed to juggle the simultaneous existence of pro-Taiwanese and pro-Peking factions and groups supporting each of the two Koreas. Yet the all-powerful role of private interests also has the effect of destabilizing Japanese society and its famous consensus, which was specifically based on a universal sense of belonging to the middle class. From the mid-1980s, when the country was swept by a vast wave of speculation, a distinct social divide set in, creating the impression of what some ironically referred to as a 'new feudal bondage'. Despite the fact that the standard of living has risen by 5 per cent per annum, the Japanese 'salaryman' clearly has little opportunity to prosper: buying a modest apartment is enough to exhaust his entire savings and credit capacity. In 1989–90, the banks occasionally granted mortgage loans spread over 100 years, the repayment costs of which will also be borne by future generations. Conversely, both small and large land and property owners, the professions, shopkeepers and other small businesses all profited from the extremely widespread practice of tax evasion, to which politicians and officials turned a blind eye. All in all, Japanese social customs are such that the very notion of 'insider dealing' is non-existent in the financial world, allowing those with influence to become rich very quickly. The stockmarket crashes of 1987 in Wall Street and in particular 1990 in Tokyo showed how *keiretsu* connections, or even simply personal contacts, shelter the major players from losses, leaving the ordinary saver to foot the bill. In 1990–1, under pressure from American financial institutions trying to achieve openness and transparency on the Kabutocho (the Japanese stock exchange), several incidents were exposed where losses had been compensated. These revelations led to a drop of almost 60 per cent in Japanese share prices. In fact, it was these guarantees, disclosed or otherwise, which shielded the leading players against loss, just as much as the cross-holdings between them, allowing share prices which bore no relation either to dividends or to company profits. Japan's stock market was still capitalized at US$1.86 trillion in January 1992, but successive scandals have continued to weaken share prices.

Once again, Japanese society appears to be trapped in an insoluble dilemma. There are particular human factors which have produced spectacular successes, with less imagination than is generally acknowledged: social cohesion, personal contacts, informality, pragmatism and an ability to adapt to crisis, a disinclination for ideological and political swings and a capacity for hard work. The LDP's extraordinary skill at consensus, income redistribution and the granting of political favours ensures that the less fortunate groups in society do not lag too far behind. Through patronage it provides the equivalent of the state safety-net found in the major European economies. It has an electoral system based on the continuity of quasi-feudal fiefdoms and the dominance of the rural vote (not only in the LDP but also in the JSP), which makes Japanese politics immune to discontent and urban tensions. The extraordinary dynamism of the economic giants, their unrivalled capacity for technological innovation, and their ultra-rapid introduction of new products and production methods is only possible due to the countervailing presence of this great shock-absorber: cut-throat competition and rivalry do indeed exist in a society which remains obsessed with its quest for collective and individual security.

However, comparisons with the standard of living and working hours of other industrialized countries now less advanced than Japan, the introduction of political and legal standards imported from the West (especially the American model), financial liberalization and the huge profits resulting from it, as well as structural corruption in politics – all cause the Japanese people to feel bitter. In 1989, at the time of the trade negotiations with the United States, a majority backed the American position rather than support the Japanese government. Even though the LDP may still have appeared invincible, its popularity was very low, particularly in the major cities. The employees of the major firms and senior civil servants were the two groups responsible for the Japanese miracle. The former still work 2,100 hours per year each (compared with fewer than 1,700 hours in Germany) and secretly envy the standard of living enjoyed by Westerners, when they are not casting a jealous eye at the Singaporeans or the middle classes of Korea and Taiwan. It is surely no coincidence that within a few years, a man with the intuition of Akio Morita, the celebrated founder of Sony, has switched from the anti-Americanism articulated in *The Japan that can say no* (Morita and Ishihara, 1989), written with Shintaro Ishihara, an ultra-nationalistic right-wing LDP member of the Diet, to arguing for wages, working hours and lifestyles that would reflect the wealth Japan has accumulated. Senior civil servants, their status undermined by the influence of their private sector counterparts, are more sensitive than politicians to international threats against Japan's aggressive trade behaviour. Admittedly, there does exist a *nouveau riche* class based mainly on property ownership: a few acres of building land or a handful of apartments are a passport to riches, since ultra-stringent legislation and urban planning guarantee a permanent housing shortage. Meanwhile, those who have abandoned the notion of buying their own apartment will often divert their purchasing power into luxury cars, the race to acquire imported goods, and holidays abroad. In fact, they achieve nothing like the assets which the European or American middle classes can possess.

The very success of the Japanese economy has brought with it strategic and social choices. The cohesion of the post-war years and the supremacy of the LDP were assured by a sense of inferiority and the need to catch up with the rest of the world, as well as by a fear of communism. The disappearance of Japan's inferiority complex *vis à vis* the United States has the potential to cause nationalist tensions and a predisposition to resume pre-war ideas, which are still very much alive. Yet the bulk of Japanese urban society, and before it the environmentalists, artists and intellectuals of the 1960s, has expressed above all the wish to end Japan's status as the odd one out. This is what provides the justification for a highly formalized democracy and the fact that Japanese society is still run along particularistic lines. We may be seeing the end of the era which Japan's founders knew, of conformist wage-earners in thrall to an exclusive caste of law graduates from prestigious Todai University, populist politicians with their noses in the public subsidy trough and speculators as ruthless as the Osaka merchants of old. At any rate, it is an era which is now failing to satisfy the majority, despite its economic success.

Wealth and power: the controversy

To describe Japan's enhanced role in the world since 1973 means repeating a litany of figures, which would appear to speak for themselves. At any rate, they show that the Japanese economy has played a key part, perhaps even the central part, in the international system of technology, trade and capital. Japan has become the world's leading producer or exporter in many industrial sectors – steel, car manufacturing, machine tools and electronics for example. It is the major net holder of financial assets overseas (approximately US$500 billion in 1990) and the leading donor of international government aid. Between 1987 and 1990, the level of transactions recorded on the Tokyo stock exchange equalled that of Wall Street. It was Japan alone which financed one third of the cost of the international expedition against Iraq in 1991 with a contribution of US$13 billion.

This perspective is clarified further by the emergence of a new angle: the newly-industrialized countries of Asia are advancing on Japan in formation, like a 'flight of geese', to quote the quaint and vivid phrase of the late Foreign Minister Saburo Okita, who became the unofficial guru of Japanese relations with the rest of Asia. They certainly seem to be moving fast: having achieved rapid growth of nearly 10 per cent per annum in the 1960s, the 'Four Dragons' – Taiwan, Korea, Hong Kong and Singapore – have kept on growing ever since. Other economies, for example Thailand, Malaysia, even Indonesia, as well as a considerable part of mainland China, achieved a similar developmental rate during the mid-1980s, and moreover their growth has been much more export-driven than Japan's. All in all, their economic interdependence with Japan is increasing, returning in times of freedom to a plan sketched out before and during the Second World War, starting with the role of the yen as a regional reserve currency and lending instrument, and progressing to more intensive trade and Japanese direct investment in industry and distribution. Overall, Japan's share of industrial exports as a proportion of world trade rose from 5.6 per cent in 1960 to 9.4 per cent in 1970 and nearly 20 per cent in 1990, while that of the 'Four Dragons' rose from 5.4 per cent to nearly 11 per cent between 1980 and 1990. In 1991–2, the ASEAN countries envisaged forming a free-trade zone, particularly for manufactured goods, while maritime China is taking an increasing part in East Asia's economic expansion. All in all, this would appear to place Japan at the head of the world's most dynamic region (or at least in the lead), although without weakening its international role.

Modern-day Japan combines a renewed sense of superiority with a continuing awareness of its own vulnerability. The spectre of natural disaster (especially of an earthquake worse in its effects than that of 1923), an obsession with the country's supplies of natural resources and the probing of *nihonjin* (or Japanese identity), which is a choice publishers' market, are ever-present anxieties: they seem to have replaced history, and particularly attempts to elucidate the militarist era of 1931–45, which is still intellectually and socially taboo. Yet the Japanese have become the most avid producers and consumers of futurology, ranging from modern technology (particularly the information society) to systems of power for the twenty-first century. The pursuit of these themes, epitomized by the 1985 World's Fair at Tsukuba and the university established there, is also visible in the urban development of Japan's vast, densely-populated cities: fast-renewing, gleaming and apparently chaotic, all at the same time. There is cultural debate, and a questioning of the national role, but virtually no social debate, which instead seems to have been completely replaced by the race

for commercially viable technologies and for the innovations which market-
ing engenders. Although the pure sciences appear to be dominated by the
United States, Japan would appear to have cornered the market in applied
technology. When Minolta and Sony found themselves facing lawsuits
brought by American defence companies concerning the misuse of technologies such as auto-focusing devices, infra-red and high-definition, the
episode above all showed that Japanese firms were offering the consumer
technology which in the United States was only accessible to the
Pentagon itself.

In the quest for identity, modern-day Japan seems caught between wealth
and power. These two concepts – *fokuku kyohei* in Japanese, *fuqiang* in
Chinese – lay at the heart of the industrial revolution of the Meiji era as well
as other attempts at modernization in Asia during the nineteenth and
twentieth centuries. In those days they were inseparable, and they are still
associated today in Chinese minds, even though the People's Republic has
not moved very far towards putting them into practice. In Japan, on the
other hand, the dislocation which occurred in 1945 still lingers on. In almost
every international sphere, the advocates of a low profile, co-operation and
diplomacy vie with the supporters of a new stance more in keeping with
national ambitions. This does not mean that the line represented by Shigeru
Yoshida and his successors has failed: on the contrary, the commercial
dynamism which grew out of Japan's perpetual role as second fiddle to the
United States has taken it so far that it is now increasingly less adaptable to
its new role. For some, the future lies in an internationalist breakthrough
for Japan, which would become the leading world power (or at least a
power equal to the United States), while exercising that responsibility in a
manner unprecedented in human history. For the advocates of 'globalism',
the technological era has gone beyond the nation states inherited from the
nineteenth century, creating a global society founded on trade in goods and
services. Japan, positioned in the vanguard of this transition, must act as
the donor of aid on a world scale (which indeed it already is), yet it must
also advance the major causes of the international order: the environment,
disarmament and international law. Unfortunately, this vision soon clashes
with some mundane realities: Japan is still one of the 'enemy states' cited in
the original United Nations Charter, along with Germany and Italy, and
has no permanent seat on the Security Council. To claim a place in the new
world order inevitably implies a devaluation of those who won in 1945, or
at least the former Soviet Union, France and the United Kingdom. Even in
regional crises such as the Cambodia question, Japanese diplomats still only
assert themselves indirectly, protected by their country's considerable financial contributions. Furthermore, Japanese public opinion still rejects any
notion of Japanese participation, peaceful or otherwise, in international
conflict. This was shown once again in 1991, at the time of Iraq's invasion
of Kuwait, as well as in the wrangle the following year over Japan's provision of peacekeeping troops to the United Nations. The text of the motion

as finally voted upon ruled out any commitment to Japanese armament or direct combat, in effect creating a humanitarian contingent rather than an international peacekeeping force. After all, some of Japan's closest neighbours – Korea, China, Singapore – quail at the slightest hint of an enhanced military role for Japan, whatever form it might take.

There remains the option of realism, either diplomatic or military. Within the LDP and among defence experts in the big industrial firms and the Foreign Ministry, there have always been a significant number who have criticized the Constitution and the official pacifist line. Yet over several decades, this realism has split into two distinct schools of thought. First there are those, notably LDP politicians and the Foreign Ministry, who are in favour of the security treaty with the United States, viewing it as an ideal defence umbrella, and who unequivocally support America's international lead. Yet there are also those who advocate a realism based on the more military means of Japanese defence and regard Japanese rearmament as vital, something which would also allow Japanese diplomacy to become more independent. America's budgetary difficulties are increasingly forcing it to fund its Asian military presence through financial contributions from its allies in the region. The disappearance of the Soviet Union and of the threat which it embodied has likewise reduced the tendency to automatic unity. A growing gulf is now emerging between these two parallel realist views, the diplomatic and the military. Being richer than its partners, Japan can no longer evade the consequences of power: if it restricts defence expenditure, it will face accusations (as it already does) of unfair economic advantage; if it increases it, its motives will be open to question. Japan has become the arbiter of the various modes of organization, diplomacy and politics within the Asia–Pacific region. Poised between a vision of the Pacific Basin which sees both shores united (one which it has itself advocated) and the creation of a free-trade zone, or even an East Asian bloc (essentially the economically productive part of Asia), Japan has considerable power to influence the world's future. Although it has not devoted a great deal of effort to aeronautics or space, its acquisitions and co-operative links (until now oriented almost exclusively towards America, rather than Europe) will tend to favour one or other of the world's poles. While Japanese society would still prefer to envisage its future as being that of a large Switzerland, rich and neutral, its leaders are being forced to make choices which often overwhelm them: the elusive nature of political power, which since 1945 has often made it possible in the past to preserve the autonomy of the losing side, now prevents them from taking these international decisions in a coherent way. The Japanese economy is currently equivalent to two-and-a-half times that of Germany, yet Japan is a long way from attaining (or re-attaining) Germany's diplomatic and political influence, and has not had the advantage in recent years of the framework of a European Union to help anchor its relations with its neighbours. This conclusion, far removed from the aggressive image which is wrongly conjured up by notions of 'economic warfare' (a highly inaccurate term for corporate dynamism), presupposes internal developments within the Japanese archipelago. In contrast to Victorian England, Japan – the great transoceanic commercial power of the late twentieth century – is seeing its own society permeated from top to bottom by the powerful solvent of modernization. The cultural uniqueness often claimed by the Japanese as by many other Asians, for example in terms of the importance of the family unit, the unity of the local community, social cohesion and patriotism without social disharmony, may be receding. Will this favour the emergence of an international society of individuals living on unearned income, resting on their technological superiority and their financial surplus, which would lead to a short-lived heyday? Or will Japan transform its own society sufficiently to acquire real cultural and political influence over the rest of Asia and the world? It may be too easy to answer these questions, but they are already being asked.

These questions became even more urgent in 1992–3: once the speculative 'bubble' of the 1980s had finally burst, Japan embarked on its first real post-war economic recession, longer-lasting than the aftermath of the 1973 oil shock. The fall in profits (or the losses, more or less thinly disguised) suffered by the major banks, insurance companies and property firms led to a general slump. There is a shortage of markets both in Japan and the West, and East Asia is the only growth area which remains as vigorous as ever. As it reduced its imports due to its stagnant domestic market, Japan's trade and financial surpluses continued to increase, almost to a burdensome extent, reaching an unprecedented high in real terms in 1992, even in the midst of the economic crisis. Shaken by repeated and ever more explicit scandals, Japanese politics seems to be approaching a turning-point. The arrest of Shin Kanemaru, the LDP's venerable godfather figure, and the discovery of vast hoards of gold and cash at his home, appears to have been a clearer repudiation than in similar incidents in the past. Strangely, this did not work to the benefit of any of the political alternatives vying with the LDP moderates over the path to be taken. After the demise of Mrs Doi, the only influential woman in Japanese politics, the Japanese Socialist Party seemed divided and forgotten by public opinion. The defeat of the LDP old guard (after Tanaka, Nakasone, Takeshita and more recently Kanemaru) actually benefited the pro-Westerners represented by Prime Minister Kiichi Miyazawa. While this uncharismatic figure may seem incapable of injecting new life into Japanese politics, he did on the other hand prevent it from veering towards nationalism or adopting a more social-democratic programme in spite of the crisis. President Clinton and his running-mate Al Gore, who were elected on an implicitly protectionist ticket, would no doubt welcome the chance to cross swords with Japan, but Japanese society did not give them the pretext of a Japanese nationalist revival. On the contrary, they found themselves confronted by the archetypal representative of the advocates of democracy and free trade which the post-war era has bequeathed to Japan. Though part of the Far East, Japan was not far off being a Far West in the early 1990s, while the United States and Europe were going through an introspective phase. It was also not far off experiencing the splendid isolation of Victorian England.

This situation has seemed to intensify in 1995. Japan has been hit hard by a domestic economic crisis which has brought with it a seemingly neverending revaluation of the yen. However, this tendency has its roots in the commercial vigour of Japan, whose trade surplus, though no longer on the increase, still indicates its strength on the major world markets. Having become, of necessity, an advocate of free trade, Japan has managed its financial wealth much less effectively: several times since 1985, foreign investments in dollars have suffered a monetary crisis, while domestic recession has created a mountain of debts payable in yen. Because of having refused to divert its capital elsewhere other than the United States, since that would have given the yen the status of a reserve currency and would have forced Japan to assume concomitant political responsibility, it did not utilize its full economic strength on the international level.

The hesitation and calculation involved in domestic political transition – ever since the LDP lost its political monopoly in 1993 – have also impacted on Japan's international standing. Its application to become a member of the UN Security Council was accompanied by reservations over a possible military role, and it appeared cautious over the approach to take *vis à vis* a highly self-assertive China. But does this transition, prolonged by the LDP's return to power alongside the socialists, mean that Japanese politics is incapable of making strategic choices? At this time, actual public opinion – pacifist yet disillusioned with regard to the United States, hostile to political parties but more modest in its aspirations than ever before – is expressing the uncertainty characteristic of large democracies. However, it seems likely that Japan, forced by currency speculation to open up its economic system more widely, and facing the rise of China and possible Korean reunification in the vicinity, will have to make choices. Either it will have to complete its international symbiosis with the United States in order to avoid the consequences of possible American isolationism, or it will have to develop in the direction of the theory of the 'normal state', with the responsibilities and risks that such a development would entail.

SELECTED READING

Alletzhauser, A. (1990) *The House of Nomura*, London: Bloomsbury.

Baerwald, H. (1986) *Party politics in Japan*, Boston: Allen & Unwin.

Berque, A. (ed.) (1987) *Le Japon et son double*, Paris: Masson.

Choate, P. (1990) *Agents of influence: how Japan's lobbyists in the United States manipulate America's political and economic system*, New York: Alfred Knopf.

Coriat, B. (1991) *Penser à l'envers: travail et organisation dans l'entreprise japonaise*, Paris: Christian Bourgois.

Curtis, G. L. (1988) *The Japanese way of politics*, New York: Columbia University Press.

Cusumano, M. A. (1985) *The Japanese automobile industry: technology and management at Nissan and Toyota*, Cambridge, MA: Harvard University Press.

Dore, R. P. (1987) *Taking Japan seriously: a Confucian perspective on leading economic issues*, London: Athlone Press.

Emmott, B. (1989) *The sun also sets: why Japan will not be Number One*, London: Simon & Schuster.

Esmein, J. and Dubreuil, R. (eds) (1986) *L'évolution des systèmes japonaises*, Paris: CESTA.

Hrebenar, R. J. (1986) *The Japanese party system: from one-party rule to coalition government*, Boulder: Westview Press.

Inoguchi, T., Okimoto, D. and Patrick, H. T. (eds) (1987) *The political economy of Japan*, 3 vols, Stanford: Stanford University Press.

Ishihara, S. (1991) *Le Japon sans complexe*, Paris: Dunod.

Katzenstein, P. J. and Okawara, N. (1993) *Japan's national security: structures, norms and policy responses in a changing world*, Ithaca: Cornell University Press.

Lincoln, E. J. (1990) *Japan's unequal trade*, Washington: Brookings Institution.

Nora, D. (1991) *L'étreinte du samourai*, Paris: Calmann-Lévy.

Okimoto, D. I. (1989) *Between MITI and the market: Japanese industrial policy for high technologies*, Stanford: Stanford University Press.

——and Roheln, T. (1988) *Inside the Japanese system: readings on contemporary society and political economy*, Stanford: Stanford University Press.

Patrick, H. T. (1986) *Japanese high technology industries*, Seattle: University of Washington Press.

Pempel, T. J. (ed.) (1990) *Uncommon democracies: the one-party dominant régimes*, Ithaca: Cornell University Press.

Postel-Vinay, K. (1994) *La révolution silencieuse du Japon*, Paris: Calmann-Lévy.

Prestowitz, C. V. (1988) *Trading places: how America allowed Japan to take the lead*, New York: Basic Books.

Sabouret, J. (1988) *L'état du Japon*, Paris: La Découverte.

Sautter, C. (1987) *Les dents du géant: le Japon à la conquête du monde*, Paris: Olivier Orban.

Seizelet, É. (1988) *Les petit-fils du soleil*, Paris: Publications orientalistes de la France.

Stockwin, J. A. *et al.* (1989) *Dynamic and immobilist politics in Japan*, Honolulu: University of Hawaii Press.

Suzuki, Y. (ed.) (1989) *The Japanese financial system*, Oxford: Clarendon Press.

Touraine, A. *et al.* (1984) *Japon, le consensus: mythes et réalités*, Paris: Economica.

Turcq, D. (1992) *L'inévitable partenaire japonais*, Paris: Fayard.

Vogel, E. F. (1983) *Le Japon médaille d'or*, Paris: Gallimard.

Wilkinson, E. (1992) *Le Japon face à l'Occident: images et réalités*, Brussels: Éditions Complexe.

Yachi, H. and Sautter, C. (1991) *L'état et l'individu au Japon*, Paris: Éditions de l'École des Hautes Études en Sciences.

8 The take-off of maritime Asia

In his monumental trilogy entitled *Asian Drama,* Swedish economist Gunnar Myrdal (1968) described the vicious circle in which Asia's underdeveloped societies struggled: population explosion, underequipment and technological stagnation in agriculture and a downtrodden underclass created by rural–urban migration. Agrarian revolts and communist guerilla movements sprang from this seemingly endless tide of rural poverty, further exacerbated by the expansion of the cities, which fed like parasites both on the influx of unemployed workers and the bounty which the United States was beginning to hand out in its war on communism. Hopes of a brighter future were raised during the Kennedy era, for example with the appointment of the economist Kenneth Galbraith as ambassador to India, and the activities of the Peace Corps, a volunteer youth organization devoted to Third World co-operation, but they were overtaken by the rise of neocolonialism which, despite sincere good intentions, committed some catastrophic mistakes. The stereotype of the naïve American citizen grappling with the mysteries of the Orient had already been created by Lederer (1959) in his novel *The Ugly American,* which is set in a fictitious Laos post-1954. Several years later, the great Indonesian novelist Mochtar Lubis, who was imprisoned first during the Sukarno era and again in 1965, offered a different perspective in *Twilight in Djakarta* (Lubis, 1963), illustrating to Indonesia's student population, with their American values, the impossible dilemma – corruption versus communism – which they would face on coming into contact with Indonesian bureaucracy.

In addition to the communist threat and the spread of anti-Americanism, post-colonial rivalry also began to develop between the new states, generally transcending the battle lines of the Cold War. There were, for example, doubts over the future viability of Singapore, which was evicted from the Malaysian Federation in 1965 because of Sino-Malay antagonism: unemployment in the city-state stood at 16 per cent and its per capita GNP at a mere $500, while its regional trade prospects were limited. The future looked grim for the Chinese enclave, whose population were frequently inclined to favour Peking in any case. The period of hostility between Indonesia and Malaysia, known as the Confrontation, lasted until

September 1965 and the downfall of Indonesia's President Sukarno, while the Philippines and Malaysia were involved in a dispute over the territory of Sabah on the large island of Borneo, which led to various outbreaks of armed conflict.

Future developments were to belie Myrdal's pessimistic socio-economic diagnosis. Admittedly, although his study was focused on Asia as a whole, and the Indian subcontinent in particular, it did not include Taiwan, Korea and a few other pockets of industrial progress. Furthermore, even in East Asia itself there are communities which are barely subsisting, especially in border areas and regions which still remain peripheral to the economic boom. The examples of the Khmer Rouge in western Cambodia, selling off their rubies and diamonds via their Thai sponsors, using business and financial networks which extend to Hong Kong and Saigon, and the Burmese generals trading precious woods and heroin, notably for the latest Chinese weapons, illustrate the way in which the oldest bandit traditions are interwoven with the realities of modern economic and political life. Some regions have seen an increased destruction of natural resources, for instance Thailand's forests were reduced from 55 per cent to 16 per cent of its total area between 1970 and 1990, leading a number of environmental organizations to obtain a ban in 1988 on any felling of trees in the virgin forest of the north. Today, however, it is the neighbouring forests of Burma and Cambodia which are being devastated with the connivance of local officials. In a more systematic way, the vast forests of Malaysia, Sarawak and Borneo are being rapidly depleted. The insatiable demand from the Japanese, who are aficionados of precious woods, for articles ranging from plywood to toothpicks, entails a high environmental price. At times, this exploitation of the environment has led to some of the biggest forest fires in the world, such as the one in Borneo in 1991 which destroyed an area of 50,000 square kilometres, 9 per cent of the size of France.

The social inequalities evident in most newly-industrialized countries are in many cases still as widespread as they were before industrialization. In Indonesia, as in the Philippines under Ferdinand Marcos, the extent of corruption, from the presidential family itself down to local bureaucracy, has imposed a heavy burden on society. Although Corazon Aquino herself managed to avoid any accusation on this score, her supporters have come in for heavy criticism. When Thai soldiers overthrew Prime Minister Chatichai in 1991, allegations of large-scale corruption, which had already been drawn up on the basis of public rumour, were regarded by observers as an open and shut case. In South Korea, although former President Chun Doo-hwan initially escaped corruption charges by retiring to a monastery, he is now, along with his successor General Roh Tae-woo and the heads of the seven biggest industrial groups, indicted for corruption. Thai society, with its considerable middle class in Bangkok cheek-by-jowl with rural poverty and cruel ill-treatment of children and minorities, is just one of many examples of flagrant inequality which economic development has failed to eliminate. Throughout the region, local patronage – the traditional response to food shortages and general insecurity – is still there, but is usually manifested in mafia-style connections between the police, the army and local gangsters. The fight against crime is sometimes even bloodier, much as it sometimes claims to control it. In Java in 1983, for example, death squads murdered several thousand criminals, including a number of political opponents, with the connivance of the army. The same phenomenon has recurred at various times in the Philippines where, in August 1992, the newly-installed President Ramos was forced to purge the entire police hierarchy. As has already been seen in the context of the Khmer Rouge, the pattern of mafia activity is not unique to the societies of South-East Asia undergoing rapid transformation, but is also likely to follow from the collapse of communist rule. At a time when the central authority of Peking is on the wane, southern China is seeing old customs re-emerge, as well as trafficking with neighbouring countries: local cadres and also new secret societies such as the Great Circle, which is recruiting members among former members of the People's Liberation Army, are involved in drug running and prostitution, especially with Indochina's Golden Triangle. Police and customs officials in Guangdong province and also on the large island of Hainan deal in illegal imports from Hong Kong. On one occasion in 1988, when caught red-handed on the dockside, they took the over-zealous Hong Kong customs officials hostage, only freeing them after various intercessions.

Overall, some countries have failed to follow the general trend of growth, or have even regressed, due to special political circumstances. The Philippines, which long held the lead in political modernization and education, falls into the first category, while the exhausted states of Indochina (Vietnam, Cambodia, Laos and especially Burma) belong to the second.

None the less, most of the developing societies and régimes of maritime Asia have evolved much more coherently and positively, starting with those which passed the development stage in the 1980s. There is hardly a single conflict between the countries of East Asia which has not been resolved, or at least put on the back burner, from the Japanese–Korean border disputes and the Thai–Malay frontier question to the quarrel over Sabah and the delimitation of the Indonesian archipelago. While the anti-communist alliance could hardly be said to have produced genuine joint action (each country preferring to operate within the framework of its own security relationship with the United States or the United Kingdom), it has at least helped to promote a readiness for dialogue and compromise among its members. The main symbol of this is ASEAN founded in 1967 by Indonesia, Singapore, Malaysia, the Philippines and Thailand, and joined by Borneo in 1984 and Vietnam in 1995. Great economic progress has led to increased trade as well as new hopes of establishing a common economic area at international level. Not only have communist attempts at armed revolution been successfully quashed everywhere except

Cambodia, but Asia's communist countries, from North Korea to China and Vietnam, are currently on the defensive, both ideologically and in their dealings with the rest of Asia. It is now they who live in fear of potentially subversive or spontaneous influences spreading from their far more prosperous neighbours.

EAST ASIA: BETWEEN AUTHORITARIANISM AND DEMOCRACY

The various governments of East Asia have passed through several stages. The first was a quasi-parliamentary phase, which occurred either in the immediate post-war period, in South Korea, the Philippines and Thailand, or after independence, in Malaysia, Indonesia and Singapore. The second phase involved a shift to authoritarianism, such as in the Philippines, Thailand and Malaysia, which in some cases was accompanied, or succeeded, by full-blown dictatorship, for example in Indonesia, Singapore and South Korea. At the time, both these phases were justified on the grounds of the anti-communist struggle: Taiwan was the only government in the region to move straight to dictatorship in 1947, due to the Chinese civil war raging on the mainland. In each instance, though at varying intervals, this second phase gave way to political liberalization. At any rate this phase came after early indications of the political failure of the United States in Vietnam (marked by the Tet offensive of 1968), when a number of the region's governments realized that unconditional American support would not last forever. However, in some cases, such as in South Korea, Taiwan and the Philippines, liberalization led to a full-blown democratic transition, while elsewhere, in Indonesia, Singapore and Malaysia for example, it has remained inconclusive and provisional. Thailand temporarily switched from the first to the second of these groups in 1991, when a military coup interrupted its parliamentary development.

In most cases, the post-war era and decolonization gave rise to governments which were founded on principles of democratic legitimacy, even if these principles were not always strictly observed in practice: a host of national founders relied on their own personal popularity. Parliaments and political parties assumed an important role throughout South-East Asia, but the resulting instability either led directly to, or provided a pretext for, a shift towards authoritarianism.

Sukarno's Indonesia

Under Sukarno (1949–65), Indonesia's original 1945 constitution, written in the midst of anti-Dutch ferment, was liberal yet vague, with a host of political bodies which met infrequently. Sukarno, a President endowed with sweeping powers, initially governed by playing the army and the nationalists off against the Islamic and communist forces, the latter having undergone a major revival since their defeat at Madiun. In 1951, there were thirteen parties, and despite discontent among the army, which would rather have had him overthrow the entire Indonesian political order in 1952, Sukarno decided on the election of a Constituent Assembly in 1955. In the event, the Masjumi Muslims and the nationalists came out equally, but the communists also won 16 per cent of the vote, and in years to come the PKI amassed as many as three million members, as well as 16 million sympathizers in affiliated mass organizations. The United States, concerned at this state of affairs, first backed a local uprising at Sulawesi in 1958, then the army, while simultaneously supporting the Masjumi. Sukarno became an international spokesman for the Third World following the success of the Afro-Asian conference at Bandung in April 1955, and began to develop a close relationship with the People's Republic of China, whose efficiency he, like many others, admired. In February 1957, he abandoned his plans for Western-style democracy in favour of 'guided democracy', based on the *Pancasila*, the *gotong royong* (mutual help and consultation) and, early on, a system of 'functional groups' – socio-economic organizations whose appointed members had to be free of political affiliation. At the same time, he adopted the idea of *dwi fungsi* (two functions) for the army, one being defence, the other economic and social construction. The programme was reintroduced wholesale by General Suharto in 1965, and still forms the cornerstone of his régime's official ideology. In 1959, Sukarno abandoned all notion of a new constitution, opting for what was termed a 'return to 1945', which effectively meant a quasi-military government and a political shift towards the PKI and Peking. Ideological and verbal ingenuity were never a weak point with Sukarno, who concentrated on his simultaneously romantic–revolutionary and anti-imperialist rhetoric while neglecting the domestic economy. In 1959, in association with his ideologist Mohammed Yanin, he developed an eight-year socio-economic plan consisting of eight volumes, 17 chapters and 1,945 measures – 17 August 1945 being the date of the declaration of independence (Shaplen, 1969). In 1960, parliament was dissolved and the Masjumi Party was outlawed. While the functional groups joined the new assemblies, the communists consolidated their influence, including within the army. After an attempt to recapture West Irian from the Dutch in 1962 (land which the United Nations handed over to Indonesia in 1963), Sukarno embarked on a disastrous conflict with the embryonic state of Malaysia, with the result that he also had to seek help from China. The economy continued on its downward slide, and Sukarno appeared to make a rash move in promising the communists a major stake in the country's political future. All the signs seemed to indicate that Indonesia was switching sides internationally. In January 1965, it withdrew from the UN to set up a rival organization called the 'Conference of Emerging Powers'. In August 1965, Sukarno announced the formation of a 'Jarkarta–Phnom Penh–Hanoi–Peking–Pyongyang axis'. The Indonesian communists, on the strength of their popularity and considerable articulacy despite a conspicuous lack of any real strategy, could one day look forward to reclaiming the keys of power, not through revolution or electoral success but by virtue of an irresistible shift by existing institutions. Only Nikita Khrushchev uttered a warning note on a visit to Indonesia in 1960, when he said: 'The Communist Party is not a grocer's shop where the more customers you attract, and the more soap and herrings you sell, the more money you stand to make'.

This state of perpetual improvization by the PKI casts doubt on the official Indonesian version of the coup which took place on 30 September 1965. A group of officers, backed by the PKI, assassinated five senior generals but failed to get General Nasuntion, who alerted Suharto, Commander-in-Chief of the special troops known as Kostrad. There was thus *de facto* evidence implicating the PKI and its leader Aidit. However, one of the officers involved was in fact a close associate of President Sukarno, while one subsequent interpretation (Wertheim, 1979) suggested the possibility of intrigue by Suharto himself, who, surprisingly, was not targeted in the first place: he was alleged to have manipulated those responsible for the putsch, turning against them when his old enemy General Nasuntion survived. It was only after this theory had been made public that General Suharto claimed to have been one of the targets of the conspiracy. The theory of a CIA plot, much favoured in progressive circles, was never substantiated either, although the United States certainly seemed extremely satisfied following the coup.

The backlash was unquestionably horrific. The ABRI (the Indonesian army), reinforced by leagues of Muslim activists and local rivalries, staged the worst massacre since 1945. In Java, and in Bali particularly, whole villages were subjected to lynchings and executions. The number of deaths totalled 80,000 according to official estimates, one million according to opponents of the régime, with special hatred being targeted at the Chinese community, exacerbated by accusations against the PKI and China. However, the repression was much more long-drawn-out and deep-seated than this. In Java, 58,000 out of 120,000 teachers were sacked, while hundreds of thousands of people, labelled 'tapols' or political prisoners and classified by their degree of guilt, were imprisoned and deported to the outermost reaches of the archipelago. Most of the survivors remained detained until 1977–9, when the Carter administration put heavy pressure on the Indonesian government. However, there was a special group of detainees, made up of some of the most heavily-implicated senior members in the PKI, who continued to be tried and executed by General Suharto until the end of the 1980s, often as a warning to the opposition. Every Indonesian citizen is obliged to carry a 'certificate of non-participation' relating to the coup of 1965.

One further peak of repressive violence was yet to come. Following the forced annexation in 1975 of the former Portuguese colony of Timor, not far off the Australian coast, more than 10 per cent of the island's Melanesian and Christian population were killed during the struggle against the FRETILIM guerillas, who have claimed independence for Timor ever since. In 1991, the army once again massacred over a hundred peaceful protesters who were gathered together in a cemetery. This violence was the legacy of the forced unification of Indonesia's 14,000 islands from 1945 onwards, but what is less well known is that similar brutality has also been used against attempts at secession in Aceh, north-west of Sumatra.

General Suharto, a wily and inscrutable peasant obsessed with astrology, who rarely mentions his aristocratic background, spared Sukarno's life when the latter was deposed in 1966, and built a mausoleum for him on his death. He continued all the nationalist themes developed since 1945, backed by the officer caste and a mushrooming bureaucracy organized into functional groups (the Ministry of the Interior, for example, had 800,000 members in 1971). Moreover, 'Bapak' (Father) Suharto, like his wife and sons, has reportedly gone on to accumulate a huge personal fortune with the help of his Chinese business advisers: if, apropos of this, it is possible to evoke the old tradition of the privileges of the kingdom of Java (Vatikiotis, 1993: 201), the intrusive nature of this family has become a topic of open debate twenty years later. Politically, Suharto is supported both by the officers and the Muslims against the third member of the Indonesian trinity, socialism. However, the bulk of his policy since 1965 has been to restrain the political zeal of the Islamic militants, while at the same time allowing them religious influence. The Kopkamtib (secret military police) is all-powerful, and the Law on Internal Security still permits the death penalty for any infringement or 'deviation' from the five principles of the *Pancasila* as laid down in 1946. In 1980, a petition was circulated, signed by fifty prominent figures including General Nasuntion, the hero of independence and the target of the 1965 coup, calling for greater human rights and democratization. On a more general scale, Bapak Suharto has, one by one, ousted all the generals who have served as his number two. Each of the first three national elections resulted in 62 to 63 per cent of the vote going to the official party, Golkar, to which all civil servants are required to belong. In 1988, this percentage rose even further, though not without prompting a certain amount of scepticism among all observers of the system. The other parties, including the liberals and the Islamic parties which succeeded the Masjumis of the 1950s, were either forced to join with government organizations or were banned. In 1989, Suharto alluded to the possibility of his retirement in 1993 and since then, several senior army personnel have alluded to the time when he will be replaced. However, the fact that he is still supported more than ever by loyal staff makes it very hard to foresee this happening. In 1993, moreover, he won a further presidential mandate by democratic means, thus postponing his departure until the end of the millennium. This is certainly the most tangible deadline for the liberalization of the New Order, which has none the less opened up considerably since 1965.

Malaysia, Singapore and Brunei

Malaysia and Singapore, which, like Brunei, are both members of the British Commonwealth, inherited two major assets on independence: first, a British-style civil service, highly-educated and free of serious corruption, and second, a competent professional army which was relatively uninvolved in politics, if not against communism. However, the parallel does not end there. The two countries were linked in a federation from 1963 to 1965, but split as a result of Malay fears at the prospect of the Singapore Chinese and the brilliant Lee Kuan Yew upsetting the peninsula's ethnic balance. Both possess majority parties which have dominated the political scene since independence, but by due democratic process. They observe the form of democracy, if not its substance, something which Malaysian politicians refer to, somewhat ambiguously, as 'the rules of the game'. The problem is more severe in Malaysia, where the broad ethnic spectrum means that politics is structured along the lines of the various communities, thus marginalizing parties which attempt to introduce multi-racial, assimilationist policies. In a country where the Muslims have a slight majority, the constitution enforces Islam and the continuation of nominal rule by the sultans. In Singapore, on the other hand, Lee Kuan Yew and his PAP (People's Action Party) advocate multi-racial co-operation and in particular held back Chinese cultural nationalism for a long time before giving in to it in the 1980s.

In Malaysia, the ethnic question has totally dominated the political scene, although the communist uprising of 1948–60 did provide some respite in the early days. UMNO, the Malayan pro-independence party which was established in 1948, had no difficulty in forging a political alliance including, most importantly, the Malayan Chinese Association (MCA created in 1949), a party made up of businessmen and prominent Chinese figures who opposed communism. In addition, special emergency laws, still actively in force in the 1990s, have enabled an all-out campaign against subversion. The critical phase in the confrontation with Malaysia and the simultaneous impact of the abortive attempt at federation with Singapore further reinforced a shared sense of nationality.

However, the disappearance of all immediate threats after 1965 led to a rise in ethnic tension. The Chinese community in particular resented an education system which applied what today would be termed reverse discrimination in favour of the less-educated Malays. The MCA was rivalled by two other Chinese-run parties including the DAP (Democratic Action Party), an offshoot of the Singaporean PAP. In the 1969 elections, for the first time, UMNO lost the two-thirds majority required for a revision of the constitution. The days immediately following the election were marked by race riots and the appearance of a radical Malay nationalist wing. Its leader, the future Prime Minister Muhammad bin Mahathir, was duly expelled from UMNO. Malay supremacy was re-established with the suspension of the constitution, followed by a tightening of emergency measures, including a ban on all public debate of racial problems.

Malay supremacy has continued to assert itself ever since, but at the cost of a decline in democracy, which one Malay commentator has described as a 'lame duck' (Ahmad, 1985), with considerable restrictions on opposition speaking time, brief election campaigns and widespread gerrymandering which discriminates heavily against Chinese and Indians. UMNO has continued to strengthen its power, and a new alliance named the Barisan (National Front), which it formed in 1974, propounded a doctrine based on Islam. This trend became particularly marked as Islamic movements began to emerge, winning elections in Kelantan and Terenganu in the north-east. UMNO's economic policy, biased in favour of Malays, involves a strong element of state control of the economy, coupled with efforts to attract international investment, a feature also shared by Singapore and Indonesia. In 1982, eager to counterbalance the West as well as the Chinese community, Mahathir launched his 'Look East' policy, designed to emulate Japan and South Korea. This complement to the existing policy of systematic support for ethnic Malays, expressed in the form of a large public and state-aided sector, became enormously successful in the second half of the 1980s. Conversely, all political initiatives by the Chinese collapsed, apart from the DAP, and the small Chinese family-run enterprise appeared less healthy than in the past, while the Barisan increased its support in this sector. Not one government-sponsored bill was rejected by the Assembly. However, authoritarianism has increased since 1980 under Mahathir, precipitating a rift between the UMNO wing, led by Razaleigh, the moderate Minister of the Economy, and the rest of the party. In 1987, more than 100 politicians on all sides were arrested and several influential newspapers were closed. Mahathir subsequently came under criticism from all Indonesia's first-generation politicians, such as Abdul Rahman, Abdul Razak and Datuk Onn. UMNO split into two wings, but Mahathir appears to enjoy extremely firm backing from a civil service that has since been highly politicized, as well as drawing on fears that a more radical brand of Islam might sweep the political scene: he won a further victory in the elections of 1990, endorsed by observers dispatched by the Commonwealth to ensure that there was no irregularity.

This development became accentuated further in 1994–5. UMNO, which some saw as being jeopardized by a new rivalry between Muhammad Mahathir and his more technocratic, less authoritarian Finance Minister Anwar Ibrahim, actually won a broader victory in the national elections, taking the state of Sabah from the opposition and resisting an onslaught from the Democratic Action Party, the Chinese-dominated opposition party, in Penang. These successes have clearly enabled the Mahathir government to put up more effective resistance to the excessive demands of the Muslims: at any rate, it has demolished the Islamist Al Arquam sect.

In external affairs, Malaysia has also enjoyed noticeable success. Mahathir, admittedly, cannot resist getting involved in a good dispute when he gets the chance, whether it be the row with the United Kingdom over press articles querying the Prime Minister's integrity, barbed comments on Europe's role in Bosnia, or his relentless defence and demonstration of Asian 'values' in contrast to the lessons offered by Western democracy. Yet Mahathir has also achieved a reconciliation between his own country and China, and instigated the formation of a free-trade association within ASEAN. While he was the only head of state in the region to refuse to attend the summit meeting of APEC (Asia–Pacific Economic Co-operation) in Seattle in November 1993, he seems less isolated today, now that the ASEAN Regional Forum seems to be becoming the focus for debates on Asia's strategic direction. Mahathir's nationalism and authoritarianism are irksome, yet they also provide a realistic counterpoint to the pan-Pacific rhetoric of the United States.

In Singapore, the internal situation appears more stable, no doubt because Lee Kuan Yew has always convinced his people of the impending threat of communism, Malay nationalism and other external forces: military expenditure reached 11 per cent of GNP in the 1970s. However, the trappings of Singapore's British-style democracy contrast sharply with underlying reality. What is more, Lee burned all his boats as far as the Commonwealth was concerned, to avoid being constrained by appeals to the Queen, as happened initially. A confirmed advocate ever since 1950 of a political path appropriate to the country's particular stage of economic development, Lee Kuan Yew managed the feat of duping the communists and progressives who joined forces with him in the run-up to independence, then maintaining a monolithic unity within his People's Action Party, based on structures as tightly closed as those of a traditional communist party. As for elections, a majority rule for every seat has ensured that very few opposition candidates are ever allowed to win seats. In 1991, for example, the opposition made great progress to obtain four out of eighty seats, despite having won 40 per cent of the vote. The state-owned national press is tightly controlled and the international press frequently muzzled. In this haven for multi-nationals, reception of CNN television has long been banned, and remains controlled. For a generation, opposition supporters deemed subversive were interned, often for long spells, on the small island of Sentosa, now converted into a theme park. Yet Lee Kuan Yew's almost Victorian prudishness, which none the less fails to include the political implications of *habeas corpus,* has also kept him from overstepping certain boundaries, so there are no political executions and not even any real physical abuses. Intimidation has been more the PAP's style, for example cuts in public expenditure for districts which vote the wrong way, or charges of fraud or assorted moral transgressions levelled against leading members of the opposition. Yet for all its lack of any real cultural vitality, Singapore has become the most prosperous and peaceful country in the entire region.

Lastly, we come to the sultanate of Brunei, a hereditary monarchy and Asia's equivalent to a Gulf emirate, which stands totally apart from the above typology. With a population of 250,000 inhabitants and a GNP per capita of US$25,500 in 1990 due to its vast oil and gas reserves, this absolute monarchy, which at one time ruled the whole of Borneo, has managed to avoid extinction. Its sole period of liberalization, in 1962, ended in repression. Having learned from past experience, it is xenophobic in its outlook, despite the fact that it is dependent on foreigners. Its oilfields, for example, are wholly owned by Royal Dutch Shell and guarded by British Gurkhas, while its jungle provides a training-ground for both Singaporean and American troops. In the long term, the main threat facing Brunei, whose sultan tacitly opposed Iraq in 1991, is that of potential territorial claims by Malaysia, which continues to shelter the country's tiny political opposition. Nevertheless, by acting as regional paymaster, currently backed by over US$30 billion in foreign investment, and indispensable to the United States since events in the Persian Gulf, the sultan can still hope to avoid the hostility of its neighbours.

The Philippines

Although politics in the Philippines operates more openly than in some other countries, parliamentary activity has appeared highly artificial since the Marcos era (1972–86). Successive governments have been undermined by oligarchy, political cliques, corruption and above all the inefficiency of the social infrastructure, and the Philippines have frequently been referred to as the 'sick man of ASEAN'. Yet despite this, the 1950s and 1960s were a period of economic growth and electoral propriety. However, the central government, weakened by political debate, failed in its attempts to impose taxation and legislation on the local chiefs. The country was dominated by charismatic individuals, within a presidential system that had gone unopposed since independence. Quezon, Magsaysay and the young Marcos in his early days in office in 1965 were classic examples of this, as Corazon Aquino would later prove to be in 1986–92. The way the parties alternated in office often came about through deals struck between the leading families which traditionally controlled the Filipino Senate. In 1972, Ferdinand Marcos dissolved the Congress and declared a state of martial law, which remained in force until 1981. His party, which was formed at the beginning of the 1970s, went on to triumph in rigged elections which were only seriously contested in Manila. The first phase of his dictatorship was nevertheless economically successful, although it did little to change the problem of social inequality: 50 per cent of the population received less than 20 per cent of the income, but the wealthiest 10 per cent, who accounted for 27 per cent of income in 1956, were receiving 37 per cent by 1985. In the same period, the real value of Filipino salaries fell by 50 per cent in real terms while GNP went up. From 1968 onwards, the Filipino Communist Party rose from the ashes. Backed by the guerillas of the New People's Army (whose methods were inspired by Maoism, although it received no significant aid from China) the Party regained control of a section of the peasant population on the archipelago's 6,000 islands. An international campaign against the abuses of the Marcos régime, the increasingly flagrant nepotism and corruption by the presidential couple, and finally the army's assassination of opposition leader Benigno Aquino in full view of the world's television cameras, all ended in disaster. Foreign investors withdrew and the United States threw Marcos to the human rights lobby. After an attempt to organize elections in the presence of international observers, Marcos was forced to flee in February 1986 in the face of the rise of 'people power' represented by Corazon Aquino, the murdered Benigno Aquino's widow, who was firmly backed by the Catholic Church.

After 1986, Corazon Aquino succeeded in re-establishing political democracy. A new constitution, with a president elected for a single six-year term, two chambers (including a twenty-four-member Senate, which in practice would be an oligarchic chamber) and a completely free press, marked the Filipino nation's return to its democratic roots. Seven attempted military coups were foiled and Mrs Aquino served out her term. However, despite this, there was a failure to solve the problems of insecurity, rural poverty and the rebellion endemic in the communist New People's Army with its 15,000 guerillas. In particular, the Aquino government procrastinated over the issue of land reform, implementing only a very limited version in 1988. In an attempt to tackle security-related problems, the government itself encouraged the re-emergence of local militias, which were often more akin to death squads or the landlord-owned private armies of the past. The country's political classes preferred to focus on the renegotiation of the vast American bases at Clark Airfield and Subic Bay. As nationalist feeling became whipped up, a number of political leaders hoped above all to raise the stakes, but to no avail. In early 1992, after the disastrous eruption of the nearby Pinatubo volcano, the United States announced that it was abandoning the bases in order to save costs, and it started using other harbours, notably Singapore, as maintenance centres. The post-colonial ploy of making constant appeals to the United States seemed well and truly over, and the Philippines were effectively marginalized as a security partner. However, with the orderly election of General Ramos in July 1992, political stability began to lure foreign investors back, especially the Taiwanese, and the country is now joining the regional trend of economic growth.

Thailand

Thai politics, played out in the shadow of the army, has been heavily marked both by the struggle against the communist guerilla forces, which in the north-east lasted into the mid-1980s, and by the presence and subsequent withdrawal of the American GIs in 1974. There are other reasons too, the most important being the ethnic factor. In a country where a highly-assimilated 40 per cent of Chinese Thais hold the economic levers in Bangkok, the monarchy and the officer caste (whose military academy remains barred to new immigrants up until the third generation) serve to create a *de facto* ethnic balance between Chinese and Thai. The civilian democracy, restored in 1945 on the arrival of the Allies, ended in 1948 with the return to power of General Phibun, who had been dictator since 1932 and went on to stay in power until 1957. The devolution of political power was subsequently determined by the growth of new cliques within the military caste. Social advancement and army promotion depended on membership of one or other of these cabals, which often centred on a particular graduating class in the military academy. However, after the young king Ananda was assassinated in 1947, the monarchy remained extremely stable. Ananda's successor, Bhumibol, enjoyed considerable longevity and became highly influential, both as a result of his role as mediator and through the private fortune owned by the royal family. In 1973, following the violent suppression of a student revolt in Bangkok, the King introduced a period of more open democracy. Those years, which coincided with the American débâcle in Vietnam, were a period when Thailand broadened its foreign relations, particularly with Vietnam and China, and insisted on the withdrawal of US troops. The country's left wing, with its base in the student and urban communities, adopted as its rallying cry the poverty which existed in the shanty towns and among landless farmers. The army for its own part organized conservative populist leagues in the cause of 'King, religion and nation', the fundamental principle of modern Thailand. This liberal phase ended in 1976 with the downfall of Prime Minister Sarit and the ascendancy of Generals Kriangsak and Prem. They were brought to power by army officers known as 'Young Turks', who were weary of corruption and wanted a settlement with Vietnam. The movement disintegrated in a failed putsch in 1982. The influence of King Bhumibol subsequently became ever more marked: it was his support which saved Prem, while he also took on the extreme right-wing leagues.

Electoral competition was reintroduced with a proliferation of parties which owed more to political favours than to ideological debate. This trend appeared to be confirmed by the 1979 and particularly the 1988 election results, which showed a victory for Chatichai, the leader of the Chart Thai party. Although he was himself a former officer, Chatichai did not rely directly on the army for his power. Under his leadership, as its economy gathered pace, Thailand increasingly laid claim to hegemony over its Indochinese neighbours with the slogan of the 'golden peninsula': an alliance with the Burmese generals against the democrats and a shift towards closer links with the government in Phnom Penh (and even Vietnam) formed part of the new strategy of an economically confident Thailand. This development was interrupted by bitter struggles for power between Chatichai and part of the army, particularly General Chaovalit who had secretly initiated contact with Cambodia and Burma. Chaovalit, who was opposed to any *rapprochement* with Hanoi (in which respect he sided with the Minister for Foreign Affairs, Sidhi Savetsila), led a dogged struggle against the Prime Minister.

It was ultimately General Suchinda who seized power in 1991, backed by his comrades from the Military Academy's fifth graduating class, driving Chatichai briefly into exile and forcing him to promise his complete withdrawal from politics. Observers have tended to rationalize this struggle by citing the political and financial conflicts of interest which prevailed between the fourth and fifth graduating classes of the Military Academy. The latter group, which staged a coup with minimal bloodshed, early on had the initiative to instal a known technocrat as Prime Minister, thus reassuring foreign investors. But General Suchinda modified the constitution to make sure that elections would include a contingent of officers appointed to the Assembly. The General then came under pressure to restore democracy, almost as much from other members of the army as from opposition democrats. The conflict became a tragedy in May 1992 in Bangkok, when several hundred unarmed demonstrators were shot down by the army. The army thought it could apply the political model which had been used in Burma on the occasion of the massacre in Rangoon in August 1988, and in China at the time of the Tiananmen Square crackdown in June 1989. However, it also found its path blocked by the Chinese–Thai commercial bourgeoisie as well as by the new middle classes, armed with their cellphones and backed by the international and local media. The King then ordered Suchinda's resignation, thus living up to his role as arbiter in a crisis.

In pursuing both its tradition of putsches and a culture of compromise and public order, Thailand is therefore a striking example of a failure to achieve full democracy, in contrast to its rapid modernization. Since 1946, in defiance of all attempts to categorize it, it has managed to combine, whether successively or simultaneously, a hereditary monarchy, military government, multi-party politics and patronage, as well as a remarkable balance between its constituent ethnic groups.

Taiwan and South Korea

Taiwan and South Korea, both of which were positioned on the front line in the Cold War, are states which evolved out of the divisions created by the Second World War and the Chinese civil war. In the 1950s and 1960s, they were generally regarded as the prototypes of the national security régimes. Yet they also belong to the sphere of Chinese cultural influence, as well as benefiting from the more positive effects of Japanese colonization, in terms of their economies and their education systems. In both cases, there has been ruthless dictatorship and an extreme militarization of society. For a long time, the safety-valve for the educated classes was the 'green card', or residence permit for the United States, a brain-drain which long hampered both economies until it began to be reversed in 1985.

Both countries are also classic examples of economic mobilization in a capitalist setting, albeit retaining considerable dirigiste and protectionist features up until the 1980s. Culturally they are torn between two influences. One is that of American culture, now spurned because it was primarily epitomized by the GIs stationed on the two territories, but which persists in the form of a sizeable community of trans-Pacific émigrés. Second, the protection of the values associated with Confucianism and traditional culture is especially vigorous since both governments have long regarded themselves as having a duty to defend their national heritage in the face of the tyranny of Mao and Kim Il Sung. This conservatism is also a weapon used by the nationalists to restore the status of national culture *vis à vis* Japanese influences, which are suppressed and thereby forced underground; for example in Taipei in the 1970s trademarks were still being removed from lorries and buses imported from Japan.

Yet both countries have attained total democracy, without any revolutionary phase comparable to the celebration of 'people power' which chased away Ferdinand Marcos in the Philippines. Not only is their press free, it is also prosperous and competitive. The major Korean dailies, like their Japanese counterparts, have a circulation of up to several million copies and are major institutions. Taiwanese politics is highly adversarial, with frequent Brazilian-style fistfights breaking out in the Taiwanese parliament, and waves of strikes in South Korea rival those seen in Latin America in the 1970s. They are accompanied in both cases by an excessive tendency to violent street demonstrations. However, whereas in Taiwan it is mainly farmers, environmentalists and activists in the pro-independence party who resort to this type of demonstration, in Korea it takes the form of generational student action and extra-parliamentary workers' protests. This new-found mood of political and social volatility has led to many reservations as to whether the boom in these two Asian 'dragons' is likely to continue. However, this has not prevented compromise solutions taking effect, nor stopped the economy from growing.

Both countries, particularly their conservative parties, did, admittedly, have hopes of introducing a Japanese-style political system and thus achieving the stability and electoral legitimacy of the Japanese LDP. In pursuing this path they went through two main stages. In South Korea, these occurred when a moderate opposition party (including Kim Jong-pil, the former Prime Minister from the 1960s and a close ally of both the business community and Japan, and Kim Young-sam, the eternal rival of Kim Dae-jung in opposition to the military) joined forces with Roh Tae-woo's conservative party to found, right on cue, a Liberal Democrat Party. This took place in January 1990, and the resulting alliance, identical to the conservative grouping which was formed in Japan in 1955, ruled out any possibility of a rapid change of government, as most South Koreans would not trust the remaining opposition which was much more doctrinaire. In Taiwan, the turning-point came with the legislative elections of November 1991. For the first time, all seats were contested and voting was free and open. It resulted in a majority of nearly two-thirds for the Kuomintang, the Progressive Democratic Party (*Minjindang*) having become bogged down in a high-risk bid for a referendum over the island's self-determination *vis à vis* the People's Republic of China. In Taiwan, as in South Korea, politics is sometimes highly Japanese, even in its negative aspects: the two-seat constituencies which existed in Korea until 1988; the local members' organizations and the bonds which exist with the electorate all show analogies with Japan. In Taiwan, patronage, including vote-buying during election campaigns, remains an important factor as used to be the case in Japan, while dependency on financial contributions and the business community is total and continues to be completely unregulated.

The cases of Taiwan and Korea: reunification or war

The main irony of the post-Cold War period is that it is precisely the two Asian countries which have been most fully converted to democracy that are most seriously threatened by the fall-out from the communist system. In South Korea, the democratic government of Kim Young-sam is having to face blackmail from North Korea with its acquisition of a nuclear capability: between 1991 and October 1994, there was alternately tension and negotiation between the Pyongyang régime and the United States, still the guarantor of security in the Korean peninsula. Apart from the final agreement concluded at Geneva in October 1994, the possibility of North Korea possessing nuclear weapons has been neither excluded nor verified. South Korea has been forced to go along with the United States, whether it is brandishing threats (sometimes for domestic political ends, as when President Clinton appeared in uniform on the demarcation line between the two Koreas) or signing an agreement that fails to satisfy Seoul's demands. By effectively postponing the deadline for the verification of radioactive materials generated by North Korean nuclear reactors by as much as five years, the Geneva agreement has actually enabled North Korea to keep its nuclear card at the ready, whether for real or as a bluff. On the other hand, the United States, South Korea, followed by Japan and the European Union are beginning to equip and finance replacement civilian nuclear installations for North Korea.

This exercise might remain hypothetical. Following the death of Kim Il Sung in July 1994, his son Kim Jong Il, a capricious and sickly playboy, delayed in achieving an effective succession. The country's economic situation disintegrated to the point where, in 1995, North Korea requested food aid from Japan and South Korea, an admission of weakness which was none the less consistent with the régime's decision to force the international community to finance its political survival. In fact, the South Koreans are as horrified at the prospect of reunification under disastrous conditions as they are patriotically determined to pursue that reunification – but not yet.

This is not so in Taiwan, where more and more open pressure is emerging for independence. The government of Lee Teng-hui, no doubt to counter the propaganda of the pro-independence opposition, has agreed to lead a campaign for Taiwan's admission to the UN. It has only replied to the proposals of China's President Jiang Zemin on reunification in the most formal terms. Thanks to commercial competition between Western suppliers, it has secured the sale of 150 F-16 fighters and AWACs reconnaissance aircraft from the United States, as well as 60 Mirage-2000 jets from France, following in the wake of a major contract for naval frigates. The prospect of seeing Taiwan both rearmed and en route to independence or international legitimacy aggravated the leaders in Peking.

From July 1995 to March 1996, while Taiwan was holding legislative elections and its first direct vote presidential election, China staged a series of intimidating exercises in the Taiwan straits clearly deisgned to simulate a naval blockade of Taiwan, including the firing of land-based missiles close to the major cities of Taipei and Kaohsiung. These threats backfired, however, when the US sent two aircraft carriers close to the scene, thus reinforcing the credibility of America's security commitment to Taiwan. Even more significantly, the presidential election turned into a personal triumph for Lee Teng-hui, against whom China had waged a political campaign. Taiwanese by descent but a member of the Kuomintang, he has acquired international stature, pursuing a dialogue with Peking and lobbying internationally towards a new status for Taiwan. In the long term, however, Peking's actions offer a reminder of the limitations on Taiwan's decisions. Moreover, it is likely that Taiwan, whose economy today is increasingly invested in China itself, will seek a compromise. Yet the years ahead, with the reunification of Hong Kong, are dangerous ones. And it is unthinkable that Taiwan, although democratized, would give up its quest for security.

Politics: the cultural dimension

While democracy cannot be said to be fully established in Asia, it is equally true that most of the region's political systems cannot be classified as totally authoritarian. The prime characteristic of non-communist Asia continues to be the uncertainty of its political and institutional structures. Schematically speaking, as in the controversy over the Near East among orientalists, two main approaches predominate. First there is the democratic vision of Asia's political systems, convinced of the universal quality of values and the need to combat political repression, and second there is the culturalist interpretation, which defends a diversity of values, be they Confucian or Malay–Islamic. It is clearly wrong to argue that East Asia has never experienced calls for democracy or even democratic phases in the past. Even excluding Japan, bids for democracy have come from political forces in China, from the Philippines (inspired by the United States), from Thailand (following European models) and from certain elements within the Indonesian and even Vietnamese national liberation movements. There is no schematic framework for interpreting post-colonial Asia's democratic aspirations, merely a few broad lines of influence. First, there is the role played by the Christian churches, particularly the Catholic Church, from the Philippines to South Korea and Vietnam, although the Buddhist clergy can also be seen as acting as a democratic opposition force from South Vietnam to Burma. Equally unmistakeable is the periodic resurgence of democratic challenges and human rights within the Chinese and Vietnamese Communist Parties, as well as in the societies which they govern. Such a phenomenon seems unthinkable in North Korea or under the Khmer Rouge, where communist totalitarianism meets traditional despotism. Yet there are societies which continue to straddle the dividing line between Western-style democracy and native culture, most notably in Malaysia. A striking example is also offered by Lee Kuan Yew of Singapore, a brilliant advocate of his own theories since 1950. He now openly rejects any westernization of his country's political culture, even though Singapore's dazzling economic success stems from its position at the crossroads between East and West. By now a veteran of Asian politics, albeit a controversial one, Lee Kuan Yew tells the West to its face what many other Asian leaders are thinking in private, accusing human rights campaigners and pro-democracy supporters of practising political imperialism and ignoring the orderly nature of development in Asian societies. While he had long opposed any influences which came from communist China, after reform commenced in Peking he began to assume a new, Confucianist sense of civic responsibility which was actually very close to the moral code constantly preached by the old Chinese Kuomintang. Aspects of the Lee Kuan Yew model include social eugenism (with initiatives to favour a higher birth rate for the educated relative to the rest of the population), close watch on all media (the low status of bookshops contrasts with the pursuit of science and leisure in Singapore) and understanding for the Tiananmen Square crackdown of June 1989. In fact, this model is a problem not so much in terms of its effect on Singapore, which is relatively benign, but in terms of the support which it represents for all the governments in power throughout the region. Its lead is followed, albeit with caution, by most members of ASEAN, which have produced a collective response to American, and in some cases European, criticism on human rights. Strangely enough, this means that the progressive anti-Americanism of the 1960s has sometimes given way to an authoritarian anti-Americanism, arising out of fears over the impact of public opinion in the United States and over positions adopted by Congress. This hostility is also provoked by what are seen as the decadent aspects of American society, for example crime, racial conflict and the demise of work in favour of leisure.

Sometimes ASEAN pursues a separate line from the United Nations, as in 1992, when it refused to condemn the military régime in Burma. However, it is important to remember that there are enormous internal differences between the governments of Asia. If the East Asian countries were to introduce the right to intervene in the name of democracy, or even of human rights, they would inevitably come into conflict among themselves. Propaganda promoting neo-Confucianism, neo-authoritarianism and supposedly Asian values should not be allowed to obscure the fact that necessity knows no law.

The role of charisma

Another characteristic shared by almost the entire region, and one which is also common to Asia's communist régimes, is the highly personalized nature of political power. This may be part of the legacy bequeathed both by the Confucian and Hindu cultures, but it is striking that the more modern societies of the region – Japan, South Korea and Taiwan – have made considerable progress towards making politics a normal part of everyday life, thus approaching a situation where politicians are blandly indistinguishable, as they are in the Western democracies. However, this is not true of their less-developed neighbours. Kim Il Sung in North Korea (from 1946 until his death in 1994), Deng Xiaoping in China (though including some spells out of the limelight, and now officially retired), Suharto in Indonesia (from 1965), Lee Kuan Yew in Singapore (from 1959 onwards, and still influential despite being retired), Ne Win in Burma (from 1962 onwards, and now also officially retired): all went on to enjoy a similar political longevity unparalleled in the contemporary world. This longevity often coincides with dynastic patterns: it is both the modern-day expression of the patronage tradition and the outcome of efforts ever since 1920 to raise the revolution or the struggle for independence to the status of heroic myth. However, new democratic leaders, aided by the resonance-box effect of the modern media, are able to benefit from this in their turn. Indeed, the most striking examples can be found in democratic opposition forces as well as in dictatorships.

Taiwan (until 1987) and Singapore are representatives of these newer developments. Marshal Chiang Kai-shek, who died in 1975 after having governed the Republic of China since 1925 (and Taiwan since 1946), saw his son Chiang Ching-kuo, the former head of the political police, take his place. Ironically, it was the young Chiang who presided over the most delicate stages of the liberalization process before his death in 1988. His first successor, Prime Minister Yu Kuo-hua, had also been Chiang Kai-shek's private secretary during the 1930s. In Singapore, Lee Kuan Yew has held the reins of power since 1959 and is the most eminent statesman in the region, albeit at the head of its smallest state. Lee Kuan Yew has groomed his own son, the brilliant technocrat and Deputy Prime Minister Lee Hsien

Loong, to succeed him eventually. Disease, however, has led to a stronger role for Prime Minister Goh Chok Tong.

In a more diffuse sense, present-day China is largely dominated by the influence and privileges of what are called the *gaogan zidi*, the sons of senior cadres, who play a particularly influential role in all the commercial enterprises connected to the Party and the Army. As for North Korea, it appears to have succumbed to the prospect of hereditary despotism with the official appointment of Kim Il Sung's son, Kim Jong Il, as his successor.

In some cases, the personalization of politics has coincided with an increase in standing for royal families. In Thailand, for example, although the institution of royalty began to decline after the overthrow of the absolute monarchy by young nationalists in 1932, King Bhumibol, who has reigned since 1946, enjoys high prestige. As the deified patron of Thai Buddhism, and immensely wealthy, he periodically acts as an arbiter behind the political scenes. The return of Norodom Sihanouk to Cambodia in December 1991 further illustrates this to the point of caricature: for his re-entry into a country still ravaged by civil war, Sihanouk's chosen mode of transport was the same white Chevrolet convertible which the young prince had so enjoyed riding in before 1970. The Khmer royal family was once again caught up in its traditional internal disputes over the succession. The two princes – Ranarridh, who has taken over as leader of the Funcinpec opposition movement, and Chakrapong, who has sided with the Phnom Penh government – represent opposing political options, as the Laotian princes did in the past. Chakrapong had to leave the country in 1993 after plotting a coup. Another royal prince, Sirivuth, was forced out in 1995.

Alongside these examples of governments in power, however, there also exist certain figures among the democratic camp who display the same tendency to personalization. Corazon Aquino (*née* Cojuangco), from one of the richest Filipino families, is the widow of Senator Benigno Aquino, who was himself the descendant of one of the country's most prominent oligarchic families before he raised the democratic standard against Ferdinand Marcos. After her husband's assassination by Marcos' henchmen in 1983, her symbolic value, and her human and political qualities, led to her being appointed President of the Philippines in 1986. In Burma, the opposition figurehead Aung San Suu Kyi is the daughter of Aung San, the leader and hero of the national independence movement until his assassination in 1947. After having lived in both India and the United Kingdom since 1960, she returned to Burma in 1988 at the time of a democratic uprising. She was placed under house arrest in July 1989, yet it was in her name that the opposition won the national elections of February 1990 after which the army intervened and arrested most of the opposition candidates. Aung San Suu Kyi, who was awarded the Nobel Peace Prize in 1991, might have had a similar destiny to that of Corazon Aquino if the countries of ASEAN had been willing to boycott Burma's generals. It is how an open question in Indonesia whether Megawati Sukarnoputu, the daughter of former president Sukarno, will play a similar role. Both instances are strikingly reminiscent of South Asia, with the long line of democrats, the Gandhis in India and the saga of the Bhutto family in Pakistan.

Democracy and integration

The ethnic problem is not the only factor to raise doubts about rapid convergence between the states and societies of South-East Asia. A common regional structure, although partly the result of economic development, also requires a political standard which is common to, or at least compatible with, all the states concerned. Yet there is no such model, nor is there any such common point of reference linking the political systems of non-communist Asia. While the national security demands associated with the anti-communist struggle have been removed for the most part, the governments and societies of East Asia are following several divergent political paths. On the one hand, there are the authoritarian, paternalistic systems (Indonesia, Brunei and Singapore), which in principle put emphasis on economic growth and ensure cohesion in societies which are undergoing modernization. On the other hand, there is democracy, in some cases (for example South Korea and Taiwan) based on the long-term influence of a conservative majority party aspiring towards the Japanese model, but elsewhere (for example Malaysia) still founded on ethnic and religious divisions. Only the Philippines, back in the days before Marcos' long reign (1966–86), had a political system based on principles clearly inspired by Western democracy. However, it failed to live up to these principles in practice, and its long-running economic decline has meant that other South-East Asian countries have tended to steer clear up to now.

This attempt at a systematic classification does not fully take account of the comparative dangers of these various situations. The wide differences in the brutality of the societies concerned may be more closely linked to the extent of their economic development and to local cultural traditions. The latter are clearly important, since for example no Asian country (not even the British colony of Hong Kong) has abolished the death penalty or witnessed the emergence of an abolitionist movement. Moreover, the countries of South-East Asia use capital punishment as a matter of course, notably in cases of drug trafficking. Even in politics, in Indonesia and Malaysia for example, the level of local protest is limited due to the way that the opposition itself is forced to argue its case within the existing judicial and legal framework. This serves to explain the resentment felt by the governments in power at what they perceive as blatant interference by the US Congress and the European Union.

Confucian Asia belongs to a tradition which gives much more weight to the conduct, good or bad, of individuals (and especially those in authority) than to the law of the state. This tradition has been openly criticized by Chinese advocates of democracy such as Fang Lizhi, the astrophysicist whose human rights petition marked the start of the Chinese demonstrations of 1989. Even in a society as modern as Taiwan there are few civil and criminal lawyers, and mediation rather than arbitration is widely practised. South-East Asia also continues to be influenced by the absolute rulers who divided up the land prior to colonization: the tendency towards authoritarianism manifested in all the military castes which grew up after independence was also more pronounced among indigenous politicians than among those educated in the colonial, and particularly the British, system. The ordinary people, regardless of their cultural tradition, often take a highly pragmatic view of both the real dangers and the political successes of their masters, especially since they have no utopian expectations of the role of the state. By this standard, a true classification of the various states bears no relation to their official political philosophy, nor to any formal criteria of political freedom. The most democratic state in South-East Asia, the Philippines, remains an extremely dangerous society, while the most controlled régime, Singapore, also offers the greatest degree of personal safety.

Taken together, these situations are incapable of being reduced to a single common thread, whether this be the authoritarian state inherited from the anti-communist era, the problems of democratic transition or the theory of an Asian (that is, Japanese or Confucian) political model. None of these labels is adequate to describe a political history that has been extremely varied since decolonization. Throughout South-East Asia, the lack of a clear political model has thus become a major issue for the future, and one to which proverbial Asian pragmatism does not offer a satisfactory answer.

ECONOMIC TAKE-OFF

The rural miracle

Within a quarter of a century, the relative balance between sectoral underdevelopment and the factors of economic dynamism has been reversed. In East Asia at the end of the 1980s, agriculture accounted for just 25 per cent of GNP in China, Indonesia and the Philippines. The absence of a primary sector in the case of entrepôt cities (Hong Kong and Singapore), rapid industrial growth (South Korea and Taiwan), and industry combined with the exploitation of other raw materials such as oil, natural gas and tropical timber (Thailand, Malaysia and Brunei) have led to a rapid reduction in the economic and political importance of Asia's farming communities, even though they still constitute a major social and local problem. The fact that tariff barriers and quotas on imports of agricultural and raw materials continue to be enforced, not just in Japan but throughout East Asia, and South-East Asia especially, is an indication of this persistent problem and the desire for social stability by governments which are, moreover, founded on exponential growth. This was how Indonesia became self-sufficient in 1984, even though it was consequently forced to pay over the international going-rate for its domestic grain. Furthermore, despite the threat of a possible opening-up to the global market, the farmers of South Korea, Taiwan and Thailand have performed a record technological leap, like some of their counterparts in Luzon (Philippines) and Java. The green revolution instituted by the so-called 'miracle rice' made famous by Manila's Institute of Rice in the 1960s, transformed their lot, while requiring them to re-enter the trade circuit, producing an influx of fertilizers, pesticides and machinery. After several decades which marked a heyday for small family-owned farms, based in some cases on early land reforms, new advances are now possible as the result of more intensive land use, first introduced in the great central plain of Thailand, and land restructuring, which was initially carried out in Taiwan. China is also beginning to face a similar prospect, although in its case there is also an ideological dimension. Having had their virtues lauded by post-communism, individual Chinese farmers enjoy only a brief heyday before entering a decline similar to that which has affected agricultural workers in Europe since 1945 and in South-East Asia since the 1980s.

Shortly before Gunnar Myrdal set out his gloomy vision of rural Asia, another economist, Walt Rostow (1960), had applied his take-off theory to non-communist Asia as a whole. Inspired by Schumpeter and Marx (whose arguments he skilfully turned round against Marx's disciples), rather than neo-classical or liberal economics, Rostow, an academic who advised Lyndon Johnson during the Vietnam War, predicted increasingly rapid growth based on industry, trade and the urban economy rather than on a boom in the rural economy. He was right, apart from two points: first, the South Vietnamese economy which he took as his case study fell victim to American hypertrophy before foundering on the reef of reunification in 1975; second, it is Japan which has led the field by a long way since the beginning of the 1980s, not only in its exports to the rest of Asia but also in its investment in industry and in the transfer and sale of technology. East Asia's economic growth over a number of distinct phases has made it the most dynamic zone in the world today, even if in purely quantitative terms it has not yet caught up with North America or the European Union. Japan's role in this overall achievement is clearly overwhelming: it alone accounts for almost 70 per cent of the total GNP of East Asia, including China. However, the boom in Japan's maritime and peninsular neighbours reaches far beyond the 'Four Dragons', known since the late 1960s as the NICs, or newly-industrialized countries. Today these four have actually attained the status of developed countries, overtaking most southern European countries both in terms of per capita income and, to an increasing extent, in terms of manufactured exports. Hong Kong (with an income of US$22,000 per capita in 1995), Singapore (US$25,000 per capita in 1995), Taiwan (US$13,000 per capita in 1995, plus almost a third more if account is taken of the vast amount of undeclared income) and Korea

(US$10,000 dollars per capita in 1995) have all witnessed a period of rapid growth longer than that seen in post-war Japan, stretching from the 1960s up to the early 1990s. In some cases, there has also been greater industrial growth: in the 1980s it reached an average of 13 per cent in South Korea, and nearly 12 per cent in Taiwan. This may not be enough to enable them to catch up with the Japanese economy, which currently leads the region, but in the short term it is quite enough to put them on a par with the rest of the world's industrialized countries.

In addition, a second potential wave of newly-industrialized countries emerged in the second half of the 1980s, including Malaysia (with a per capita income of US$4,000 in 1995), Thailand (US$2,400) and even Indonesia (US$900 in 1995), the population giant of South-East Asia with 189 million inhabitants. The Vietnam War and the consequent impact of military spending and American aid on the ASEAN countries had already brought in considerable resources. The positive effects of the first oil shock in 1973 on countries which were producers of primary products enabled a second phase of economic growth, including exports of manufactured goods. Between 1965 and 1980 the 'Four Dragons' and the ASEAN countries, excluding the Philippines, saw a growth in industrial production of over 10 per cent per annum across the board. At the beginning of the 1980s exports to the United States rose considerably, not only from Japan but from the region as a whole. The 'Four Dragons', like the South-East Asian NICs, are now heavily dependent on these exports for their domestic growth.

Urbanization and education

The transformations taking place in Asian societies have proceeded in parallel at a rapid pace. Two phenomena in particular serve to illustrate this point: urbanization, with its advantages and its disadvantages, and education, which has even greater implications for the future. Vast urban agglomerations have sprung up as the result of rural–urban migration and the concentration of economic activity, especially in the tertiary sector. Many of these agglomerations appear to be modelled on the Japanese examples of Osaka–Kobe or Tokyo–Yokohama, which have as many as 25 million inhabitants within a radius of 50 kilometres. Thus Seoul has expanded to over ten million inhabitants, while Taipei has reached five million. These cities, which are like permanent building sites with new business districts constantly under construction, have fallen victim to a frenzy of property speculation, destroying all their old quarters, and both are building costly underground systems, with five lines laid in Taipei within five years. Both sited in basins, Taipei and Seoul suffer from pollution caused by core industries established in the past and from a huge increase in car traffic. South Korea had already made the use of catalytic converters compulsory at the time of the Olympic Games in 1988, five years before the

European Community. Hong Kong, with its six million inhabitants, and Singapore, with two and a half million, are both examples of successful urbanization. Hong Kong's large-scale public housing policy and vast investment in infrastructure, including three underground lines, numerous bridges to link the islands and the planned Lantao airport, all add up to what is, physically speaking, probably the most impressive urban agglomeration in the region. Singapore has 75 per cent of its public housing in pristine condition (which is sold to residents), a model public transport network and strictly-regulated private transport, the best airport in the world, and spotless streets and green spaces due to the fact that infringements are heavily penalized. In terms of socially-inspired, utopian urban planning, Singapore represents the pinnacle of the pre-war Viennese socialist tradition. It is no accident that Lee Kuan Yew, a member of the Socialist International until 1979, has, through authoritarian yet visionary state control, perfected the model pioneered by Red Vienna during the 1920s.

Much more problematical is the situation in Bangkok, with its eight million inhabitants, Jakarta with nine million, and above all Manila with ten million. In these cities, the paramount importance of the business districts and tourism, coupled with a high degree of social segregation, has created enclaves of luxury and middle-class life, yet their choked transport systems, the unregulated pollution of their air and water supplies, their shanty towns and the living conditions of their underprivileged classes, all continue to tie them to the rest of the modern-day Third World. Each of these agglomerations also features a so-called middle class, whose standard of living now exceeds European and Japanese levels, alongside a much less privileged proletariat. At the same time, there are widespread aspirations towards social advancement, justified by the high wage increases of the 1980s. In 1993, the average worker's salary in Taiwan was equal to the French statutory minimum wage, while South Korea is also catching up after several years of continuous social change. In both Singapore and Hong Kong, the salaries of qualified professionals now exceed European levels.

An even surer sign of confidence in the future clearly lies in the amount of public and individual effort put into education. Primary school education was available to all by the beginning of the 1980s, except in some jungle regions and urban shanty towns. Numbers enrolled in secondary education are almost as high in Taiwan and Korea, while they are rapidly improving elsewhere. However, it is in higher education that progress has been most dramatic. The numbers of students at university in South Korea, Taiwan and the Philippines are equal to those in the industrialized world at over 20 per cent of the corresponding age bracket. The unusually high concentration of universities in Seoul, with a student population of over one million, is one of the reasons for the large amount of political unrest and street protest in that agglomeration. Student demonstrations in Thailand resulted in a violent crackdown in October 1973, while students in Manila also played a part in the downfall of Ferdinand Marcos in 1986. The teaching staff of some universities, such as Chulalongkorn in Bangkok and the national universities of Singapore, Taiwan and Seoul play prominent roles, either as government advisers or as critical voices inspiring the opposition. Conversely, education in South-East Asia is not immune to ethnic conflict. This was the reason why Lee Kuan Yew curtailed the independence of Nanyang University, which he regarded as both too pro-Chinese and too progressive, in favour of the melting-pot of the Singapore National University. Meanwhile in Malaysia, the status of Chinese schools and the Chinese language has been challenged since 1989.

Regional dynamism

The mid-1980s were less favourable for the South-East Asian economies than for the rest of East Asia. While Japan and the North-East Asian NICs concentrated on penetrating the American market, the ASEAN countries were handicapped by the drop in prices for oil and raw materials, as well as by their own persistently low level of technological development. Singapore, a country hypersensitive to regional economic fluctuations, even underwent a full-scale recession (-1.6 per cent) in 1985, as did Malaysia and the post-Marcos Philippines. However, the crisis was short-lived. Indeed, from 1986, all international forces started to work in favour of South-East Asia. A major revaluation of the yen in 1985 was followed by similar trends in Taiwan and South Korea, two of the three economies which usually posted high trade surpluses. Only the Hong Kong dollar escaped this trend owing to doubts over the colony's future following its reversion to China in 1997. Japan, Taiwan and Korea all embarked on a major policy of direct investment in the ASEAN economies and China, not only to lower their direct trade surpluses with the United States but also to cut their own labour costs. In Japan, this policy of industrial relocation particularly affected four key sectors: the electrical and electronics industry, the car manufacturers and their subcontractors, the machine tool sector and also the major department stores, which launched fashion lines aimed at well-heeled consumers. Taiwan and Korea frequently invested in labour-intensive industries for consumer goods, but their investments are now about to overtake those of Japan. The relative share of American and European direct investment in the ASEAN economies has tailed off since the beginning of the 1980s. At the same time the domestic markets of Japan, Taiwan and Korea have opened up under the influence of liberalization measures called for by the United States, and also as a result of monetary revaluation. This benefited the manufacturing output of the 'Four Dragons' and South-East Asia between 1985 and 1990: their share of manufactured exports to Japan rose from 50 per cent to 73 per cent between 1980 and 1988, with

ASEAN's export share increasing from 6 per cent to 20 per cent over the same period.

The dynamism of the South-East Asian economies is also reflected in an even greater increase in imports from Japan. Factories and machinery ear-marked for the setting-up of new Japanese companies, Japan's monopoly on certain advanced manufacturing techniques and the success of its consumer goods have also played a part. In 1989, Japan exported the same amount to the 'Four Dragons' as it did to Western Europe, to the tune of nearly US$60 billion in both cases, while in 1991, its second-largest foreign trade surplus was with Taiwan at US$10 billion. The export success of the South-East Asian countries has often assisted the strategies of the Japanese firms which have set up business there. In 1987, for example, 30 per cent of their output was destined for third countries, with less than 16 per cent being sold in Japan, while 45 per cent of their supplies were Japanese in origin. In February 1988, the Japanese MITI set up a study-group to draw up proposals for a unified system of patent legislation which would be applicable to all Asian countries, a project which was crucial in spreading the transfer of technology throughout the region. South-East Asia's economic growth since 1986 has therefore been unusually strong. For the first time, the ASEAN countries (excluding the Philippines) have forged ahead of the first genera-tion of Asian dragons, Taiwan, South Korea and Hong Kong. It has not so much been a series of separate economic miracles as a process of regional synchronization, largely dominated by Japanese firms and considerable quantities of Japanese government aid. The yen has also become a regional trade and reserve currency, alongside the dollar which previously dominated all transactions. In February 1991, the governors of all the region's central banks held a joint meeting for the first time since 1945.

The limits of regional integration

One might argue that we are seeing the rapid emergence of a single market, something which it has taken the European Union nearly a quarter of a century (1958–93) to achieve. In January 1988, the Japanese government put forward the idea of a free-trade zone with ASEAN. Australia and New Zealand, keen to be integrated with the rest of the region, took up this proposal, which was welcomed equally enthusiastically by Prime Minister Lee Kuan Yew of Singapore: naturally, it was the stronger economies which reacted most positively. In 1991, Prime Minister Mahathir of Malaysia gave the theme an unexpected twist by proposing a fully-fledged economic bloc, consisting of the whole of East Asia and excluding the United States, Australia and New Zealand. This idea was seen as a clumsy reaction to concerns over the possible erection of a 'fortress Europe' after 1993. A compromise was decided by the six members of ASEAN in 1992 to establish a free-trade zone within fifteen years, but with a great many restrictions and exclusions.

In actual fact, the entity being created is more limited, even if it does already mark an impressive achievement. Rather than a common market, it is a single Asian workshop, enabling the main export industries to operate a truly horizontal division of labour throughout the region and to trade products and components across borders, the best example being the electronics industry. Virtually all the countries in the region have taken major steps to liberalize their controls on foreign investment in industry. This is much less true of Taiwan and South Korea, which both have mature industries to protect: 26 per cent of Taiwan's economic activity remained closed to foreigners in 1989, as against 20 per cent in South Korea. The financial markets, artificially boosted by the wave of speculation sweeping the globe in the 1980s, have been liberalized, to a high degree in the case of Bangkok, Kuala Lumpur and Jakarta, less so in Taipei and Seoul.

The concept of free zones is experiencing a new heyday, and affects a much wider geographic area, including the east coast of Thailand, the region between Kuala Lumpur and Ipoh in Malaysia, and even an ideal international prototype: on the island of Batan, between Singapore and Indonesia, a vast industrial zone has been developed, based on low Indonesian wage levels but without the usual delays and bureaucratic corruption. Technical staff and executives arrive by ferry in thirty minutes from Singapore, while all company headquarters remain in the city, the great favourite of the multi-nationals. The economic area which has evolved as a result, known as the 'growth triangle' (which also includes the neighbouring zone of Johor in Malaysia) is primarily geared to exports for the world's markets, although it also has the more immediate effect of generating regional prosperity. In the longer term, the opening-up of China's coastal areas to foreign investment and the increasing osmosis taking place between Hong Kong and its Cantonese hinterland (the colony actually employs over three million workers from Guangdong) could indeed represent a similar phenomenon. Following the revival of indirect links between Taiwan and China, Taiwanese investors are storming the continent, channelling over US$10 billion in 1990–2 into what is still in theory a communist-run economy.

However, the countries of ASEAN, like Japan in the 1950s and the first generation of NICs, have shown little enthusiasm for free trade. They are frequently in competition with one another in the sale of agricultural products and raw materials and have a need to protect their own farmers. The joint ventures of the 1970s, for example to establish a common car industry, ended in failure. ASEAN increased its notoriety in many quarters with its announcement of a reduction in tariff barriers between member states, for just 71 products in 1976, rising to 18,000 in 1986. Sceptics had a field-day pointing out that the list of products covered was so bogus that it included items such as snowploughs which were of little use in the tropics. Export to American and European markets remains a top priority: the possibility of the number of major international blocs being reduced to three – North

America (already a free-trade zone), the European Economic Area and East Asia – would heavily penalize the Asian economies.

At an even more fundamental level, the internationalization of East Asia has, outside Japan, only permeated the thinking of a very few people. The obstacles in this case are both political and cultural. They include, first and foremost, the growing gulf separating Islam from other cultures in South-East Asia and also in western China, particularly Xinjiang province. Since 1980, Malaysian public life has been islamized both at the instigation of Prime Minister Mahathir and as a result of heavy pressure from extremists. This growing trend has created renewed tension with the influential Chinese community. In Indonesia, with the world's largest Muslim community at 140 million, Islamic pressure is sufficiently strong to force General Suharto into new declarations of faith. Both Indonesia and Malaysia have also modified their foreign policies accordingly. Even the tiny sultanate of Brunei, one of the world's top ten oil-producing countries, has, since 1987, implemented a policy of islamization to the detriment of its other ethnic communities. Moreover, it is no longer the syncretic and tolerant Asian form of Islam which is preached there. Indeed, Islam is frequently blurred with an anti-Western nationalism, sometimes approaching paradox: for example, the great majority of the people of Brunei supported Saddam Hussein and Iraq in 1991, even though their tiny kingdom occupies a similar position to Kuwait. The growing extremism among popular religious movements and the fundamentalism of religious leaders and governments signal much more fraught relations with Confucian and Buddhist Asia, which is founded on pragmatism and tolerance. Not only is there a danger that regional political integration will remain strictly limited, but in the case of certain ASEAN member states there is even a potential threat to national unity. Against the prototype of the 'growth triangle' as represented by Singapore, one might cite the triangular relationships which link Japan, the Chinese and the Malay–Islamic communities.

Other obstacles are caused above all by problems of cross-border communication. It is only since the end of the 1980s, for example, that the people of South Korea have been free to travel abroad and export foreign currency in the process. ASEAN's international conferences bring together senior officials, professors and journalists, yet the intermingling of the different societies has scarcely begun. There is also no system of town-twinning or exchanges similar to those which paved the way for the building of Europe. The one exception to this is with Japan, which conjures up the possibility of regional integration on a much broader geographic and political scale, to which South-East Asia does not hold the keys. Tourism statistics themselves are misleading, as visits very often consist only of short stays in capital cities or on beaches. Immigration, though much debated in Taiwan and Singapore due to its novelty, is still small-scale. Part of the success of the free zones stems precisely from the fact that it has so far been a case of the factories relocating towards supplies of cheap labour, rather than of the poor gravitating towards the more advanced economies. Lastly, the wide expanses of ocean separating the countries of maritime Asia preclude the same advanced level of integration achieved in European trade. However, this hindrance has, admittedly, brought about the remarkable success of container shipping (since the 1980s, Evergreen of Taiwan has been one of the world's leading maritime freight companies, while Singapore is one of the two leading international ports along with Rotterdam) and South-East Asia's airlines are the fastest-growing in the world (again, Singapore Airlines, a publicly-owned company and the city-state's major employer, is one of the largest airlines in the world). For the time being, South-East Asian integration consequently remains an industrial phenomenon linked to international trade, rather than an institutional or cultural reality.

SELECTED READING

Alagappa, M. (ed.) (1995) *Political legitimacy in Southeast Asia: the quest for moral authority*, Stanford: Stanford University Press.

Achara, A. (1994) *An arms race in post-Cold War Southeast Asia?*, Singapore: Institute of Southeast Asian Studies.

Bartholomew, J. (1984) *The richest man in the world: the Sultan of Brunei*, London: Viking.

Beauregard, P. de *et al.* (1986) *La politique asiatique de la Chine*, Paris: Fondation pour les Études de Défense nationale.

Bedeski, R. E. (1994) *The transformation of South Korea – reform and constitution in the Sixth Republic under Roh Tae Woo. 1987–1992*, London: Routledge.

Bonner, R. (1987) *Waltzing with a dictator: the Marcoses and the making of American policy*, New York: Times Books.

Broinowski, A. (1982) *Understanding ASEAN*, New York: St. Martin's Press.

Cayrac-Blanchard, F. (1991) *L'Armée et le pouvoir en L'Indonésie*, Paris: L'Harmattan.

Chalfont, A. (1989) *By God's will: a portrait of the Sultan of Brunei*, London: Weidenfeld & Nicolson.

Chan, H. C. (1984) *A sensation of independence: a political biography of David Marshall*, Singapore: Oxford University Press.

Cheng, Y. and Aubert, C. (1984) *Les greniers de Mancang: chronique d'un village taiwanais*, Paris: INRA.

Chew, E. C. T. and Lee, E. (eds) (1991) *A history of Singapore*, Singapore: Oxford University Press.

Fabre, A. (1988) *La grande histoire de la Corée*, Lausanne: Favre.

Fukui, H. (ed.) (1985) *Political parties in Asia and the Pacific*, 2 vols, Westport: Greenwood Press.

George, T. J. S. (1973) *Lee Kuan Yew's Singapore,* London: Andre Deutsch.

Girling, J. L. S. (1981) *Thailand: society and politics,* Ithaca: Cornell University Press.

Gold, T. B. (1986) *State and society in the Taiwan miracle,* Armonk: M. E. Sharpe.

Goodno, J. B. (1991) *The Philippines: a land of broken promises,* London: Zed.

Guzman, R. P. and Reforma, M. A. (eds) (1988) *Government and politics of the Philippines,* Singapore: Oxford University Press.

Hsiung, J. C. (ed.) (1981) *The Taiwan experience, 1950–1980,* New York: American Association for Chinese Studies.

Huntington, S. (1991) *The third wave: democratization in the late twentieth century,* Norman and London: University of Oklahoma Press.

Joaquin, N. (1983) *The Aquinos of Tarlac: an essay on history as three generations,* Mandaluyong.

Karnow, S. (1989) *America's empire in the Philippines: in our image,* New York: Random House.

Kim, Q. (1983) *The fall of Syngman Rhee,* Berkeley: California University Press.

Koon, H. P. (1988) *Chinese politics in Malaysia: a history of the MCA,* Singapore: Oxford University Press.

Kressler, R. J. (1989) *Rebellion and repression in the Philippines,* New Haven: Yale University Press.

Kuo, S. W. Y., Ranks, G. and Fei, J. C. H. (1981) *The Taiwan success story,* Boulder: Westview Press.

Lai, T., Myers, R. H. and Wei, W. (1991) *A tragic beginning: the Taiwan uprising of February 28, 1947,* Stanford: Stanford University Press.

Lee, K. (1984) *A new history of Korea,* Cambridge, MA: Harvard University Press.

Leifer, M. (1995) *Dictionary of the modern politics of South-East Asia,* London: Routledge.

Lintner, B. (1989) *Outrage: Burma's struggle for democracy,* Hong Kong: Far Eastern Economic Review Publishing Co.

Margolin, J. (1989) *Singapour 1959–1987: genése d'un nouveau pays industrialisé,* Paris: L'Harmattan.

Mauzy, D. K. and Milne, R. S. (1978) *Politics and government in Malaysia,* Singapore: Times Books.

May, B. (1978) *The Indonesian tragedy,* London: Routledge & Kegan Paul.

Mody, N. B. (1987) *Indonesia under Suharto,* New York: Apt Books.

Mutalib, H. (1990) *Islam and ethnicity in Malay politics,* Singapore: Oxford University Press.

O'Brien, H. (1991) *Forgotten land: a rediscovery of Burma,* London: Michael Joseph.

Okabe, T. (ed.) (1988) *Twenty years of ASEAN: its survival and development*, Tokyo: Japanese Institute of International Affairs.

Régnier, P. T. (1987) *Singapour et son environnement régional*, Paris: Presses Universitaires de France.

Scalapino, R. A., Sato, S. and Wanandi, Y. (eds) (1986) *Asian political institutionalism*, Berkeley: University of California Press.

Schwarz, A. (1994) *A nation in waiting: Indonesia in the 1990s*, Boulder: Westview Press.

Seagrave, S. (1988) *The Marcos dynasty*, New York: Harper & Row.

Shaplen, R. (1969) *Time out of hand: revolution and reaction in Southeast Asia*, London: Andre Deutsch.

Song, B. (1990) *The rise of the Korean economy*, Hong Kong: Oxford University Press.

Turnbull, M. C. (1979) *A history of Malaysia, Singapore and Brunei*, Sydney: Allen & Unwin.

Vatikiotis, M. R. J. (1993) *Indonesian politics under Suharto: order, development and pressure for change*, London: Routledge.

Vorys, K. von (1976) *Democracy without consensus: communalism and political stability in Malaysia*, Singapore: Oxford University Press.

Wade, R. (1990) *Governing the market: economic theory and the role of government in East Asian industrialization*, Princeton: Princeton University Press.

Winckler, E. A. and Greenhalgh, S. (1988) *Contending approaches to the political economy of Taiwan*, Armonk: M. E. Sharpe.

Wong, J. (1984) *The political economy of China's changing relations with Southeast Asia*, London: Macmillan.

Wurfel, D. (1988) *Filipino politics: development and decay*, Ithaca: Cornell University Press.

Wyatt, D. K. (1984) *Thailand: a short history*, New Haven: Yale University Press.

Xuto, S. (ed.) (1987) *Government and politics of Thailand*, Singapore: Oxford University Press.

Zakaria, H. A. and Crouch, H. (eds) (1985) *Military–civilian relations in Southeast Asia*, Singapore: Oxford University Press.

9   Post-communism in Asia

The Chinese film director Tian Zhuangzhuang, also known abroad for *The Horse Thief* and *The Blue Kite* and now prevented from filming, has told the life-story of Li Lianying, the 'imperial eunuch' who was steward to Empress Cixi throughout her reign. The Japan of the post-war economic miracle inspired Mizoguchi, in *Street of Shame*, to create a melodrama about the collapse of traditional values, while post-Maoist China in turn, caught up in the relentless pursuit of prosperity, has an insatiable appetite for historic scenes of (almost) bygone days. However, in this particular case, Tian Zhuangzhuang's scenario conceals an allegory about Deng Xiaoping, now in his nineties, and his Prime Minister Li Peng, hated for his official part in the Tiananmen tragedy of June 1989. In the most violent scene of the film, Li Lianying, on the orders of Dowager Empress Cixi, has the advisers and servants of Prince Guangxu beaten to death, though not without himself fainting at the sight. In 1898, Prince Guangxu, the son of Cixi and the titular Emperor, had backed a brief bid for reform, which lasted a hundred days before Cixi put a stop to it, and the episode consequently became known as the Hundred Days. Guangxu himself was put under house arrest in the Forbidden City and is reputed to have been poisoned. The liberties which Tian Zhuangzhuang takes with historical fact only emphasize all the more clearly his intention to represent the post-Tiananmen period. The portrayal of Cixi's flight after the ransacking of the Summer Palace by the Anglo-French forces is intended as an analogy to the departure of China's leaders from the Forbidden City in May 1989, which the government itself maintained was the result of a Western-inspired plot. The whole of China knows that Li Peng, the person nominally responsible for the June 1989 crackdown, was on the verge of a nervous breakdown when he appeared on television, convulsed with nerves, to give an impromptu speech on environmental protection, at the very moment when the tanks were in action. They also know that Zhao Ziyang, the reformist leader appointed as Deng Xiaoping's successor to head the Communist Party, was immediately put under house arrest, while several of his close advisers were imprisoned and many activists were killed. In Tian Zhuangzhuang's film, Cixi, an intelligent tyrant who no longer has any rivals to fear, eventually becomes physically dependent on her entourage and in particular Li Lianying, who carries her on his back, reminding her of songs from her childhood – an allusion to the communist veterans and their past. Meanwhile, beyond the walls of the Forbidden City, China undergoes increasing transformation, in a scene which itself also evokes the present gulf between the old generation of leaders and the dynamism of their country. Just as Li Peng was long reputed to be, Li Lianying is portrayed as a man of rare integrity, ever delivering homilies to the distant relatives who come to seek his help. He thus remains loyal to bureaucratic prescription, just as Li Peng remained loyal to the morality of Maoism. Neither have received any thanks for this, for they also violate both the Confucian duty to offer help and the principle of family unity which is so important in Chinese society. In the end, Li Lianying outlives his mistress but is immediately forced to give up his post, bemoaning his life as a eunuch deprived of all feeling, both literally and metaphorically. It is fairly obvious here what fate Tian Zhuangzhuang was imagining for Li Peng.

China thus seems to be entering the post-communist era against its will. It is still led, albeit from 'behind the curtain' (that is, from unofficial positions), by the same men who introduced communism there in the 1920s.

But is the situation any different in the three countries of Indochina? Vietnam has been governed by the last survivor of the three brothers who have dominated the country since 1975: General Le Duc Anh, the President of the Republic who, in 1993, played host to François Mitterrand, the first Western head of state to visit the country, was the real Vietnamese administrator for Cambodia and Laos from 1979 onwards; his brother Le Duc Tho was the signatory to the Paris agreements of 1973 along with Henry Kissinger, while Mai Chi Tho was South Vietnam's much-feared security chief as well as Party Leader for Ho Chi Minh City. General Vo Nguyen Giap, after years spent playing tennis in semi-retirement in Hanoi appear to have kept him well-preserved, smiles enigmatically at his Western guests. Do Muoi and Vo Van Kiet are also still senior members of the Vietnamese communist movement. And what of Cambodia, notwithstanding the upheavals of the Khmer Rouge downfall and international involvement in the conflict? Since the Paris Agreements of October 1991, the chief arbiter has once again been Norodom Sihanouk – the key actor in the Khmer drama, former protégé of Admiral Decoux in 1941, advocate of 'Buddhic socialism' during the Bandung era, and first the enemy of the Khmer Rouge (up to 1970) then its ally (1970–79). Having walked a tightrope between the French and the Japanese, then between the Americans and the North Vietnamese, he headed, from 1991 to 1993, a system of four Khmer factions, once again including the Khmer Rouge and the pro-Vietnamese faction in Phnom Penh. Pol Pot, the historical leader of the Khmer Rouge, spent time in Thailand and probably even in Cambodia, while Khieu Samphan rubbed shoulders with world leaders on his diplomatic travels.

Their lieutenants control the population of western Cambodia, while the ruling party apparatus in Phnom Penh has assassinated a few troublesome opponents. An open and democratic election backed by the UN in May 1993 has legitimated both Sihanouk and Hun Sen's rule. But in the capital city corrupt officials and Thai businessmen are rapidly privatizing what remains of the Cambodian state. It is time to do business, and ASEAN is in such haste that it has already admitted Vietnam as a member, and considers Cambodia and Laos as well. After harbouring hopes of a second march into Phnom Penh and assassinating families of Vietnamese civilians settled in Cambodia, the Khmer Rouge show signs of disintegrating themselves, under the attraction of money deals. The most extreme communism in Asia may be ending with a whimper rather than a bang.

THE END OF THE CHINESE REVOLUTION

It is just over forty-five years since Henri Cartier-Bresson took his memorable photograph of Shanghai investors storming the banks to withdraw suitcases full of banknotes, amid the spiralling inflation which gripped precommunist China. This mythical snapshot of a devalued currency served better than any rational argument to justify the introduction of the Chinese communist régime, which, along with Fidel Castro's Cuba, was one of the few to actually try to abolish money as a means of exchange, in one still-famous episode of the Great Leap Forward. In a sense, communism was not only morally desirable given China's feudal oppression, but even inevitable considering its economic disintegration. Like the fascist régimes of Europe and their productivist philosophy after 1918, it presented itself as a short cut out of underdevelopment, while simultaneously avoiding both democracy and disorder.

In August 1992, however, international television cameras filmed 100,000 Chinese as they flocked from all over the country to the famous special economic zone of Shenzhen to buy lottery tickets, the prize for which was the opportunity to acquire newly-issued shares in private companies. The return of the cult of Mammon, along with a penchant for gambling and lotteries, and the blatant misappropriation of public funds by officials (in Shenzhen, the state security services apparently seized most of the shares at source in order to re-sell them) indicate that a new Chinese revolution is imminent.

However, whereas the evolution of Chinese political thought shows signs of Western influence, albeit hidden, the development of its economy since 1978 bears little resemblance to the Western model of industrial revolution and liberal capitalism. Rather, China's economic boom since 1978 is an example of the traditional phenomenon of catching up with more advanced economies, as experienced by southern Europe and maritime Asia.

The waning of the Maoist economy

Not that the Maoist period saw the economy stagnate: by means of a huge programme to mobilize collective labour for the grain harvest (increasing the yield from 110 million tonnes in the 1930s to 270 million in the 1970s, over an area much the same size), it continued the race to feed its growing population, without resolving the dilemma. The fact that China's GNP increased by roughly sixfold was proof of the régime's efforts to industrialize, largely in accordance with the Stalinist model. This growth was extensive rather than intensive, devouring the capital which the government had extracted from the population, demanding an excessive volume of labour and freezing civilian technology (and even military technology, apart from that connected with nuclear and space activities) at Soviet levels as they had been in 1959. Later improvements, which Maoism presented as the flowering of the genius of the popular masses, were more to do with random tinkering than systematic innovation. Almost everywhere in China, five-tonne 'Liberation' lorries were still being driven in the 1980s, the direct descendants of a 1930s Dodge lorry donated in 1942 to the Soviet Union, which then passed it on to China.

Similar development without transformation is equally noticeable in Chinese demographic and social trends. If the urban Shanghai of 1978 (and even of 1985, for reform came later there than elsewhere) looked physically the same as the Shanghai of the Concessions in the 1930s, this was because all urban development was frozen under Maoism. In great contrast to Stalinism, which drafted the peasants to work in the factories after the massacre of the *kulaks*, Maoism kept the peasants in the rice fields, even though it also meant sending down millions of city-dwellers deemed to be superfluous. City-dwellers represented 17.3 per cent of the total population in 1962 and 17.4 per cent in 1976: as several sociologists of rural China have shown, at the latter date the vast majority of peasants still continued to live in their ancestral villages (Banister, 1987). This freeze was, of course, only possible as a result of ubiquitous bureaucratic control and because China was largely isolated from the world economy: at the same period, with a quarter of the global population, it accounted for a mere 0.5 per cent of international trade.

There was likewise considerable untapped productivity, both in agriculture and in industry. The forced enrolment of the rural population into the collective squads of the people's communes had certainly made it possible to find everyone a place in the systems of employment and resource distribution, but at the cost of excess labour, underemployed on wages which still went up to the old maximum levels. The complete lack of chemical fertilizers (the first factories to manufacture them were purchased from the United States in 1972–3) and mechanization (the few tractors China possessed were used for transport rather than for agricultural work) also contributed to this stagnation in productivity, the sole advantage of which was that it minimized financial investment in the rural sector. As far as industry was concerned, technology largely stagnated at the level reached by the Soviet equipment delivered in 1959–60, the last year of Sino-Soviet co-operation. Western imports in the years following the Sino-Soviet rift were too sparse to make any difference to this situation, and harassment in the fields of education and science (apart from the areas of nuclear and space technology) prevented any independent progress. As a result of this policy, industrial growth, which had been spectacular in the 1950s, slowed down increasingly in the 1960s and particularly the 1970s. At some years' remove, China was heading for the same economic stagnation which the USSR experienced during the Brezhnev era.

The phases of reform under Deng and the economic revolution

The reform of the Chinese economy is inextricably linked to the de-Maoi-zation of the régime, even though it stopped short of political reform. Each new phase has brought about an imbalance with the bureaucracy and economic behaviour inherited from the Maoist era. Instead of the vicious circle which many Sinologists predicted, these tensions have prompted an overwhelming dynamism among the people and new proposals from the advocates of reform. Whereas the problems of reform could have resulted in it being cut short, as was the case with all the East European precedents, they instead served to spur on the process with the headstrong pursuit of new policies, an example subsequently followed by Gorbachev and Yeltsin.

China's post-Maoist boom is, of course, inseparable from its political direction, even though reform has fallen short of the political system. Furthermore, certain aspects of the reform programme date back to 1974–5: at that time, when Deng Xiaoping first returned to power, both education and science and technology policy in China were undergoing modernization. This became the major issue in propaganda campaigns between moderates and radicals, with the latter ousting Deng Xiaoping again in April 1976. De-Maoization, official and otherwise, generally went hand-in-hand with economic and social liberalization. In February 1978, the real power was still in the hands of an *apparatchik* close to Mao: Hua Guofeng had been chief of the Great Helmsman's own native district, Shaoshan, and had transformed that overcrowded upland region into a showcase for the régime and a place of political pilgrimage. In what appeared to be a political rallying strategy, Hua Guofeng and Deng Xiaop-ing together launched an ambitious ten-year plan, based on a large-scale opening-up to imports of technology from abroad and on labour mobiliza-tion. Conceived without any preliminary reform of an economic bureau-cracy exhausted by the Cultural Revolution, the plan ended in chaos. Overproduction and unsold stock coincided with huge shortages in sectors such as energy and transport, while the trade balance tipped drastically in favour of uncontrolled imports. This could have been another experiment like that of Gierek, as experienced in Poland in the early 1970s, but Deng, ever the political tactician, used this failure as a means to attack his enemies, the heirs to the Maoist legacy. In December 1978 there came the second phase: the Communist Party announced a rise in the prices paid to farmers for their produce and the reopening of private markets in the countryside, at the same time as the purge of some Maoist leaders and the reinstatement of those who had been victimized by the régime since 1957. The rural population extended these early reforms, carrying out a return to the system of family-run farms from the spring of 1979, a move which was officially decreed in 1980–81. The trade imbalance resulted in multi-year economic planning being suspended for three years between 1979 and 1981, while under the leadership of Zhao Ziyang in Sichuan, and later throughout the rest of the country, there were experiments into managerial reform in state-run enterprises. Deng Xiaoping and his colleagues showed no hesitation in closing off the Democracy Wall in March 1979, imprisoning a number of its supporters. In June 1979, however, they created special economic zones and mixed enterprises using foreign capital, adopting some of the methods applied in Taiwan and Singapore in the 1960s. Until 1984, the agricultural economy literally soared under the impetus of the rural population and the revival of private activities – canteens, trading, haulage, peddling, construction and specialized agriculture – around which small private enterprises were rebuilt on the fringes of the official economy. The fact that this phenomenon was not recorded statistically explains the subsequent boom in private enterprises, these being incorporated into the statistics once they had become politically correct. Industrial reform stagnated, especially in Manchuria and Shanghai, the last bastions of the state-run economy, where Soviet-style connections between cadres and firms made it more difficult for a real market economy to emerge. The new-found willingness to accept foreign capital primarily benefited the south of the country, notably Shenzhen, a hitherto obscure place near the border with Hong Kong which suddenly turned into a fast- growing city. However, a number of leaders criticized this open door to capitalism in the south. Deng Xiaoping obliged them by launching two campaigns, one after the other, beginning in the summer of 1983, the first against petty crime and the other against imported 'spiritual pollution'.

In 1984, however, he relaunched the reforms. This was the year which saw the abolition of the requirement for farmers to surrender the profits from their sales quotas and also the legalization of private enterprise. In October, a Party directive, couched in the language of French-style incentive planning, extended the market economy to the industrial, urban sector. The privileges formerly granted to state-run enterprises were phased out and steps were taken to encourage the meeting of consumer needs. A year of unrestrained growth ended with a tremendous rise in inflation (with an increase of 50 per cent plus in the money supply) and a greatly increased trade imbalance, with a trade deficit of no less than US$15 billion in 1985.

Even so, huge numbers of new enterprises were set up, creating new jobs, while the living standards of the urban population, long constrained by central planning, began to rise sharply. It was at this time that – as well as the phenomenon occurring in the south, in the area backed onto by Hong Kong – people began referring to the economic miracle of Jiangnan, the area south of the Lower Yangtse. From Nanjing to Shanghai, the rural population were abandoning the fields for the new enterprises, and two regions – the Pearl Delta and Jiangnan – started to take off, just as the Korean and Taiwanese economies had done in the 1960s.

Deng Xiaoping attained political supremacy in 1984, keeping a visible grip on the army and ruling the Party via Hu Yaobang and the General Secretariat. However, the unexpected success of the reforms and the spontaneous impetus given to them by the people resulted in a new struggle over party line. This time, the split was no longer between die-hard Maoists and their victims, but rather between reformists and conservatives. Many of the latter, such as the economist Chen Yun and the ideologist Hu Qiaomu, had supported de-Maoization during its initial phase. However, whereas Deng's anointed successors, Zhao Ziyang and Hu Yaobang, wanted to forge ahead both to extend the reforms and to replace a generation of cadres promoted by the Cultural Revolution, the conservatives reacted against any threats to the political and social stability of the country. It was a question of the accelerator or the brake. From 1985 until the end of the summer of 1988, Deng failed to choose either of these two manoeuvres, ultimately causing the violent swerve of spring 1989 and the collision between the young proto-democrats and the paleo-Maoists on 5 June.

Tiananmen and the small-scale restoration of 1989–91

From the original petition signed by thirty-three intellectuals, calling for the release of Chinese political prisoners, to the public uproar of those heady May days, the protest movement of spring 1989 clearly had complex roots. None the less, each new generation of Chinese pro-democracy supporters tends to disregard its predecessors: for example the name of Wei Jingsheng, which was in the air at the start of the 1989 movement, virtually became ignored along the way, just as the victims and political prisoners of 1989 themselves appear in turn to have been largely forgotten a few years later.

The first forerunner to the events of 1989 was the May Fourth Movement of 1919, that protest against the Versailles Treaty by the teachers and students of Peking – clad in traditional long robes but brandishing English-language placards – which was destined to end in the upheaval of Chinese culture and its frenetic modernization. The bloody crackdown by the authorities in 1989 was by no means a traditional response: the legitimacy of the intellectuals was too strong in May 1919 for direct military force to be used against them. At the very most, there was the republican government of Wang Jingwei in Nanjing which, under pressure from Japan, brutally suppressed a number of anti-Japanese student demonstrations in 1935. Memories of the days following the death of Zhou Enlai in April 1976 were a further factor in bringing about the mass mobilization of 1989: the protesters timed their initial action, in April, to follow on from a posthumous tribute to Hu Yaobang, whose portrait, depicting him in a three-piece suit, hung overlooking Tiananmen Square, just as that of Zhou Enlai had done in April 1976. There was also the reopening in 1978–9 of the Democracy Wall, whose success had been largely encouraged by Deng Xiaoping himself as a means of undermining his opponents.

Another durable aspect of China's political life lies in the sponsorship, albeit indirect and implicit, provided by certain high-ranking government leaders, depending on their own motives: each time, this enables the launch of a fresh wave of opposition while limiting its scope for independent political action. The best example of continuity in the use of this tactic, even more so than Deng Xiaoping, was unquestionably General Secretary Zhao Ziyang himself: as a senior provincial cadre in Guangdong during the Cultural Revolution, he had already given tacit encouragement to the 'democratic manifesto' of the Li Yizhe faction, which was unique of its kind in the Maoist era. Although Hu Yaobang died shortly before the 1989 Second Spring took place, many of its leaders were veterans of the 1956 generation who sympathized with the bid for democracy, without joining in themselves. A prominent member of this group, the writer Wang Meng, who had begun his literary career at the time of the Hundred Flowers in 1956–7 and had become Minister of Culture in 1986–9, was a hate figure in the eyes of the conservative communists. The declaration of martial law on 20 May 1989 ultimately led, among other things, to a hostile petition signed by some of the most influential names in the People's Liberation Army and to open resistance from some of the army units charged with enforcing martial law. This was particularly true of the Thirty-Eighth Regiment appointed to guard Peking, many of whose officers, and also the Defence Minister and the Minister for State Security, had sons or daughters of their own among the protesters in Tiananmen Square.

Tiananmen was ultimately one in a series of several peaceful pro-democracy movements to occur in East Asia: in Taiwan, where the lifting of martial law in September 1987 and the introduction of complete freedom of the press marked the run-up to the introduction of a democratic political system; in South Korea, where General Chun Doo-hwan's government gave in to pressure from student demonstrators; and above all in Manila, where Corazon Aquino's 'people power' and the presence of electoral observers from the United States enabled proper elections to be held, overthrowing the Marcos régime. These movements also attested to the fact that the region was becoming less preoccupied with anti-communism and security. Since 1978, the audience for foreign radio stations (for example the BBC, Voice of America, Radio-France, and Taiwan) had grown in China. The television power of CNN did the rest: coincidentally, the Second Spring of 1989, which began with the anniversary of April 1976, followed by that of May Fourth 1919, also featured the first meeting in Peking of the Asia Development Bank, attended by the Taiwanese Finance Minister and also Mikhail Gorbachev, the first visit by a Soviet leader since 1969. All these media events acted as a shield for the protesters. The papier-mâché replica of the Statue of Liberty, dubbed the 'Goddess of Democracy', which they erected in Tiananmen Square, was the ultimate extension of this: in the absence of any coherent political strategy, it seemed to be the Chinese version of a 'cargo cult', where a raised effigy is supposed to bring about the real thing. It also significantly aggravated Chinese nationalism.

Another, less visible episode in May–June 1989 marked a more important precedent for the establishment of the rule of law in China, and that was the attempt by the protesters to call a meeting of the People's National Assembly in order to oppose the introduction of martial law. This incident was indeed the first step along the road to parliamentary government. The People's National Assembly, headed by a Standing Committee (the equivalent of the Supreme Soviet in the former USSR) was in practice nothing more than a rubber-stamping body, while the indirect election of representatives was largely controlled by the Party. Its rare meetings (no more than two brief sessions a year under Deng Xiaoping and even fewer during the Maoist era) were also determined by the Party. However, one article in the 1982 constitution made provision for a meeting of the Standing Committee of the Assembly to be called by a majority of its members, and it was this which the more radical reformists tried to achieve, notably abetted by Wang Runnan, the director of China's first private computer firm, Stone, who sent faxes the length and breadth of the country in order to track down potential signatories. This attempt was blocked by the Party, which accused those responsible of conspiracy, but it nevertheless gave a foretaste of the future parliamentary legitimacy which might develop out of existing institutions, such as by avoiding the chaos of a revolution. At any rate, the advocates of repression were sufficiently concerned to delay Wan Li, the President of the People's National Assembly, in Shanghai: on his return from an official visit to the United States, he was regarded as hostile to martial law. His timely U-turn provided an opportunity to suppress the opposition within the Assembly.

The massacre of 4–5 June, which ended with a spate of arrests and the temporary return by the régime to propaganda and Maoist purging tactics, was accompanied by an economic freeze. Not only did most foreigners flee the country and temporarily withdraw their investments, but fears of a debt crisis and the threat of inflation which was causing unrest among the urban population led the government to implement a policy of uncontrolled deflation in order to curb consumption. It was initially targeted at the new private and semi-private enterprises, and the vast majority of independent workers within that sector – rural migrants, building workers seeking construction sites and, more generally, the so-called 'floating population' (estimated at 55 million in September 1988) – found themselves forced to return to their native rural districts. Prime Minister Li Peng spoke out in favour of restoring financing and vital resources for state enterprises as a major element in the Five-Year Plan. This attempt at recentralization also had a clear political dimension, successfully curbing the growing influence of the provincial authorities, including along China's maritime border, and slowing down the privatization of the economy. The policy of 'cooling' the economy, as it was called, continued until spring 1991. It made it possible to bring foreign trade back into balance: although the leading Western powers punished the Chinese government by suspending all new loans (Japan was the first to resume them in July 1990), China eliminated its trade deficit and reduced its debt, although the latter still remained in excess of US$50 billion. With an irony accepted by its main trading partners and encouraged by the competitive devaluation of the RMB, China's trade surpluses continued to rise steeply, reaching, for example, nearly US$30 billion with the United States in 1994, over US$15 billion with the European Community and over US$5 billion with Japan. From 1991, China had the world's second largest trade surplus with the United States after Japan.

1991 onwards: the great capitalist bazaar

In the meantime, however, the remainder of the policy of authoritarian recentralization either failed or had its effectiveness reduced by other factors. Admittedly, between the aftermath of Tiananmen and the Fourteenth Congress of the Chinese Communist Party in October 1992, the country's leadership appeared to become completely fossilized: since the downfall of Zhao Ziyang and a small number of scapegoats, there had been no further departures or major promotions. The country had been ruled from 'behind the curtain' by a few elderly retired men, dubbed the 'eight immortals' by the Hong Kong press. Apart from these eight, Li Peng, despite being protected by fears of a repudiation of Tiananmen, was not really taken into consideration, and initially neither was the new Party General Secretary, Jiang Zemin, who confessed after his appointment to a feeling of walking on a surface as fragile as the ice on a lake. China's shadowy state security chief, Qiao Shi, has avoided any involvement. Although General Yang Shangkun and his half-brother, Yang Baibing, seized political control of the army in June 1989, the Yang clan has prompted opposition from an army reluctant to put itself at the service of a single individual, a situation which the sharp rise in military expenditure from 1989 has done nothing to improve. In 1992, Deng Xiaoping himself further justified this caution when he forced Yang Shangkun out of the Politburo into semi-retirement, and inflicted semi-disgrace on Yang Baibing by entrusting the Party's Military Committee to a modernizing admiral and demoting subordinates of the Yang clan throughout the army. More than ever before, the elderly Deng

Xiaoping appears as the remote yet undeniable creator of China's transition.

Furthermore, the small-scale socialist restoration of 1989–91 failed to produce the anticipated results. The central government has no control over the expenditure or investments of the local authorities, metropolitan and provincial, which now exceed the central budget. State enterprises, once again favoured in principle by economic planning, have nevertheless incurred ever-increasing financial losses, both overt and hidden, as local party bosses and state leaders grant favours to their political supporters and then force the official banks and the state to subsidize them. The threat of social unrest has prevented loss-making enterprises from making redundancies. Between 1980 and 1992, state employees accounted for approximately 19 per cent of the total labour force, amounting to a considerable body of labour in China's cities and at the same time acting as a shock-absorber for the new economic tensions. Despite its unfavourable treatment, the private or semi-private sector has finally forged ahead since the relaxation of monetary policy in 1991. Individual small business owners and village or district enterprises, while subject to incessant demands for money from the local authorities, have only come under slight fiscal pressure from central government. The latter has no real control over revenue collection, and is only able to have funds transferred from local budgets to the central Treasury, just as it did in the days of the Empire.

The Chinese economy also has never solved the problem of overheating (*guore*), and the expansion of the non-state sector has continued, despite the orthodox speeches of 1989: market forces have proved stronger than the forces of stagnation. Reform gathered renewed force following a series of statements made by Deng Xiaoping on a tour of southern China in February 1992. These statements, pieced together by Deng's followers into the fictitious 'Shenzhen speech' (so-called after the special economic zone), constituted a new political offensive: glorifying the market economy, extolling the adoption of capitalist methods, Deng harked back to the frenetic growth of 1984–9, calling it a 'genuine Great Leap Forward which has not harmed the country'. His supporters, along with a number of potential nominees for a reformist succession, immediately launched a critique of economic 'leftism' which the whole leadership was promptly forced to join in, even Li Peng, who displayed unexpected flexibility in what was, for him, a very difficult task. A small group of orthodox cadres who tried to stop the publication of a collection of Deng's sayings were sacked a few months later. Li Peng's flagship project to construct a huge hydroelectric dam at Sanxia, on the River Yangtse, came under renewed and heavy criticism in Peking, with 177 deputies voting against the scheme in the National Assembly, 664 abstaining and seventeen not voting at all. The episode became a symbol of Li Peng's wavering authority. The plan was nevertheless approved, but not without the New China News Agency issuing a press release the next day announcing a need for further pilot studies on the grounds of 'environmental impact'. The central technocracy again found itself in deep water. The veteran Deng Liqun, one of Deng Xiaoping's supporters during the early stages of reform and a reluctant opponent of political liberalization, burst into tears in the middle of an extended meeting of the Politburo, denouncing those of his colleagues who practised 'feigned Marxism' in contrast to the true believers, doubtless pointing the finger primarily at Deng Xiaoping.

Once again, however, Deng acted with skill, dividing his enemies and forging a pact with the older generation of leaders. The 'eight immortals', all indeed over eighty years of age on average, who made up the Planning Committee for the Fourteenth Congress in 1992 included Chen Yun, Bo Yibo and even Li Desheng. Chen Yun, a former architect of Chinese economic planning in the 1950s, had also been one of the few to oppose the Great Leap Forward in 1958, and was responsible for introducing economic reforms in the style of Khrushchev. Though a mainstay of the 1978 reforms, he subsequently parted company with Deng Xiaoping once they were generally implemented. For Chen Yun, the market economy and economic planning were like the proverbial bird and cage: the cage must be large enough to allow the bird to fly, but open the door and the bird will be lost. Bo Yibo was China's answer to Suslov. The favoured prosecutor of disgraced colleagues, he brought about the political downfall of Defence Minister Peng Dehuai in 1959, Hu Yaobang in 1987 and Zhao Ziyang in 1989. Yet he was also a skilled tactician, quick to spot the winning side. As for Li Desheng, he proved the major surprise of this political phase of 1992, appearing on the scene like a Maoist 'Last of the Mohicans'. As a general he was for a long time the commander of the North-East region, the most important in China, and hence also controlled Manchuria and its industry. It was to him that Deng Xiaoping had turned in June 1980 to quash appeals to the army by the conservative Hua Guofeng on the eve of his political downfall. Despite this, Li Desheng, who also harboured an ideological loyalty to Maoism, was excluded from the leadership after 1985 and was subsequently appointed President of the new National Defence University in Peking.

It was from there that Deng summoned him to the rescue in 1992, and his unexpected presence on Deng Xiaoping's tour of the south was reported by the Chinese news agencies, although it went unnoticed in all the Western media. The two seemed to strike an unlikely alliance. In fact, Deng was once again attempting the old political tactic, borrowed from Mao, of the grand alliance, which involved, as a first step, encircling the enemy of the moment with a coalition that was then strengthened even further by the inclusion of the maximum range of tendencies, united above all by bonds of personal loyalty. The pivot of this manoeuvre was the army: its regional commanders had been pressurized, and its leaders spoke out in favour of the so-called 'Shenzhen speech' in May–June 1992. The few who directly opposed it, such as the Chinese-Korean General Cho Namqi, Yang Shangkun's successor, were punished the following autumn. Deng also sought out the last remaining supporters of nationalist Maoism, of which Bo Yibo and Li Desheng were the jewels in the crown, as opposed to the cadres who were tainted with Stalinism, such as Yang Shangkun himself, the last survivor of the Group of Twenty-Eight Bolsheviks from the 1920s, and Li Peng, who had studied in a Soviet school in 1955. Deng Xiaoping's alliance had a single purpose: to liberate the Chinese economy once more from the strait-jacket of state control. Yet this was carried by promising all communist veterans that by rallying to the new cause they would avoid the humiliation of political impeachment that formed the stuff of their worst nightmares: the unimaginable banning of the Communist Party and the transformation of *apparatchiks* into destitute private citizens, as happened in Russia in 1991.

At that point the Chinese economy became gripped by something akin to an undeclared revolution. Although the growth in GNP slowed down in 1989–90, it picked up by 7.7 per cent during 1991 to rise above 12 per cent in 1992, something it had not done since 1984–5. This growth was even more marked in twelve provinces, eight of them coastal ones (Jiangsu, for example, showed a 27 per cent rise). The same was true of industry, which was stimulated by a 30 per cent increase in investment, and above all in private-sector construction, with the number of dwellings built for sale rising by 93.6 per cent in 1992. With the exception of the major cities, the regions of the interior, like the state enterprises, experienced growth below the average rate. Foreign trade and exports, for which there is no shortage of corroborated data, soared by 22 per cent. Most significantly, the difference in the sizes of the state and private sectors became greater than ever before: whereas in 1978 the state sector accounted for 78 per cent of industrial production, in 1991 the figure was 53 per cent and by 1992 it was reduced to a mere 46 per cent. Rural industry underwent a massive boom, absorbing a quarter of the total industrial workforce. Amid this welter of statistics it is all the more difficult to assess the exact share accounted for by private enterprise, since many collective and co-operative enterprises are actually run as private enterprises, while at the same time benefiting considerably from inputs channelled by state cadres and the state sector.

The dividing line between the public and the private sectors has become very much a grey area. On the one hand, thanks to the two-price system, state enterprises sell their own supplies at a profit. On the other hand, however, the public authorities have stepped up their investments (infrastructure, construction and financial inputs) in semi-private enterprises which include a large number of cadres. The obvious corruption resulting from this is a form of privatization which is concealed from the economy. In many cases, the enterprises themselves have become empty shells, offering guaranteed employment as economic activity shifts to the newly-formed private sector. The state has encouraged this transition by scrapping all but the most essential fixed prices in 1991–2, the second time this had been done since 1984. By the end of 1992, the state controlled only 10 per cent of all prices (30 per cent for primary products and building materials), while central planning applied to a mere 12 per cent of production as a whole and less than 50 per cent in the case of primary products. The state is increasingly limiting itself to providing broad geographic and macroeconomic guidelines and objectives. Characteristically, however, it always reserves the right to restore the old controls, and occasionally does so in limited circumstances.

In finance, developments have been just as marked. The volume of personal saving in China is enormous, even allowing for the lack of a social security system and the traditional shortage of consumer goods, amounting to RMB116 trillion in 1992, 23 per cent more than the total volume of retail sales. However, saving by the rural population, which played such a decisive part at the beginning of 1980, is much less important today: in 1992, 10 million small urban entrepreneurs had accumulated the same amount of savings as the whole rural population put together. In order to prevent capital flight, the state offers more attractive interest rates (of nearly 9 per cent in 1992) and in 1991 legalized the holding of deposit accounts in foreign currency. Most inhabitants of Peking, Shanghai and in particular Canton have opened such accounts, and the real exchange rate for the RMB is freely quoted alongside the official one. China's currency is thus gradually moving towards free convertibility. It is nevertheless freely accepted as a means of payment for most transactions, even for the scarcest imported consumer goods. In February 1993, it became legal to transfer the RMB abroad, marking a decisive step along the road to free convertibility.

There has, so far, been no more reform to the banking sector than there has been to the management of the state enterprises. Although the directors of the People's Bank of China, no doubt out of political cautiousness, give the impression of being orthodox monetarists, the money supply grew by 30 per cent in 1992. While the state needs to pour subsidies into loss-making state enterprises if it wishes to avoid them going under, bank loans are at the same time seen as money down the drain. This was shown, for example, in the stampede by the local authorities in 1992 to create investment zones aimed at attracting foreign capital and factories. What is more, it appears that as in 1988–9, many of these local governments gave in to the temptation to pay for farmers' harvests with mere debt notes (*baipaio*), in order to save their ready cash for new projects. Like the 'communist wind' of old, the 'capitalist wind' has brought with it some extravagant behaviour.

China victorious?

How is it that this dislocation of state control, accompanied by the obsessive pursuit of wealth, has not ended in chaos, as it has in Russia since 1989? Some of the same dangers are present, including those of continuous devaluation, which could well lead to capital flight, soaring prices bringing the risk of hyperinflation, mafia corruption, the irreformable nature of the state economic sector and a workforce ill-adapted to the social constraints of the market economy. China's very borders have become dangerously permeable: the most visible signs of this are the luxury cars which are systematically stolen in Hong Kong and turn up registered in China (even though their steering-wheels are on the right hand side), and the contraband which is spreading out from Hong Kong along the coast of Fujian and even throughout Vietnamese territory. Like the vast numbers of foreign bank accounts held by Chinese enterprises and cadres, these *shuihuo* (water goods) are clearly a drain on the national economy, and consistently prevent the state from conducting a policy of controlled growth as carried out by East Asia's 'dragons'. China may be communist in name, but its economy is far less tightly regulated than those of its neighbours have ever been.

None the less, there are some differences between China's transition and the present chaos in Russia. The most fundamental of these lies in the spirit of initiative and adaptability shown by a large section of the Chinese people. Just as the rural population grasped the new economic freedoms which came after 1978, the urban population and the host of migrants from the interior have scrambled to create brand new sectors of production which are labour-intensive and economical in terms of resources. The Chinese proverb 'The phoenix flies towards the south-east' has proved an apt metaphor for the lure of the new regions in the Hong Kong hinterland. Shenzhen, the most important of all the special economic zones, has grown from 70,000 inhabitants in 1978 to more than three million in 1992, who are spilling over chiefly into neighbouring Guangdong. All over the country, Cantonese-language schools are being opened to encourage access to this Eldorado. The phenomenon is not solely a provincial one, however – quite the opposite, in fact. In Peking, for example, groups of workers from Zhejiang (in fact, the same *Wenzhouren* whose work travels as far as Paris's Sentier quarter) are renting dozens of new suburban premises in order to set up textile workshops. Their plentiful and relatively low-priced products find instant buyers among provincials who travel up to Peking as well as the hawkers who pack out the Trans-Siberian railway twice a week. These textile workers are by no means an isolated case. According to the Chinese press, 'the mobile army of workers from Sichuan (the most densely populated of all the provinces) is the largest workforce in the country'. Conversely, the Lhassa riots back in 1986–8 were primarily due to the influx of Chinese settlers setting up businesses and workshops among the less entrepreneurial Tibetans. The vast surplus rural population combined with the assiduous pursuit of individual profit create an abundant supply, slowing down price rises for everyday consumer goods. Production costs stay low as the more backward regions join in, and because there are no trade unions and no political framework to protect wage levels. This is precisely the sort of supply-side economy which has so far been lacking in Russia, where, admittedly, the age profile of the population and the scale of public-sector employment are not strictly comparable. What seems to be developing, in rural China particularly, is protocapitalism, as seen in Europe at the start of the Industrial Revolution, but a protocapitalism which is being directly stimulated by access to modern techniques and markets. In some respects, in bastions such as the Pearl Delta and the Lower Yangtse, it also resembles Italy's economic miracle in the 1960s and Taiwan's in the 1970s. In some cases it is fuelled by similar products: within the space of forty years, world production of toys, Christmas decorations, shoes, handbags and electric lamps shifted away from Italy (and Japan) towards Taiwan and Korea; now, over the last ten years, it has been shifting to China. From the outset, this new industrial centre has been more internationalized than its predecessors. In fact, it is already possible to predict that Chinese protocapitalism, which has been emerging since 1978, will, in terms of labour-intensive industry, become the world number one between now and the year 2000.

As in 1978, China's growth is therefore dependent on the rapid mobilization of forces of production which have hitherto remained dormant or paralysed. In the longer term, it is a vulnerable process: if only for want of adequate legal and political guarantees, the new entrepreneurs prefer short-term profits and will rarely undertake long-term, fixed investments such as plant and technology; also, by remaining rudimentary and small-scale, industrial growth ensures an increase in employment. However, there is a noticeable shift by Chinese private-sector initiatives towards the mixed-enterprise sector in collaboration with foreign partners. Thanks to legislation passed in 1979, this is paradoxically the sector which benefits from the clearest legal status as well as from the widest range of regulatory, customs and fiscal exemptions. There are many Chinese who will produce the capital required to set up a mixed enterprise (US$130,000 in 1993) for the sole purpose of being able to import freely and register a car. Increasingly incapable of controlling production, the Chinese state is now being forced to rely on certain specific sectors (the best example being the defence industry, with its mercantilist system of exports) and on a policy of heavy investment in infrastructure. Recent examples include the Daya Bay nuclear power station and the highly controversial Yangtse dam which will provide electricity for the whole of central and southern China. Forthcoming projects include ambitious plans for railway building and mineral and oil prospecting in western China: it will be vital to supplement traditional coal supplies in order to provide the fuel for growth, and China could well find itself competing with the peoples of Central Asia – Uighurs, Mongols, Kazhaks, Uzbekhs and Tajiks – for control of its deserts, if it does not exploit the latter more effectively.

At the beginning of 1993, two options fought for precedence within the government. The former mayor of Shanghai, Zhu Rongji, favoured both by the West and by Taiwanese investors, who had been put in charge of economic policy at the Fourteenth Congress of the Chinese Communist Party, called for the entire central economic administration to be merged into a vast Chinese equivalent to the Japanese MITI. This would involve shedding more than a third of the central departments of the civil service, opening the way for an export strategy linked to a dismantling of state enterprises, although this point remained unclear. Prime Minister Li Peng, although a convert to the language of reform, preferred to put the accent on the establishment of a central state fund equivalent to the French Caisse des Dépôts or the Japanese Fiscal Investment and Loan Programme (FILP), that would be separate from the general budget and intended for carrying out major public works and investments. It was a choice between export-driven dirigisme versus state-run construction sites: although the dilemma appears less stark than in 1984–9, it did actually conceal fundamental clashes. The conservatives, rather than questioning inflationary growth, could draw attention to the fact that those members of the population who stayed on the land, especially in the leading grain-producing regions, were now the victims of an explosion in urban growth. The reformists could argue that it was primarily the fiscal irresponsibility of the state-run enterprises and the cadres which created inflationary pressure and cyclical crises in the economy. After the still-born boom of 1978–9, followed by the overheating of 1984–9, 1991 marked the start of a new cycle of rocketing growth. Instead of moving towards a decentralization of decision making, which would merely shift corruption out of central government and into local government, some Chinese economists have been daring enough to advocate, if not the unattainable goal of privatization, then at least the conversion of state-owned property into a system of share-holding that would be part public, part private. All, admittedly, are convinced that, given Russia's headlong rush towards disaster after 1989, the gradualism which has characterized China's reforms since 1978, though dependent on the survival of the one-party system, still offers the best chance of a successful transition.

The end of the Chinese revolution

Let us pause for a moment to examine the portrayal of the Empress Cixi's steward, filmed barely two years after the Tiananmen massacre. Tian Zhuangzhuang is far from explicit, and this allows his work to pass through the censor's hoops prior to filming, even though it may not always be seen by Chinese audiences. His melancholy vision of a bureaucracy increasingly cut off from reality, but which lives on despite its growing lack of purpose, strikes a chord with the political disillusionment of many Chinese, for whom the present régime seems interminable. What is more, it is one of the present régime's leading protagonists who told them so: Zhu Rongji, Vice Premier in charge of overall economic policy since 1993, and who, as Mayor of Shanghai in 1989, had acquired a favourable reputation by acting as the shock absorber in the clash between the protesters and the government, made it clear to his subjects in a televised speech that they 'should not hope for a change of dynasty'. This fit of openness conveyed the political dimensions of the problem better than any official pronouncements on the building of socialism .

But is it not a further paradox that Zhu Rongji could speak these words, stripping away the mystique of communist legitimacy, while at the same time it was possible for Tian Zhuangzhuang's film to be produced in China? Is Deng Xiaoping really the old man collapsed on his throne which he seemed to be during the heady June days of 1989? Or is he still a born strategist, possessing a vision of the future yet lacking the specific framework and vocabulary necessary to articulate it, who leads the country blindfold, piloting the ship's course more or less skilfully? The régime has undergone profound change, through a combination of voluntary reform and involuntary disintegration. If communism still officially rules in China, it is because it is already defunct as far as the economy and society are concerned. Its remains now only concern those involved with politics, particularly advocates of political democracy. What is more, the corpse is still moving, with China scoring considerable diplomatic successes: the explanation for this is that it benefits from the passivity of the Chinese people, fearful of the chaos which a political changeover might bring and unfavourably impressed by the fate of the former Soviet Union. Hence we have the paradox of post-communism Chinese-style. Economic reform is only tolerated by the party organization because it steers clear of politics. The people continue to accept the political status quo because economic growth offers everyone a hope that is far more tangible and immediate than the quest for new institutions, and so communism, though decaying, maintains its legitimacy by default. However, if reform or the economic boom were to end, as was the case in 1988, social frustration and unrest would result in a political explosion. This, for all the democratic slogans, would be not so much revolutionary as corporatist: intellectuals and modern bureaucrats, individual traders, private entrepreneurs and workers on commission are all signalling to the Communist Party that there is just one option left, and that is to continue to extend the market economy to accommodate them, alongside the communist edifice that has been in place since 1949.

Neo-authoritarianism

The narrow path from reform to post-communism, between the twin precipices of a return to Maoism and the inevitable chaos of a political revolution, has taken on the guise of 'neo-authoritarianism', borrowed from the rapidly industrializing national security states of Asia. Although the watchwords of Maoist communism still occasionally resurface in government propaganda, the unspoken ideology of the régime is now to emulate the dictatorships of South-East Asia, especially since it found itself temporarily isolated by the West after the Tiananmen tragedy and deprived of the support of Europe's communist governments as they disappeared one by one. Today, China's communists might well cite also the conversion to nationalism by President Khravchuk of Ukraine, formerly First Secretary of the Communist Party of the Soviet Union, or by President Nazerbajev of Kazakhstan who, like several other leaders of new states in Central Asia, also came from the upper echelons of the Communist Party.

They do not do so, for several reasons. The chief source of national pride, and Deng Xiaoping's personal boast, is to have instigated the end of communism since 1978 through pragmatic economic reforms, while avoiding democratization. China's condescending attitude towards Mikhail Gorbachev and its disdain for Soviet political reform, which it saw as paying lip-service to change without turning around the system of production, combined to turn the ex-pupil into the new master: this reversal of roles is unmistakeable, since certain key elements in China's economic reforms, for example mixed enterprises based on foreign capital, special economic zones and co-operative enterprises, have also been taken up by virtually all communist economies in transition. It took the political scare of Tiananmen in 1989 to persuade certain veterans of the régime (including the President of the Republic, Yang Shangkun, who is in fact the last remaining survivor of the partisans of Moscow from the 1930s) to appeal to their former Big Brother the Soviet Union for help, apparently in the hope of building an ideological bloc – a lost cause, because at that same moment, Gorbachev and some of his advisers were beginning to instigate the downfall of Ceaucescu in Romania, the abandonment of Honecker in East Germany, tacit support for Czechoslovakia's 'velvet revolution' and, more generally, the dismantling of the Soviet empire beyond the borders of the USSR.

During the days and months of official agonizing, first in the wake of Tiananmen, then following the collapse of European communism in the autumn, there was a ban put on all reference to the changes taking place within communism. Admittedly, China did show some worrying parallels with these changes it had sometimes unwittingly inspired. It, too, had witnessed constant rivalry between conservatives and reformers in the Party since 1978 (this opposition was only revealed in the Soviet Union after Brezhnev's death); the threat of a split in the régime's armed forces in 1989 (as in Romania at the end of the same year); and also a strange inertia on the part of the Gonganju, the Chinese state security service, from the time of the student demonstrations in November–December 1986 up until Tiananmen, as was the case in Leipzig in 1989, when a refusal to carry out orders from the top to open fire on the protesters marked the collapse of the régime. Lastly, from 1986 onwards, China witnessed the formation of circles in Peking led by prominent dissident intellectuals, echoing the eighteenth-century salons of the European Enlightenment: although they ostensibly kept out of tactical decisions concerning the demonstrations during the spring of 1989, the stimulus offered by these Chinese 'think-tanks' in association with certain reformist government bodies was undeniable. A few months later, Vaclav Havel followed suit with his famous Magic Lantern

Theatre, which became allied increasingly closely with the communist reformers and their symbol, Alexander Dubcek.

East versus West?

Mao's heirs pioneered the reform of communism from within, but they
none the less took inspiration from the many previous abortive attempts
scattered throughout history, ranging from the New Economic Policy
(NEP) and Bukharinism to the reforms of the economist Libermann during
the Khrushchev era, via the year 1956 which was a dress rehearsal for the
revolution of 1989. Yet just as Chinese society shaped the course of communism in its own way, so it took a different route out. A society of
factions, it spawned a régime whose history proved far more turbulent than
that of Stalin's bureaucracy. It also pioneered a way of pinpointing the
demolition of communism in the same way that nowadays huge tower
blocks are dynamited without causing any shock waves in the vicinity.
Despite failing to complete this act of demolition in 1989, China has none
the less provided the precedent, and in some ways the inspiration, for
Eastern Europe to follow the same route.

This in itself should be enough to disprove the superficially westernizing
yet fundamentally racist argument which claims that genuine democracy is
the preserve of the West and of those countries which belong to European
civilization: a favourite *leitmotiv* of the great novelist Milan Kundera and
other slavophobic intellectuals, for whom the Slavic world no longer forms
part of Europe and must be abandoned to the oriental despotism represented by Asia. Strangely enough, the Far East, made up of the Chinese
world, is a major factor in the long-standing dispute between slavophiles
and westernizers which is currently convulsing the bulk of the former Soviet
empire. It can also be seen in the sudden enthusiasm of Russian conservatives for the Chinese model, after similar effusions in favour of the Pinochet
model.

More than ever before, Chinese culture is itself racked by a similar
dispute, between the heirs to the cultural legacy of the Han – bureaucratic,
continental, agrarian – and those in favour of maritime, westernizing openness. The westernizers are certainly not in the minority, as proved by one of
China's most popular television series, *Heshang* (Yellow River Elegy), in
1988: throughout its journey down from the desert uplands of north-western China until it flows muddily out into the Gulf of Tianjin, the great,
unpredictable river serves as a pretext for a portrayal of the conflict between
two Chinese cultures. The makers of the series were quite open in their
condemnation of the feudalism, chauvinism, inertia and conformism of
continental Chinese society, instead extolling westernization and the reform
of Chinese thinking in the tradition of the great May Fourth Movement of
1919. Having won the approval of General Secretary Zhao Ziyang and
his followers, the series was broadcast to overseas Chinese communities

worldwide, as well as to the general public in China itself. A Chinese equivalent to films such as *The Sorrow and the Pity* in France or the West German *Heimat*, it provoked bitter controversy, with some individuals coming down on unexpected sides: it was thus possible to witness the President of the Taiwanese National University, a Chinese-American Nobel prize winner and the historian Ho Ping-ti, author of a classic work on the origins of Chinese civilization, all denouncing what appeared to them to be a despicable work of caricature. The makers of the series, who were forced to emigrate in June 1989, have since toned down their argument somewhat by affirming that the key to the evolution of Chinese culture does not lie purely and simply in the rejection of its historical roots. Thus the extreme westernizers have returned to the fold. Yet conversely, most of the intellectuals who first introduced the notion of 'neo-authoritarianism', centred around Zhao Ziyang, took part in the events of 1989 and were forced to leave China. In the final analysis, the rejection of the optimistic philosophy of Marxism played a more important part in their thinking than political realism.

As a general rule, the further the overseas Chinese move away from the stifling control of the heavenly bureaucracy, the more they indulge their nostalgia for their great, timeless culture. The leading Chinese entrepreneurs of South-East Asia are the world's greatest collectors of celadon pottery, while the Chinese of Malacca, faced with the problems of assimilation into the Malay community, are creating a sacred burial ground right in the centre of the city, a veritable altar to the traditions of their Chinese-born ancestors. As for the Chinese in China, they show far less interest in their own past, their current fascination being with the outside world: initially, at the beginning of the century, it was America; then, during the first decade of the communist régime, it was the Soviet Union; now, once again, it is America.

In any case, not just the intelligentsia but Chinese society in general is linked, both to the West and to maritime, capitalist Asia, by a thousand invisible threads. The intellectual revolution is certainly the easiest to discern. China's leading dissident, the astronomer Fang Lizhi, is a very different personality from the physicist Andrei Sakharov. Whereas Sakharov started out as the father of the Russian thermonuclear bomb, a figure respected by the establishment, who only later came to question the validity of the Soviet military effort, Fang Lizhi played the part of a Chinese Galileo from the very outset. In the early 1960s, after initially being purged for 'rightism', he spoke out in favour of the early versions of the theory of 'black holes' as the origin of the universe. Marxism–Leninism in its Maoist form rejected this hypothesis. This atheistic response might have been due to the fact that the idea of the universe having one single origin could all too easily suggest the existence of a creator. Alternatively, it could have been because the notion of the universe originating in a non-being was too close to classical Taoist philosophy. Whatever the case, Fang Lizhi's views again made him the victim of purges during the Cultural Revolution. A theoretician first and foremost, sequestered away in a large but second-rate university in Hunan, he concentrated all his later arguments on the theory of law and the individual. When, in the aftermath of June 1989, the government wanted to organize a national political campaign against Fang Lizhi, who by then had taken asylum in the United States Embassy, they produced their own edited collection of his works, thus spreading their notoriety throughout China. What in Fang Lizhi's case was the fruit of scientific logic became very much a cult of the West for the young generation which had grown up after the decline of Maoism. Although many students and intellectuals have in the past looked to Japan or, to a lesser extent, Europe, it is today the United States which acts as the focus for the fascination and interest of the Chinese people. One only has to think of the way in which the Chinese public, more so than other Asians, supported the allied expedition against Iraq in 1991: quite apart from the cult of military might which remains a perpetual feature of Chinese popular culture (books on Napoleon, for example, always sell well throughout the Chinese world), the defeat of a military dictatorship belonging to the Third World, which the Chinese people are adamant they have left behind, coupled with Western supremacy, suited them to perfection.

In view of this fascination with the West and its own distaste for the consequences of Gorbachevism, the régime's only option was to seek refuge either in Chinese tradition or in the authority-figures of South-East Asia. Local cults were established in honour of Confucius and Sun Yat-sen, and Chiang Kai-shek's house was even turned into a museum. Just as the Honecker régime in East Germany spent the last few years before its collapse trying to recreate the architectural splendours of East Prussia as a contrast to Western decadence, even if it meant fabricating them out of nothing, the Chinese government went back to its traditional roots: before long, the main tourist attraction could well be the project currently underway in Xian to completely excavate the tomb of the brutal dynastic founder Qin Shihuang.

Strangely enough, in this respect China's post-communist government finds itself in the company of Lee Kuan Yew rather than the Kuomintang in Taiwan from which it remains divided by too many conflicting interests. The neo-Confucianism favoured by Singapore and the hostility to European and Western ideas which accompanies it take on a whole new significance for the Chinese leadership, since they have not prevented a windfall of foreign investment and model growth. For his own part, Lee Kuan Yew, having spent much of his life resisting the impact of Chinese communism on his own territory, may be rediscovering the pull, whether real or imaginary, which many overseas Chinese feel towards their mother country. In 1984, he dispatched his deputy, Goh Keng Swee as economic adviser to the Chinese government, and in the aftermath of June 1989 he acted as an apologist for his senior Deng Xiaoping, claiming that the protesters had shown him a 'lack of respect'. Both leaders also have a number of international interests in common: the fear of seeing Japan one day resume political leadership in Asia; the fear, ever since 1975, of Vietnamese hegemony over the Indochinese peninsula; and, increasingly, a common concern to preserve the easiest possible access for exports to the North American internal market.

Thus, for a host of domestic and international reasons, the government has decided to gamble its survival on a rejection of total westernization, just as China and Japan have done whenever confronted by the West ever since the nineteenth century. The problem is that this line of argument above all thwarts intellectuals and bids for democracy in China, yet coincides with a huge-scale Western-style economic revolution. Although in this respect also the government would rather see its economic growth in the context of the newly-industrialized countries of Asia which it so closely resembles, there is no escaping the fact that Western technology and the outlets offered by the United States and the European Community are the main forces driving China's economy.

THE END OF COMMUNISM IN INDOCHINA

While China appears to be in the throes of a dynamic, albeit uncertain transition, the countries of former French Indochina (or rather former Vietnamese Indochina as it should be called from now on) have faced a crisis which threatened their very existence. Things have changed considerably since the victory of April 1975, when the Vietnamese communists and the Khmer Rouge embarked on their race against time to seize control of the cities of Saigon and Phnom Penh respectively. In both cases, rapid victory gave rise to a form of hubris. In the case of the Vietnamese communists, this consisted of wanting to fulfil the late Ho Chi Minh's hope of a Vietnamese Indochina, accompanied by an absolute faith in their own invincibility. For the Khmer Rouge, it involved implementing an ultra-Maoist programme, cut off from the outside world, coupled with a reckless disregard for the regional balance of power. Both strategies collided head-on at the height of the South-East Asian economic boom, preventing any measure of post-war reconstruction. Not only that, but the clash between the nationalist communism of the Vietnamese and the rampant genocide of a Kampuchea (as Cambodia was now known) caught in the grip of political and ethnic purges, triggered the first international war to be fought in the communist world, between Cambodia, Vietnam and China, in the winter of 1978–9. While the victors of 1975 believed themselves to be founding communism in Indochina, they were in fact heading straight for xenophobic Balkanization. The last regional vestiges of Chinese imperialism and the genocidal streak of the Khmer Rouge played just as important a part in this crisis as Vietnamese hegemonic ambitions.

The end of the second Indochina War

The Paris Agreements of 1973 had paved the way for the 'Vietnamization' of the second Indochina War and the withdrawal of the United States land forces: an immediate ceasefire led to South Vietnam being oddly partitioned into zones of influence, with an international contingent of observers representing both sides as well as other countries, charged with overseeing the implementation of the agreements. Nixon and Kissinger's objective in doing this is still a matter of debate. Did they hope to marginalize the rural zones, which were already seen as a lost cause, and consolidate the South Vietnamese government with military and economic aid? This was the view consistently argued by advocates of urbanization and modernization as a response to communism, such as Samuel Huntington (1968) and Walt Rostow (1960). Or were they simply looking for a 'decent' breathing-space in order to withdraw United States troops and extricate the United States from any direct responsibility for later developments? Despite the many accusations levelled against the Nixon–Kissinger duo, for example by William Shawcross (1979) and Frank Snepp (1977), the bulk of North Vietnamese testimonies and sources generally shows that nothing could have made it possible to anticipate such a rapid victory for the communist forces, if not the loss of political will in the United States, among the followers of President Thieu of Vietnam and most of all in the camp of Marshal Lon Nol.

Contrary to Chinese and Soviet advice, and despite the scepticism of the many members of the Vietnamese Politburo who predicted a much longer war, General Tran Van Tra launched the strategy of the 'flowering of the rose', a major offensive by the North Vietnamese regulars against Banh Me Tuot, a town situated amongst the high plateaux of South Vietnam, which appeared to be of little importance in itself, except that it commanded the region's main roads. The sudden fall of Banh Me Tuot triggered psychological shock-waves throughout South Vietnam. The North Vietnamese troops spread out like the petals of a rose from the high plateaux to the South Vietnamese coast and its towns, routed the South Vietnamese army and took the Americans in Saigon by surprise. Even more so than Dien Bien Phu in 1954, Banh Me Tuot appeared on the surface to be a military victory for Vietnam, but deep down it was a political one. In the Saigon camp there was no longer any will to continue the war. Most of the communist militants in the South had also been eliminated, either in the 1968 Tet offensive and the crackdown which followed, or in the internal purges by the North, and it was the *bo doi* and their political police from the North who immediately took control of the country.

Cambodia: encounter with death

Meanwhile, the Khmer Rouge were not so much planning the total upheaval of their country as improvising it in the name of a principle: the 'old people', the Khmer peasants who were already grouped together in the guerilla zones, were, for example, given the task of indoctrinating the 'new people' (also known as the 'people of 17 April' after the date when the capital was seized), in other words the bulk of the inhabitants in the regions and especially in the towns, which were suddenly conquered. Most of those who had been 'servants' of previous governments, from the Prime Minister down to the lowliest public official, were immediately put to death, while a similar fate awaited the ethnic minorities. Just as Ieng Sary, the Kampuchean number two, was actually presenting Vietnam's premier, Phan van Dong, with the gift of a crocodile during an official visit (Chanda, 1986), the Khmer Rouge were carrying out the first programme of ethnic cleansing in the history of communism. In retrospect, it is curious that they did not spare the numerous Vietnamese peasant and fishing communities in the east, nor the Chinese traders, nor even the chiefs of the mountain tribes who belonged to FULRO (Oppressed Races United Liberation Front) and had seen them as an ally against Vietnam. The evidence suggests that the blood lust of the Khmer Rouge did not conform to any geopolitical logic or foreign policy strategy, even though their leaders had adopted a crazed view of a world, committed to inevitable and universal war. Numerous historical accounts and works such as those of François Ponchaud (1977), Laurence Picq (1984) and Chandler (1992) have traced the deadly rampage by Pol Pot and his followers between 1975 and 1979, as well as the methods which they used: Angkar, the anonymous organization which even enabled them to dispense with a Leninist political front; banishing the entire urban population into rural labour; the slaughter of educated Khmers, for whom a feature as innocent as a pair of glasses or an over-pale complexion could result in death; torture sessions and inquisitions resulting in the progressive elimination first of countless fellow travellers, then of actual party members and cadres. Records survive of torture sessions carried out in the main prison at Tuol Sleng, where 14,000 prisoners were registered by name, six of whom are known to have survived. These records show that at the end of 1978 the interrogations conducted by the chief executioner, 'Brother' Deuch, started to implicate Son Sen, Deuch's own superior and number three in the Khmer Rouge, who doubtless owed his survival under Pol Pot to the fact that the régime collapsed. Pol Pot himself – 'Brother Number One' – fluent in Vietnamese, Chinese and French, and so secretive that no biography has yet fully explained his psychological make-up (Chandler, 1983), appears to have embodied several attitudes and ideologies: his ritual impassivity, possibly gained in the spectacle of the royal ballet, where his sister once performed; the early nationalism espoused by the few Cambodian students; the Stalinism picked up first in France and Yugoslavia from 1948 to 1952, then in Vietnam; and the Maoism which gave the Khmer Rouge its most extreme characteristics. Anti-intellectualism, self-sufficiency, xenophobia justified as anti-imperialism and the immediate abolition of the currency – all were aspects of the radical upheaval of the post-1975 period which bore an obvious resemblance to China. Yet it is also important to stress the parallels with the absolutist slavery of the kingdom of Angkor, although there was never any explicit reference to this by the Khmer Rouge.

In the course of 1977, the Pol Pot régime, doubtless blinded by paranoia and disregarding the balance of power in the real world, embarked on a series of violent forays into Vietnamese territory, notably in the so-called 'Duck's Beak' region of Cochinchina, which the Cambodians traditionally regarded as belonging to them. This was his downfall. While international opinion was slow to realize the extent of the 'autogenocide' carried out by the Khmer Rouge (Lacouture, 1978), Hanoi took advantage of some ideal pretexts – the massacre of its citizens, violent acts of aggression and Kampuchea's almost total international isolation – to extend its influence over the Cambodian plain. Diplomatic relations were severed in December 1977 and Vietnam began to prepare for a counter-offensive. Pol Pot's decision to launch a large-scale political and military purge in eastern Cambodia made the task easier, as hundreds of Khmer Rouge cadres, including Hun Sen and Heng Samrin, the future leaders of the Phnom Penh government, fled to form a resistance movement under Vietnamese auspices. On 24 December 1978, the Vietnamese took Cambodia by storm, liberating it in under a fortnight. However, over 100,000 Khmer Rouge soldiers, cadres and hangers-on found asylum in Thailand, along with the movement's leaders. Norodom Sihanouk still remained alive after having been under house arrest for nearly three years, whether due to pressure from Chinese diplomats or because of the satisfaction which Pol Pot, the former poor relation of the Royal Palace, gained from keeping him in his clutches. Sihanouk, dispatched by Pol Pot to plead the cause of the defunct state of Democratic Kampuchea to the UN, managed to evade his entourage in order to negotiate with the American government and prepare for the future.

The death toll was horrific and at the same time unquantifiable, as no population census, however rudimentary, had been carried out in Cambodia since the 1960s. In 1962, the population had been put at 5.7 million, which, assuming an annual growth rate of 2.2 per cent, would suggest that the population in 1970 must have stood at roughly seven million, the same as the estimate for 1992. The mass bombings by the United States during the Lon Nol era (1970–5) undoubtedly helped to reduce this figure. After the collapse of Democratic Kampuchea in 1979, panic and general chaos reigned as everyone attempted either to return to their homes and families or make their way to Thai refugee camps. This resulted in widespread famine which undoubtedly claimed several hundred thousand victims in 1979–80. American Air Force aerial reconnaissance photographs taken at that time showed that the Cambodian population was less than five million. Erring below the estimates of many survivors, we may conclude that between April 1975 and December 1978 the Khmer Rouge either murdered, or caused the deaths of, at least one in seven of the Cambodian population – over one million people. The victims included nearly all the ethnic minorities, the Buddhist monks and the educated. A controversy blew up between the first historians to study the period: while many subscribed to the theory of unrelievedly murderous totalitarianism, some, such as Michael Vickery (1984), pointed to a less black-and-white picture, with the level of oppression varying considerably between one region and the next and between the successive phases which rapidly followed 1975. The dispute is significant, since it was possible for selective allocation of responsibility to result, among other things, in the exoneration of certain Khmer Rouge cadres who were subsequently readmitted into the government after 1979. So many Khmer patriots and progressives were deceived by Khmer Rouge propaganda (often paying for this lack of perspicacity with their lives when they returned to Cambodia after 1975) that it is not unreasonable to suppose that the Khmer Rouge cadres were themselves utterly overwhelmed by the paranoia which set in at the top after victory. Because the parallel between the Khmer Rouge and the Nazis so often figured in Vietnamese propaganda (on the advice of East Germany) it was often regarded as suspect, and, it must be admitted, the Khmer Rouge had access to almost none of the modern methods used by Nazi Germany. Their supremacy was largely the result of a juxtaposition of local authorities which were all-powerful, except in relation to Angkar, its agents and its ideology, the latter being undeniably modern. Ultimately, once it goes beyond circumstantial details, the attempt to relativize the Khmer Rouge genocide soon leads to a denial that it ever took place, with the result that the countless testimonies of survivors are effectively buried, like the bones of the dead victims. In the United States, the linguist Noam Chomsky, a fierce critic of America's role in Indochina, destroyed his reputation by underestimating the tragedy. In France, it is worth noting that Serge Thion, the chief spokesman for this cause, was later involved in a similar attempt to deny the Jewish Holocaust.

A bridge too far: the plan for a Vietnamese Indochina

The Vietnamese offensive was a liberation – as it was seen by most Cambodians present at the time – before becoming an occupation in the eyes of the same people. However, it also marked a further victory for Vietnamese arms. This view was reinforced by the partial failure of a Chinese attack on Vietnam. Deng Xiaoping, angered by the overthrow of China's Kampuchean allies, waged a three-week war from February to March 1979, with troops being hurriedly mobilized from as far afield as Fujian province facing Taiwan. They raided Langson and the Honggai coalmine (which was ransacked by the Chinese army) before being withdrawn. Yet China's attempt to teach the Vietnamese a 'lesson', as Deng Xiaoping put it during a visit to the United States, had little effect. Even though the Chinese army did not take on the Vietnamese élite units concentrated in the Red Basin, it suffered nearly 30,000 casualties at the hands of Vietnam's second-grade forces. This shook the Chinese military and temporarily weakened Deng Xiaoping, while further bolstering the Vietnamese government's sense of invulnerability. However, the Soviet Union, Vietnam's ally, had ostensibly stayed on the sidelines at the time of the Chinese offensive, thus defining the limits of its support from the outset, although it was subsequently forced to give Vietnam enormous military and financial aid.

The Vietnamese government was thus inevitably closing the trap on itself. After defeating the French, the Americans and even the Chinese, it succumbed to the temptation of a pan-Indochinese plan. Several arguments were put forward in favour of this: the threat of the Khmer Rouge, with an international coalition backing the legitimacy of Democratic Kampuchea, which was represented at the UN by Norodom Sihanouk but largely sustained by the renewed guerilla warfare of Pol Pot; the need for a buffer zone to ensure the security of Vietnam's long, narrow territory (Vietnamese occupation being the sole guarantee of unarmed neutrality for Cambodia); also, less ostensibly, the need of a *Lebensraum* for Vietnam's overabundant population. In the years following 1979, some of the rural Vietnamese population was resettled in eastern Cambodia, and the hevea plantations near the Vietnamese border began to be exploited, as did the fish-rich waters of the Tonle Sap, Cambodia's great lakeland region. The three governments of Laos, Cambodia and Vietnam held regular 'Indochina conferences'. Vietnamese diplomats worked hard at persuasion. However, if not the charismatic Foreign Minister Nguyen co Thach, appointed to work his charm on the foreigners, then certainly former general Vo Dong Giang who seconded him, made it absolutely clear that if Vietnam could not resolve the Cambodian crisis peacefully, it would do so by force. Vietnam's admission to the Warsaw Pact and the large-scale re-equipment of an already hypertrophied army gave a certain amount of credence to these warmongering comments. Since 1975 Vietnam has set record rates of annual population growth of between 2.4 and 3 per cent per annum, and its expansion might well seem written into the region's destiny. Furthermore, the generals in power in Indonesia, obsessed with the threat from China, often expressed the view privately that Vietnam was carrying out a kind of Indochinese unification similar to their own formation of the Indonesian archipelago after 1945. Although this remained a minority view within ASEAN, it gave Vietnam room for manoeuvring.

On paper, the Vietnamese army became no less than the third largest in the world at that point. It particularly benefited from the vast stockpiles of American weapons recovered in 1975, and was a power of its own throughout Indochina. However, the troops assigned to Cambodia were suffering from malaria, malnourished and had badly-maintained equipment. The offensives launched against the Khmer resistance during the dry season and the occasional incursion into Thai territory were followed by months of static withdrawal. It is one of history's ironies that in order to prevent guerillas infiltrating the western frontier, the pro-Vietnamese government in Phnom Penh built a string of strategic villages and displaced the rural population, a throwback to the 'new villages' created by the British counter-guerilla campaign in Malaya and the 'strategic hamlets' of the United States in South Vietnam. At international level, an unlikely coalition was formed, although its members denied its existence. China donated aid to the Khmer Rouge, the ASEAN countries backed the two other resistance factions (the followers of Sihanouk and the conservative nationalists), while the latter received arms from the United States (and later France and Britain too) through various channels. As for Thailand, it formed the hub of all these alliances, being forced to admit several hundred thousand refugees onto its territory who, though protected by the UN, were often under the control of one or other faction. As in all previous wars in Indochina, Vietnam, the new colonial power, could not win, as the enemy possessed a secure rearguard and an inexhaustible fund of support.

Furthermore, while there could be no comparison between the Vietnamese dictatorship and the infamous deeds of Pol Pot, Vietnam also lost most of the support it had previously had among Western public opinion. The repression which followed 1975 and the opening up of new cleared zones on the high plateaux were certainly nowhere near the 'bloodbath' forecast by Cold War hawks. Nevertheless, several hundred thousand people were imprisoned and the forced collectivization carried out in the south prompted the flight of hundreds of thousands of others: these were the 'boat people', whose emigration was from the outset the result of a complex mixture of political and economic motives. The lack of any legal programme of direct emigration to the United States, the Eldorado of a new life in the West and also the connivance of local officials, who often robbed the would-be emigrants of their money before they had even started, produced an endless saga. Unknown numbers of boat people were lost at sea, the victims of storms, pirates in the Gulf of Siam and the indifference of many international vessels. Even before the military response by China, the 1978 offensive against Cambodia coincided with a xenophobic attack on the 'Hoas', the Chinese of Vietnam. The nationalization of the food trade, managed in the South by the Chinese traders of Cholon, disrupted supplies even further. In the North, the Hoas of Hanoi were forced to flee to China, while their brethren in the South in turn became a new generation of boat people.

The three countries of Indochina thus became more and more bogged down in underdevelopment, at the same time as their South-East Asian neighbours were really taking off economically. With an income of less than US$200 per capita, a crumbling urban and transport infrastructure, a foreign debt which had prompted the West to freeze all financial aid, and galloping inflation, Vietnam was at its nadir. It had in fact long been dependent on the goodwill of Moscow for its survival, and from the Brezhnev era until Gorbachev came to power in March 1985 this aid was considerable. The Soviet Union had secured stopover rights (in effect, a permanent base) at Da Nang, giving it renewed access to the Pacific more than seventy years after its naval defeat at Tsushima. However, the fact that this aid was stopped, owing to reform and the subsequent disintegration of the Soviet Union, ultimately had some fairly positive effects for Vietnam, forcing its leaders to adopt pragmatic measures in order to save the economy. In 1991–2 inflation slowed and exports (mainly in agriculture) increased. Once financial sanctions were lifted (and Japan and France declared a willingness to do this early on) the country could look forward to a Chinese-style economic boom, although it still lacked the necessary infrastructure. In Laos, which falls within Thailand's commercial orbit, the communist leadership have carried out a similar pragmatic programme of modernization. The situation is far more serious in Cambodia, which has an income of less than US$100 per capita. The never-ending civil war has bled the population dry, and statistical records are piling up: there are 200,000 orphans, 35 per cent of the female population over 18 are the heads of families and infant mortality stands at 200 for every 1,000 births, while one Cambodian in every 240 has already had a limb amputated as a result of the anti-personnel mines which maim approximately 9,000 people a year. The Soviet Union had extended its own sphere of influence to include Cambodia and Laos, with the result that the peasants in Luang Prabang's old kingdom could receive satellite broadcasts from Moscow's first channel; as for the Cambodians, they can watch the television news on the French channel Antenne 2. Following the collapse of the Soviet Union and the signing of the Paris Agreements, a host of businessmen and speculators have descended on the country, mainly from South-East Asia. While Cambodia's forests are rapidly being felled, Phnom Penh's public buildings and sparse public services are largely being 'privatized'. The influx of 20,000 highly-paid UN personnel has pushed inflation and conspicuous consumption to the limit in what is a devastated country.

The third conference on Indochina

The Cambodian conflict lasted eleven years, from 1979 to 1991. Reasons for this included Hanoi's intransigence, the fears of ASEAN member states concerning Vietnamese expansionism, and the new overtures being made by Deng Xiaoping's China to some of its old anti-communist rivals. The government of Singapore in particular was extremely vocal in its opposition to the Phnom Penh régime, as were most of Thailand's generals. Public opinion in the West was coloured by testimonies of the Khmer Rouge genocide, epitomized by the film *The Killing Fields* in 1985. Yet Norodom Sihanouk, the little king with the silver tongue and the stature of a David battling against a Vietnamese Goliath, shrewdly bandied references to the Free French as well as to his protectors Kim Il Sung, Ceaucescu and Deng Xiaoping and succeeded in upholding the diplomatic credentials of the state which had been overthrown in 1979. Diplomatic wrangles over the Cambodian question became an international preoccupation, though ASEAN made them a speciality. Until 1986, Vietnam skilfully took advantage of this, pretending to listen to anyone if it would help to avoid any opening up to the outside world which might force it to compromise. Deep down, the Vietnamese were convinced that time was on their side, and countries like Sweden and France which wanted to practise 'open door' diplomacy on them were merely wasting their time.

However, the rise to power of Mikhail Gorbachev altered the whole nature of the problem. In January 1986, he forecast a reduction in Soviet commitments, both financial and military, in the Third World. China then called on the Soviet Union to put pressure on Vietnam and thus remove what was seen as the 'third obstacle' to Sino-Soviet relations. However, although the Soviet Union announced the withdrawal of Soviet troops from Afghanistan and a reduction in the forces concentrated on the Chinese border, Vietnam's occupation of Cambodia continued. The threads of many separate negotiations began to come together in so-called 'informal discussions' conducted under Indonesian auspices and in preparations by France for a new international conference, which led to the first meeting between Sihanouk and Hun Sen, the Prime Minister of Phnom Penh, at Fère-en-Tardenois in December 1987. One major obstacle was removed when Vietnam withdrew all its troops from Cambodia in July 1989. A series of meetings in 1990 between the foreign ministers of the five permanent members of the Security Council produced a preliminary outline for a diplomatic solution to the conflict, while Australia put forward a plan for UN intervention which bore a strong resemblance to the final agreement. It then remained for the four fundamentally irreconcilable Cambodian factions to agree to comply with the wishes of the international community. This was accomplished at the Paris conference, which finally ended in agreement in October 1991. At this point, rather than trusting to diplomatic optimism, those involved might have been better advised to remind themselves that the ordinary Cambodian people, whom foreign domination and successive crises had robbed of all political identity, had a long history of superficial compliance with the wishes of the Great Powers, whoever they might be.

Furthermore, the Paris settlement of 1991 was inevitably complex, given the large number of parties to be reconciled. Legitimate authority in Cambodia was placed in the hands of the UN, although the cadres of the Phnom Penh administration still remained in post. The four factions came together to form a Supreme National Council, headed by Norodom Sihanouk, but it had no power and was effectively a permanent negotiating body. UN troops and a number of observers were charged with safeguarding the basic aims of the peace, namely disarmament and the partial demobilization of each faction on the ground, followed by elections which were naturally to be free and democratic. Give or take a few modifications, this was, in fact, the same formula already adopted by the 1973 Paris

Agreements on Vietnam. The Paris settlement of 1991 made no reference to the genocide committed between 1975 and 1979, nor did it make provision for any punishment. The Khmer Rouge were thus granted an amnesty, with the result that the Khmers were effectively prevented from exorcizing their past. In order to facilitate the process of reconciliation, provision was made for vast amounts of international aid for reconstruction, with over US$2 billion injected within a very short space of time. As the process went along, the impracticality of these schemes soon became obvious.

For Vietnam more so than for Cambodia, the Paris settlement of 1991 closed the final chapter in the third Indochina War. Soviet aid was brought to a virtual standstill by the crumbling of the Soviet empire in 1989–91, and, whereas the Vietnamese government had previously been reluctant to introduce Chinese-style economic reforms except on paper, it was now forced to embark on a process of economic openness and liberalization simply in order to survive. There was a tentative normalization in Sino-Vietnamese relations, but this failed to eradicate either the mutual suspicion or the maritime territorial disputes between the two, although the Chinese Prime Minister Li Peng did visit Hanoi in 1992. Vietnam's huge population increase (rising to over 70 million, compared with 45 million in 1975), the gradual wearing down of those in power and the partial demobilization of its armed forces have in fact acted as a spur to economic and social development. As the result of agricultural liberalization, Vietnam has once again become a rice exporter, while international détente has prompted the arrival of the first foreign capital: one source has been the Viet Khieu, who emigrated in 1975 and in many cases enriched themselves in the United States and Australia, while other sources include Taiwan, which has relocated a number of its manufacturing industries to Saigon–Ho Chi Minh City, and also to some extent France and Japan. The persistent crises in Vietnam's domestic finances have made the *dong* a worthless currency, prompting officials and cadres to seek additional sources of income. Although the government continues to enforce a dictatorship far more thoroughgoing than that of China, its ideological pretensions have collapsed. In fact, it is not so much the improvement in Vietnam's relations with China which is protecting it, but its *rapprochement* with the six member states of ASEAN: having attained observer status in 1994, Vietnam became a full member in 1995. Similarly, the United States is re-establishing diplomatic relations with its old enemy, paving the way for commercial links. China was fully conscious of what it was doing in 1995, when it likewise redirected its military pressure in the South China Sea towards the Philippines: by gaining a foothold on Mischief Reef, in the maritime zone claimed by the Philippines, China has brought into play an ASEAN member state allied to the United States, and no longer simply the relatively isolated Vietnam.

Cambodia: war in peace

Was the implementation of the peace plan issued in December 1991 by the International Conference in Paris a success or a failure for the UN? The international dimension of the plan was a major success: by stopping China's political and military backing for the Khmer Rouge, and likewise by curbing Vietnam's support for the Phnom Penh régime, the Paris Agreements put an end to the international rivalry which fanned the flames of the Cambodian civil war. Yet there still remained the task of putting into effect the internal dimension of the agreements, that is the political co-existence of four factions which was beleaguered on all sides: the communists installed, with the help of Vietnam, the Khmer Rouge, the supporters of Norodom Sihanouk and the republican resistance. To this end, the international community launched one of the biggest operations ever overseen by the UN, involving the dispatch of thousands of UN troops together with a military commander (first French, then British) and a political envoy, Yasushi Akashi of Japan. The plan was accompanied by a special effort to support Cambodia's economic recovery: more than US$800 million were pledged for this purpose in 1992, but changing circumstances on the ground meant that this sum of money was never actually committed. Conversely, a high proportion of Cambodian refugees, especially in Thailand, were repatriated. The UN, particularly the French contingent, carried out difficult mine-clearing operations: the country is littered with anti-personnel mines which stand to claim victims from the civilian population for a long time to come.

Up to the time of the national elections in June 1993, nothing could convince certain Cambodian factions to comply with the Paris Agreements. The Khmer Rouge in particular evaded them at every opportunity, the first of which was provided by the Phnom Penh administration when it organized the spectacular, albeit interrupted, lynching of Khieu Samphan and Son Sen, the Khmer representatives in the capital. In 1992, the Khmer Rouge refused to implement programmes of disarmament and demobilization, refused UN personnel access to any of the zones under their control, apart from one showcase region on the Thai border, and finally announced their refusal to take part in the national elections. Their pretext for this was that Vietnamese civilians were being planted, supposedly in order to be falsely entered on the electoral roll. Documents which were seized, and a speech attributed to Pol Pot, revealed that they were once more planning to seize power until the political and social disintegration of urban Cambodia had been achieved. The Phnom Penh administration, similarly divided and riddled with corruption, adopted an ambiguous stance. While on the one hand it was willing to tolerate the emergence of new parties and the presence of a small number of human rights observers, it also appeared to be resorting to covert attacks on troublesome opponents, even moderates within its own camp. Norodom Sihanouk, ceremoniously installed in

Phnom Penh, possessed few political or human resources of his own: one might also point out that his own family was divided, as his son Ranarridh continued to lead the Funcinpec resistance and had adopted ideas sometimes closely linked to the diplomatic wing of the Khmer Rouge, while Prince Chakrapong became a member of the Hun Sen government. What might have seemed further proof of the old King's legendary tactical skill was also a mark of political powerlessness. International intervention has been large-scale yet ineffective: of the forty or so nationalities involved, many have been limited to a very formal presence, and the UN contingent in any case had no mandate to engage in military action. The clearing of landmines, let alone reconstruction, has proved an even more enormous task given that the Cambodian factions have by no means abandoned their civil war: in fact they continued to fight, sometimes even in the vicinity of the UN forces. The role played by Thailand represented a further unknown quantity: the civilian government failed to persuade the army to end its support of the Khmer Rouge and its business community was systematically milking Cambodia dry. After all, western Cambodia originally belonged to Siam before becoming a French colony, and a *de facto* partition of Cambodia would mean recreating a Thai protectorate in the region. The countries which donated the bulk of the financial resources and, in some cases, the personnel for UN operations in Cambodia, notably Japan, the United States, France, Indonesia and Germany, did so for a period which ended in principle in September 1993, and were unwilling to commit themselves to any further military involvement. The Indochinese quagmire continued to instil fear, and this largely gave the Khmer Rouge their trump card. Sitting on their income (from teak, ruby mines and foreign bank accounts) and controlling their troops better than the other factions, they were counting on the general mood of weariness in order to persevere, if not prevail, on this, South-East Asia's final frontier.

And yet the miracle came true in May–June 1993. The Khmer Rouge brought intimidatory pressure to bear on the elections: they assassinated a Japanese member of the UN troops, prompting the Japanese self-defence forces to withdraw to their camps. They kidnapped a number of Western tourists and threatened the country with a wave of violence, calling for abstention from the elections. However, the rural population of Cambodia turned out at the polls en masse, temporarily protected by the UN presence. They proceeded to grant a new mandate to the régime, leading to a political coalition between the party inherited from Hun Sen's communist administration and Norodom Sihanouk's royalists. This coalition established a constitutional monarchy, with a two-headed government consisting of former communist cadre Hun Sen alongside Prince Ranarridh, son of Norodom Sihanouk and formerly a professor of law at Aix-en-Provence. The UN was thus able to conclude the military phase of its intervention and withdraw, as all the countries involved wanted to do, from taking part in an operation against the Khmer Rouge that was threatening to become bogged down.

In the process, the UN and the West actually learned an Asian secret of conflict resolution, that of solution over time. Though weakened politically, the Khmer Rouge were by no means weakened in the field. The new government proved fairly incompetent as far as Cambodia's development was concerned: investment often gave the impression of being a frequently corrupt auction. Furthermore, the régime split with its Ministers of Foreign Affairs and Finance, Prince Sirivuth and Sam Rainsy, both well known for their personal integrity.

Yet the worst predictions have failed to materialize. The Khmer Rouge are certainly not short of money, sitting as they do on a border region rich in wood and precious stones. However, Cambodia's neighbours –Thais, Singaporeans and Malays especially – have an interest in investing in central Cambodia, which is also a main line of commercial penetration through to Vietnam. The problem of the Khmer Rouge is becoming a permanent scourge, but the insecurity which reigns over one part of the country is no different from other situations in South-East Asia, the Golden Triangle for one. In what is a sign of the times, Khmer Rouge troops are increasingly affected by the desertion of their soldiers, a problem which was always more serious for their rivals. This incomplete dénouement to the Cambodian conflict looks set to drag on, vindicating those who denounce the hypocrisy of the UN's involvement as well as those who stress its positive results in practice. In the summer of 1996, while Pol Pot's death was rumoured, then denied, several Khmer Rouge commanders inside Cambodia defected – lending credence to the solution of attrition through time.

The history of communism is also coming to an end in Asia, even though the upheavals of 1989 only produced cracks in the façades of governments whose legitimacy and political bases remain independent of Moscow. The respective party organizations are nevertheless surviving surprisingly well not only the collapse of their ideology, but also the political currents undermining the economic and social structure of past decades. In some cases the emperor is without clothes, abetted by the apparent complicity of some reformers. In 1992, an American journalist revealed that Bo Yibo, China's answer to Suslov, was selling works of calligraphy for hanging above the doorways of newly-established shops and private enterprises at US$100 dollars apiece, while another report in 1993 announced that Yang Shangkun, the eighty-year-old president of the People's Republic of China, and Jiang Zemin, number one in the Chinese Communist Party, were both buying jacuzzi bathtubs at US$7,000 each, two object lessons in the fact that the communist leadership has reached the absolute limits of its original ideology. What remains is not communism, but rather the authoritarianism and patronage that have always been endemic in that bureaucratic society. In another sense, the coverage of the 'bathtub affair' by one foreign newspaper in February 1993 was also (no pun intended) a leak such as only

Deng Xiaoping was capable of engineering, targeted against his colleagues on the eve of political change. Since 1978, he has cajoled and coerced them by turns in the pursuit of China's transformation. Instead of the familiar image of an ageing Deng Xiaoping hunched on the back of his own bureaucracy, a better metaphor would be the ferryman in the Peking Opera, steering his boat over the perilous waves. To the very last, Deng Xiaoping will have guided his country towards the future.

WHITHER POST-COMMUNISM?

Although the post-communist era has already begun, it has been slow to find political expression. In China, parliamentary democracy seemed still-born in June 1989, and the major issue in Chinese development – namely to raise the standard of living of the rural masses to the level enjoyed by the most highly-developed regions – has not yet really been tackled, either by the reformers or by their opponents. Partly due to government repression, but also a tradition dating back to the end of the Qing, this political vacuum constitutes the major uncertainty for the future of China, while its economy represents one of the fundamental building blocks of the twenty-first century.

The situation in Vietnam is increasingly becoming comparable with that of China, although the relatively recent memory of an earlier form of society in the South is still apparent, as is the fragile nature of Vietnamese national unity, with the continuing existence of the 'three Kys', the divisions of Annam, Cochinchina and Tonkin. Other communist régimes are faring even less well. North Korea, firmly locked under the despotic yoke of Kim Il Sung until his death in July 1994, and his family, continues to sink ever deeper into isolation and poverty, and regardless of any diplomatic expedients used by a government with its back to the wall, it is hard to imagine that the sudden opening up of the country to its South Korean neighbour and the modern world in general would not cause the explosion of that suffering society. North Korea's arms build-up and nuclear development certainly seem to be one enormous bluff bequeathed by the elderly Kim, an expert at this kind of sleight-of-hand for over half a century. Its unravelling could unleash more chaos than has been seen anywhere else in the former communist world. As for Cambodia, now that the intellectuals and fledgling democratic parties have resumed their marginal role, it remains torn between two bids to re-establish communism. While the first, in Phnom Penh, no longer really exists apart from its security apparatus, the other has, thanks to the war, managed to preserve, in the countryside to the west and on its Thai bases, the conditions necessary for Maoist guerilla warfare to continue: xenophobia, an impoverished rural population and urban and political corruption. Pol Pot and Khieu Samphan are as much of an anachronism in Asia as the Burmese drug baron Khun Sa, yet they have managed to survive amid the quasi-indifference of the surrounding region, situated on the final frontier of industrial Asia, on a peninsula where national issues continue to burn almost as fiercely as they do in the Balkans. At the outset, Maoism clearly recognized that rural bandits, many of whom were outcasts bred by a ruthless society, could be recruited and transformed into brave guerilla fighters – indeed some of the best Red Army generals came from this background. What Mao failed to foresee was that political guerilla activity might revert to full-scale banditry, as has happened in Indochina.

The interpretation of the declining communist régimes and the background to the development of post-communism is only just beginning. Two perspectives predominate, both of which, paradoxically, take their inspiration from the immediate phenomenon of the old European revolutions. The first is derived from Albert Soboul's view of the preliminary introduction of political democracy through class rebellion: in the past, it was the bourgeoisie and the people coming together against the monarchist aristocracy; today, it is the same classes amassed against the communist *nomenklatura.* These forces had sometimes been rallied by enlightened aristocrats (for example the French Constituent Assembly) and sometimes by communist reformers of the same ilk, such as a Dubcek, or some of the movers behind the 'salons' in Peking in 1988–9. This schema, which was visible in Vaclav Havel's velvet revolution in Prague (albeit abetted by Mikhail Gorbachev), might easily have transpired in Peking in 1989. Yet Deng Xiaoping is no Gorbachev, and although Zhao Ziyang certainly shares the latter's cautious style, he was General Secretary of the Party in name only.

The second, Burkean view is that put forward by conservatives, who are worried by any political transformation, and includes the countless ludicrous 'analyses' of the years 1985–9, which attributed to Gorbachev an evil plan to restore an archetypal Leninist dictatorship. There has also been a profusion of dark warnings about coups – conservative, restorationist, military or ultra-nationalist – which seem to be conjured up by any hint of progress east of the Vistula. In an even more surprising move, ex-Maoists in the West who reverted to the defence of liberal democracy clearly felt a need to depict Deng Xiaoping as a bloodthirsty despot, since the uproar created by the all-too-real flaws in the present régime would also allow them to dispel the memory of their own enthusiastic support for the Maoist era, including its mass crimes.

In the post-1989 world, many former Communist leaders have been surprisingly able to adapt and even profit from new political conditions. They now run nationalist states, succeed in elections where social welfare is a key issue, or profit from their former connections in the brave new world of business.

As for Deng Xiaoping, he is the archetypal political survivor. As far as China is concerned, and perhaps in future Vietnam too, instead of relying on an upside-down version of the French Revolution, it may be preferable to use another interpretation, that of the historian of the French Revolution, François Furet. He has reasoned, rather conclusively, that the French

Revolution was less a matter of class struggle than a process of competition between several élites – and first of all between the landed aristocracy and a new educated merchant class. For this, one need only cite the characteristically premeditated plan to mould the politico-hereditary Yenan aristocracy, which has held sway since the revolution (or, in Vietnam's case, the Tonkin aristocracy which has ruled since the Vietnamese war of independence), into the new and (socially and politically) greater task of rebuilding – or in Vietnam, building – entrepreneurial capitalism. It is easy to spot the Girondins, played by the leaders of southern China, and the Thermidorians, played by the heirs of the Maoist régime, sitting on their unearned bureaucrats' income. Not surprisingly, given the major role played by the military in Chinese society since 1850, there are several possible candidates for the role of Bonaparte. Lastly, as has often been observed, there are the famous words of Guizot himself, 'Get rich', which can almost be read on Deng Xiaoping's lips. In this schema, the notion of full democracy is as illusory as the social equality which constituted the great utopian dream of revolutionary movements. What we are about to see in China is the fusion of several bourgeoisies: the old bourgeoisie of the intellectuals and the Shanghai weavers with, in the phrase of Milovan Djilas (who first identifies the trend in his native Yugoslavia of the Tito era), the 'new class', made up of the post-1949 Communist Party and the *nouveaux riches* created by the frantic race for growth since 1975.

As in France in 1815, it is hard to discern the role of the people in this union. However, the obvious difference is that China is much younger and more exposed to the changing winds of the world economy and modern technology than was the exhausted France of the Restoration. In the current era, with communications allowing all worlds to interpenetrate, it will no longer be possible for the virus of democracy to be contained or held back for half a century as it was in France until 1871 and in South-East Asia post-1945. As yet, it is uncertain what direction this speeding-up of history will take, but it will definitely happen.

SELECTED READING

Aubert, C. *et al.* (1986) *La société chinoise après Mao: entre autorité et modernité*, Paris: Fayard.

Banister, J. (1987) *China's changing population*, Stanford: Stanford University Press.

Becker, É. (1986) *Les larmes du Cambodge: l'histoire d'un génocide*, Paris: Presses de la Cité.

Beer, P. de (1989) *La Chine: le réveil du dragon*, Paris: Centurion

Beja, J. *et al.* (1991) *Le tremblement de terre de Pékin*, Paris: Gallimard.

Brosseau, M., Pepper, S. and Sho-Ku, T. (eds) (1996) *China Review 1996*, Hong Kong: The Chinese University of Hong Kong Press.

Brown, F. Z. (1989) *Second chance: the United States and Indochina in the 1990s*, New York: Council on Foreign Relations.

Burke, E. (1912) *Réflexion sur la révolution française*, Paris: Nouvelle librarie nationale.

Cabestan, J. (1992) *L'administration chinoise après Mao*, Paris: Éditions du CNRS.

Carrère d'Encausse, H. (1992) *Victorieuse Russie*, Paris: Fayard.

Chanda, N. (1986) *Brother enemy: the war after the war*, San Diego: Harcourt Brace.

Chandler, D. P. (1992) *Brother Number One: a political biography of Pol Pot*, Boulder: Westview Press.

Chen, L. and Thimonier, C. (1990) *L'impossible printemps: une anthologie du Printemps de Pékin*, Paris: Rivages.

Djilas, M. (1956) *The new class*, New York: Praeger.

Elliott, D. W. P. (1981) *The third Indochina conflict*, Boulder: Westview Press.

Furet, F. (1978) *Penser la révolution française*, Paris: Gallimard.

Gentelle, P. (ed.) (1989) *L'état de la Chine*, Paris: La Découverte.

Giafferri-Huang, X. (1991) *Le roman chinois depuis 1949*, Paris: Presses Universitaires de France.

Goldman, M. (ed.) (1987) *China's intellectuals and the state*, Cambridge, MA: Harvard University Press.

Goldman, M. (1994) *Sowing the seeds of democracy in China: political reform in the Deng Xiaoping era*, Cambridge: Harvard University Press.

Goodman, D.S.G. (1994) *Deng Xiaoping and the Chinese Revolution – a political biography*, London: Routledge.

Halpern, N. (1985) *Economic specialists and the making of Chinese economic policy, 1955–1983*, Ann Arbor: University Microfilms.

Hamrin, C. L. and Cheek, T. (eds) (1986) *China's establishment intellectuals*, Armonk: M. E. Sharpe.

Harding, H. (1992) *A fragile relationship: the United States and China since 1972*, Washington: Brookings Institution.

Hicks, G. (ed.) (1990) *The broken mirror: China after Tiananmen*, London: Longman.

Jackson: K. (ed.) (1989) *Cambodia 1975–1978: rendezvous with death*, Princeton: Princeton University Press.

Jacob, A. (1982) *Un balcon à Pékin: le nouveau pouvoir en Chine*, Paris: Grasset.

Joffe, E. (1987) *The Chinese army after Mao*, London: Weidenfeld & Nicolson.

Joint Economic Committee (1991) *China's economic dilemmas in the 1990s: the problems of reforms, modernization and interdependence*, 2 vols, Washington: USGPO.

Lacouture, J. and Lacouture, S. (1976) *Vietnam: voyage à travers une victoire*, Paris: Le Seuil.

Lardy, N. R. and Lieberthal, K. (eds) (1983) *Chen Yun's strategy for China's development: a non-Maoist alternative*, Armonk: M.E. Sharpe.

Li, Z. (1994) *The private life of Chairman Mao: the inside story of the man who made modern China*, London: Chatto & Windus.

Lieberthal, K. and Oksenberg, M. (1988) *Policy making in China: leaders, structures and processes*, Princeton: Princeton University Press.

Link, P. (1984) *Roses and thorns: the second blooming of the Hundred Flowers in Chinese fiction, 1979–1980*, Berkeley: University of California Press.

Martin, M. (1989) *Le mal cambodgien: histoire d'une société traditionelle face à ses leaders politiques, 1946–87*, Paris: Hachette.

Okonogi, M. (1988) *North Korea at the crossroads*, Tokyo: Japanese Institute of International Affairs.

Peschoux, C. (1991) *Enquête sur les nouveaux Khmers rouges (1979–1981)*, Paris: Handicap International.

Pike, D. (1986) *PAVN: People's Army of Vietnam*, London: Brassey's.

Pin Yathay (1979) *L'utopie meurtrière, un réscapé du génocide cambodgien témoigne*, Paris: Robert Laffont.

Ponchaud, F. (1977) *Le Cambodge année zéro*, Paris: Julliard.

Regaud, N. (1992) *Le Cambodge dans la tourmente: le troisième conflit indochinois, 1978–1991*, Paris: L'Harmattan.

Rocca, J. (1991) *L'empire et son milieu: la criminalité en Chine populaire*, Paris: Plon.

Rozman, G. (1985) *A mirror for socialism: Soviet criticisms of China*, London: I. B. Tauris.

—— (1987) *The Chinese debate about socialism*, Princeton: Princeton University Press.

Ruan Ming (1992) *Deng Xiaoping: chronique d'un empire, 1978–1990*, Paris: Éditions Philippe Picquier.

Scalapino, R. A. and Kim, J. (eds) (1983) *North Korea today: strategic and domestic issues*, Berkeley: University of California Press.

Shawcross, W. (1979) *Sideshow: Nixon, Kissinger and the destruction of Cambodia*, New York: Simon & Schuster.

Sidane, V. *et al.* (1980) *Le printemps de Pékin*, Paris: Gallimard.

Snepp, F. (1977) *Decent interval*, New York: Random House.

Soboul, A. (1981) *Comprendre la révolution: problèmes politiques de la révolution française, 1789–1797*, Paris: F. Maspéro.

Vickery, M. (1984) *Cambodia, 1975–1982*, Boston: South End Press.

Vo, N. T. (1990) *Vietnam's economic policy since 1975*, Singapore: Institute of Southeast Asian Studies.

Yang, R.H. and Segal, G. (eds) (1996) *Chinese economic reform – the impact on security*, London: Routledge.

Yang, Z. (1988) *Hu Yaobang: a Chinese biography*, Armonk: M. E. Sharpe.

Epilogue: towards Asian integration

To err is human. Following the Second World War, American advisers in Korea saw that country's future principally as that of a rice producer, while French trade advisers posted to Tokyo decided to aid Japan's ailing motor industry by handing over the blueprints for the Renault 4CV. Joseph Laniel, the President of France's Council of Ministers under the Fourth Republic, refused to acknowledge the strategic implications of China's support for the warring Vietnamese, thus ruling out any possibility of a French victory in Indochina. In the 1960s, General Curtis LeMay, the leader of the United States Strategic Air Command, who had experienced aerial bombardment during the Second World War, once said that America would solve the Vietnamese question by transforming the northern half of the country into a 'parking lot'. At the same time, population growth in rural Asia, coupled with a levelling-off in farming yields, prompted frequent predictions from economists of development entering a 'vicious circle' or a dead end. Even today, there are still European firms willing to head out to Taiwan or Korea, in the hope of setting up business locally on the basis of low wage levels, whereas local industrialists are relocating their own factories to South-East Asia and China.

THE HISTORICAL LEGACY

These reminders emphasize the fact that the modern history of East Asia has taken the West by surprise. They also show that this is not only true of the mistakes made by Western admirers of Maoism, peasant revolution and autarkic development in a wider sense, but also of the frequent tendency among Western politicians and economists to underestimate the region. The speed of the changes which have occurred in Asia in the twentieth century, unparalleled elsewhere in the world, has created layer upon layer of mutually contradictory historical strata: the feudal despotism of Kim Il Sung and the benevolent yet archaic system of colonial rule in Hong Kong coexist alongside the successes of the electronics industry and the information-rich societies, which indeed include Hong Kong. The pace of change has meant that attention has become focused on the immediate present, on current economic conditions or the day's turnover. The headlines may read 'Japan – champion of the world' or, alternatively, 'Japan at the end of the line': it all hinges on the Nikkei Index. China can be caught in the grip of a group of retrograde geriatrics, as in 1989 after Tiananmen, or it can be China the herald of market capitalism, depending on the latest political cycle in Peking. South-East Asia – in transition towards democracy, or at the mercy of authoritarian castes? Here, too, the winds of history blow hot and cold. Admittedly, it is becoming increasingly absurd to claim that Asians have a different conception of time: on the contrary, the frenetic speed of growth is drastically compressing the stages experienced within a single generation. The benefits, as economists well know, of having come late to industrial revolution are also still very much in evidence: there are many more mobile telephones, photocopiers and satellite dishes in Asia than in our 'old' world, since there are no vested interests there to block them. This argument is also true of the generations of Asians who have recently joined the industrial world: creating their own markets to a large extent, many have seen their prospects transformed within the space of a single career span, without any corporatist power-struggles with their elders. This rapid rise in living standards and social status is a major factor in Asia's political and social stability.

Does this therefore mean that Asia, swept by the winds of technology and capitalism, might become a *tabula rasa,* devoid of any memory or legacy of the past? When the Paris Agreements on Cambodia were signed in 1991, some observers predicted that the Khmer Rouge soldiers would become tradesmen, lorry drivers and so forth, but so far they have failed to change their occupation, still murdering the unfortunate hostages who occasionally fall into their hands. Even newly-restored Cambodia offers an all-too-vivid reminder of the extreme disintegration and corruption which enabled the Khmer Rouge to seize power in the past. A similar disintegration could also occur in Chinese society as a result of the recent economic boom, the collapse of official ideology and demographic intermixing, a prospect feared by the Chinese leadership. These are the famous 'shifting sands' which Sun Yat-sen feared for his country and against which he pitted a legitimacy which, though populist, was undeniably authoritarian in nature.

In order to interpret the phenomenon unfolding before our eyes, it is vital to have a conceptual framework that is empirically-based. Fifteen years ago, our instantaneous sociology of Japan was full of observations on the rising suicide rate, the level of juvenile delinquency and the novelty of hippies appearing in Tokyo's Harajuku underground station. In fact, it was not hard to notice that in the latter case the phenomenon only occurred on Sundays, leaving six days of the week for more conventional lifestyles. Fifteen years later, although Japanese public opinion has seen many changes, social behaviour remains closer to tradition, as witnessed by the stoicism of the survivors following the massive Kobe earthquake in January 1995. The place allotted to fringe groups and harmless deviance in this society will probably never change, even though the precise make-up of such groups and forms of deviance tends to reflect the whims of the day.

ASIANISM: AN ALTERNATIVE POLITICAL MODEL?

The psychological and cultural constants present in Asian societies are surely at least as real as long-term demographic and production trends in Europe: so goes the main argument used by the apostles of a new Asianism, notably the ruling classes in Singapore. Yet in East Asia, as elsewhere, the birthrate is falling fast and divorce rates are rocketing, while the ravages of consumerism are just as visible as they are in Western societies. The governments of Malaysia and Singapore, to quote but two examples, may be right to invoke the maximum penalties for drug trafficking, an area in which, in the West, and especially in Europe, leniency is now the order of the day. Yet if this is the case, how can one justify the fact that their pragmatic doctrine of non-intervention in Burma and southern China is encouraging the growth of the world's most virulent hotbed of mafia activity, founded, above all, on drug trafficking? In fact, South-East Asia's conservative élites rediscovered an enthusiasm for Asia's cultural constants – family, Confucianism, a hierarchical society and the paternalism of 'good government' – at the very moment when the anti-communist struggle was abating and Western support becoming less crucial. Their attitude also corresponds to political fears at the prospect of problematic successions in several countries: for example, the restlessness in Indonesian politics after nearly thirty years of rule by President Suharto, and the problems the Singaporeans have in seeing the overpowering personality of Lee Kuan Yew in perspective, both provide internal reasons for avoiding foreign interference and criticism, particularly from the West.

Examining these Asian constants does not explain all recent developments in East Asia. History still has a role to play between, on the one hand, the short-termism sometimes dictated by the current Asian economic situation, with its succession not just of national miracles but also of sudden cyclical crises, as seen in Japan, China and certain South-East Asian countries, and, on the other hand, the temptation to reduce explanations of Asia's successes to a unique cultural anthropology. It is worth remembering that while today the shelves of our bookstores are packed with works offering undiluted praise for Confucianism as a factor in economic development, it was only seventy years ago that Max Weber, followed by a long line of orientalists, actually blamed Confucianism for Asia's economic stagnation.

A great controversy broke out in Asia at the beginning of the 1990s between, on the one side, advocates of democratization which was supposedly due to follow on from the economic boom, bringing inevitable convergence with the Western market democracies, and, on the other, believers in an Asian political model with particular characteristics of its own which, in their eyes, offered the best rationale and guarantee for the region's economic growth. This debate was complicated by one further factor, namely intervention by the international community (and, in practice, by the Western democracies) in the domestic political problems of Asian societies and especially in the matter of human rights.

However, the autonomous political development of Asian societies and the means by which Western democracies might influence it are two quite separate problems. As far as the first is concerned, it is clear that the states of East Asia are not all currently following the same path. First there was Japan, founding a pluralistic democracy in the aftermath of the Second World War based on a complete separation of powers and total freedom of information, then Taiwan, South Korea and the Philippines which opted for full democracy. To protest that their democracy fails to extend to social issues, or that it embodies customary limitations, would be just as unfair as it would be to disqualify the Latin American democracies by comparison with the Westminster parliamentary model. In contrast, in South-East Asia, while there are, admittedly, sizeable bodies of opinion demanding similar choices, this is decidedly not what is wanted by the governments in power. All justify a very wide range of restrictions on political freedoms: in Malaysia, because of its vulnerability to possible ethnic conflict; in Singapore, in order to protect a model of enlightened despotism which has achieved impressive economic and social results; in Indonesia, in order to defend itself against threats of centrifugal explosion within its vast archipelago. As for Thailand, throughout its recent history, symbolized by the Bangkok riots of June 1991 and the failure by the military government to deal with these protests, it has since chosen to follow a dual path as far as its political development is concerned, with indisputable democracy in its Parliament and in Bangkok, but accompanied by the persistent influence of the military establishment in matters of vital self-interest, including the Thai position on Burma and Cambodia. China, Vietnam and, of course, Burma draw a clear boundary between economic openness, which they are pursuing at all costs, and political liberalization, fearing its implications for their own domestic legitimacy.

On the second issue – the influence of international opinion, the universality of human rights and pressures from overseas public opinion – the differences between Asian countries are smaller, particularly in practice, as one Malaysian researcher has pointed out (Alagappa, 1994). Even Japan took until 1978 to ratify the United Nations Conventions on Human Rights. Although the latter became an explicit policy objective from 1986 onwards, culminating in Japan's participation in economic sanctions against China in 1989–90, it remains a qualified stance, liable to U-turns, particularly where Japan's big neighbour, China, is concerned. Even more recently, the government of Kim Young-sam in the Republic of Korea, and in particular his liberal Foreign Affairs Minister Han Sung-joo, have made human rights policy an integral part of South Korea's international goals.

Although it offers very useful evidence of the recent political transformation of their country and its new international ambitions, this change has yet to stand the test of time. As for the Philippines, they lack the real leverage needed to support the positions they have adopted in principle.

Much more significant is the charge of hypocrisy levelled by many Asian critics against Western attempts at interference. The failure of human rights to acknowledge socio-economic constraints and the right of the individual to economic subsistence constitutes a 'materialist' theme which unites those communist régimes of Asia undergoing economic transition, as well as the governments of South-East Asia which have scored considerable successes in that respect. The famous proverb quoted by Brecht in *The Threepenny Opera* – 'First comes food, then comes morality' – has found unlikely echoes in an Asia that remains authoritarian, despite already being largely post-communist. Another rallying theme relates to the very inconsistent attitude of Western countries to the implementation of democracy and human rights. Many Asian leaders are fond of recalling the fact that the West remained silent following the annulment of the 1992 election results in Algeria and has stood by almost impassively as the Bosnian Muslims have been massacred. This criticism temporarily unites the views of Asia's Islamic societies (Malaysia, Indonesia and Brunei) with those of their more Chinese-influenced neighbours. Yet the argument least cited by Asian advocates of the neo-authoritarian state in support of their views is, in fact, the most obvious one: that in order to square up to the threat of internal economic decline, sluggishness in domestic markets, and a general climate of gloom and economic recession, most Western countries have embarked on a frantic commercial race towards Asia. One after another, Western governments have thus abandoned their human rights policies towards China and instead begun to engage in mutual competition for contracts. The height of this U-turn is epitomized by the Clinton administration which, having led an electoral campaign critical of the Republicans' willingness to compromise on this issue, is now moving much closer to Peking than its predecessors. After several years of American pressure for the renewal of the 'most favoured nation' clause, giving China concessions in the areas of human rights and arms proliferation, the United States decided in June 1994 to give priority to trade, just as Germany and France had done in the previous year. 'In the end, Beijing was prepared to give President Clinton just enough "face" by way of concessions that he would heave a sigh of relief and reverse his policy permanently... The fact is that they didn't believe they needed to pay much – and they were right' (Lampton, 1994: 613, 620).

In order to extricate themselves from a crisis, while avoiding the temptation towards protectionism demanded by populist tendencies, Western governments are currently operating an aggressively mercantilist policy towards Asia. In these circumstances, human rights policies may now only be applied to states devoid of all economic appeal, such as North Korea and Burma. The European Union, also stimulated by this competition, is likewise in the process of revising its Asian policy to place economic penetration and dialogue with Asian governments at the top of its external agenda. However, this realist turnaround implies that European positions on human rights must now be articulated more tactfully, thus forming part of the 'political dialogue' with Asia, without any explicit link being made between it and economic or trade negotiations (Commission of the European Communities, 1994: 24).

In a seminal, visionary article Samuel P. Huntington predicted the imminent outbreak of a 'clash of civilisations between the West and the rest' (Huntington, 1993: 22–49). This article was nowhere so warmly welcomed as in Asia, where it gave rise to a great many conferences, even in the absence of the author himself. Whereas Huntington was describing a development which he feared, and against which he advocated coexistence, many thinkers and unofficial commentators in South-East Asia apparently saw it instead as a guide for the future, asserting a modern-day Asianism which would break free of the influence of universal (and, in their view, excessively Western) values. Meanwhile, Western states have been extremely reluctant to 'support in other civilisations groups sympathetic to Western values and interests' (Huntington, 1993: 49). On the contrary, one by one they have been urgently planning an economic assault on Asia's key markets, with transport and energy infrastructures, arms and high technology spearheading this competition. Five years after the fall of the Berlin Wall and the collapse of communism in Europe, there is no longer any real external pressure being put on Asia's authoritarian régimes.

This new age of international mercantilism will undoubtedly put the brakes on the internal development of Asia's political systems by emphasizing national and state structures at the expense of intellectual and social advances. Some struggles, such as that of the post-Tiananmen political dissidents in China, are petering out, starved of the support and legitimacy conferred by international public opinion, yet Chinese society, caught in the grip of frenetic economic growth, has never before been so diversified as it has been since 1991. In Indonesia, as the time of President Suharto's succession inexorably approaches, the government is tightening the pressure on an international press that has become daringly critical. After an informal period of transition towards democracy during the 1980s, South-East Asia may well find its political system facing deadlock in the 1990s. The chief danger would then, of course, be an increase in internal tensions and frustrations, whether expressed in a revival of nationalism or in an assault on the established order. The violent strikes against Chinese employers at Medan, Indonesia, in 1994, similar protests in China (albeit largely non-violent) against foreign employers, and renewed battles between the Malaysian government and Islamic fundamentalist organizations all signify a possible renewed rise in tension in Asia, both social and nationalist-ethnic in nature.

There are two extreme responses to this undeniable threat. The first is the nationalist, authoritarian one represented by Mahathir, who has, for example, argued against the 'unbelievably arrogant attitude of Europe'[1] and even 'the North which is subjecting us to imperial pressures',[2] no doubt to preserve the freedom of action of Asian governments and muster a sense of communal or regional unity. The second, more qualified response is that of keeping Asian societies open to the future and to international influences. Whereas the President of the Philippines, Fidel Ramos, was very much in tune with the national mood when he stated, for example, that many Asians admire Europe 'for the way you have softened individual enterprise with compassionate social values',[3] it is somewhat more surprising to see Tommy Koh, one of Singapore's leading diplomats, launch into a positive portrayal of American society, so often said by his colleagues to be in decline: 'in spite of its shortcomings, the United States is the most admired nation on earth . . . because of its ideals, altruism, magnanimity and generosity'.[4]

This debate is is not only about the dominating role of the editorial pages of the international press, or the creation of a new set of philosophical values aimed at the new middle classes and other Asian 'yuppies'. Although they usually deny its importance, most of the authoritarian governments in Asia are currently extremely sensitive to public opinion, first because of the loss of face which a negative international campaign can cause, and second because it was clashes of opinion which produced the rise of democracy in Taiwan, Korea and the Philippines in the mid-1980s and prompted the downfall of European communism in 1989. The information revolution has created new communications media which transcend national boundaries. For example, CNN and the BBC, each in their different spheres, played a major role in the events of 1989 in China. The fact that the BBC's new global news network has been banned from channels broadcast in China via the Asiasat satellite, and also from other Asian countries, is indicative of this unease. New technologies, such as the fax and the mobile telephone, are making it much more difficult to exercise political control over communication in Asian societies: another reason, as many of the region's governments see it, to stem the tide of foreign influence and pressure being exerted on Asia. If necessary, the individualism, sexual licence and fascination with violence glorified by so many products of Western culture are used as a moral justification for such control, even though its main goal is a political one.

PROSPECTS FOR ASIA–PACIFIC INTEGRATION

This debate over the universality of human values versus their cultural relativism, which has attracted so much media attention, clearly has implications for the future political situation in Asia. Yet it should not obscure the existence of much more directly quantifiable issues, one of the most important of which is the direction of regional integration, which is

currently underway. The level of common economic and political organization in Asia has always been low. On a security level, the failure of alliances
such as SEATO, Asia's answer to NATO, which actually brought together
the major Western powers as well as Asian states hostile to communism,
bequeathed nothing more than a system of bilateral alliances, with the
United States acting as the pivot. Exceptions to this rule include ANZUS,
made up of the United States, Australia and New Zealand (the latter later
withdrawing at the instigation of David Lange's Labour government) and
the Five Power Defence Agreement (FPDA) combining Britain, Australia
and New Zealand, together with Singapore and Malaysia, with the aim of
protecting the area around the Strait of Malacca. Between 1967 and 1989,
the sole political organization in the region was ASEAN, a grouping of five
South-East Asian nations that were joined in 1984 by Brunei. Based on the
principles of non-intervention, neutrality and peace, ASEAN has been
extremely effective in resolving, or more often burying, the territorial disputes which used to simmer between several of its member states; but it has
never been a military alliance. It only achieved greater international status
through the active diplomacy which it carried out during the Cambodia
crisis between 1979 and 1989, in conjunction with the major countries of the
Security Council and with Australia. As for North-East Asia, split over the
Korean peninsula and its two enemy states and ravaged by mutual mistrust
between Chinese and Japanese, Japanese and Korean and especially
Chinese and Russian, it was incapable of any integration whatsoever during
the Cold War.

Now, for the first time, the end of the Cold War and the prospect of an
American withdrawal necessitated by the United States budget deficit are
prompting the countries of South-East Asia to embark on a dialogue over
regional security. Other factors include the prospect of a revival in Chinese
military power. This is still some way off: China's military establishment
currently constitutes a state within a state, with its own economic ventures,
a commercial profit motive and an agenda which is political rather than
strategic. As a result of the great international sell-off of Soviet weaponry,
China's share of the arms trade has shrunk considerably, while it is also
under pressure from the United States to show a more responsible standard
of behaviour by refraining from the continued sale of ballistic missiles.
China is none the less worrying its neighbours with island-hopping forays
in the South China Sea, even reaching as far as Filipino waters in February
1995, accompanied by short but violent skirmishes with the Vietnamese
navy and a resolution by the Chinese National Assembly calling for the use
of force to defend so-called 'national territories'. An analysis of China's
future oil requirements – for, like Indonesia, it is set to experience shortages
in future years – lends weight to theories of economic imperialism in the
making in the South China Sea. The much more conciliatory stance
adopted by Chinese diplomats towards peaceful solutions succeeds neither
in persuading nor in offering reassurance. It has thus been up to the

members of ASEAN (often defined as a club of small nations in relation to their powerful neighbours) to take the initiative for a political and security dialogue. After every ASEAN summit meeting, a post-ministerial conference is held, bringing together its own members along with Japan, the United States, Australia and the European Union.

As for the United States, it is aiming much higher in terms of regional integration, welcoming with open arms the establishment of APEC (Asia–Pacific Economic Co-operation) in 1989, at the instigation of Australia's Labour government. This much broader grouping, which has since been joined by China, Taiwan, Korea, Canada and Mexico, is primarily a forum for discussion and co-ordination: 'four adjectives in search of a noun' as one Australian observer has jokingly observed. However, it is already starting to worry ASEAN's member states, which fear they may be seeing the regional initiative slip away from them. It is no doubt for that reason, as well as out of opposition to United States human rights initiatives, that Prime Minister Mahathir proposed a community restricted solely to Asian countries, entitled the East Asia Economic Caucus (EAEC), which critics soon dubbed 'a caucus without Caucasians', referring to the exclusion not only of the United States and Canada, but also Australia and New Zealand. With its existing global as well as regional commitments, Japan did not respond to the proposal, though neither did it condemn it explicitly. A compromise began to develop from 1993 onwards: on the one hand, in place of the EAEC scheme, ASEAN adopted a fifteen-year plan for free trade, the precise shape of which remains extremely vague. APEC, on the other hand, dropped most regional security issues, while in 1994, ASEAN created the ASEAN Regional Forum (ARF). This new grouping, geared to matters of regional security, includes most APEC members, but also includes Europe, which was already involved in political dialogue with ASEAN.

These developments illustrate not only a willingness to compromise on the part of most ASEAN members and Japan, but also their freedom of manoeuvre, which is ultimately considerable compared with that of the United States. Thus, at the APEC summit in Jakarta in October 1994, they agreed to set a deadline for the full introduction of free-trade arrangements between all member states by the year 2010 in the case of the developed economies and by 2020 for the developing economies: South Korea managed to find its way into the second category despite its hopes of soon becoming a member of the OECD, in other words the international club of rich nations. Shortly afterwards, the post of Secretary-General of APEC was awarded to a Japanese, who was given the task of steering the organization's work in the run-up to the Osaka summit in 1995. The Japanese government took pains to stress that the deadlines of 2010 and 2020, which President Clinton had gone to such great lengths to secure, were merely notional targets, and that agreement on a common economic integration policy was still a long way off. On the evidence, it would appear that the quest for a consensus between APEC's Asian partners is more important than the strategic lead given by the United States.

It is still hard to imagine what the precise make-up of an integrated Asia might be. Admittedly, even though it was affected by the recession of 1992–3, Japan has clearly hung on to unrivalled reserves of potential investment and productivity. The very fleeting drop in Japanese company profits reflects the frenetic pace of investment in the 1980s, which was self-financing until the Japanese speculative bubble burst in 1987. It only needed a very slight reduction in investment and in the rate of plant renewal to sustain the record-breaking cost–benefit ratio of Japanese industry. Problems such as unemployment are appearing – 3 per cent of the Japanese workforce were out of work at the end of 1994 (still the lowest rate of all the industrialized countries) due either to technological advances or to the recession – but these will soon be solved by the rapid ageing of the Japanese population. Following a further revaluation of the yen in 1993, confounding all expectations, Japan's trade surplus, particularly with the United States, stayed the same at over US$60 billion per annum. In 1994, the Japanese currency dropped to a new low of less than ¥100 to the dollar, but this did not halt the determination of the major exporting industries to sustain productivity at all costs. In 1994, with the rate standing at less than ¥100 to the dollar, the leading Japanese car manufacturer, Toyota, once again showed overall profits, an achievement which would have been unimaginable a few years earlier. Toyota immediately set itself the publicly-declared aim of building new, affordable models with the dollar as low as ¥80. In March 1995, the wishes of Toyota and some others were unintentionally fulfilled, as the dollar fell to ¥83, before picking up a few months later.

This speedy adaptation prompts us to consider the limits of a policy of monetary devaluation as a weapon of trade warfare. Admittedly, more than ever before, Japan is finding itself in the role of an absentee landlord, whose financial credits greatly exceed its overseas industrial assets, and which has neither natural resources nor geographic area. None the less, with its financial surplus Japan is still better able to guarantee the retirements of its ageing population than anywhere else in the world.

As we enter the twenty-first century, Japan will no longer stand alone in Asia. The way that the newly-industrialized countries are catching up has altered in pace and method. It is no longer simply a question of expanding the geographic scope of their international trade, driven by differences in wage levels and leading to an international division of labour: in this classic scheme, leading-edge technologies remained the preserve of the most advanced economy, while the techniques and processes discarded by the latter were transferred to the developing economies. The technological ambitions of these emerging countries, coupled with massive investment in all levels of education, from nursery-age through to university, is modernizing most Asian societies at a rate faster than the economic boom alone could achieve. Moreover, such investment in education is at least as much an individual and family phenomenon as it is a matter of public policy. There are fewer functionally illiterate people in Malaysia than there are in the United States, while South Korea (with a population of 44 million and a GNP of US$10,000 per capita) has as many students as France (with its population of 56 million and a GNP of US$20,000 per capita). On a technological level, the path taken by Korea and Taiwan is significant: the former has become the world's leading manufacturer of electronic components, while the latter is the world's foremost producer of computer workstations. Malaysia's ambitions in the automobile sector must still be qualified in terms of the fact that the leading national manufacturer, Proton, is a dependent company of Mitsubishi. However, the same used to be said of the Korean manufacturer Hyundai, which now designs and builds all its own vehicles. The scheme of a division of labour between more and less developed economies is thus being severely challenged. Not only Japan but several countries in the region are heading the rush towards industrial relocation, and such moves are not solely confined, as they were in the 1960s, to environmentally harmful industries and second-rate consumer goods. The leading investor in China is not even Japan, but Taiwan, and Taiwanese investment in South-East Asia is almost equal to that of Japan. Threats of tariff protectionism issued by Europe and the United States are serving to accelerate and extend this process of relocation, as Asian industrialists are keen to avoid the risk of trade sanctions or quotas being imposed on the most visible exporting countries. This political as opposed to directly economic factor, which is set to reduce the marked trade surpluses posted by countries such as Japan and Taiwan with Western countries, has created a clear triangular pattern of production and trade in Asia. As a result, the accumulated trade surpluses of China, Taiwan and Hong Kong *vis à vis* the United States were scarcely any greater in 1994 than they were five years before: however, it is China which accounts for the bulk of this (to the tune of US$30 billion) while the Taiwanese trade surplus has shrunk considerably. In certain cases, it is Asia's developing countries which are in turn investing in the old industrialized countries of Europe: for example, there are Korean investors in Ireland and Lorraine and Taiwanese investors based around Schipol Airport in the Netherlands. Although minimum wages remain low, those of workers in the major firms (the ones most vital to exports) have passed the US$1,000 per month mark in Korea and Taiwan. The low wage argument invoked by advocates of protectionism in Europe and the United States is gradually ceasing to exist, just as it has already done in Japan.

In the background of this regional integration process, China figures as another major force. Not that it will be free in future, as it was in the past, to determine its own political actions – on the contrary, the same factors which are contributing to its boom are also those which bind it to the international community, that is, the role of foreign capital and the overseas Chinese communities, and the importance for the latter of keeping open access to external markets. Here, too, politics plays a vital role. After the dark days of Maoism ended, the disappearance of all ideological references and the devaluation of the past meant that the world's most flexible workforce was launched on to the labour market. Although wages are rising fast, China is still the country where the lack of welfare rights is most strongly felt. Its overall stability depends on the rate of growth and the maintenance, for the time being, of a large state-run industrial sector which, despite its low productivity, still employs no less than 20 per cent of China's industrial workforce. This sector is still taking on workers, for example to compensate evicted peasants living in the suburbs of the major cities. Growth is not going to occur at the same rate across the whole of China, and at present it is highly dependent on external support. Yet today, China and the overseas Chinese communities together form a growth centre to supplement Japan. As for the other South-East Asian nations, they will soon be able to balance some of their own links with Japan by means of this China factor.

A great danger none the less looms over the future of China's development. Is the West (or rather the United States) ready to accept in China what it has already accepted in Japan, Taiwan and Korea? The Cold War no longer makes it necessary to reinforce Asian allies, while the lead of the United States and Europe can no longer be taken for granted. In addition, the supply of Chinese labour appears inexhaustible. China is facing the barriers of protectionism much sooner than its Asian predecessors. Admittedly, the risk of political and social crisis in China may worry its trading partners, leading them to be cautious. Even so, China will need to give unaccustomed priority to its own domestic market, and even accept the maximum range of foreign imports. It will consequently be unable to apply the protectionist 'industrial cocoon' strategy which helped to create Asia's post-war economic miracles. For the time being, the technological requirements of Chinese industry and the Chinese people's hunger for consumption will coexist alongside a need to balance foreign trade. But what of the future? A new economic recession in China, whatever the cause, could arouse bitterness in society along with its political consequences.

These consequences are of two kinds. An airlock occurring in the middle of such a rapid economic boom could destabilize a government whose political legitimacy is already somewhat fragile. Alternatively, in order to close ranks, the government might encourage a vindictive nationalism directed against the West, or against overseas Chinese, who are seen as overprivileged: Hong Kong and Taiwan are two potential targets. Even with the safety-valve of an electoral system, it would be a monumental task to steer Chinese society along the long road towards development without a hitch, but the present communist government is unstable, especially in a period of succession. For this very reason, it is attempting to transform itself into a neo-authoritarian régime based on a privileged caste, a marriage of convenience that would make it much less vulnerable to internal political challenge.

This major uncertainty, which has greater implications for the future than the development of former Indochina, South-East Asia's final frontier, is a factor in the regional political organization of Asia. The reason that ASEAN, Japan and some others are currently joining together and broaching the question of their own regional security, formerly the preserve of the United States, is not solely, or even primarily, to form a bloc or union against the United States and Europe. Even if the United States perceives the advantages of remaining Asia's policeman, particularly to maintain a strong position in trade negotiations with the region, a certain level of disengagement seems inevitable, although the rate at which it happens will naturally depend on United States budgetary constraints and the strength of isolationist feeling. It would, after all, be no more than a return to the ranks for the United States, which up to now has had special influence. It is therefore vital for the maritime states of Asia to affirm their positions and come to a viable form of relationship with the less predictable countries of the region. This is why, at a time when the West (along with Japan, out of international obligation) was imposing sanctions on China in the wake of the Tiananmen massacre, the Asian maritime states were conversely strengthening their relationship with it. It is also the reason why former (and existing) anti-communist governments are holding out a hand to Vietnam and bringing it into the dialogue with ASEAN. The same policy could be applied to China. Conscious of their future importance, China's leaders, among whom the army plays a major role, are taking every opportunity to provoke mild fears in their neighbours. The task of keeping the communist guerillas going has now been superseded by the issue of China's maritime territorial claims, which is at least as important for the messages it sends out as it is for the small islands and reefs at stake.

Lastly, the rise of Asia also affects the planet as a whole. The choice which we in Europe and the United States seem to be facing between protectionism and free trade is a false dilemma, because either way they only involve our own markets. Although in their affinity with the under-developed world Japan and the Asian dragons show major deficiencies in human terms, they offer a low-cost alternative to Western capital and technologies, often without political conditions attached. Unencumbered by lobbies and interests handed down from a colonial or neo-colonial past, they are finding it to their benefit to develop the South. The most sophisticated strategy is that of Japan, which is currently recycling a growing proportion of its financial surplus in that direction (and, one might add, is proving much less open-handed than Western Europe as far as Eastern Europe and Russia are concerned). Yet Japan does not see this policy as competing with Western interests. In the Near and Middle East particularly it has come to an understanding with the West. Instead of going it alone and simply defending its own access to vital oil supplies regardless of who owns them, it has rallied behind the Western allies over the necessary control of the wells. Meanwhile, in almost every case, it is also attaching certain political conditions to economic aid, particularly for terrorist states.

This development is a recent one, and remains to be confirmed. In the 1970s, Japan, convinced that it was more vulnerable in terms of primary resources than other developed countries, made overtures to Middle Eastern governments, regardless of their identity. Other Asian countries have still not reached that stage, whether owing to their religious make-up (as in Malaysia and Indonesia) or because they have not yet affirmed an international aid strategy. No doubt they, too, will come to see the need for a coherent international order in a period which is seeing the rapid disintegration of the pluri-national states and political régimes inherited from the past.

As this issue shows, the attitude of Europe or the United States towards the Asian economies cannot be determined solely by trade considerations, nor by the domestic question of employment, however critical these may be. Whether with us or without us, an international realignment is taking place in terms of who the winners and losers at the end of the century will be. Joining in this process through realistic negotiation is preferable to facing it with an imaginary denial.

NOTES

1 *International Herald Tribune*, 14 October 1994, p. 1
2 *Far Eastern Economic Review*, 14 March 1992, p. 22.
3 *International Herald Tribune*, 14 October 1994, p. 10.
4 *International Herald Tribune*, 8–9 October 1994, p. 4.

Note on the spelling of proper names

Finding a way through the maze of conventions governing the transliteration of Asian languages is no easy task. This note outlines those chosen for this book, which in some cases are the result of compromise between rules and ease of usage.

As far as Chinese names are concerned, we have in general adopted the *pinyin* form of transliteration as used in the People's Republic of China. However, in certain cases the traditional Wade-Giles form of transliteration has been retained, e.g. Peking, the Yangtse River, Chungking, Canton, General Chiang Kai-shek, etc. In all personal names, the family name comes before the given name, e.g. Deng Xiaoping. For all personal names and placenames outside the People's Republic of China, we have adopted the customary form of transliteration, e.g. Taipei not Taibei.

Singaporean names are given using the usual English form, separating the two syllables of the given name, which comes after the family name, e.g. Lee Kuan Yew not Lee Kuan-yew.

In the case of Korean names, the two syllables of the given name are linked where appropriate, the family name coming first, e.g. Roh Tae-woo not Roh Tae Woo. North Korean personal names, however, are given as three separate words, with the family name once again coming first, e.g. Kim Il Sung.

For Japanese names we have followed the Western convention, which is also the one used by some Japanese when writing in Western languages. The given name precedes the family name, e.g. Shigeru Yoshida.

For Vietnamese names, we have adopted the romanized form as used in Vietnam, but without any accents or other typographical marks. As far as personal names are concerned, e.g. Nguyen Co Thach, the family name (Nguyen) comes first and the given name (Thach) last, but it is almost invariably the latter by which the person is known, e.g. Giap for Vo Nguyen Giap.

For Malay and Indonesian names we have adopted the most current form of romanized spelling. Indonesians are often known simply by their family name, e.g. Suharto or Sukarno. However, many Malay names incorporate a variety of honorifics or titles of nobility which we have understandably shortened.

For Laotian and Khmer names the customary English form of transliteration has been used.

As for Thai names, contemporary usage fluctuates between phonetic transliteration and the standard rules of romanized spelling, and no attempt has been made to choose between the two.

FG/EJP

References

Ahmad, Z. A. (ed.) (1985) *Government and politics of Malaysia*, Singapore: Oxford University Press.

Alagappa, M. (1994) *Democratic transition in Asia: the role of the international community*, East-West Center Special Report no. 3, Honolulu: East-West Center.

Banister, J. (1987) *China's changing population*, Stanford: Stanford University Press.

Bastid-Bruguière, M. (1980) 'Currents of social change', in J. K. Fairbank and K. Liu (eds) *The Cambridge History of China* vol. 11, *Late Ch'ing, 1800–1911*, part 2, Cambridge: Cambridge University Press.

Benedict, R. (1946) *The chrysanthemum and the sword*, Boston: Houghton & Mifflin.

Bergère, M. (1989) *The golden age of the Chinese bourgeoisie*, Cambridge: Cambridge University Press.

—— (1989) *La république populaire de la Chine de 1949 à nos jours*, Paris: Armand Colin.

Bianco, L. (1987) *Les origines de la révolution chinoise, 1915–1949*, Paris: Gallimard.

Carrère d'Encausse, H. (1986) *Ni paix ni guerre - le nouvel Empire soviétique ou du bon usage de la détente*, Paris: Flammarion.

Chanda, N. (1986) *Brother Enemy: the war after the war*, San Diego: Harcourt Brace.

Chandler, D. (1983) *A history of Cambodia*, Boulder: Westview Press.

—— (1992) *Brother Number One: a political biography of Pol Pot*, Boulder: Westview Press.

Chew, E. C. T. and Lee, E. (1991) *A history of Singapore*, Singapore: Oxford University Press.

Cipolla, C. (1965) *Guns and sails in the early phase of European expansion, 1400–1700*, London: Collins.

Commission of the European Communities (1994) *Towards a new Asia strategy*, Brussels.

Denison, E. E. (1975) *How Japan's economy grew so fast*, Washington: Brookings Institution.

Deutscher, I. (1963) *The prophet outcast: Trotsky 1929–1940*, London.

Fanon, F. (1961) *Les damnés de la terre*, Paris: F. Maspéro.

Geertz, C. (1963) *Agricultural involution: the process of ecological change in Indonesia*, Berkeley: University of California Press.

Guillain, R. (1986) *Orient Extrême: une vie en Asie*, Arléa-Le Seuil.

Horowitz, D. (1967) *From Yalta to Vietnam: American foreign policy during the Cold War*, Harmondsworth: Penguin.

Hrebenar, R. (1986) *The Japanese party system: from one-party rule to coalition government*, Boulder: Westview Press.

Hu Shih (1937) *Independence, convergence and borrowing*, Cambridge, MA: Harvard University Press.

Huntington, S. P. (1968) 'The bases of accommodation', *Foreign Affairs* 46, 4: 642–56.

—— (1993) 'The clash of civilisations?', *Foreign Affairs* 72, 3: 22–49.

Ike, N. (1972) *Japanese politics: patron-client democracy*, New York: Alfred Knopf.

Isaacs, H. R. (1967) *La tragédie de la révolution chinoise, 1925–1927*, Paris: Gallimard.

Johnson, C. (1962) *Peasant nationalism and communist power: the emergence of revolutionary China, 1937–1945*, Stanford: Stanford University Press.

—— (1982) *MITI and the Japanese miracle: the growth of industrial policy, 1925–1975*, Stanford: Stanford University Press.

Kataoka, T. (1974) *Resistance and revolution in China: the Communists and the second united front*, Berkeley: University of California Press.

—— (1991) *The price of a constitution: the origins of Japan's post-war politics*, New York: Crane Russak.

Kolko, J. and Kolko, G. (1972) *The limits of power: the world and United States foreign policy 1945–1954*, New York: Harper & Row.

Lacouture, J. (1978) *Survive le peuple cambodgien*, Paris: Le Seuil.

Lampton, D.M. (1994) 'America's China policy in the age of the Finance Minister: Clinton ends linkage', *China Quarterly* 139: 597–621.

Lederer, W. (1959) *The ugly American*, New York: Norton.

Leys, S. (1971) *Les habits neufs du président Mao: chronique de la 'Révolution culturelle'*, Paris: Champ Libre.

Lubis, M. (1963) *Twilight in Djakarta*, London: Hutchinson.

Mauzy, D. K. and Milne, R.S. (1980) *Politics and government in Malaysia*, Singapore: Times Books.

Morita, A. and Ishihara, S. (1989) *The Japan that can say no: the new United States–Japan relations card*, Tokyo: Kobunsha.

Myers, R. A. and Peattie, M. R. (eds) (1984) *The Japanese colonial empire, 1895–1945*, Princeton: Princeton University Press.

Myrdal, G. (1968) *Asian drama: an enquiry into the poverty of nations*, New York: Pantheon.

Nakano, C. (1974) *La Société japonaise*, Paris: Armand Colin.

Okimoto, D. I. (1989) *Between MITI and the market: Japanese industrial policy for high technologies*, Stanford: Standford University Press.

Ouchi, W. (1982) *Théorie Z*, Paris: Interéditions.

Picq, L. (1984) *Au delà du ciel: cinq ans chez les Khmers rouges*, Paris: Barrault.

Ponchaud, F. (1977) *Le Cambodge année zéro*, Paris: Julliard.

Pons, P. (1988) *D'Edo à Tokyo: mémoires et modernités*, Paris: Gallimard.

Reischauer, E. O. (1970) *Japan: the story of a nation*, New York: Alfred Knopf.

Roosevelt, E. (ed.) (1952) *The Roosevelt letters, being the personal correspondence of Franklin Delano Roosevelt, Vol. 3 (1928–1935)*, London: George Harrap & Co.

Rostow, W. W. (1960) *The stages of economic growth: a non-communist manifesto*, Cambridge: Cambridge University Press.

Saïd, E. (1978) *L'Orientalism: L'Orient créé par L'Occident*, Paris: Le Seuil.

Scott, J. C. (1976) *The moral economy of the peasant: rebellion and subsistence in Southeast Asia*, New Haven: Yale University Press.

Shaplen, R. (1969) *Time out of hand: revolution and reaction in Southeast Asia*, London: Andre Deutsch.

Shawcross, W. (1979) *Sideshow: Nixon, Kissinger and the destruction of Cambodia*, New York: Simon & Schuster.

Snepp, F. (1977) *Decent interval*, New York: Random House.

Starobinsky, (1964) *L'invention de la liberté*, Geneva: Skira

Stone, I.F. (1952) *The hidden history of the Korean War*, New York: Monthly Review Press.

Sukarno (1965) *An autobiography as told to Cindy Adams*, Hong Kong: Indianapolis.

——(1970) *Nationalism, Islam and Marxism*, trans. by K. H. Warouw and P. D. Weldon, Ithaca: Cornell University Southeast Asia Program, Modern Indonesia Project.

Suzuki, Y. (1980) *Money and banking in contemporary Japan*, New Haven: Yale University Press.

Van Wolferen, K. (1990) *L'Énigme de la puissance japonaise*, Paris: Robert Laffont.

Vatikiotis, M. R. J. (1993) *Indonesian politics under Suharto: order, development and pressure for change*, London: Routledge.

Vickery, M. (1984) *Cambodia, 1975–1982*, Boston South End Press.

Vogel, E. F. (1983) *Le Japon médaille d'or*, Paris: Gallimard.

Wertheim, W. F. (1979) 'Whose plot? New light on the 1965 events', *Journal of Contemporary Asia* 9, 2: 197–215.

Yoshida, S. (1962) *The Yoshida memoirs*, New York: Houghton & Mifflin.

Chronology

This chronology reviews the main dates cited in the body of the text.

1427	Victory of Le Loi in Vietnam against imperial China
1521	Death of Ferdinand Magellan in the Philippines
1603	Tokugawa shogunate begins in Japan
1644	Qing dynasty begins in China
1771	Revolt of the Tay Son in Vietnam
1802	Gia Long founds Nguyen dynasty in Vietnam
1819	Founding of Singapore
1825–30	Dutch war in Java
1839	Brooke family arrives in Sarawak
1839–42	First Opium War in China
1851–64	Taiping rebellion in China
1853	Japan opened up by Commodore Perry's fleet
1858	Treaty of Tianjin and end of the Second Opium War
1861–75	Tongzhi Restoration in China
1862	France captures Cochinchina
1864	French protectorate in Cambodia
1868–1912	Meiji era in Japan
1874	Pangkor Engagement between United Kingdom and Malay sultans
1876	Korea opens up to trade
1879	Japan gains Ryukyu Islands at China's expense
1884	French navy sinks Chinese fleet at Fuzhou
1885	Anti-French Revolt of the Literati in Vietnam
	Khmer revolt against the abolition of slavery
1886	Britain annexes Burma
1889	Meiji Constitution in Japan
1895	Sino-Japanese Treaty of Shimonoseki – Taiwan ceded to Japan
	Creation of the Federated Malay States
1898	Failure of Reform of a Hundred Days in China
	First official Japanese doctrine on Asia
	Independence in Philippines and Malolos constitution

	New Territories joined to Hong Kong for 99 years
1899	Philippines annexed by USA
1900	Siege of the Legations by the Boxers in Peking
1901	Dutch adopt 'ethical policy' in their colonies
1902	Anglo-Japanese alliance
1905	Japan sinks Russian navy at Tsushima
1906	Young Men's Buddhist Association founded in Burma
	Japanese Socialist Party founded
1907	France splits off several provinces from the Kingdom of Siam
1908	Sarekat Islam founded in Java
	Death of Empress Cixi in China
1910	Japan annexes Korea
1911	First Chinese revolution and end of Qing dynasty
1918	Li Dazhao forms Marxist study group in Peking
1919	Versailles Conference
	Anti-Japanese movement in Korea
	May Fourth Movement in China
1920	Baku Congress
	Second Congress of the International in Moscow
	Indonesian Communist Party founded
1920–21	Hailufeng peasants' revolt in China
1921	Chinese Communist Party founded in Shanghai
1922	Treaty of Washington
	Japanese Communist Party founded
1923	Constitutionalist Party founded in Vietnam
1924–27	First CCP–Kuomintang united front in China
1925	Ho Chi Minh founds League of Revolutionary Youth in Canton
	Cao Dai sect founded in Vietnam
	Death of Sun Yat-sen
	Universal male suffrage introduced in Japan
	Creation of Ministry of Trade (the future MITI) in Japan
1926	Formal beginning of the Showa era and reign of Hirohito
1926–7	Rebellion of PKI in Java and Sumatra crushed
1927	Nationalist VNQDD founded in Vietnam
	Sukarno founds Indonesian Communist Party again
1928	Foundation of Communist Party of the South Seas
	Ho Chi Minh founds nucleus of Thai Communist Party
1930	Nghe Tinh peasant revolt in Vietnam
	Saya San peasant revolt in Burma
	Formation of the Thakin movement in Burma
	Formation of the Indochinese, Malay and Filipino Communist Parties
1931	Japan invades Manchuria
1932	Coup against absolute monarchy in Thailand

	Emperor Bao Dai crowned in Vietnam
1933	Japan leaves League of Nations
1935	Seventh Congress of the Communist International and turn around by Popular Fronts
1936	A Khmer language newspaper founded in Cambodia
	Anti-Comintern pact between Japan and Germany
	Xian incident and capture of Chiang Kai-shek
1937	Marco Polo Bridge incident and start of Sino-Japanese war
1938	Burmese uprising against the British
	Foundation of the pro-independence Young Malay Union
1939	Foundation of the Burmese Communist Party
1940	Triple Alliance (Japan, Germany and Italy)
	Japan occupies French Indochina
1941	General Tojo becomes Prime Minister of Japan
	Non-aggression pact between Japan and Soviet Union
	Allied blockade against Japan
	Japanese attack Pearl Harbor
1942	Battles of Midway and Guadalcanal
	Foundation of Thai Communist Party
1943	Japan grants formal independence to Burma
	Cairo and Tehran Conferences
1945	Japan grants independence to Vietnam, Cambodia and Indonesia
	Division of Korea
	Japan surrenders
	Ho Chi Minh launches August Revolution
	Sukarno proclaims Republic of Indonesia
	Bombing of Haiphong
	Soviet Union declares War on Japan on 8 August
1946–54	First Indochina War
1946	Civil war in China
	Dialogue between Ho Chi Minh and Sainteny
	Holland recognizes United States of Indonesia
	USA grants independence to Philippines
	Shigeru Yoshida cabinet in Japan
	MacArthur Constitution in Japan
1947	Huk rebellion in the Philippines
	Short-lived coalition government with socialists in Japan
	Land reform in Japan
1948	Calcutta conference
	Revolt by Malayan Communist Party
	Rebellion by PKI at Madiun (Java) suppressed
	New Yoshida cabinet in Japan
	General Phibun returns to power in Thailand
	Burmese independence

1949	Netherlands accepts independence of Republic of Indonesia
	Parity fixed between yen and dollar (until 1971)
	Creation of MITI in Japan
	Creation of Malayan Chinese Association
1950	Sino-Soviet Friendship Treaty
	Start of Korean War (1950–3)
	Creation of Japanese Self-Defence Forces
	Creation of Eximbank of Japan
	Land reform in China
	China enters Korean War
	Kim Il Sung purges 'Yenan faction'
1951	USA signs security treaty with Philippines, Australia and New Zealand
	Kim Il Sung purges pro-Soviet faction
	San Francisco Peace Treaty and first US–Japan security treaty (ratified in 1952)
1953	Death of Stalin
	Relaxation of Antitrust Law in Japan
	Panmunjon armistice and end of Korean War
1954	SEATO formed
	Battle of Dien Bien Phu
	Geneva Conference on Indochina
	Surrender of Huk leader Luis Taruc
1955	Sino-American confrontation over Strait of Formosa
	Afro-Asian Conference at Bandung (Indonesia)
	Collectivization of Chinese agriculture
	Foundation of Liberal Democratic Party in Japan
1956	Independence in Singapore
	The Hundred Flowers in China and Vietnam
	Japanese-Soviet agreement over Kuriles
1957	Kishi cabinet in Japan
	Independence in Malaya
	Anti-rightist movement in China
	Kim Il Sung purges the Party in North Korea
1958	Great Leap Forward launched in China
	Flying Horse Movement launched in North Korea
	Bombing of Quemoy and Matsu
1959–61	The 'three black years' in China
1959	New US–Japan security treaty
	Confrontation at the top at the Lushan plenum (China)
1960	Soviet Union cuts off aid to China
	Ikeda cabinet in Japan
1962	Mao's self-criticism for the Great Leap Forward
	Sino-Indian war
	Sukarno launches Confrontation with Malaysia

1964	Olympic Games in Tokyo
	Japan joins OECD
	Sato cabinet in Japan
1965	Ferdinand Marcos elected President of the Philippines
	Downfall of Sukarno in Indonesia
	Start of Vietnam War
1966	Launch of Cultural Revolution in China
1967	Wuhan incident (China)
1968	Tet offensive by Vietcong in South Vietnam
	Chinese Red Guards sent down to countryside
1969	Guam speech by Richard Nixon and 'low profile' in Asia
	Death of Ho Chi Minh
	Anti-Chinese riots in Malaysia
1970	Lon Nol's coup against Sihanouk in Cambodia
1971	Downfall and death of Marshal Lin Baio, Mao's appointed successor
	China joins United Nations
1972	Richard Nixon visits China
	Tanaka cabinet in Japan
	Japan recognizes People's Republic of China
	Massacre of students in Bangkok
	LDP loses absolute majority in Japanese Diet
1973	First oil shock
	Paris conference and agreement to end hostilities in Vietnam
1974	Tanaka affair (Lockheed) and Miki cabinet in Japan
	Portuguese leave Timor
1975	Khmer Rouge come to power
	Reunification of Vietnam by the North
	Chiang Ching-kuo succeeds Chiang Kai-shek in Taiwan
1976	Death of Zhou Enlai
	Fukuda cabinet in Japan
	Posthumous tribute to Zhou Enlai in Tiananmen Square
	Death of Mao Zedong
	Arrest of Gang of Four in China
	Ceiling of 1 per cent of GNP placed on Japanese military expenditure (until 1986)
	Ohira cabinet in Japan
1977	Deng Xiaoping's second return to power
1978	Democracy Wall and the first Peking Spring
	Economic liberalization in China
1979	Vietnam drives Khmer Rouge out of Cambodia
	Soviet Union invades Afghanistan
	Economic zones and foreign investment zones introduced in China
1980	Suzuki cabinet in Japan

	Decollectivization in Chinese agriculture
1982	Nakasone cabinet in Japan
	G7 summit at Versailles
	Mahathir launches 'Look East' policy in Malaysia
1983	Korean Boeing 747 incident
	G7 summit at Williamsburg
1984	Sino-British declaration on Hong Kong
1985	Large-scale revaluation of yen begins
	Official visit by Nakasone to Yasukuni Temple
	Maekawa Report advocates opening up of Japanese market
1986	Downfall of Ferdinand Marcos and election of Corazon Aquino
1987	Downfall of Hu Yaobang in China
	Takeshita cabinet in Japan
	Mikhail Gorbachev announces total destruction of SS–20s
	End of martial law in Taiwan
	Stock market crash on Wall Street
1988	Roh Tae-woo succeeds General Chun Doo-hwan in South Korea
	Massacre in Rangoon (Burma)
	Olympic Games held in Seoul
1989	Death of Hirohito and start of Akihito's reign in Japan
	Kaifu cabinet in Japan
	Gorbachev visits China
	Second Peking Spring and Tiananmen massacre
	Withdrawal of Vietnamese troops from Cambodia
1990	Stock market crash in Tokyo
	Kim Young-sam founds Liberal Democratic Party in South Korea
1991	Coup against Chatichai in Thailand
	Nobel Peace Prize awarded to Aung San Suu Kyi
	Miyazawa cabinet in Japan
	Paris peace agreements on Cambodia
	Peace treaty between the two Koreas
	Free general elections in Taiwan
1992	ASEAN countries create a future free-trade zone
	Deng Xiaoping's Shenzhen speech
	Massacre in Bangkok and collapse of military government
	Election of General Ramos in the Philippines
	Vote on Japanese law concerning the sending of peacekeeping forces within the framework of the UN
	Election of Kim Young-sam in South Korea
1993	Suharto re-elected for sixth time as President of Indonesia
	First official talks between China and Taiwan in Singapore
	Free elections in Cambodia under UN auspices

First change of government in Japan since 1947

First APEC summit in Seattle

1994 France recognizes principle of a single China

Fall of Hosokawa administration in Japan

US ends refusal to grant most-favoured-nation status to China

Patten administration embarks on electoral reform in Hong Kong

Death of Kim Il Sung

Meeting between Burmese junta and Aung San Suu Kyi

Nuclear accord between US and North Korea

APEC adopts goal of free trade at its summit in Bogor (Indonesia)

1995 Kobe earthquake (5,000 dead)

Attack by Aum Shinrikyo sect on Tokyo underground

Nuclear non-proliferation treaty extended indefinitely

Temporary resumption of French nuclear testing in the Pacific

Aung San Suu Kyi freed

Vietnam joins ASEAN

APEC summit at Osaka

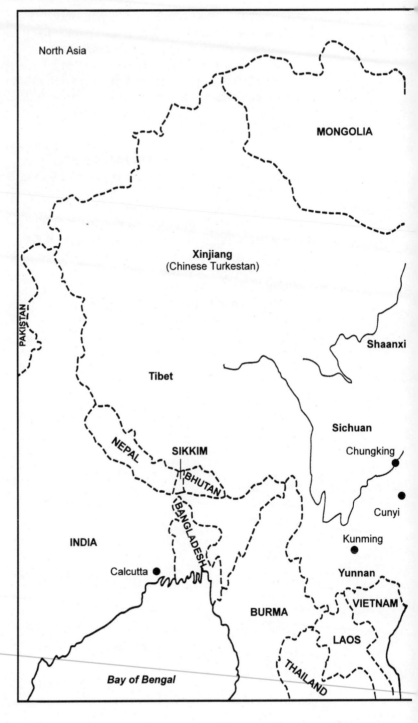

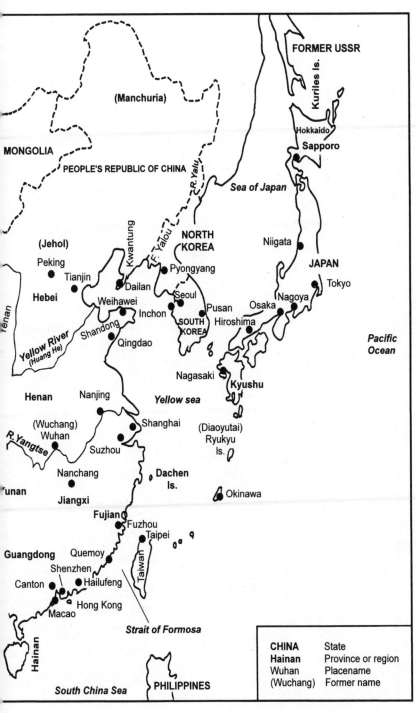

FORMER USSR

Kuriles Is.

(Manchuria)

Hokkaido

MONGOLIA

Sapporo

PEOPLE'S REPUBLIC OF CHINA

R. Yalu

Sea of Japan

Kwantung

R. Yalou

NORTH
KOREA

Niigata

(Jehol)

Peking

JAPAN

Tianjin

Pyongyang

Hebei

Dailan

Seoul

Tokyo

Weihawei

Nagoya

Inchon

Pusan

Osaka

Shandong

SOUTH
KOREA

Hiroshima

Yellow River
(Huang He)

Qingdao

Henan

Nanjing

Yellow sea

Nagasaki

Kyushu

Pacific
Ocean

Yenan

(Wuchang)
Wuhan

Shanghai

(Diaoyutai)
Ryukyu
Is.

R. Yangtse

Suzhou

Nanchang

Dachen
Is.

'unan

Okinawa

Jiangxi

Fujian

Fuzhou

Guangdong

Quemoy

Taipei

Taiwan

Shenzhen

Canton

Hailufeng

Hong Kong

Macao

Strait of Formosa

Hainan

South China Sea

PHILIPPINES

CHINA	State
Hainan	Province or region
Wuhan	Placename
(Wuchang)	Former name

South- East Asia

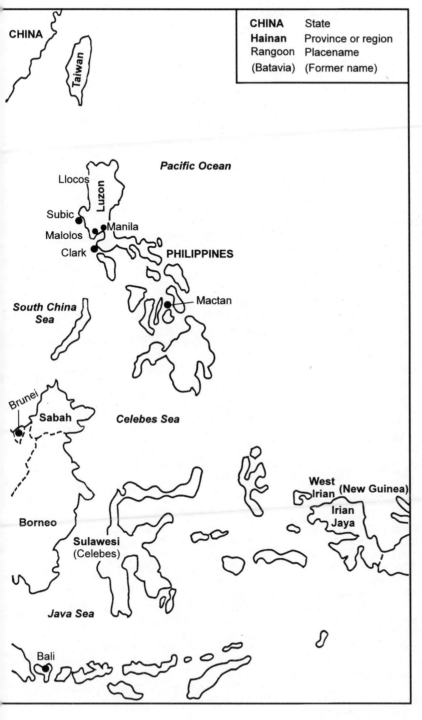

CHINA	State
Hainan	Province or region
Rangoon	Placename
(Batavia)	(Former name)

CHINA

Taiwan

Pacific Ocean

Llocos

Luzon

Subic

Malolos

Manila

Clark

PHILIPPINES

South China
Sea

Mactan

Brunei

Sabah

Celebes Sea

West
Irian (New Guinea)

Irian
Jaya

Borneo

Sulawesi
(Celebes)

Java Sea

Bali

Index